Collective
Wisdom

Collective Wisdom

Lessons, Inspiration, and Advice
from Women over 50

Edited by

GRACE BONNEY

Artisan | New York

Copyright © 2021 by Grace Bonney

All rights reserved. No portion of this book may be reproduced—mechanically, electronically, or by any other means, including photocopying—without written permission of the publisher.

Library of Congress Cataloging-in-Publication Data

Names: Bonney, Grace, author.
Title: Collective wisdom : lessons, inspiration, and advice from women over 50 / edited by Grace Bonney.
Description: New York : Artisan, a division of Workman Publishing Co., Inc. [2021]
Identifiers: LCCN 2021004796 | ISBN 9781579659431 (hardcover)
Subjects: LCSH: Older women. | Wisdom. | Conduct of life.
Classification: LCC HQ1221 .B73 2021 | DDC 305.26/2—dc23
LC record available at https://lccn.loc.gov/2021004796

Cover and book design by Shubhani Sarkar
(sarkardesignstudio.com)

Artisan books are available at special discounts when purchased in bulk for premiums and sales promotions as well as for fundraising or educational use. Special editions or book excerpts also can be created to specification. For details, contact the Special Sales Director at the address below, or send an e-mail to specialmarkets@workman.com.

For speaking engagements,
contact speakersbureau@workman.com.

Published by Artisan
A division of Workman Publishing Co., Inc.
225 Varick Street
New York, NY 10014-4381
artisanbooks.com

Artisan is a registered trademark of Workman Publishing Co., Inc.

Published simultaneously in Canada by
Thomas Allen & Son, Limited

Printed in Canada

First printing, September 2021

10 9 8 7 6 5 4 3 2 1

Photography Credits

Lisa Abitbol: Pages 375, 376–77
Holly Andres: Page 127
Todd Antioquia: Page 255
Johnny Autry: Page 178
Julot Bandit: Pages 156–57
Claire Bangser: Pages 148–49, 223
Jonathon André Beckles: Page 330
Sara Blanco: Page 72
Nicole Caldwell: Pages 137, 304
Natalie Chitwood: Pages 85, 122, 130, 161, 196, 215, 391, 394, 400
Erica Elan Ciganek: Pages 16, 203
Liz Clayman: Pages 260–61, 286, 370
Kim Craven: Page 276
Andrea Mead Cross: Page 144
Reginald Cunningham: Page 365
Austin Day: Page 303
Christopher Dibble: Page 315
Eddie Hernandez Photography: Page 271
Bill Eichner: Page 97
Laurence Ellis: Page 152
Jim Fiscus: Pages 308–9
Tomas Flint: Page 187
Peyton Fulford: Page 290
Gabriela Hasbun: Pages 76, 81, 350
Kay Hickman: Pages 354–55
Sharon Hughes: Pages 334–35
Texas Isaiah: Page 386
Sasha Israel: Pages 2–3, 10–11, 14–15, 23, 26–27, 66–67, 68, 71, 140–41, 297, 300, 341
Stephanie Keith: Page 230
Nick King: Pages 102–3
Abiola Kosoko: Page 342
Caroline Ingraham Lee: Page 226
Cameron Linton: Page 90
Lindsay Linton: Pages 237, 238–39, 349
Kelly Marshall: Pages 52, 62, 358–59
Baxter Miller: Page 218
Steven Miller: Page 208
Leigh H. Mosley: Page 248
Quince Mountain: Page 319
Rick Poon: Page 173
Kristin Powell: Page 325
Shaun Price: Pages 49, 50
Ben Ritter: Page 115
Mary Rozzi: Page 385
Jason Schmidt: Pages 266–67
Heather Sten: Page 192
Justin Sullivan/Getty Images: Page 31
Romy Suskin: Page 57
Kevin A. Taylor: Page 36, 106, 113, 118
Cassie Wang: Pages 245, 272
Carissa Wertman: Page 366
Matika Wilbur: Pages 280–81
Woodlucker: Page 380
Joshua Woods: Page 168
Josette Youssef: Pages 40–41, 45, 398

For Georgine,
who taught me that
learning never stops and
friendship has no age limit.

And for Cecilia,
who lived a life full of
bravery and beauty.

Contents

WE NEED TO REMEMBER ACROSS GENERATIONS THAT THERE IS AS MUCH TO LEARN AS THERE IS TO TEACH.

—GLORIA STEINEM

Introduction

Since the beginning of time, women have been the keepers of stories, traditions, and wisdom. And for too long, the powerful conversations women have with each other have been overlooked, because society often devalues women, age, and knowledge that is spoken rather than written. *Collective Wisdom* seeks to rebalance these scales by valuing women who have lived long and complex lives— and the experience and perspective that come with that.

My goal with *Collective Wisdom* is twofold. I want to gather and share stories and advice that we can all return to, over and over, whenever we need help finding our way. But I also want to remind anyone reading that the most powerful and life-changing tools we all have access to are the connections we form with other women. For that reason, you'll see two types of stories in this book: **individual stories** and **intergenerational group stories**. These are woven together throughout the book just as they are in real life: there are no group stories without individuals, and each individual is shaped by the communities they are a part of.

The individual stories profile women—most over the age of 50—reflecting on their lives between childhood and the present, in their own words. These stories not only include happy, joyous recollections but also touch on life's challenges and what the women have learned from them.

The group stories are all intergenerational conversations. Many are between two women, whether they're family, friends, mentor and mentee, colleagues, or a mix of each. Some are among larger groups of women, like the members of the Resistance Revival Chorus (page 160), participants in the Gee's Bend Quilting Retreat (page 66), and dancers from the Washington Wizdom (page 22). The women discuss what they've learned from each other, what they hope their relationships bring to each other, and how their lives have been impacted by their connections.

The women in these pages have blazed trails for over a century. From an Olympic athlete (Gail Marquis, page 197) and a NASA team member (Elaine Denniston, page 244) to award-winning artists (like Paula Greif, page 390), activists (like Miss Major Griffin-Gracy, page 384), writers (like Carmen Agra Deedy, page 291), and filmmakers (like Joan E. Biren, page 249), these women have been the guiding forces of so many different movements and communities.

The issues discussed throughout this book are complex. Addressing both things we all have in common, like experiencing loss and grief, and things we don't all necessarily experience, like living with a chronic illness or disabilities, *Collective Wisdom* does not shy away from difficult topics. You'll read about women's experiences parenting (and *not* parenting), how different cultures view aging, how self-confidence and empowerment change for women over time, and why so many women think the decades between 40 and 60 are the best.

As much as there are moments of uplifting advice and wisdom, there are also useful, honest, and vulnerable reflections from women looking back on their lives. These reflections serve as a reminder that while age often brings wisdom, it rarely offers closure or perfection. Every woman in this book has not only evolved but is *evolving*. They are curious about themselves and the world.

I came away from making this book with a better understanding that life is messy, and very little is linear. There is joy next to sadness, community next to loneliness, friendship alongside family. My biggest takeaway is that things won't always be okay, but that is okay.

In sharing and celebrating the stories and the lessons the women in *Collective Wisdom* have learned, my hope is that anyone reading will feel uplifted, less alone, inspired to reach out to women who are older or younger than they are right now, and moved to nourish and celebrate the relationships they already have. Your whole world can change when you change whom you listen to. Mine has changed from listening to everyone here.

—GRACE BONNEY

Cecilia Chiang

SAN FRANCISCO, CA

Restaurateur Cecilia Chiang was perhaps best known for bringing the food of northern China to America. After a harrowing escape from the Japanese invasion of China as a child, she came to San Francisco, where she went on to open and run the beloved restaurant the Mandarin, host a cooking show on television, author several cookbooks, and be the first woman to win a Lifetime Achievement Award from the James Beard Foundation. Before her passing in October 2020, at the age of 100, she sat down with her granddaughter Siena Chiang to reflect on the life she lived.

What was your childhood like?

I had never worked until I came to America. I had been a student in China, but when the Japanese occupation started, we had to leave. We had to walk to Free China, to Chongqing. That walk took us six months.

For months, we didn't have a bath. We could not travel through the big cities because the Japanese soldiers were bombing and shooting. So we walked at nighttime through all the little villages, with no maps. We found our way, though, because every little village would have some kind of a guide. We would pay them and ask, "Where is the next village?"

Just before we got to Chongqing and the Neutral Zone, we saw that the soldiers had dug a huge ditch, just like the Berlin Wall. The Berlin Wall went up, but this went way down—because the Chinese were afraid the Japanese tanks could go through a wall. So we had to cross that ditch.

The Japanese soldiers had robbed us of our luggage before we got there. But they had left us our coats. It was a miracle. My mother had sewn money—gold pieces we called "little fish"—into the linings of those warm coats.

The soldiers charged us so much money to get across the ditch, but we paid them, and they threw this big rope to us from the other side. They tied us up and pulled us over so slowly; it was so scary. I've gone through a lot. But we survived, and we were able to get to Chongqing.

What has been one of the most memorable moments from your life?

When my sister and I got to Chongqing, we registered our names. Then a military chief drove by and asked if I was Sun Yun (my Chinese name). I said yes. He handed me a letter that turned out to be from my high school classmate, inviting me to dinner that night.

The soldiers told me she was now the general's wife. In school, people had laughed at her because she was very tall. But I always said it was not right to make fun of her. "What's wrong with you all? She is just older." But I had forgotten all about that.

We were able to clean up some, but our hair was so full of fleas that we had to use gasoline to wash it. The soldiers gave us some fresh clothes, and we were able to go see her in her home. She was happy to see me, and she told me she remembered how I had protected her in high school. We ended up staying with her for over a week.

Is there something that used to scare you that you no longer feel afraid of?

No. But maybe I'm naive in a way. I always keep going back, and I don't give up. Like with my restaurant; people told me I couldn't do it, but I kept going back and never gave up. If you make up your mind about something, you can do it. I'm a fighter, you know.

What did it feel like when you decided to sell the Mandarin?

It felt like I lost a baby because I had been in that business for so long. And the staff was like family. I felt kind of lost all of a sudden. So my friend Alice Waters said, "Cecilia, you come work for me. I need somebody to work downstairs, show them how to do vegetables." I said yes, but under one condition:

no salary. So I went to Chez Panisse to work for her. I never actually retired, even now.

Do you have a mantra or any words that you live by?

I always say: Enjoy your life. Be happy. I have gone through a lot. You are lucky living in the United States. When I was growing up in China, I remember the conversation at the dinner table was always about the civil war. So now I live here and I feel safe and very happy.

Do you think people have misconceptions about getting older and what that means?

I think everybody's different. I have a few older friends, and they still worry about their health and finances. But I don't really think too much about those things. I believe when someday the Lord calls me, I'll go. I'll say fine. All that I have gone through, a lot of ups and downs, difficult times and everything—if I die, I have had a good life, I think. And also, I did something. Something I am very proud of. I have no regrets.

What was the most meaningful gift you've ever given or received?

Five years ago, I got a phone call from somebody I didn't know. He was asking me what year I was born, and I said, "What's this all about?" Finally he told me he was from the James Beard Foundation. Then I got a letter saying I had been nominated for an award—but no other details.

I was already retired then, so I wasn't thinking about awards. I never even dreamed about it. But then I found out I was being given the Lifetime Achievement Award. It was like an Oscar for the movies. My son said, "My mother is a really big deal."

I was the first woman, and also the first Asian woman, to get such an award. So I feel really proud.

What are some of your most memorable moments from working at the Mandarin?

One time, a woman came in with her three daughters to have dinner. I showed them to their table, and I had a menu in my hand, pointing out everything. The woman said to me, "Show me your hands." And then she said, "Poor you. Look at your hands. Girls, remember I told you don't spend any time in the kitchen; spend more time in the bedroom. Then you won't have hands like this."

People always look at my hands, and I say, "I don't feel anything is wrong with them. I feel that God gave me my hands, and they're for work. They're not just for being beautiful."

Who have been the most important woman mentors or role models in your life?

My mother. She taught me about life: how to get along with people and all about good food. She had a lot of influence on me. We weren't very close. We had a formal relationship, which was common in China in those days. I just watched how she did things.

One thing that sticks with me is how my father used to praise her in front of us. At that time in China, the husband never did that. My father would tell us how my mother was such a good cook, and very good at managing money. When we were kids, our parents took us to all the famous restaurants in Beijing; they explained the dishes and flavors to us. In many ways, the way they raised us was very unusual. It definitely influenced the rest of my life.

Were you treated differently as a woman business owner?

Oh yes. Everybody told me the restaurant business wasn't a woman's world. You never saw women chefs or owners in those days. Never. I went against a lot of the rules. I never thought I would fail, and I was totally naive about that, even though I didn't see anyone else doing it. I just thought I could do something differently.

One time, Norman Lear came in. He was meeting someone for lunch, and I was at the front desk. He said he was looking for the owner. I told him, "I'm the owner." He was so surprised. He said, "Wow! I was expecting some gray-haired old woman." I was in my forties. I seated him, and he asked if I knew who he was. I said, "I'm sorry, but I really have no idea." That made him laugh.

And what about now? Do you think there is gender equality today?

Young people in general are way smarter than they were when I was young. They know so much more, have so many more opportunities. But no, it's still not equal. Men get paid more for the same job. How can you explain that? They say that everyone is equal here in America, but it's not true. Race, gender, class—they all play a role.

What made you think you could succeed? Looking back, what were the keys to your success?

I always thought I could do something different. I'm not a follower. I like to create things on my own. I see so many young women today who are afraid. But you have to try. You have to focus on doing something different, and being unique. Also, always keep learning.

Are you proud to be a grandmother?

People would say you take after me, which I do think is true! But what was more important to me was that I saw that you weren't afraid. If you wanted to do something, you would just go ahead and do it. I see a lot of me in how you weren't scared to do what you want. I'm very proud of that.

Usually in Chinese families, the third generation is not close to the grandparents. The age and background difference is so big. We have a unique, special relationship in that way. You are one-third my age, but we are so close. I still remember when you were a teenager and you taught me about saying "I love you" when we talked on the phone. We didn't say that to each other in China when I was growing up; it's part of your American upbringing. But I'm so glad saying that is part of our communication now.

Margo
Real Bird

CROW RESERVATION, MONTANA

Margo Real Bird, 83, is a matriarch of the Apsáalooke (Crow) Tribe. She is known as Baahkuuwiia, "Early Morning Woman." A member of the Whistling Water clan, Margo is early to rise and reads the newspaper daily. She has resided her entire life on her family's land along the banks of the Little Bighorn River near Garryowen, Montana, on the Crow Reservation. A descendent of Chief Medicine Crow, Margo has three children and more than twenty grandchildren and great-grandchildren and is affectionately described as kaale (grandmother) to many. She was an elementary school teacher for twenty-five years, as well as a Head Start instructor, working with thousands of students. She's a member of the Crow Tribe's sacred Tobacco Society and a bearer of many traditions and stories of the Apsáalooke people. Margo sat down with writer Anna Paige to talk about her life.

What does your current age feel like for you?

I like my age, and I always tell people, I'm 83 years old. I'm doing good. I have birthday parties that last for about three days. I used to be the youngest; now I'm the oldest of the Real Bird family. I'm the last one. I could go at any time. But then I think, What if I live to 100? My granddaughters say, "Oh, that would be fun. You will have one hundred candles on your cake."

Your Crow name is Early Morning Woman—where did that originate?

From one of my clan uncles. When you're born, they give you a Crow name. And then when you reach a certain age, they give you another one. Some of these men, they have about two, three of them. One of my nephews has four. Any time they do a good deed or something, their clan uncle or aunts or somebody in the family names them.

My first Indian name was given to me by my grandfather, my dad's stepdad, and I had it all the way until about 30. Then I had a ruptured appendix. My mother said I just about died. She asked one of my clan uncles to give me a new name. And that's Early Morning Woman. In the morning, you see the sunrise, and you say, "It's a good day." That's why he gave that to me.

Your clan is Whistling Water. What is a clan?

We follow our mother's clan from way back when they were still nomads. My mother said they used to camp together. If you're a Whistling Water, you camp together. You are a child of your father's clan, but you are a clan of your mother's clan. I'm a Whistling Water and a child of a Greasy Mouth. There are ten of them.

What role do you feel your ancestors, or the women in your family who came before you, play in your life?

They taught me to be a good woman. My dad, his mother was a good woman. My mother's mother was a good woman. They provided for their kids, gave them a place to stay and a home. I think that's carried me on.

What are you most proud of about yourself?

That I was a teacher. That I earned my own living. I didn't have to depend on somebody. I got my own paycheck. I always say, "I earned my paycheck, so you be careful." I get up every morning at six o'clock. And I don't gamble; I don't like to spend my money foolishly.

Can you describe a turning point in your life, and how it changed things for you?

When my youngest one was 2 years old, I got divorced. I was about 28 or 29, and that was a turning point. If I hadn't, I'd probably be somewhere with him. Maybe the Lord put it that way so that I would be out of that family. He hurt me really bad. He broke my heart. So I don't see him, I don't talk to him. After we were separated, I said, "I'm not going to be poor. I'm going to go and do something to support my children and myself."

What is a lesson you're still learning or need to learn?

Health. You need to eat right. You need to exercise. You need to walk. That helps a lot to even your mind and your body.

Knowing what you know now, what would you go back and tell your younger self?

Start early. I should have gone to college when I graduated high school. But I was expected to get married and have kids and have a home. Then I was afraid to leave the reservation. So I was satisfied with that until later. I could have done more, but it's all right. I'm satisfied with everything.

You have been surrounded by lots of youth. What have you learned from them?

They look after me. I always think, That must be old age. When I get out of the car, they rush and try to help me to the door. Lately, I've been needing that. I fell during the winter. I landed backward. My granddaughter said, "And what did you do?" I said, "I laid there and made snow angels."

You've had a tough year—in 2020, you buried several family members, including your twin brother, and you were also hospitalized for two weeks with COVID-19. What was that like?

I was really scared of COVID, and I got it. Before you die, you complete your outfits—what you are going to wear before you go to the Other Camp. While I was in the hospital, I was lying there, and I said, "I don't have any moccasins. If I go to the Other Camp, my mother would probably get after me for not having any moccasins."

When my nephew died from COVID, we didn't get to see him. He was a strong man, a rancher with a lot of cattle and horses. That really got me.

What are some of your happiest memories?

My kids, when they were born, that's one of the happiest times I remember. I loved all of them, right then and there. I even remember what they looked like when they were born. I have three, two boys and one girl. My daughter had a lot of hair. And my older son was really big—he's still big—and I always remember his hands.

You come from a large family and grew up with eight siblings. What was that like?

On my line, I have about thirty-five relatives. I grew up with six brothers and two sisters. And my sisters each had nine kids! Seven girls, two boys. That's a lot. My siblings were a lot older than me. My sister would always say, "Don't get pregnant. Go to the clinic and get something. In my day, there wasn't any."

My mother had a brother, but my father was an only child. My dad said in those days, they didn't have any house or a stable place, so women didn't have too many children. That is why he was the only one—they were just settling down, or something like that. My grandma was the daughter of Chief Medicine Crow. They named a school after him. My mother's side is from Medicine Tail. He was a right-hand man to the chief.

Crow Fair is a century-old tradition for the Apsáalooke people. Have you always taken part?

Every year, except last year, because of COVID. We sure missed it. I think everybody missed it. The first Crow Fair, they say, was started by my mother's dad. He had a lot of ideas, and a Bureau of Indian Affairs agent came to him and wanted to gather all the people and have a contest, like gardening and horse races, so he started that.

When my daughter and, later, my granddaughter were little, I would take them to the parade. I have my whole parade outfit, elk tooth dress that was my mother's and trimmings for the horses, beaded stuff my mother made for me. She always took first place, second place. But now we have a float because there are so many of us.

Who in your family does beadwork?

My daughter does the beadwork. My mother had a lot of Indian artifacts. Her mother-in-law made cradleboards for all my mom's kids, but by the time my brother and I arrived, she had already died, so we didn't get one. But the others, they did. I say, "Where are they now?" They are at the Cody museum (the Buffalo Bill Center of the West). I said, "Why did you get rid of them?" She said, "With this many kids, I have to buy food, so I sell them." She even made dolls and cradleboards for the dolls.

One time, with my mother, we went over to the museum, and she saw her own Indian saddle. She said, "I don't know how it got there." Like the museum in Chicago with all those war shields—I don't know how they got there. Maybe they sold them.

What did you want to be when you were younger?

My dad said that a woman had to get married and have kids and stay home and cook. That's what their idea was. But sometime along the way, I wanted

to work. It must be that time where all the women want to work. I have some cousins I went to college with. They are teachers.

At what age did you start teaching?

I got my college degree at 33. I had just separated from my husband, had three young kids, and had a high school diploma, but that was about it. I had no other training or skills, except cooking. I said, "Oh my God, how am I going to feed my kids? What are we going to do with no car?" And then I said, "I'm not going to be poor. I'm going to go and get a college degree." And they all agreed, my brothers, my sisters, they said, "Oh yes! Go." So they took care of my little kids. From school to my home is about 70 to 80 miles. I stayed at the dormitory, but I would go home when I got lonesome for my kids. In the morning, I had to get up at about five o'clock to go back.

My dad used to say that it would be all right if you worked with children, because they don't gossip and don't say anything bad about you. And here I was a teacher, and my dad had died before I got my college degree. He always said, "Work with children." So I did, for twenty-five years and more. And I like all of them. I still talk to them. I want to know where they are at. I know some are in prison, some are nurses and teachers. They invite me to their graduations. And to their children's birthday parties. I am proud of them when they do something nice. When they are in trouble, I talk to them. One, I asked, "Why did you do that?" She looked at me and said, "You weren't there."

What does the land you are on mean to you?

This is where we live. This is where all my grandkids came home to. My father gave me some land for wheat, three allotments, so I get money in the fall. Whoever leases my land, I always meet them before I sign anything.

I have a son who raises horses. He goes out every morning and checks the land, across the river and along the banks, to see that there's no one trespassing, make sure there are no stray horses or cattle. Nowadays, you really have to watch your land.

What has been passed down across the generations of your family that you carry today?

All the stuff, artifacts, they go to the men, like my brothers and nephews, so I don't have any. But I was taught to never sell your land. So I don't. Where I live now is where my great-grandmother, my mother's dad, then my mother, then me, and now my children live. Six generations now. My land is adjacent to the Little Bighorn battlefield. It starts right where the line is. Some people have come and wanted to buy it. But I say no. If I did, we wouldn't have any place to go. So I never sold it.

My dad used to say, "Remember you are a Crow Indian. Don't act like you're a white person." We have religions, too. We really care more about health, wealth. I have bundles that are for wealth. And I keep them in my bedroom. In the spring, I take them out and cedar them. Then I have a lot of medicine bundles. They were made for my parents and are for good health, wealth, owning a home, and having children.

Who or what has influenced your life the most?

My parents. They made us go to school "on the other side of the world," outside our home. We couldn't miss a day of school. We had to go. If you stayed home, there was nothing to do.

I got a lot of encouragement from my family. My dad reads a lot, even though he only went as far as eighth grade. He would say it was just like high school if you finished eighth grade, in those days.

And after I started working, the school principal taught me a lot of things. And I became a good teacher. She was a mentor. She was strict. She taught me timing. If your job starts at eight o'clock, you come twenty minutes before. And she made us read.

Our grandma wanted her kids go to school, and my uncle was the first one who graduated from Hardin High School in 1924. And then my sister was the first Crow Indian girl to graduate from Hardin. I said, "We broke the ice."

We all go to school. We all have high school diplomas. But now my nephews and nieces, they have master's degrees. They ask me if I wanted to go for a master's and I say no, too much work.

I have a brother who graduated from the University of Montana. He was a chairman for six years. I graduated from Eastern (now Montana State University—Billings). I told my dad I was going to go to work. He always said I was a good cook, and there was an opening for the school cook, so I applied. But then they put me as a secretary, then from secretary, they put me as a teacher's aide. Then after teacher's aide, they told me to go back to college, and there was a whole bunch of us who were chosen to go to college, so they picked me, and I got my college degree in elementary education.

You have a heart for encouraging youth. Where did that come from?

I think it's from my mother. My dad, he's very stern, very strict. He gets after us. He doesn't hit, but he cusses. Even that hurts. My mother, she likes to laugh. And then she always says, "Have some pretty things," so I always have pretty material in my dresser, a pretty scarf. I like those pretty things.

It's a dangerous world for Indigenous girls and women, and many young women who go missing are found murdered. It's a crisis. You taught the women in your life to take good care of themselves and learn self-defense. Why did you share that kind of knowledge?

My dad used to say, "People are dangerous. You be careful. Don't go near them if they are mean." So I didn't go near people who didn't like us or who were mean to us. Then he said, "If someone hits you, you beat them up good." My granddaughter Nina, when she was a ninth grader, one girl kept fighting her, so Nina beat her up. And she had to go to the principal and the counselor. And they said, "Nina, your grandmother is a teacher. Didn't she tell you about rules?" "Yeah, she did," she said. "If anyone hits you, just beat the shit out of them."

My dad used to say that if your child doesn't come home by midnight, you get up and go look for them. I always watch my granddaughter. I tell her it's like this. She says, "Yes, Grandmother, you told me." But you have to hear it every day. Now she kind of understands.

What message do you have for women reading your story here?

Be strong. Don't gamble. Help children.

I FELL DURING THE WINTER. I LANDED BACKWARD. MY GRANDDAUGHTER SAID, "AND WHAT DID YOU DO?" I SAID, "I LAID THERE AND MADE SNOW ANGELS."

The Washington Wizdom

WASHINGTON, DC

The dancers of the Washington Wizdom are a moving and grooving reminder that the adage "age is just a number" is true. The Wizdom dance team was formed in 2019 to entertain the crowds during halftime breaks at Washington Wizards NBA games. The team comes from a diverse range of backgrounds and life experiences, but they all have two things in common: They love to dance, and they're over 50. Dancers Robin Beasley, Sheila Samaddar, Elizabeth Zucker, Dottye Williams, and Pamela Gaskins got together before one of their performances to share what dancing with the team has meant to them.

What was your earliest dance memory?

DOTTYE: In 1975, I won Miss Personality in a dance recital. I still have the trophy, and my daughter mocks me for it.

ROBIN: I studied ballet at the Jones-Haywood Dance School, one of the historical studios here in DC. I was auditioning for a part—and mind you, I was like 5 years old—and I didn't get into the show. So I left ballet forever. How dare they not choose me? But life is funny, because now I'm taking ballet again.

SHEILA: I have always been in motion. I was a majorette baton twirler and competition twirler. But my favorite event is called "Fancy Strut," and you have to strut your stuff. So that would be my first experience dancing in front of an audience.

PAM: My earliest dance memory was in the early 1970s at our community center. I was a part of a modern dance class. And I remember specifically that one of the first dances we did was to a song by Teddy Pendergrass. It was "Wake Up Everybody," and it has such an awesome meaning and was so much fun to dance to.

LIZ: I remember being a snowflake in a school play. But then at age 7, I started taking ballet here locally in Silver Spring. And I was professionally and classically trained till I was 18. I hit my turning point at that age, in terms of deciding whether to be a biologist or a ballerina. And I chose biology. So this is great because I get to dance again.

What did it feel like the very first time you stepped out onto the arena here in front of a packed house?

D: Well, actually it starts before you get on the floor. We rehearse behind the scenes, and then we get lined up. And while we are lining up, our stomachs, or at least mine, is full of butterflies. And it's like, "Do I want to throw up and do I really have to go to the bathroom?" All of this for two minutes we're doing on the floor. And so you're nervous. But the minute you get on the floor and you drop your head and the music starts—it's heaven. It's an awesome feeling to have seven or eight thousand people looking at you as you dance. I love it.

S: It's a weird calm, actually. I've danced my whole life, but this is a different kind of excitement because you get on the floor and it's sort of a melee and there's so much stuff going on around you. There are camerapeople, and there's the basketball team. It's this injection of energy that is pure magic. It's unbelievable.

What does it feel like to be a part of a team like this?

P: One of my nieces dances for the Wizards. She informed me that they were having auditions for the Wizdom, and I waited until like the last minute to put in my paperwork. When we tried out, it was just so much fun, and we all were feeling like even if we didn't make the team, the experience of seeing so many women from so many backgrounds coming together for one cause, to be a part of this team, was amazing. The camaraderie that we have, the

support, the concern that we have for each other's families and encouragement—it is a special group that I am thankful to be a part of.

L: Sheila and I are rookies. I had so many layers of anxiety about auditioning, but they were all so welcoming. Every single person on the team made us feel welcome here.

S: When we walked into the very first rehearsal, after we all made the new team, I went to shake hands with everyone. Not a single person shook my hand—they all grabbed me in a big bear hug. It made me cry.

You know, as you age, it's harder to meet friends. And I was really excited that I was going to have like twenty-seven new besties. I have my professional friends and my kids, but this is different because this is a part of me that existed before family, before kids, before my job. And it's like—I'm back. Some part of my youthful self and who I *really* am was back.

How does it feel to be something of a role model to people out in the stands watching?

P: I think each of us reflects wonderfully how things can work out even as we age. You're never too young or too old to achieve anything or dream anything.

D: I think the thing about what we're doing is that it's actually a service. You never know who, in the crowd of people, just needed a smile. People see us in the hallways after the game and ask for pictures and a hug. You never really know what that means to people. If we can bring a joyful experience to one person, I think we've achieved what this group was supposed to be about.

R: Our team is not like the Dallas Cowboys Cheerleaders. We're not all the same height; we don't all have the same hairlines. Everything is diverse in this group, and I think that helps people in the audience relate to us. Sure, some of us can dance a little bit better than others, but that's not the point. The point of it is, no matter how old you are or how your knees or back might be hurting, you can do it, too.

How has being a part of this team affected your identity and self-confidence?

P: They say that people in their sixties are their happiest, and it's true. You're finding your peak.

You just learn to let all the little challenges and anxieties of your youth go.

R: To know that I'm a part of this wonderful group and that, until the day I die, my granddaughter will be able to say "My grandma did this!" means so much. It's a big deal to me.

S: I've never really left dance. It's always been there waiting for me to come back. But after having kids, and worrying about losing baby weight, I'd started thinking I might never perform again. To realize now that I can perform, and have fun, and that I shouldn't be so caught up on the external—it's been a huge help. This team has shown me that we can still get out there and show people that we can be proud of ourselves and *represent*—and be a part of something bigger than each of us individually.

What misconceptions about aging would you like to dispel?

R: People think that you can't do the same things when you're older that you do when you're younger. But that's not true. I teach aerobics and have women in my class who are in their twenties, thirties, forties, fifties, and sixties, and sometimes it's the younger women who are groaning and moaning and I have to say, "Come on, ladies! You can do it!" I think age has little to do with it. You can still move and dance and have fun, and everyone needs encouragement now and then.

D: I think the key is to just never stop. Keep dancing; keep doing what you want to do. That's what I strive for, and it really keeps me moving and feeling good about myself.

What do you hope people watching you feel when they see you out there dancing?

S: I hope they feel happy and encouraged, and feel they, too, can do something like this for themselves.

L: I hope that people at any age are willing to take on a new challenge, because taking on something that might make you uncomfortable at first can be an amazing experience in the end. That's what this has proven to be.

D: I think when the crowd sees us on the floor, they say, "Here come the old people . . ." But then we go out there and we shake and we dance and we're all over that floor. I think they are shocked. In a way,

AS YOU AGE, IT'S HARDER TO MEET FRIENDS. AND I WAS REALLY EXCITED THAT I WAS GOING TO HAVE LIKE TWENTY-SEVEN NEW BESTIES.

YOU'RE NEVER TOO YOUNG OR TOO OLD TO ACHIEVE ANYTHING OR DREAM ANYTHING.

we are showing them that you can keep going until you drop. That's pretty much it. We are going to keep going until we drop.

R: I would like them to walk away with the same joy I'm feeling when I'm dancing. I want them to feel encouraged that this is something that, no matter how young or old you are, can still happen. There is a place where you can be out there having fun.

P: I think if we can make the audience feel better than they felt coming in, that makes me happy. You never know what a person is going through, and just being there seeing older people dancing— if we can bring a smile and some joy, I think we've done our job.

What is your favorite song or type of music to dance to?

S: I'm a disco girl. I grew up with "Do the Hustle," and I was in college and I'm teaching everybody in the dorm how to do the hustle. High energy— always twirling, moving, spinning. That's me.

L: I love hip-hop, and I love the fact that we do more current stuff, too. Even though I'm a ballet dancer at heart, I love hip-hop.

D: For me it's gotta be Motown.

P: I love R&B, but being a native Washingtonian, you have to love anything go-go and anything by Chuck Brown.

When do you feel your most powerful?

D: For me it's at church. I'm a playwright, so when I get to perform there and get standing ovations— that makes me feel empowered and lets me know I'm on the right path.

P: I feel most powerful when I can help someone. So whether it's a person on the street, a family member, or my dance team members, whatever I can do, if I can help somebody, I know my living has not been in vain.

R: I feel most powerful when I can be of service to others or serve others. I felt that the most when I was teaching preschool, and it wasn't just about the kids but the whole family. Letting parents know that they're doing a good job or helping them in situations where they just didn't know what to do with the kids—being able to help them was such a gift. And dancing out here on the floor, that's another way to help and uplift people. So I'm glad I get to do that.

S: As I've aged, it's definitely changed. When I turned 50, a lot of things happened in my career. I reached this amazing professional pinnacle and realized that I wanted to focus on what made me feel like I was more of service. I'm a dentist by trade, so I helped found a mission to Haiti, and I was able to provide service to a ton of people there.

L: Well, I had a wonderful career in conservation biology. I just retired and I did a lot of great things and saved a lot of wildlife habitat. But I'm most empowered when I'm doing Derek's choreography on the court.

Betty Reid Soskin

RICHMOND, CA

Betty Reid Soskin is, at 100 years old, the oldest National Park Service ranger serving in the United States. Though she was born in Detroit and spent her early childhood in New Orleans, Betty moved to Oakland, California, with her family after a hurricane destroyed their home.

After cofounding Reid's Records with her first husband, Mel Reid, Betty became a well-known songwriter during the civil rights movement. Her work at the music store inspired her to get involved in civic activism, which led her to work as a field representative for California state assemblywomen Dion Aroner and Loni Hancock.

Betty worked on the creation of the Rosie the Riveter WWII Home Front National Historic Park in Richmond, California, and soon after its opening, became its official park ranger. She was named California Woman of the Year in 1995 and attended President Barack Obama's inauguration in 2009. In 2018, she published *Sign My Name to Freedom: A Memoir of a Pioneering Life*, which documents her life from childhood to the age of 96.

Where did you grow up, and where do you live now?

I grew up in Oakland, California, and I am living now in Richmond, which is about two towns over, but they're all part of a big metropolitan area.

Do you remember what you wanted to be when you were younger?

I don't. I imagine it was different at different times. I can't imagine I would have ever dreamed I would become a park ranger at the age of 85, but I did!

What role do you feel your ancestors, or the women in your family who came before you, play in your life?

My great-grandmother, whom I knew as a child, was a slave. She lived to be 102. My aunt Vivian loved my great-grandmother very much, and I think it was through Vivian's interceding that, as a child, I knew my great-grandmother as well as I did. My great-grandmother grew up in a town outside New Orleans called Welcome. She worked for the village doctor. He would come through town once every three months on horseback, and her job was to go out and hang a white towel on the gate of any home where he was to stop. When he was done, he would confer with her and she would take over their care until he came back, three months later.

I always felt the need to be that person who was hanging imaginary white towels, as long as I could do so. And I think that probably was the way I handled life through all the problems that came up.

How has your sense of self-confidence or self-acceptance evolved over time?

It has changed so often, sometimes I wasn't even aware that it was happening. For example, I never intended to be a park ranger. I started out working with the state of California as a field representative and was attending meetings that were shaping the creation of the Rosie the Riveter WWII Home Front National Historic Park. I don't remember how it happened, but at some point, I left my employment with the state and became a park ranger. It sort of all fell into place. I don't remember how it started, but I know that when I arrived at the age of 85, and they wanted to put me in uniform, that would mean that I would be official. I had already followed a forty-year contract of helping to plan the park, so when that came to be, I realized that I had helped to form it, and that was quite something.

I HAVE BEEN MANY WOMEN. THEY COME AND THEY GO, AND SOME OF THEM I WOULD HAVE LOVED TO HAVE STAYED WITH ME LONGER, BUT THE FACT THAT I HAVE BEEN ALL THOSE THINGS HAS MADE LIFE, FOR ME, VERY RICH.

In looking back, it feels like a big deal, but at the time, it wasn't. I think all things feel that way. I think sometimes, we don't realize how big and life changing something is until we're much further along in it.

When have you felt the most empowered?

I think I was reborn at a point in my life where my first and second husbands and my father died, all within three months. I didn't know who I was because I had been Betty, and Betty Charbonnet, and Betty Soskin, and Betty Reid, and I didn't know who was left behind. Then one day, I woke up and I felt absolutely spellbound because I suddenly felt whole for the first time in my life. I felt free, and I didn't know I'd been bound, and nothing can feel freer than the freedom you get when you did not know you were bound. And I've been going ever since on that Betty that was freed.

What does your current age feel like for you?

It feels like I'm where I need to be in these years. But because I was a stroke victim in 2020, I had a feeling of dying and coming back. And that was something that I wasn't sure of as a state of being, except that when I finally came back and realized that I was going to be living longer, I entered a stage in life that I had never been in before. And it still feels somewhat strange, because there are days when I don't feel that I should be here and there are days when I feel that I have something left to do and I don't know what that is, and maybe I won't know. Maybe it will reveal itself at some point.

What are you most proud of in your life so far?

I think the evening when I got to sing with the Oakland Symphony. I got to sing a song that I had written, and it was as if I had all of my life leading up to that moment. I can remember sitting on that barstool on a big stage with five choruses and the entire Oakland Symphony and singing a song that only lasted three minutes and fifteen seconds. But it felt longer than that—it was so wonderful.

I also got to visit Washington and meet President Obama (and First Lady Michelle Obama) and introduce him to the nation on PBS. That was quite something.

What's the biggest risk you've taken in your life, and how has it shaped you?

I'm not sure that this applies to me, because I've taken so many risks and I've always lived my life in a *constant* state of surprise. I'm not a planner. I don't make lists. Every morning, I wake up to a brand-new day, I face it, and I'm not sure that I've ever measured any risks and what they might demand of me.

Who or what has influenced your life the most?

My children. Each of them is different. Each of them has changed so much in such a short time that each of them requires a piece of me that I didn't know I owned.

What would you like to learn or experience at this stage in your life?

I don't really think there's much left for me to experience that I haven't experienced. I'm not even sure how I would go about measuring what that might be, because I have a feeling that I've really lived so much in my life. I think that's a reason why I was willing to go when there was a chance that I might die. I had a feeling of completion.

Knowing what you know now, what would you go back and tell your younger self?

I would tell my younger self not to be afraid, because I think fear was something that was at the bottom of, or behind, so many things, and I never really got a handle on what to do with fear. I think it would be good to be able to look fear in the face and really know that I could best it.

At this point in your life, what have you made peace with that used to be a struggle for you?

I think the fact that marriage was something that I always had expected to get more from, and it never lived up to what it should have. And to have learned, after I was 70, I think, maybe 65, that it was simply never necessary. There was nothing I could do when I was married that I couldn't have done without being married, and if I had to do it over again, I don't think I would marry. I think that I would probably have children, but I wouldn't ever be married, and that surprises me, because I've always thought that life was lived in twos, and I find now that life was never lived in twos at all, that it was possible to have done everything that I have done, plus have children, and not be married. I think I would have loved that. I would like to have been able to live as that person.

What impact do you hope your life and story will have on the people around you?

That is one of the great mysteries in my life. I don't know why I have influenced people's lives. But I knew a Unitarian minister who I felt knew me as no one else did. His wife was another who knew me that way. I think they had a picture of me in their heads that I liked. I would love to have been who they thought I was, and sometimes, I really was that, but only sometimes. Most of the time, I was one of the women that I have lived my life as, because I have been many women. They come and they go, and some of them I would have loved to have stayed with me longer, but the fact that I have been all those things has made life, for me, very rich.

What misconceptions about aging would you like to dispel?

The misconception that at a certain age you stop being curious. I don't know what I would do if I stopped having questions, because the questions always push me into discovering more. But now the questions are taking on a different character. They're not demanding answers. The questions now lead to more questions, but I'm not frustrated by them. I used to be, but I'm not expecting myself to know, ever, because I'm sure that some questions are only answered collectively and that none of us has the answers to anything. But we all do have questions.

NOTHING CAN FEEL FREER THAN THE FREEDOM YOU GET WHEN YOU DID NOT KNOW YOU WERE BOUND.

Judy Heumann

WASHINGTON, DC

Author and disability rights activist Judy Heumann, 73, is one of the leaders behind the Americans with Disabilities Act (ADA) and is a tireless advocate for people with disabilities. Her lifelong devotion to fighting for the rights of disabled people has been chronicled in the documentary film *Crip Camp* and in her memoir, *Being Heumann.* Judy's work with state and federal governments, nonprofits, and disability interest groups has had a lasting and profound impact on the lives of disabled people throughout the world. Judy is a leading advocate for the independent living movement and sat down to speak with fellow disability rights activist (and founder of Alpha Studios) Kaitlyn Yang about her life and work from her home in Washington, DC.

What does your current age feel like for you?

It's a very interesting question, because my age feels different today than it did in February 2020. In February 2020, I was a 72-year-old disabled woman who was going to be traveling around the country and doing things with my book and moving as I have throughout my life. Then when COVID hit, all of a sudden it was my age and my disability that put me at greater risk. And so that's when I really had to start thinking, Okay, you are 72 years old. You did have polio, and you do have respiratory involvement. And so you *do* have to be careful. So I don't feel whatever 73 is supposed to feel like, I don't feel like that, but I do have to highlight it in my mind; I have to reconcile how I feel with what science is saying are the risks.

How has your sense of self-confidence or self-acceptance evolved over time?

My confidence level has evolved a lot over my life. And I would say I still have a lot more to learn. Having experienced segregation based on disability, I really encourage families to have their kids who have disabilities be in regular school environments and regular neighborhood environments, because I think limiting my ability to socialize with kids who didn't have disabilities—it was a failure for that to happen.

Frequently being the only one in a wheelchair, it took a lot for me to be able to enter the room. It's one thing to sit in a room, and it's another thing to *speak* in a room. So for me over the years, it's really been about having to learn to have confidence in what I'm saying.

One thing that has helped were times when I wasn't just speaking up for myself but was reinforcing things that other disabled people were saying, like with *Crip Camp.* There's a moment in the documentary where I'm wearing a red dress and I'm talking about bathroom accessibility, and that is a very indicative scene of me. I was surrounded by other disabled people, and saying what I said around other disabled people *to* nondisabled people gave me a sense of confidence that I was saying something that was relevant not just to me but to other people.

It's also been important to my self-confidence to make myself say things that are uncomfortable. For many decades, I've chosen to talk about the bathroom and bathroom accessibility. Because it's something that people don't talk about, and yet everybody uses the bathroom. And so trying to really discuss this in a way that shows the absurdity of what we have to experience as disabled people is something that is important for me. It's making people feel uncomfortable in a different way because they don't want me to be talking about the bathroom. I feel uncomfortable because I want them to understand that if you couldn't go to the bathroom for the number of hours that we can't go to the bathroom, it would alter your life. And I know that the bathroom problem would be resolved.

Would you say that you feel your most powerful within a community of disabled people?

I feel like together, we're empowered. So, it's not that I feel more empowered, but I feel the energy from the group. If I'm talking to people like myself who've been involved in the movement for a long time, that's one discussion. But if I'm talking with people who are younger and are just emerging into the movement, finding their way, then I tend to not change what I'm saying, but maybe change how I'm saying it and looking at ways of getting people more engaged. I don't like a power imbalance. So I have a habit, which not everybody likes, where if people ask me a question and I feel like they have an answer, then I'll ask them to answer their question before I answer it. Because I feel like if I answer it, I can be overshadowing what they're thinking, and I really want them to say what they're thinking.

If you could go back in your life, what would you like to do over?

I suppose in some ways I wish I had felt less shy. It kind of goes back to when I was about 9 years old and my mother, my father, my brothers, and I went to Hyde Park, where the Roosevelts lived. Mrs. Roosevelt happened to be there that day. And my mother insisted that we go over and speak with her. And I was frozen. I feel like that exact feeling is something that repeats with me, where I think in some ways, I don't see myself like other people see me. And so it does hold me back sometimes in going forward to talk with people, particularly nondisabled figures of note, even if they know me. I would say one thing I would like to go back and do is to really have that inner strength to be able to venture forth and not to feel hesitancy.

Is there something you would never do again?

I went on a blind date once that I would never go on again. It was through a dating service, and I didn't know the guy. And I had him meet me at my singing teacher's house because I thought if we met him together, we could tell if he was an okay guy. And it turned out that he really wasn't. And I was in a manual wheelchair, and it just became a potentially pretty bad situation. So it did make me decide that I would never do any kind of dating service again, because it really put me at risk.

You have been married for a long time. How has love shaped your life?

I think love is very important because it allowed me to have emotions that evolved over the years. Love, in the beginning, can be without boundaries and involve very strong emotions that are great to feel. But in long-term relationships, there's so much ebb and flow that goes on that it's really learning how to create a balance, how to continue to grow in the relationship and also, as things change, to be able to look at ways that we can evolve. So we've been married for twenty-eight years now. It is amazing, really. And I've learned a lot in those twenty-eight years.

How has loss shaped your life or your outlook on how you're fighting for disability rights?

Well, I mean loss, I think, goes beyond just disability. I'm Jewish, and my mother and father both were sent out of Germany when they were teenagers. And so my first experience with loss was when my friends had grandparents and we had none because they were all killed in concentration camps. So being able to really understand what that meant and how it shaped my parents' lives, our families' lives, was important. In the neighborhoods where we grew up, people hadn't experienced those kinds of losses. Not that people in their families hadn't died, but they died of natural causes. So for me, loss is about trying to integrate aspects of the people who were close to me who have passed away into who I am, to not only talk about them but also consciously do things in their memory. That's a big part of the custom in my family and in Judaism and many other communities. It's really "May their memory be for blessing," which for me means, What are the things they valued, and how can I help perpetuate what their objectives in life were?

What's the biggest risk you've taken in your life, and how has it shaped you?

I've taken a lot of risks, some bigger and some smaller. I was always afraid of flying. I actually was arrested on a plane in 1974 when I was flying by myself. I was working for a senator at the time and had been asked to comment on a set of proposed federal regulations that would have restricted the ability of disabled people to fly independently. I was on the plane, reading the book *Fear of Flying*, and the captain said I couldn't be on board by myself. I refused to have anybody designated as my assistant, and they called the Port Authority police. I got arrested and taken off the plane. I was so happy that I was getting arrested because I thought, Oh my God. Now we can finally get some real publicity out of this problem. But then when they found out I worked for a US senator from New Jersey—you wouldn't know this, but Port Authority police are based in New Jersey—they didn't press any charges.

Another big risk was when I made the decision to file a lawsuit against the New York City Board of Education. I had been denied my teaching license because I was paralyzed and couldn't walk. Making that decision to file a lawsuit was a very big deal for me because it meant I was going to be in the limelight.

Do you have a message for younger women reading your story here?

Tell your own story. Look at my story as an example of what I experienced. Look at what you've experienced, and take the time to try to really delve deeply into how your life has progressed, how you've gained strength, where you think you still want to grow, how you want to reach out to work with other people to enhance your growth and contribution.

We don't know what life's trajectory is going to be. I took risks like moving from Brooklyn to Berkeley, California. I had no family there. It kind of contradicted everything I had thought about previously. I was able to take that risk because I trusted that there was a community in Berkeley where there were a lot of other disabled people. That was very important to me. And I could get the support I needed to be able to move to the next stage of my life, which was moving back to Washington to work in the Senate. I've had these huge changes

in my life that I never would have had before the opportunities were given to me. And if you had said, "Would you take advantage of such and such an opportunity?" I might well have said no. But I really feel like I did push myself in a way that I think was very helpful. Taking risks is something we should all consider doing—reaching out to other people to help us feel secure in what we're doing. It's so important.

The way my life has evolved over my 73 years, I never, ever would have thought could've happened. And in many ways, on a day-to-day basis, I am still amazed by things that have happened. Be bold. Take risks.

At this point in your life, what have you made peace with that used to be a struggle for you?

I wish I could say I feel like I've addressed all the things that have challenged me, but I think some of those things still challenge me to this day. For example, my inability to say no. Sometimes I should be saying no, needing the amount of assistance that I need, because it can be difficult to find people who could be helping me. If I had the assistance I needed, I might make certain changes in my life more readily than I do, so that's definitely an issue.

Abeer Najjar
and
Huda Najjar

CHICAGO, IL

Abeer Najjar, 35, is a self-taught chef, a food writer, and the founder of Huda Supper Club. She uses food as a canvas for storytelling, and, through her cooking, works to preserve culture and inspire conversation about identity. Huda Najjar, 66, Abeer's mother, is a Palestinian American home cook and certified siti (grandmother). Originally from Jaffa, Palestine, Huda's family was displaced to the al-Am'ari refugee camp, where Huda was born and raised. In the 1970s, she immigrated to Chicago, Illinois, where she's lived for over forty years. She loves cooking, gardening, and being surrounded by her family, including her fourteen grandchildren.

Where did you grow up, and where do you live now?

HUDA: I was born and raised in Palestine. I came to America when I was 24 years old, and I've lived here for forty-one years now. My husband had brothers here in Chicago, so they helped us arrange our paperwork to come to America.

We thought we were going to live a better life, with beautiful clothes and a beautiful house. But the situation was not good, and after having our first baby, I spent a month in the hospital. Then we had to find a new apartment, and it was so hard. We started to suffer. But someone helped us find an apartment, and we lived there without a bed, without furniture, and we had to use a suitcase as a crib for our baby. Little by little, we found a way to live.

Nobody taught me how to handle the stress of all of this. So when I found out seven months later that I was pregnant again, my husband was upset. But I knew I was going to have the baby and, despite the bad situation, God gave me patience for this life. You give your life for your kids, and I enjoy them.

ABEER: For the majority of my childhood, we were on the Southwest Side of Chicago. I was very attached to living in the city. I liked that I knew how to get everywhere. I liked the diversity of the neighborhoods we grew up in. Even though we live near a predominantly Arab community, my mom encouraged us to hang out with everybody. She said, "As long as people are nice people and good people and they're a good influence on you, I don't mind." And that was kind of my experience growing up: We had this family that was so diverse, and different people, neighbors, and elders in our neighborhood. We didn't have that extended family of our own, so our neighbors and friends became our extended family.

When I was 17, we left the city for the suburbs. That felt like such a change. I went to a private Islamic school, and it was such an isolating experience because I never really even felt part of a particular brown or Muslim community growing up.

I definitely had that common experience that a lot of children of immigrants feel. There is this pull of "Are you Palestinian?" "Are you American?" "Are you what your neighborhood is?" "Are you a Chicagoan?" And ultimately as I got older and was able to start to make sense of what my identity was, I realized I can be *all* of these things. All of these things are who I am, and it's reflected in the person I am, the work I do. But then, it was really hard to make sense of because the world is polarizing and wants to put you in a box and label you, and that became really difficult for me in my teenage years.

What was it like connecting with other members of the Palestinian diaspora in Chicago?

A: When my mom first came here, she didn't wear a hijab and was not visibly Muslim. My parents lived in an ethnically mixed neighborhood, so people didn't know if they were from a Latinx background, or Arab or Iranian or Persian. There was tension, so sometimes you wanted to be ambiguous. But there's actually a significant population of Palestinians in Chicago. It's one of the most heavily Palestinian populated cities in America.

H: I made other friends that were not from Palestine. Like the older woman in our building from Lithuania who would make cookies and bring them for my oldest child, Ilham. Another neighbor, a teacher, would come and talk to me. As well as an older man who had fought in the war. We would sit outside and talk. They helped me talk and not feel depressed, and they helped me feel that I was still a human being.

But it was hard. My husband had mental health struggles and was diagnosed as bipolar. And I got sick again after the birth of my fourth child, Abeer, and spent twenty-one days in the hospital. I had a high fever. The doctor came to me and said, "Let me give you some advice, sister. Thinking about your kids doesn't save your life. Please take care of yourself." His words renewed my will to survive. I had forgotten about Huda. There was no Huda anymore; there were only four kids and a husband. But my goal was for my kids to go to college, so I went to work to support my family.

I worked cleaning houses and cooking for families, and one time one of the women I worked for asked me why I brought Abeer to work with me. She said, "Don't you worry about that? I would feel uncomfortable for my daughter to see me like that. It's embarrassing for her to see you do this work."

But I said no, I'm working to live a better life, and she knows that. And she's happy. I thank God we don't have this mentality. I'm not embarrassed of what I do. Everyone I work for respects me and loves me, and I enjoy working. It's a hard life, but it's a happy life.

And now this girl, Abeer, she is my friend. She knows me better than I know myself. And I know her better than she knows herself. We have a good history with each other. We travel with each other, and she helps me solve problems for the family.

A: My mother and I have connected in an interesting way as both being part of the Palestinian diaspora, though we're from different generations. During one of our first trips back to Palestine, we were up late one night talking over a midnight snack. The jet lag is hard to shake, but it meant we had pockets of time together, just us, without the sometimes overwhelming environment of so much family being around. I expressed to her how I'd longed to visit Palestine because I thought it would feel like "home." How I'd thought that all the identity struggles I'd had growing up would disappear and it'd all make sense. But that the reality was, I still felt all those conflicting feelings when I finally got to Palestine. She expressed how she felt the same way. And it shocked me. She said, "This is my country and my home, but it has changed, and I have changed, so I don't know how I fit in." Of course we were surrounded by family, love, the beauty of Palestine, and delicious food. And it felt like home. But while we felt the comfort of one home, we missed the other. She said, "I miss Chicago." And later on, when we were well back into the routine of our American lives, I'd say, "I miss Falastin." We've reflected on this a lot. That even though we were born in different places, grew up differently, and have our own multi-hyphenate identities, the unease and floating feeling of being a part of the diaspora is something we share. That being able to call so many places home can be a bittersweet blessing we might carry all our lives. And that we may find "home" not in physical locations but in the spaces we hold, stories we tell, and meals we share.

My mom sometimes leaves this out, but in the last five to ten years, she's done a lot of self-work.

She's doing things that other members of our community don't talk about and support. There's a certain stigma around mental health.

H: I go to a therapist now. She's good. I talk to her, and she's helped me learn how to deal with my husband, how to talk to him. All my life I thought it was okay, solving problems by myself all the time. Sometimes I cried. I didn't want to answer the phone because I didn't know what to tell my kids. But now I listen to them. I listen, listen, listen. So we can understand each other. I'm getting better, and I appreciate life a lot.

I used to ignore my family back home because they could read me like an open book. As soon as they saw me, they'd say, "What's wrong, what's happened, what's up?" Arabs like to know everything. But sometimes your family sticks their nose in and can make more problems, not solve them. That's why I thought it was better to not say anything. But I can't hide things from Abeer. If she asks if I'm okay, she knows when I am not.

A: People in our own Muslim brown immigrant community won't even pass by a mental health clinic—they don't want people to think that's where they're going. There's a stigma about treating mental health issues. So we are constantly telling my mother that we're so proud of her for all she's doing. Because in our culture, when people become elders, it's like they *stop*. It's like, "I did my life." They're just done; that's it. They're not going to do any more work. But she's like, Nah, I'm going to do more.

She started going to therapy at 65, and I've encouraged her more than once to make an Instagram video with me about it. Because so many of my friends say, "I wish my mom would go to therapy" or "I wish there were access for them to find mental health support in a language they are comfortable with." I just want to emphasize how proud we are that she's doing that, because she's one of the only people in our family to go to therapy. She's reconnecting with Huda and finding out who she is now and will keep living a flourishing, fulfilling life. It's definitely helped our relationship so much.

What role do you feel your ancestors, or the women in your family who came before you, play in your life?

H: From my mom, I learned patience and how to do things. She taught me to live a simple life—you don't have to have *everything* in the house to have a good life. Life goes on, whether you have something or not. My grandma said, "Sometimes you only have one or two ingredients to cook. You have to cook them in different ways so that your kids won't get bored with them." Because sometimes there's a rough time, and they eat the same thing for a month or two months. I know ten different ways to cook chicken and potatoes.

A: When my mom went to Palestine one time, my brother did most of the cooking while she was gone. We didn't have a lot of money, but my brother found chicken breasts on sale for 29 cents a pound. He bought twenty pounds of chicken, and he had to get *so* innovative cooking chicken breasts. And this was pre-internet, so we didn't know a lot of recipes. But we survived on just chicken breasts for a month. He found so many different ways to make them, and I'm just now connecting that memory to what my mom is talking about with her grandmother's advice.

As I've gotten older, I've gotten more in touch with what being Palestinian means to me. I'm really getting in touch with what this generational and ancestral influence is. I can listen to a sad song and miss family that I don't have one memory with that I can 100 percent recall.

But then I realized that cooking from the soul is cooking from an ancestral fire, and it lights that ancestral connection. Obviously my mother telling me all these stories of my grandparents makes me feel I know them. It's about being with family and making connections. So anytime we have gatherings, like for Ramadan, we will invite so many people. Like a hundred friends. And I always think, We don't even have space for fifty, or have fifty chairs, how will we do this? But everybody is able to pack in and find space, and we will always fill our home with friends and family, and it will be so beautiful.

When any of these memories of family and food pop into my head, I realize that in a way, you really do become your mother, your grandmother, and your great-grandmother. I think that's beautiful— what a way for them to live on. Those traditions can transcend cultures, borders, and even language.

What are some of the most meaningful lessons you've learned from each other?

A: One of the meaningful things I've learned from my mom is that even when everything's stacked against you and you don't think things can get better, you have to persist and have hope and faith. You can hold space to both be persistent and resilient but also give yourself grace. It's especially difficult for me to listen to her stories about when she first came to America, when she refers to herself as being a blind cat, just trying to find her way. I'm so upset at a world that did that to her. And at the same time, I'm so proud that she's my mom.

There could be injustice, there could be such difficult things that weigh you down and make you feel helpless and hopeless, but you find strength within yourself. And sometimes you end up being that person who gives hope to other people or inspires love and the desire to grow and change in people. I think also, not having shame around having a life that's not perfect and not performing for other people is something I learned from her.

I think that planted the roots for me around my new career in food and in writing. I do not have shame to speak up about injustice, even if I'm the only one saying something. I'm not afraid that I'm not going to be accepted into certain rooms that want me to be a token Muslim, or be a token Arab or brown person.

The way we've been able to relate our love for food and our food experience and how it connects to our identity is just a joy. Right now for me it's just about connection and joy. And I think that is revolutionary. She has shown me how to reconnect with our food and also how food isn't only about what is on the plate or in the bowl. It is that this is *home*. This is safe. This is nourishing. And this is keeping us connected and moving forward.

What are you most proud of about yourself and about each other?

A: I am most proud of my confidence to identify as Palestinian and express my Palestinian identity, despite so many efforts to tame that, invalidate it,

I'M PROUD OF MY MOM FOR DECIDING THAT IT'S NEVER TOO LATE FOR HER TO FIND HERSELF, AND TO FIND HER WAY HOME. AND TO CONTINUE TO LIVE A LIFE THAT'S FULFILLING, AND FULL OF JOY, AND FULL OF NOURISHING FOOD.

dismiss it, and erase it. I'm proud of myself for still being able to utter the word "Palestinian," to utter the word "Palestine," despite everything that comes with that. I'm proud of being able to change my definition of success, so that I am not afraid that I won't be "successful" if I stay connected to this part of my identity.

I'm most proud of my mom for her decision to continue her journey in life, despite whatever cultural baggage may try to hold her back. Whether that's American, Arab, or Muslim culture telling her that her life is over because she's completed this service to her kids and her husband. And I'm proud of her for deciding that it's never too late for her to find herself, and to find her way home. And to continue to live a life that's fulfilling, and full of joy, and full of nourishing food.

H: I'm proud that I raised my kids and that I'm a good wife—and I hope I can be a good grandma. I'm proud of myself because I had the courage to leave and move away from my family. I miss them a lot. But I hope I did a good job.

This girl, Abeer, I'm proud of her because she's still listening. I'm proud of her because she's good with her religion, with her choices, and with choosing good friends. And she's good with people. I trust her. But the worries of being a mom never stop. It doesn't matter that she's older. You always have that same feeling of worry.

I'm also proud that she did something on her own. I think she's the first one in our family. Whenever I watch her videos online, I think that I've never seen somebody do what she does. She connects people with Arabic food and with one another. She relaxes people. She cooks our food, but in a different way. Maybe it's better. Her food tastes so good! And she did everything by herself.

Amy Denet Deal

ALBUQUERQUE, NM

Amy Denet Deal, 57, is the founder of 4Kinship, a sustainable fashion brand focused on repurposed and upcycled pieces, based in New Mexico. After leaving the corporate world in Los Angeles behind to support and re-embrace her Diné community, Amy has found a new purpose and mission in her work and life: to support her family and bring awareness to the Navajo community. Amy sat down to talk with Tyra Blackwater, a fellow Diné creative, about her life and work.

What does your current age feel like for you?

I feel like a baby. I feel like a little toddler. Actually, in my Diné years, I'm 2 years and 3 months old. So, I think that since I moved back to New Mexico, it feels like I'm a naked baby in a meadow, chasing butterflies, because I'm so happy every day. I look around, and everybody looks like me. I never had that experience as a baby. So, this is what 57 feels like to someone who has taken that journey home, somebody who's come home to relatives. It's bliss.

Are you comfortable with aging?

Absolutely. I feel like I get wiser every year. I look back at my 20-year-old self, and I'm like, "Who was that person?" So, where I am right now is, I feel like I'm the most authentic I've ever been. I'm not really pulled in different directions based on what other people tell me to do or by what I watch on social media. I get to wake up every day, be in my own space and place, and do what I'm supposed to. But it took a long time to get here.

When do you feel most yourself?

When I'm alone; when I'm completely by myself. When I'm in nature. When I can feel the sky and I can feel the earth. When I sleep on the earth. That's probably my best feeling, when I can camp out and be literally on the ground. Because I feel like Mother Earth is holding space for me.

What are your hopes for your future and the future of the world?

I hope I continue to be strong and healthy so I can keep doing this important community work. If I look at the whole world of "What are my hopes and dreams?" it's really for our tribe. It's for our people. I hope we find long-term sustainable solutions for the future. I don't want to have any more Band-Aids or any more patchwork. I want to really get down to the bottom of this thing, this inequity, this inequality. And I really want to figure some shit out through creativity. And I think through creativity, through entrepreneurs, through people who are futurists, we can come up with amazing ideas about how to make things better for your children, for my grandchildren, for the future generations of the Diné tribe. We will rise. We will be empowered. We will be strong. We will be resilient. We will be the future. Ancestral wisdom is the old *and* the new way.

What impact do you hope your life and your story will have on those around you?

That we all need to be better humans, and we all need to be connected to our community. We need to find our authentic self. We need to stop listening to everybody telling us what we need and who we should be, and how we should be. As Indigenous people, we need to listen to who our ancestors are guiding us to be for the future. I just find that such an important part of what the legacy is. It's to really be authentic, to be who you're supposed to be. Every single day, I wake up. And I stand side by side with my sisters of my tribe, and we make a difference. And it's that community. It's that sisterhood. It's that connection that we have as humans, that it's not just about ego and self. It's about being connected to others, service to our community, service to our tribe. Service to the future. It's bigger than us.

What would you like to learn or experience at this stage in your life?

I need to learn more about other things that will help elevate these creative ideas I have. Either that, or surround myself with more people who are really brilliant, who can just *be* that thing, and we can all move together as a team. I want to learn how to build a sustainable house. And even if I fail, it's going to be that beautiful process of learning how to do a new thing.

Who or what has influenced your life the most?

So many people. But the most? Mother Earth, Father Sky. I mean, it comes down to us all basically going back to our ancestral wisdom of where we come from and where our culture is based. It's in everything around us. So by coming back to New Mexico and getting out of an urban capitalistic environment, I feel like I've learned more in one year just by being here than I did in all those years before.

What is the most important part of your daily routine?

Waking up. When I wake up, I automatically have about a hundred thoughts in my head that my ancestors planted there overnight. And then I know exactly what I need to do. And I'm super excited to get going. It's almost like that feeling you'd have right before Christmas where you couldn't wait to wake up to get your presents. I feel like that every day, because my ancestors are planting these little presents in my head of what I'm supposed to do or how to fix something or how to connect the dots.

What has resilience looked like in your life?

You lean into things that make you uncomfortable. And when you fall down, you get back up. Because if you don't fall down, you're really not trying hard enough. You have to fall down a bunch of times in order to be whoever you're meant to be in your life. I try to tell my kid that all the time. Like, "Do not get comfy. Do not get cozy. Try new things." And she's like, "But Mommy, I'm not good at that." I say, "How are you ever going to be a complete person if you don't allow yourself to fail all the time?" You don't have to succeed. You can be a complete and total failure in things and still be so joyful in that failure. And I want that all the time in my life.

What's the biggest risk you've taken in your life, and how has it shaped you?

Selling all my belongings, leaving all my friends, and moving to a state where I knew nobody at 56. I think that was a pretty big risk. I had a feeling I would find my place here. I felt I would find relatives and family. But I never thought it would be like this.

You feel like you've landed on an alien planet, but everyone looks like you. And I can't explain what that's like after being out of that my entire life, even as a child. It's groundbreaking. I went with the way my heart felt, and I felt like my heart needed to come home, and all the answers would be here. And that's exactly what's happened. I'm never leaving now. I'm going to be buried here among the trees on the mountains.

How have your ideas of success and happiness changed over time?

It has nothing to do with stuff. It all has to do with people. When people are nearly ready to die or they're at the final stage, they realize that all the ideas they had about materialistic things are meaningless. It's all who you have around you. It's all about the memories you have, a family, and togetherness. It's not stuff. It's not wealth. It's not houses. It's not your social standing. It's none of that. It's who's there with you when you go.

Do you have a message for younger women reading your story here?

I have a lot of hope that young women now will find their authentic selves at a much younger stage, because they need to. We really need them to be the warriors that are going to fix all of this mess that we're in right now. They need to be resilient. They need to be strong. They need to be truly who they were meant to be. I want to encourage young women to not listen to what other people think you should be. Be your authentic self, and be connected to your community. Listen to your heart. Listen to your own mind, and everything will be there. And if you ever have a question about who your authentic self is, go out and go camping. Sleep on the ground. Be in nature. Be really quiet. Do that by yourself.

Dr. Jessica B. Harris

BROOKLYN, NY

Dr. Jessica B. Harris, 73, is a culinary historian, retired college professor, cookbook author, and journalist who divides her time between Brooklyn, New York; Martha's Vineyard, Massachusetts; and New Orleans, Louisiana. Her work focuses on the food of the African diaspora, and her writing has provided a foundation for so many to learn about and better understand the true roots of food traditions in the United States. She was formerly a member of the faculty in the English department at Queens College, City University of New York, and has hosted a radio show on Heritage Radio and published eighteen books. She was awarded the Craig Claiborne Lifetime Achievement Award by the Southern Foodways Alliance in 2004 and received a James Beard Foundation Lifetime Achievement Award in 2020. Her memoir, *My Soul Looks Back*, chronicles her life to date. She sat down with chef, producer, and writer Elle Simone to discuss life, work, family, and how she sees her place in history.

Where did you grow up, and where do you live now?

I grew up in Queens, as the child of "aspirational" African American parents, let's put it that way. My folks were, I guess nowadays people would say old-school, but they were people who believed you had to be better. If you were better, you might have access. But you had to be twice as good to get half as much. That's not necessarily a good way to come up or a good paradigm for raising anybody, and it's certainly not about equality, but that was how it was. You had to be twice as good to get half as much. So they raised me to be twice as good.

My parents met in Brooklyn. They were both a part of the very vibrant cultural life there in the 1920s and '30s. There were jazz clubs. There were all kinds of things that people don't really think about nowadays in terms of Brooklyn. But it was very much an aspirational place. They moved to Queens because it represented the George Jefferson type of moving on up. It was out of Brooklyn, into Queens. Queens represented a private house, a backyard—a different thing. And the irony now is that I moved right back to Brooklyn pretty much where they started out. I've been here for more than thirty years.

How do you describe the work you do these days?

I am by avocation a food historian, which means I study history through the spyglass of food. That's me paraphrasing Zora Neale Hurston. I look at history through food and food through history. My specialty within that is the food of the African diaspora. So it's the food of the African continent itself, and then where that food went through the scattering of Africans through the various slave trades, through migration, through all sorts of things. I've done a variety of cookbooks on a variety of topics ranging from the food of Africa itself to the food of the Caribbean, the food of Brazil, a whole kind of gumbo, if you will. About three years ago, I wrote a memoir called *My Soul Looks Back*. I was looking back, and I was fortunate enough to have had an extraordinary experience.

What's the biggest risk you've taken in your life, and how has it shaped you?

I am not always a risk taker. But the biggest risk I ever took was going to France for my junior year of college. I'm an only child, and I'm very attached to my family. But I picked myself up and went, negotiated another culture, another language, met a new family and stayed with them. I still wonder how I did some of it.

More recently, I have taken the risk of allowing myself to be enamored of someone—we'll see if he responds.

How has not raising children affected your life? Do you feel like you've played the role of a parent for other people?

Well, I have a student who refers to me as her New York mama. And she has been very much like a daughter for many years. I have a lot of younger people that I think of as being Auntie to. I'm at this age and stage where it would be nice to have attentive biological children, but not all biological children are attentive. So that's a crapshoot. But honestly, at this point in time, I would like to have more family. I can't say I'm suffering from a lack of family—I have a multitude of friends—but there is something about the African American family dynamic that I don't have.

But I have been very fortunate in that a lot of young people take care of me, pay attention to me, and treat me honorably and with respect. And that is glorious. That they're not the children of my body, as it were, is what it is.

At this point in your life, what have you made peace with that used to be a struggle for you?

I think my hair used to challenge me. I mean, I've always had very, very thick hair that I've never been able to do very much of anything with. I've just made peace with it. I'm letting it do what it does, and I'm going to do what I do, and we're going to get along.

What would you like to learn or experience at this stage in your life?

I would like to have a partner. I really want to walk hand in hand into the sunset with somebody. I hope it happens. You know, I'm doing my bit. I'd also like to feel comfortable with myself, and I'm getting there. I'd like to not worry about what people think or wonder, Is this okay? I'm not there, but I'm working toward it.

I'd also like to be able to afford my life. Without making myself go overboard. I've got a taste for antique stuff that I can't afford. I like to be, in strange ways, a custodian of history.

I get a lot of very interesting, very wonderful things that people give me. I have a very full life, and I mean that in any number of ways, but equally in terms of things. But I don't mean only things when I talk about wanting to afford my life.

I have friends all over the world, and I'd like to be able to just visit them and spend time with them in other kinds of ways. I'd like to not worry about roofs on houses and plumbing problems and to have enough to take care of those things. I'd like to feel comfortable enough to be philanthropic and give here and there. Maybe once I'm gone—because it seems as if I'll be worth more when I'm gone than while I'm here—I'll be able to step up to the plate and actually make another kind of difference.

Knowing what you know now, what would you go back and tell your younger self?

Don't be so timid. Stand up for yourself more. Know your worth.

What does the future look like for you?

The good days are tomorrow. If we stick in the past, we can get stuck and we can continue to look backward. Looking backward so you can see where you're going is a good thing. It's the same thing with culture. Go back and snatch it, go back and get what you're going to move forward with. But to think that the best is behind you . . . I'm a whole lot older, and I still think the best is in front of me.

THE GOOD DAYS A[RE] TOMORROW. LOOKING BACKWARD SO YOU CAN SEE WHERE YOU'RE GOING IS A GOOD THING. BUT TO THINK THAT THE BEST IS BEHIND YOU . . . I'M A WHOLE LOT OLDER, AND I STILL THINK THE BEST IS IN FRONT OF ME.

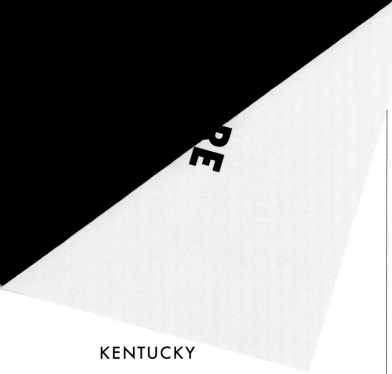

KENTUCKY

Sign painters and friends Norma Jeanne Maloney, 59, and Melissa Eason, 35, march to the beat of their own drums. Norma Jeanne's career began in 1984 when she started painting signs for the racetracks of Lexington, Kentucky. After moving to San Francisco in 1990, Norma Jeanne attended the California College of Arts and Crafts (now called California College of the Arts) for design and worked as a scenic artist for the film industry after graduation. She opened her sign-painting business, Red Rider Studios, in 1996, and she's been creating custom signs in her trademark vintage style ever since. Melissa, a graduate of Houston's Kinder High School for the Performing and Visual Arts, often works in wood, but she trained as a painter. After doing chalkboards for a national grocery store chain, Melissa took a class in sign painting with Norma Jeanne, and the two became fast friends.

How did you first meet?

NORMA JEANNE: I gave a free workshop for women to talk about tips of the sign-painting trade and about how to run a business—and Mel showed up.

Can you describe a moment when you realized that your friendship was going to be significant?

NJ: For me it was just watching Melissa during the workshop. She was so excited to be there. There was something about her that lit up the room. I couldn't wait for the class to be over so we could actually talk.

MELISSA: I knew from when I walked into Norma Jeanne's studio. She was hosting a free workshop for women—just that act is so generous, because most people charge an arm and a leg for that kind of thing. I knew that this was going to be an important person in my life. After the class, we sat on her back porch and started jamming on the guitar and singing a bunch of songs we both knew. She was a deeper version of the person I thought she might be, and I thought, Wow. I hope I know this person for a long time.

What are some of the most meaningful lessons you've learned from each other?

NJ: Most young people today want something without working for it; they want instant gratification. Mel just wanted to learn and do everything right. I was at the point where I thought, I'm not going to have any more young folks around me who want to just take from me and don't really appreciate this craft. But what I learned from Mel is that there are still people out there who do it right and who give back. She's done more for me than people I've known for thirty years have done for me. It's just remarkable.

M: My grandpa is my hero in my life. He is the hardest-working man I know. I had never known another human being like my grandfather who worked in that way, until I met Norma Jeanne. I started understanding more by watching her interact with her clients. She's a do-gooder, and she loves giving in her work. And that's really special and unique to me.

What makes you proud to call each other friends?

NJ: You can't teach integrity. And Mel is just ate up with integrity. I'm so proud to introduce her to people because she's so genuine and she fills up a room with this love and light. She gives back, and she can't do enough for people. I just feel really blessed and honored to know her.

M: She embodies the person I would like to be. She believes in giving; she believes in quality; she believes in integrity. She's so authentic. She connects with people in special ways. She remembers things about people that other people might just pass over, and she holds those things dear. That's a beautiful way to live your life, because the stories you tell about people and the way you portray them and the way you think about them defines you as a person.

What advice do you have for someone who is curious about or interested in making new friends of different ages?

NJ: I think you have to meet every person without any kind of baggage about anything else. You're meeting that person, and it's a fresh start—every person is a fresh start. Everyone has something to teach you and show you. Everyone can give you the experience of life through their story, regardless of whether they're 20 or they're 90.

M: Approach each and every human being with absolutely no prejudgment. You know, no matter who they are, no matter how old they are, no matter what they believe or what you might think they believe, just drop it and show them love. That's all we really need to do as humans: Just show everyone love. It's really simple.

What do you each hope your friendship brings or gives to the other person?

NJ: I know I'm never going to stop learning from her. I know there are so many things we're going to do together. I look forward to them so much. Sometimes when I'm having a hard day, I'm like, You know, one of these days, you're going to meet Mel on the river—just think about that. She's my best pal.

M: I want to give her the assurance that I will carry on her authenticity and her work ethic and the way she does life. I want her to know that I'm going to carry that on to the next generation. I want her to know that I'm her ally.

What are you most proud of about yourself?

NJ: I'm most proud of my relationship with my mother. I'm proud of how I can tell her anything, and how she carried me and now I carry her. It's my touchstone for my whole life, my relationship with my mom.

M: I think I'm really proud of the way that if I choose to bring joy to another person, then I can do it. I really, really, really think, just personally, that the reason I'm here and the way I feel about myself and my life and almost kind of like my purpose, when I really home in on it, is to lift people up. I love doing it, and when I do have the chance to lift someone up with joy and laughter, then I feel like I'm my whole self.

How has your sense of self-confidence or self-acceptance evolved over time?

NJ: I think that over time, I've learned that those aren't things you get from other people. You have to love yourself, and it's been really, really difficult for me to not always want acceptance from other folks. I'm not even quite there yet, and I'm 59. I think that when you have a day where you're okay with yourself and the decisions you made without anyone saying "good job" and you just saying it to yourself, you've had a good day.

M: Well, I have two answers to that. First, I finally, at 35, can look at myself in a swimsuit and be like, All right, you're fine. And second, the more I focus on uplifting myself and others, the less I care about the little shit and the bad decisions I made and the dissatisfaction with whatever's going on in my life.

At this point in your life, what have you made peace with that used to be a struggle for you?

NJ: If I can live to be 115, I would love that. Give me all the time in the world. I used to really stress out that there wasn't enough time. That I was never going to have enough time to do all the things I want to do for myself and for other people. I finally got to the point now where I'm like, All I got is today. All I got is today, and I'm just going to do the best I can

DON'T LEAVE THIS WORLD NOT DOING SOMETHING YOU LOVE.

EVERY PERSON IS A FRESH START. EVERYONE HAS SOMETHING TO TEACH YOU AND SHOW YOU. EVERYONE CAN GIVE YOU THE EXPERIENCE OF LIFE THROUGH THEIR STORY, REGARDLESS OF WHETHER THEY'RE 20 OR THEY'RE 90.

today. No promise for tomorrow. Don't sweat it.

M: I had this hang-up about making money. I always thought I was broke. I always saw myself as poor, and so I always was poor. Then I met Norma Jeanne, and she started talking about self-worth and valuing your work and valuing yourself, and I started seeing myself as more valuable. Once I started doing that, I started charging more, and now I'm actually living a semi-comfortable life, and it just gets better every day. I really believe that you actually do create your own reality and perception of yourself, which plays out into what happens to you.

NJ: I used to get in a room full of people and be like, I'll never be as good as that person. The cool thing about the last probably six years of my career is that I'm never going to stop learning, and I'm getting better all the time. I'm uniquely Norma Jeanne, and there's only one Norma Jeanne. And there's only one Mel. There's this thing that we do that no one else can do, and that has to be good enough. You have to really value your own experience and what you were given as a human being that's unique to you, that only you have, and you have to just keep growing with that. That's good enough.

What do you hope people reading this book take away from the story of your friendship?

NJ: I hope that people remember there's only one you. Every person has a purpose. If you're not happy doing what you're doing, stop doing it. Please stop doing it now. Literally. Ask yourself what you wanted to be when you were 5, what you wanted to be when you were 12. Follow what makes *you* happy. If that means you downsize to a studio instead of a one-bedroom, if that means you get six roommates who share your passion, then live like a teenager. Start over. Don't leave this world not doing something you love.

M: Spend your days in a daydream. Daydream about who you want to be, and be that person in your mind. That goal will come to you so much faster if you can just learn to daydream.

JoAni Johnson

NEW YORK, NY

Model JoAni Johnson, 69, is proof that beauty knows no age. After first attempting to enter the modeling world in her twenties, JoAni made an international splash at the age of 67 as a model for Rihanna's 2019 Fenty campaign. She has now modeled for Ozwald Boateng, Pyer Moss, Eileen Fisher, and *Essence* magazine, among countless other brands and fashion outlets. JoAni is redefining what life and a career arc can look like later in life, and doing it all with grace, class, and style. When she isn't modeling, JoAni is blending her own teas, designing jewelry, and supporting her daughters in their career paths from her home in New York City's Harlem neighborhood.

Where did you grow up, and where do you live now?

I grew up in Harlem, in an area now called Hamilton Heights. Gentrification has changed our name. I've lived in Brooklyn, Riverdale, and Syracuse—but Harlem is my place. I've always loved its diversity. We've always had pockets of different cultures. It's a vibrant community where there's *always* something going on.

What did you want to be when you were younger?

I wanted to be an artist; I was influenced by my first-grade art teacher. I absolutely adored her, and I loved the whole concept of creativity and of putting color and movement on a page.

Do you see yourself as an artist now?

Some people call me that, and I feel fine about that label. Whether it's my tea blending or the jewelry I create or what I do in front of the camera—there is an artistry there.

What does your current age feel like for you?

My age feels like endless possibilities. I grew up in a time where we always looked for possibilities, and the possibilities that happen through change. So that's continuing. And now with the youth that we have, just continuing that change, you know, you've got to get on the bandwagon.

What misconceptions about aging would you like to dispel?

That it's too late to explore opportunities and new experiences. When I was growing up, it seemed like there were always set rules for people of a certain age. For example, there seemed to be a rule that after you reach a certain age, you must have short hair. And you can see how I feel about that rule. . . .

How has your sense of self-confidence evolved over time?

In my life, I've had many experiences and done many different things. And just being able to take risks and explore new opportunities provides me with new self-confidence. It enhances my confidence within. You know, once you've done something and come through it, whether it's the good, the bad, or the ugly, it helps to grow your self-confidence.

What are you most proud of about yourself?

My resilience. When you've been around the sun so many times and have a variety of experiences and you're able to stay standing—that's resilience. The passing of my husband was a prime example. That was not a planned situation. And I had to reinvent myself and re-create my plans. It was difficult, but I'm still standing. Having the open-mindedness and willingness are major factors that helped build me as a person. And being able to do these things takes a lot of practice. But like I said, every experience reinforces who you are.

What role do you feel your ancestors, or the women in your family who came before you, play in your life?

When I was growing up, we had extended family within our community. Most of us lived near each other. My great-grandaunts and my grandaunts were very influential. They also took care of us after school. They showed me, in many ways, what it was like to be resilient—to stand up for yourself. They showed me how important it was to be able to do a job to the best of your ability and shine at it.

When do you feel your most powerful?

Oh dear. Power, to me, comes with freedom. You know, to be able to make your own choices for yourself, and to be able to stride toward your dreams. I find power when I'm in front of the camera creating something. Creativity is powerful to me.

Can you describe a turning point in your life, and how it changed things for you?

Having my daughter Joya was a turning point that definitely changed many aspects of my life. For me, there was the bond of creation. It took sacrifice, focus, research, and lots of love. She is one of my most stellar achievements. She's a rare human being who shares her gifts by educating others. I have another daughter, my youngest, who's also on her road to great things. I look at both of them as being inspirations to me because they've chosen paths that are truly nontraditional. And with that, they are keeping activism as part of it.

At this point in your life, what have you made peace with that used to be a struggle for you?

I'm challenged by putting words on a page, expressing my thoughts and truths in words. I can do that up here, in my mind, but when it comes to putting it down on paper, it's challenging. I now try to address this by allowing my words to just flow. Let an editor do the rest.

What is a lesson you're still learning or need to learn?

We always can learn. You know, I think there's a sage within the tea world who says when you stop learning, it's over. So, you know, life holds, for me, no guarantees. And that's a lesson that I learned very strongly, and I'm still learning.

What impact do you hope your life and your story will have on those around you?

You know, I hope my life and my story will always remind people of three things: To always be prepared and to be open for whatever the next step is (and many times we don't know what it is). To not be deterred by failures along the way in this thing called life. And to place more importance on nurturing your beauty from within. The beauty within is the beauty that you give without. It's the most valuable asset that you can have, as you go through these seasons of your existence.

Do you have a message for younger women reading your story here?

Never give up.

WHEN YOU'VE BEEN AROUND THE SUN SO MANY TIMES AND HAVE A VARIETY OF EXPERIENCES AND YOU'RE ABLE TO STAY STANDING— THAT'S RESILIENCE.

The Gee's Bend Quilting Retreat

RAYMOND, MS

The Gee's Bend Quilting Retreat, held outside Jackson, Mississippi, may be one of the most truly intergenerational creative experiences operating today. Founded around two members of the Gee's Bend Quilting Collective, China Pettway, 69, and Mary Ann Pettway, 64, the retreat offers quilters of all ages and experience levels a chance to come learn with quilting legends.

China and Mary Ann hail from Gee's Bend, the local name for the hamlet of Boykin, Alabama. After emancipation in 1863, Gee's Bend was an area where formerly enslaved Africans worked as sharecroppers and eventually became landowners. In the mid-nineteenth century, the quilters of Gee's Bend created a distinctive style of quilting that has finally been getting the reverence, appreciation, and celebration it deserves.

At these biannual retreats, quilters from around the world come to join Mary Ann, China, and organizer Anne Robertson, 65, in a communal space for two days where they can quilt, connect, collaborate, and join in song (led by Mary Ann and China, who are accomplished gospel singers).

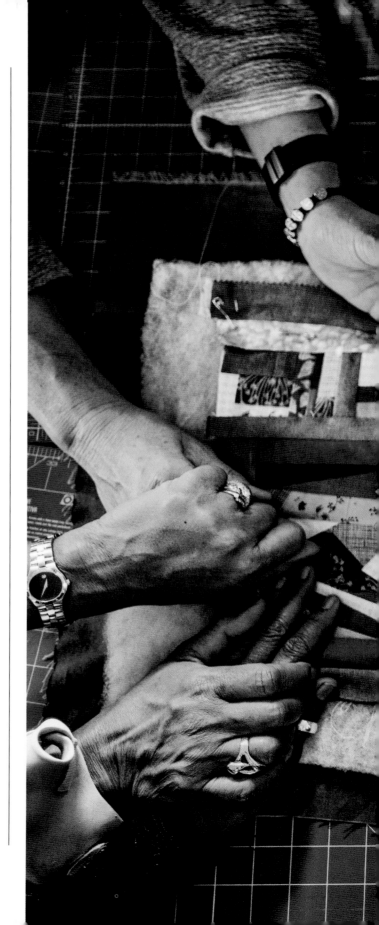

How do you feel when you're sewing?

MARY ANN: I feel relaxed. I suffer from arthritis, and when I start working on my quilt, I just forget all about it.

How do you feel being in this room with all these women?

ANNE: One of the layers of gifts of this retreat, and there are many, is the diversity of people. The racial diversity, the geographic diversity, the age and background differences, cultural differences. It's so powerful. Where else do you do this? We all come together with a common thread of loving to quilt. And somehow when we get here, we all connect and share these gifts and it's really powerful.

Is quilting a skill you've learned from other generations or see yourself handing down to younger generations?

A: Well, I would say that this art form has always been passed down from generation to generation. Usually orally. Someone taught you to quilt, someone taught you to sew, you watched them, you sat in their lap or you had the interest or they've made you do it or whatever it is. They wanted you to do it. And so we've lost some of that interconnectedness in the way we live and how full our lives are. And we don't know that we could know someone, an elder, who could teach us a meaningful thing.

There's this interesting thing about quilting: People say that it skips a generation. I sew, but my mother does not. But her mother, my grandmother, did. I have one of her quilts, and it makes me feel connected to her.

Making quilts, especially making quilts for other people, is important work. It's powerful work. Quilts are powerful. It's bigger than us, and it's an honor to have been able to pull an event like this together.

People come in and see the quilt someone has made them and they burst into tears. They treasure it like it's the most valuable thing they have. And let's get real: It's pieces of fabric sewn together. But for them, it's really powerful and it's something that they'll have for generations. And their children's children will say, This was my great-grandmother or -grandfather's quilt, and I think that's so meaningful.

What do quilts represent to you?

A: Everyone needs a quilt. Multiple quilts. And not one that you put up in a box; that's the worst. You need to use it, and you need to be under it when you're happy, when you're sad, when you're tired, when you need replenishing, when you're cold, when you're making out, whatever it is that you're doing. I mean, nothing's better than hot sex under a quilt, right?

Has quilting taught you any bigger life lessons?

CHINA: Well, I know I learned everything important I've learned from quilting. When we were coming up, my mother and I, we didn't have any sewing machine. Everything we did was done by hand. We pieced the quilt with our hands and quilted the quilt with our hands. Now people have so many different tools and different ways to do things, and I guess that's just life. But in my heart, I always hear my mama saying, "Do it your way. Ain't no wrong way to do it. You got to do it your way."

And remember: God didn't make everybody to quilt. God didn't make no two people alike. That is why he made all of us different. Because some quilt, and some take pictures. Some write. God didn't want all of us to be the same. If all of us had been the same, what type of world would we have had?

What's been your experience with making friends as you've gotten older, or making new friends here?

C: In my experience, meeting these new friends, when they say they love you, they really do love you. When people hug you, you can feel their love. When people say they love you, you can feel their love. In the Bible, they say a stranger can treat you better than people in your own home. That be the truth.
A: And at the end of the day here, it will all be something that none of the things by themselves were. It is like nature. We become stronger when we work and spend time together. You can really find your heartbeat here.

And these two phenomenal women, China and Mary Ann, they are carrying a forgotten language. They're carrying a language that people all over the world should want to remember.

What has this retreat meant to you?

MA: Being here is the flowers you give us. Have you ever heard that song? The one that says, "Give me my flowers while I yet live"? That is what this place is. They keep wanting us to come back, and they're showing us love, and it makes us feel like we are getting our flowers while we are still alive.

Overheard at the Retreat

"When I'm sewing, I feel calm and relaxed, and sometimes I can feel out of my body, too. Because as tactile as quilting is, I just daydream more. It's meditative. I don't often sew with people. I'm usually by myself."

"Quilting is an escape thing for me, and a terrific expression of my creativity. I don't really see myself as being particularly creative when you look at what I'm making now. But it feels really good to put the colors together and to put the squares together. And I've never done a planned pattern—I just make it up as I go along."

"The acoustics of this space bounce the voices around. So I know that there are people who are sewing and socializing. It buoys you to have all this creative energy swirling around."

"Being here is quite an experience. It's not what I expected. It's *more* than I expected. It's much more than I expected."

"Being here makes me feel like I can walk up to somebody and smile and ask 'Will you be my friend?' without feeling embarrassed. Here there is just that comfort of being accepted by others. And as adults, we can lose that. Being here brings me back to the playground and how free I felt as a child."

"Being in a room with all of these women is definitely out of my comfort zone. I'm usually a loner. So this has been really good for me. It feels like a safe space to branch out and just talk to other people. That's one of the reasons I decided to come: You don't have to quilt. You can just watch other people quilt, and you can talk about

quilting. There is no animosity or judgment here. We all came together to create something, and that is such an honest, special energy that nothing negative can come out of it."

"What's great about this retreat is that it doesn't matter where you're from. Because once you meet somebody, you touch them emotionally, and then we're all the same."

"My daughter just started to sew, and it's been such a special way to connect. She's in a stage of life where we don't see each other often, but I can see this being a really fun thing to do together. My sister sews as well, so I'm hopeful that we can all get together and do this together."

"Being here and quilting together, we're showing how age doesn't make a difference. And it's good to see that the younger ones are attempting to do what we've been doing a long time. It's something that's being handed down, not just with the mother-daughters but with all of these friendships. This will close the generation gap, coming together like this."

"My son died two years ago, and Anne made him a tribute quilt. I called her and said, 'I have all these T-shirts of my son's; will you do this?' And she said, 'Of course.' It was really fun because my husband, my daughter, my son's girlfriend, and I laid out all the T-shirts. And we put them in the order we wanted and took a picture and shipped them off to her. And it came back and it's this huge family memento that she was able to give to us and it became a family relic. That quilt gives me such a warm feeling."

"Hand-stitching goes back to my mother and my grandmother. I tried not to do it when I was younger, but after my mom died, almost immediately I felt like something got transferred at that time. And I have been stitching ever since. I said to my husband, it's like I still feel connected to my mother. Like that the thread connects us."

"Quilts are a time capsule. They tell family history. They're a piece of comfort and home."

Norma E. Cantú

SAN ANTONIO, TX

Writer and educator Norma E. Cantú, 74, has focused her life's work on the issues of borders and boundaries seen through a Chicana feminist lens. Born in Mexico and now based in San Antonio, Texas, Norma believes passionately that words have the power to create change in the world. After studying abroad on a Fulbright scholarship, Norma returned to the United States, where she has worked at the National Endowment for the Arts, authored and coauthored over two dozen books, and now teaches at San Antonio's Trinity University as the Norine R. and T. Frank Murchison Distinguished Professor of the Humanities.

Where did you grow up, and where do you live now?

I grew up in Laredo, Texas, right on the border, and now I live only 150 miles north in San Antonio, Texas.

What did you want to be when you were younger, and what do you do now?

I always wanted to be a teacher—and in some sense, that is what I am as a professor! I had an escuelita [little school] when I was in seventh grade. I also wanted to be a physicist, but at that time, women were not encouraged to go into science. The counselor at my junior high told me that since I was good in English, I could be a science writer, and that physics was too difficult for me. I believed her, and although I did well in the sciences, I didn't pursue it.

What does your current age feel like for you?

I am 74, and it feels great! I keep thinking I am still in my forties. When I had my cincuentañera [fiftieth birthday party], I thought it was like a marker into elderhood, but I have done so much since then!

What misconceptions about aging would you like to dispel?

Most of all, that things are over as you get older. For me, getting older has given me freedom. I have continued to write and publish as well as teach. Another thing to dispel is that just because others tell you you're old and can't do certain things anymore doesn't mean it's true. Only you know what you can or cannot do.

What are you most proud of about yourself?

That's a difficult one, because I have so many stories of things I've done. I taught an octogenarian how to write her name when I was part of a literacy project in Laredo—it was the most rewarding educational experience ever! I also walked the Camino de Santiago ten years ago, and I am so very proud of walking almost 500 miles—during the winter, no less! Of course, I am proud of my books and my work as a professor, but I am also very proud of my students.

How has your sense of self-confidence or self-acceptance evolved over time?

I am so much more confident now than when I was in my twenties! But even now, I do get nervous when speaking in front of a large group.

What role do you feel your ancestors, or the women in your family who came before you, play in your life?

A major role! My grandmother, mother, aunts, and even neighbors played a huge part as role models and guides. For instance, my mom, who was very wise, through her actions and ability to navigate the world as an at-home mom (to eleven children) and still earn money sewing and helping her neighbors, taught me that you don't have to have a degree to be wise.

What message do you have for women reading your story here, and what impact do you hope your life and story have on those around you?

I would say the message is si se puede—yes you can! Be true to yourself and to your goals. I've also learned that even when I thought things were not going well, in the end it was that contretemps, that apparent setback, that made it all go well. When we believe in our ability to do things, we can! Another of my mom's dictums: Si otros pueden, porque tú no? (If others can do it, why not you?)

When do you feel your most powerful?

I feel the most powerful when I am writing.

Can you describe a turning point in your life, and how it changed things for you?

The change points in my life are many: when I graduated from college against all kinds of odds; when I went to Spain on a Fulbright; when I moved to DC to work at the National Endowment for the Arts; when my first book, *Canícula*, was published; when I got married.

Who or what has influenced your life the most?

I would say my family. My mom and grandmother. Also, mentors like Alan Briggs, who believed I could go to graduate school.

What's the biggest risk you've taken in your life, and how has it shaped you?

One of the biggest risks was moving to DC. I left my safe and comfortable life in Laredo to go work outside of academia. Although it was temporary, it changed everything. I met my spouse then.

If you could go back in your life, what would you like to do over?

I don't think any of it. It has all been for a reason, and I wouldn't be who I am. Now, if I could change things, my brother's death in Vietnam would be one thing that I would love to change. He was a genius, and he would've done great things; plus, he would've helped me with the family obligations.

How have your ideas of success and happiness changed over time?

Not much. To me, success is doing what you love. Happiness is the same—being totally engaged in "work"—for me, that involves writing and helping community. When I was young, I did think that making a lot of money signaled success, but I don't think that now.

How has not being a parent affected your life?

I chose very early on not to be a parent. I am the oldest of eleven, and so I knew I didn't want to have children. I just knew it was not for me this time around.

At this point in your life, what have you made peace with that used to be a struggle for you?

I've always been challenged by a sense of duty. I do many things because I feel I "must"—perhaps due to being the eldest. But now it's different. I don't feel the same sense of obligation.

What would you like to learn or experience at this stage in your life?

I would love to learn Nahuatl, the Mesoamerican language, and I would love to experience more travel to places I've never been, like Africa.

What is a lesson you're still learning or need to learn?

So many! I'm learning to be more patient—still! And also to let go, to just know when it's time to move on, to let go of what I think ought to be. I started testing the #3 rule a few years ago, and it helps. That is, I try three times, and if it is not happening, then I let it go.

Knowing what you know now, what would you go back and tell your younger self?

Mostly, I would tell that office clerk typing away on customer contracts at Central Power and Light Company that it was going to turn out okay. That regardless of what appeared to be insurmountable odds at that time, I would get my degree and go to graduate school. That I would have my dream job— reading and writing and talking about what I read and write! That I wouldn't have to worry so much about money. That my siblings would be fine. That life is short and one must live it to the max. Usually when given a choice between doing two or more things, I try to do it all.

How has love shaped your life?

Significantly. Family love was everything until I was in my late twenties, when I left home. Then friends and their love, as well as lovers and their love, became the focus, and finally after my forties, the deep and settled love with my spouse. I'm not talking sexual love, but a deep kinship and oneness that is incomparable. I think my life is better for having had all these loves in my life's path.

How has loss shaped your life?

Indelibly. My brother's death in the war, my parents' passing, and even friendships that I have lost still pain me, and I feel a void. On the other hand, I do believe that these losses taught me invaluable lessons.

How has friendship shaped your life?

In so many ways! I've had friends come and go throughout my life, but some remain and endure. That is a salve and a comfort, especially when going through a rough time.

How has work shaped your life?

My work is my life. My reading and writing and teaching are "work," but more than that, they are my reason for being. I cannot imagine not having these in my life. That must be why I haven't retired.

Meg
Rahner

and

Michelle
De Marco

SAN FRANCISCO, CA

Meg Rahner, 33, and Michelle De Marco, 73, bonded over a shared love of San Francisco. While they started as roommates, they developed a deep and loving friendship that has lasted over a decade. Through years of bike rides, visits to the farmers' market, and enjoying as many "firsts" together as they can, Meg and Michelle have formed a connection that helps them both feel safe, at home, and supported. Their thirty-nine-year age difference has allowed them to learn, and reexperience, countless life lessons together as they explore the city they both love so much.

How did you first meet?

MICHELLE: We met through Meg's uncles. She's got two uncles who live here in San Francisco, and they had her come as a guest for Gay Pride one year.

MEG: My uncle John and his husband, Mike, flew me and a friend out to San Francisco. We just happened to pick Pride weekend. We didn't really know; it just worked out timing-wise. We were there for four or five days visiting, and just had such a blast. I was 18, I was such a wide-eyed kid, just soaking it all up and soaking it in, and I loved it. It was just such a positive experience.

When I was a senior at Penn State, I was trying to figure out what to do. I wanted to position myself in a city that I wanted to be in. I was trying to figure it out, and then one day it dawned on me: "I have family in San Francisco, I can go there!" Everything just started falling into place.

I called my uncle Mike and he said, "You should definitely come out to San Francisco. I'll help you find a job, and you can live with Michelle." I think he offered before he even asked Michelle. So that was sorted!

Michelle picked me up from the airport, and that night I went to her house and it was amazing. It was just an instant connection. She made me dinner, and that was the start.

MD: My daughter, who is ten years older than Meg, had been living with me. She had moved out on her own maybe six months before Meg showed up in town. So I had this big empty room, and I was knocking around in this big apartment, and really didn't have anybody to keep me company. It was a very transitional time; my whole life is sort of transitional, but this was an even more transitional time for me. So when Mike, Meg's uncle, said to me, "Look, my niece Meg wants to come back to town. You already met her; why don't you rent a room to her?" I said, "Okay!" And that's how it started.

What were your first impressions of each other?

MD: I thought Meg was sweet and fun, and I was at a point in my life where it was nice to have some companionship. And I guess with my daughter moving out, I was feeling like an empty-nest person. I'm not the most social person in the world. So it was nice for me to have company, and to have a young person around. And Meg's got a really nice attitude—she's always looking for something interesting to do and has interesting ideas about things. We clicked immediately.

MR: I remember getting to Michelle's apartment and just being so taken by all the amazingly bright decor. The apartment had a personality in and of itself, which was telling of Michelle. I just remember immediately connecting. I think it was the second day I was there, we went for a bike ride down Market Street, which can be very scary to bike down. But Michelle just seemed so adventurous, which was exciting for me because I was fresh to the city and really thrilled to see it.

In the first few days I was there, Michelle told me, "I love seeing the city through new eyes."

Can you describe a moment when you realized your friendship was going to be a significant one in your lives?

MD: I knew it right from the very beginning. Just because we connected so nicely, and it was very relaxed and comfortable and fun, and we could talk about pretty much anything. So it was always pretty great.

MR: I also knew right away. I have always enjoyed Michelle's company. Whether it was sitting down and having dinner or something bigger, I felt like we took care of each other in different ways. We would have wine and eat dinner and have all these amazing conversations learning about each other's lives. And Michelle has such an interesting life, and she was such an open book with me. And I was just really soaking that in.

Michelle and I would go to the farmers' markets on Saturday and Sunday mornings, and we'd go on bike rides, or go to festivals. We just were spending a lot of time together, instead of just going about our separate days and then coming home and having dinner. I felt like we spent a lot more time together than the typical San Francisco roommates.

MD: Meg's uncles are like family to me. They've moved away, which has become a big void in my life. But I'm so glad to have Meg in my life. I tease her sometimes and call her my second daughter, because it's almost like a continuation of having another young woman in the house. My daughter is

also very independent, and she's got her own ideas about things, just like Meg.

MR: I had a realization after spending all this time with Michelle. I had been trying to meet people, but not really hitting it off. And then I realized, "Wow, my best friend is a 62-year-old trans woman. How many young twentysomething cisgender women can say that?" I just thought our friendship was really cool, and I was really proud of that.

Was there anything you were surprised to learn you have in common?

MD: It was effortless for me, because I enjoyed Meg so much. And having the influence of a young person is always nice. Having kids and being around younger people was the best thing that could have happened to me in my life, because it's like getting *another* life. You raise your children, and you teach them, and you play with them, and you can be a kid again with them when they're small. And you can help them learn things, so you learn all your stuff again. I always thought that was a really neat part of life. And I like that about Meg, too, because she was starting to make friends, and I got to meet a lot of her friends because they would come stay with us.

It was like Armistead Maupin's *Tales of the City*. Meg always reminded me of Mary Ann, because she was from a small town in the country, coming to the big city. I got such a kick out of showing her all the different things about San Francisco that I could.

MR: I feel like that book was our lives.

What are some of your most fun memories together?

MR: One of my favorite memories with Michelle was from 2017, during the great eclipse. There was a big festival in Oregon, but I wasn't able to get time off work to go, so I asked Michelle, "Do you want to go somewhere and see the eclipse?" I knew it would be too foggy to see it in San Francisco, so she picked me up in the morning and we drove 40 miles northeast to Pittsburg, California, to see the eclipse.

When the fog finally broke, we were on this country road. There were cars pulled over everywhere doing the same thing. It felt really meaningful. I had just gone through a hard time a few months before, so I was really looking for inspiration. It was such a beautiful moment, grounding and connecting, and it was so nice to be there with Michelle. Then we met a cowboy! It was just a day full of firsts. That's one of the things Michelle has taught me that has resonated the most with me: The best days are the days when there are a lot of firsts.

MD: It was really fantastic. We ended up parking in a gated drive to a big field. We were blocking the gate, and a guy rolled up with a trailer full of horses. He was a cowboy who managed this big ranch. So he pulled his horse off the trailer and went to take care of the cattle. But when he came back down, we were still there watching the eclipse. So he started doing what felt like a rodeo show—all sorts of rope tricks with a lasso. Then he looked at Meg and said, "You want a ride on the horse?" Of course Meg said yes. She jumped on the guy's horse; it was hilarious. And to think, there we were in San Francisco, and now we're all of a sudden out on a ranch, and there's this guy with a lasso and he's taking Meg on his horse. And then we saw the eclipse. It was a great day.

How has your friendship helped you through tough times?

MD: A number of my friends have passed away, and it was always nice to have Meg as company because she's always upbeat. I hardly ever see her depressed. That's always been a big help for me. And it was nice having someone that close. Even if it's unacknowledged, it's nice to have somebody there who you know can support you if you need it.

MR: Only three days after I moved to San Francisco, we witnessed a terrible shooting that solidified our friendship, in a way. It was in 2010 during Pink Saturday, a street party held during Pride week. We went into the Castro to see a movie at the Castro Theatre on the last night of Frameline, the gay film festival.

We were all standing around talking in the street after the movie, and then suddenly the shooting happened. It was probably five to ten gunshots, and people scattered, seeking cover and shelter everywhere. It was really primal, and really intense. And then it was just chaos, and I lost everybody. I walked home and kind of shut down a little bit after that. But Michelle and I were able to work through it all together. I just wanted to compartmentalize it and put it away, but we were able to talk through it because we were both there, and I think that was really helpful.

MD: It took a while to process, because it was just so surreal. We were standing in a circle, and my back was turned away from the shooter and the victim, so I didn't see anything. I just heard the shots and saw everybody run. We definitely had some PTSD, but it was good to be able to work through it together.

MR: Outside of that traumatic event, Michelle helped me get through a really difficult breakup in 2017. I feel like she really held a lot of space for me. I actually wrote down something that she said that I didn't want to forget: "Surround yourself with people who care about things and people who care about you, and work outward." Michelle's one of the wisest people I've ever known. I feel like I learn something new every time I spend time with her. I'm really lucky.

MD: If you're lucky enough to get old and you stay a little bit busy, you end up doing and learning a lot of stuff. It just piles up.

Can you share something meaningful you've learned from each other?

MD: I like the way Meg is open to new experiences. She gets me thinking about different aspects of my life that maybe I don't think about so much as I grow older. She's always into such new things, and she keeps me in the loop about the different places that she goes and different places in town. She keeps me involved, and almost makes me feel young as well, so that's a good thing.

MR: I was born and raised in Erie, Pennsylvania, and came from a really loving and open-minded family, but I didn't know any trans people growing up. Michelle's friendship, openness, and vulnerability really expanded my worldview. Knowing her has helped me be compassionate and empathetic to her experience. She can't represent all trans people, but she's helped me better understand different aspects of the trans community that I hadn't considered. She's also helped my family understand. It's rewarding on so many levels to have a genuine connection to a community or identity that you were not previously familiar with. Michelle has also helped me understand how multidimensional people are.

What does your current age feel like for you?

MD: Well, I have to say I would rather feel young. My physical ailments have knocked me down a few pegs. I've always, my whole life, been a carpenter, and San Francisco's been really great for me. I've had lots of people hire me, and at one point I had three other transgender people working for me on one of my construction jobs. One of my buddies said, "You know, Michelle, you may have the largest transgender construction crew in the United States!"

I always loved my work, I always tried to be physically strong, and now that my strength is leaving me, it makes me start to feel older. Although I went out on my canoe for the first time in a while a few weeks ago; I've been canoeing for more than sixty years. It was a very difficult day for me because I hadn't been doing it in such a long time, so my muscles were sore, the weather was bad, the tide was wrong, I got stuck in the mud—it was a real disaster. I was gone for thirteen hours.

I was talking to my eldest son, who is now 49, and I said, "I'm a little bit sad because I'm wondering if it's my last canoe ride." And he said, "How old are you now?" I said, "Well, I'm 73." He said, "Look, if you're 73 and you're going canoeing for thirteen hours and you're climbing out of the mud, I don't think it's your last canoe ride." So that was really nice to hear, and it made me stop and realize that maybe things aren't that bad for me. I've got a beautiful little place—I live out by the beach now—and I'm pretty self-sufficient, and I can still take care of myself so far, and I'm helping my daughter by watching my granddaughter. I watch my little 4-year-old granddaughter every day. And she is, right now, the bright spot in my life. We have so much fun; we laugh and play all day. I tell her, "Play, play, play all day, day, day." And that's what we do. So I guess when I stop to really analyze it, I do not feel in my seventies. Maybe physically I feel in my seventies, but mentally, I feel like I'm, I don't know, in my forties or fifties.

MR: Before the pandemic, I loved to go see live music once or twice a week. I've started to feel old now, though. I can't go to shows on Mondays anymore. So the past year, I've really settled in and learned a lot about myself and cooked a lot. I feel like a solid 33. But I wish I had the energy I did when I was 22.

What do you each hope your friendship brings or gives to the other person?

MD: I think as a more grown-up person, it's always my responsibility to try to be supportive and help younger people. So I just want to be supportive of Meg. I'm really trying to pay attention to my life and pay attention to the things I say to people, because once upon a time I was much more abrupt and off the cuff, and I would say things without really thinking about it. And I don't want to do that anymore, so I try to embody that these days. I'm not completely successful, but I try.

MR: Trust and consistency. I feel like we've been through a lot together, and I'm not going anywhere. I feel like this friendship is something we'll have forever. And part of friendship is just being consistent about making sure you're connecting with each other, and checking in, and seeing each other. And luckily for Michelle and me, our interests are the same in regards to going to the farmers' market, and that's just a nice way that we've always spent time together. So I just want to continue to do that, and as our lives evolve and we grow, I just want to grow together in our own way, and have our friendship evolve in its own way. I know she'll always be part of my life.

What advice do you have for people who want to find a friendship like yours?

MD: Meg is always asking questions, so she pulls all my life stories out of me. I enjoy talking about all the silly things, and the wild things, and the bad things. If you ask questions, and listen, it'll make people want to be part of your life, and be part of that story.

MR: I love asking the questions because I feel like there's always something to learn. So just be a sponge. And I would say keep an open mind with friendships. Don't limit yourself to having friends within a five-year age range just because that's how it has always been for you. Age really is just a number, and I feel like deep down we're just a couple of souls on our own journeys. Just be open to that soulful connection that isn't defined by age.

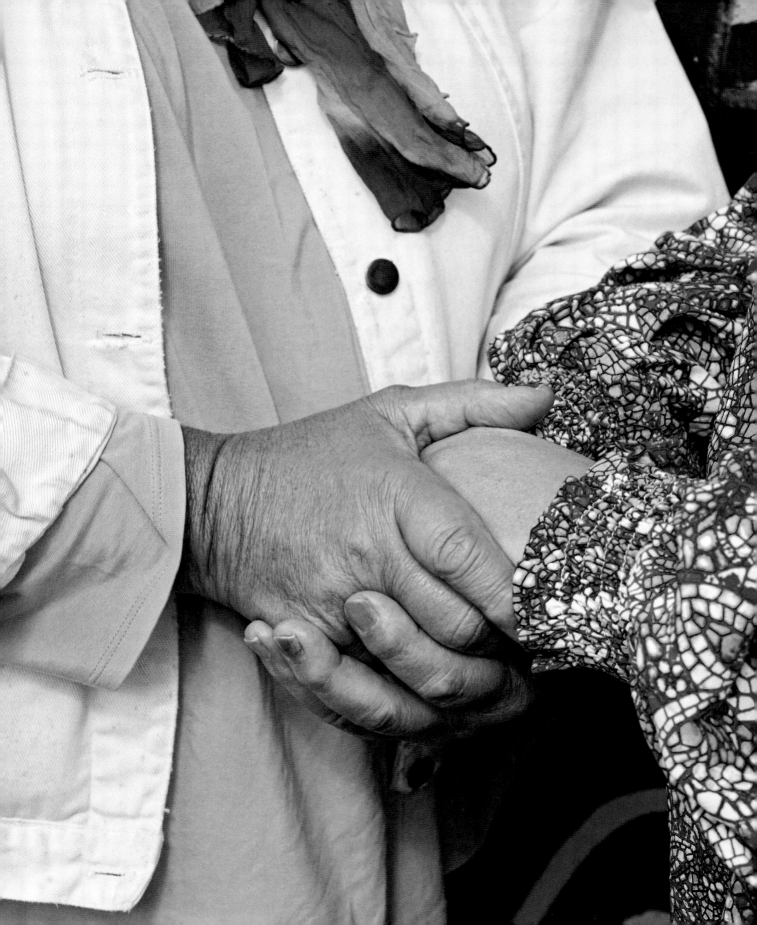

HAVING KIDS AND BEING AROUND YOUNGER PEOPLE WAS THE BEST THING THAT COULD HAVE HAPPENED TO ME IN MY LIFE, BECAUSE IT'S LIKE GETTING *ANOTHER* LIFE.

What makes you proud to call each other friends?

MD: I am proud to call Meg my friend because, number one, she's very liberal. She's got a wonderful family, and through the years I've met her sisters, her mom, her dad, her uncles, and her aunts. Whereas with my family, we had a pulling apart. I left them to become Michelle, and they left me when I became Michelle. It's more than a little bit unfortunate, but a lot of the members of Meg's family have stepped in in their place. I always tease her uncles, who are the age of my children, and tell them I'm old enough to be their mother *and* their father. So I've met all those people, and they really have taken me in and accepted me.

MR: I'm proud to be Michelle's friend for so many reasons. Michelle brings so much to a room and an environment. My uncle Mike always says Michelle has more stories than the Bible, which I love about her. So with her, it's always an interesting conversation. I feel like everyone I love can learn so much from her, and she's just such an important part of my life that whenever anyone visits San Francisco, Michelle is one of the first people I want them to meet. She's had such an impact on my life in so many ways. She's part of the reason why I'm here in San Francisco, and one of the main reasons I'm still here ten years later. I just love Michelle, and I feel like everyone would be fortunate to get to know her like I do.

Maria Hinojosa

NEW YORK, NY

Award-winning journalist Maria Hinojosa, 60, began her career as the first Latina reporter hired at NPR. She has hosted countless radio and television shows, including *America By The Numbers*, and in 1992, she helped launch the groundbreaking radio program *Latino USA*. In 2010, Maria founded Futuro Media, a nonprofit media organization committed to telling stories often overlooked by mainstream media. Futuro has produced Peabody Award–winning programs like *Latino USA*; *In The Thick*, a political podcast from the perspectives of journalists of color; Latino Rebels, a pioneering digital news outlet founded by Julio Ricardo Varela; and PBS's *America By The Numbers* and *Humanizing America*. In 2020, Maria published her first memoir, *Once I Was You*, and had a role in the film adaptation of *In the Heights* by Lin-Manuel Miranda.

Where did you grow up, and where do you live now?

I grew up on the South Side of Chicago in a neighborhood called Hyde Park, which back then was multiculti before multiculti was a thing. Once my father got a car, though, we became very mobile. I was not one of those kids who grew up only in their neighborhood. I grew up going to the Mexican neighborhoods on the weekends, and then we would go to South Chicago to get cheap gas. We would drive throughout the entire United States to get to Mexico.

Throughout my life, I was always crossing borders, which gave me a much broader perspective, and I think that's what allowed me to make the leap and move to New York to go to school in 1979, and apart from five years when I was in DC and San Diego bopping around, I've always been in New York, most recently for the last thirty years in West Harlem.

What did you want to be when you were younger?

There's actually documentation of this. A local newspaper came and did a story on my first-grade class, and they interviewed me. There's a picture of me saying, "I want to be a nurse so I can give shots to people and then give them lollipops."

I think it had to do with the fact that my dad was a medical doctor, and I couldn't see myself doing what he did, which was to look through electronic microscopes (he helped create the cochlear implant). So I think I was like, Well, I'll be the woman, caring version of the scientist, and I guess that was a nurse, but I never really wanted to be a nurse. I think I probably said that because I thought that's what I should say.

We didn't have a wide spectrum of choices when I was 6 years old. It wasn't like, "I want to be president," or "I want to be a TV newscaster," or "I want to be a writer," or "I want to be an artist." When I was 6, I guess it was pretty badass of me to even have some sense of wanting a profession.

What does your current age feel like for you?

Oh, what it feels like is 30. I have more energy now. I mean, when I was 30, I had a lot of energy, but I was using it differently. I would party a lot more. My husband and I had a very active social life. We would hang out a lot with artists. Every weekend, some kind of something was happening. So I remember sleeping late on Saturdays and Sundays.

But now I'm up super early. I use my energy differently. I'm boxing in the park at 7:00 a.m. for an hour. I never think I'm a good enough boxer, but I have to remind myself, Dude, you've been boxing for five years. You know something about what you're doing. But I say that because I'm always like, "You need to get better," which is maybe not

THROUGHOUT MY LIFE, I WAS ALWAYS CROSSING BORDERS, WHICH GAVE ME A MUCH BROADER PERSPECTIVE.

what people think about people in their sixties. I just turned 60. Even saying that is hard, because I'm like, No, that's not true. Because I honestly do not feel 60. Except for sometimes after I've been boxing, I say to myself, "What is that? Is that Arthur? Oh, it's Arthur Itis that came to visit." But I'm not going to let it stop me. So the way my day is spent might look different, but the energy capacity of what I can do in a day is completely equal to what it was when I was 30.

What misconceptions about aging would you like to dispel?

The truth is that I'm obsessed with aging and completely freaked out. But I try not to let it get to me. Because if I were to sit here and say, "Well, shit, I turned 60 this year" . . . that means that in twenty years, I'll be fucking 80! But then I'm like, "Okay, you *are* going to turn 80, so what is 80?" And I'm like, "Well, it's going to be a Rita Moreno 80."

When they were casting Rita for *One Day at a Time*, she said, "I'll play your octogenarian grandmother. But she's going to be a sexy bitch." And I was like, All right. I want to be that type of 80. I'm actively trying to change what people think certain ages look and act like.

How has your sense of self-confidence evolved over time?

Bar none, that is the best part about getting older. The reason I can be so self-confident and really *own* it is because I did decades of work to receive all the awards named after white men. So no one can question my integrity, my fairness, my objectivity, my professionalism—my anything.

If you talk to any woman, and you ask them to think about their younger years, what they all say is, "I would have told myself to get with the program, enjoy it, stop being so insecure, stop second-guessing everything." To me, that would be the best gift that I could give my daughter.

I completely love the fact that I do not battle impostor syndrome. I love, at this point in my career, just being able to feel like, So what do you want to do next? That boundless part of life feels great. I'm afraid of *other* things, but even the things that I'm most terrified of, I remember that I've

already lived through some of the worst things that I could have imagined, so there is that sense of awareness of maturity that I'm appreciative of, and that allows me to move in life with less fear.

When do you feel your most powerful?

The truth is that I feel the most powerful when I am responding to my family, when they are making demands of me. So when my family reads me the riot act, which they do not hesitate to do, and it's about, you know, "Come down off that pedestal and be here with us, and see us, and thank us, and be grateful for us," that's when I'm like, "Oh boy; you have the power to really go slugging it out with your ego. Good for you."

It might be a roundabout way to feel powerful, but it actually makes me feel like I'm using my power for good by not trashing and walking all over the people who actually love and adore me.

I would say I feel powerful when I'm working with my team. Having the capacity to have created a company, to now be expanding that company, to now be employing more people, hiring more women journalists of color—in that sense, I can easily feel like I have power to wield. Having said that, I am a Mexican immigrant woman journalist in the United States of America who's been living under the Trump campaign and presidency for the last five years. And so there's been a bit of a beatdown as well. So not feeling powerful is also part of the picture.

What role do you feel your ancestors, or the women in your family who came before you, play in your life?

In terms of my spiritual cosmology, how I see the world, the role of ancestor and ancestor worship is actually really important. I learned this mostly from cluing in to the Yoruba Santería tradition when I got to New York and hanging out with a lot of Afro-Latinos and Afro-Caribbean folk. That kind of matched with my sense of my ancestral self.

But then Henry Louis Gates Jr. [host of PBS's *Finding Your Roots*] called, and we had a very interesting experience. And basically what I've had to come to terms with, and am actually in the process of coming to terms with, is what do you do with the ancestors in your past who were horrific? What do you do with the ancestors in your past who were men, who were sexually violent? Who were physically violent? Who were men of privilege?

So Henry Louis Gates Jr. actually asked me that question: What do you think you get from your ancestors? He asked me that question before he revealed his research findings. So what I said was: When I think about my father, he was very mission-oriented and very passionate. I feel like I get that drive and push from him. And from my mother's side I feel like I get my curiosity and openness. Then Henry Louis Gates Jr. revealed some of the ugly stuff that was a part of my family history—conquerors and men in power—and it was a lot to take in. But I guess what I see there is a strong mission and strong drive. There's still that capacity my male ancestors had to leave, explore, find, and, yes, *conquer*. That's horrible. I had to make some peace with that. The other side of that story is that, ancestrally, my maternal line is Indigenous. And that, to me, was very important and very grounding.

So I'm in the midst of attempting to do some spiritual work around that. There's a saying in Mexican Spanish: "Tienes pata de perro"—"You have a dog's foot"—which means that you are out and about and all over the place. My maternal grandmother had pata de perro, and my mother had pata de perro, and I believe I have pata de perro. In other words, I believe the world is to be explored, and that is something that I did get from my maternal line, and I believe I'm working out how that connects to my Indigenous roots. I have an ancestor altar up all the time in my home—it's not just for the Day of the Dead.

Is there anything that used to be a challenge for you that you've now made peace with?

When I was hired at NPR as the first Latina correspondent, I had to write my scripts for my news spots. My husband would say, "You don't have PMS, you have PSS: pre-story syndrome." All the time I would be like, "Oh my God, I have to write a story, I have to write a script"—it was so stressful.

But I don't have that anymore. It's not to say that I don't feel fear, or that I don't procrastinate, or that I don't try to delay having to do something that I don't necessarily want to do. But it just doesn't bother me the same way anymore.

> There are certain things I don't want to conquer. Like, for example, don't ask me to learn how to roller-skate. I knew how to roller-skate once. I would love to go ice-skating again, but I don't want to risk breaking a wrist. I don't think it's worth it. Don't ask me to learn how to ski.

What's the biggest risk you've taken in your life, and how has it shaped you?

Emotionally, I would say the biggest risk was choosing my family. Again, you can choose to have all the fame and success—but it can be very lonely. So I feel like that really is a choice. It comes with a lot of things, but it is a *choice*, and I do think that for many women in positions of power, it can feel like a risky choice. So I want to talk about these things more publicly, because it's actually kind of dicey.

Besides that, forming my own company was insane. It was a huge risk. I had no idea what I was doing. I had never done anything like that. I think calling it a risk would mean that I understood just exactly what I was getting into. But I didn't. Sometimes it's better if you don't really know exactly everything that you're risking, because then it might actually stop you in your tracks.

But I think that the immigrant nature of my experience makes me feel like I'm not going to take things sitting down. In some ways, the reason I created Futuro Media was that I did not want to go on unemployment. I was at a tough place in life and was considering going on unemployment, and

I called my sister to tell her and said, "I cannot call Dad and tell him that at this point in my life I'm going on unemployment. I just cannot tell Dad that." Even though I'd worked so hard in my life and I really deserved it, I could not take the risk of telling my father I was going on unemployment. So I took a different risk and started Futuro.

What are you most proud of about yourself?

A dear friend of mine, Farai Chideya, a journalist, writer, and intellectual, called me "a queen of never giving up," and I really like that. I like that notion of just not giving up. My husband this weekend was doing some scrounging around in old boxes in our little place in Connecticut, and he pulled out a cassette from 1998. It was me getting ready for a sixty-hour music festival on WKCR that I was a part of.

I heard myself saying, in Spanish, on the air, "So we're just starting out our sixty hours here," and I was like, Sixty hours? That's crazy—I was crazy! But in many ways, there was something in me that just knew I wanted to help. I think it comes from the fact that I understood the privilege I had. I knew I had to do something with my privilege. And I think that's the thing that has allowed me to, again, be really bold, to push, and to not give up.

What is a lesson you're still learning or need to learn?

To manage my ego. In order to make it in this kind of business, in this kind of world, you have to have a very big ego. You have to believe that you are a badass, that you have a lot to say, and that you know how to make things happen. Because at this point in my life, I've made a lot of shit happen. A lot of the early part of the career was using that ego to go into the rooms with CNN executives—*all* of the executives—and that takes a lot of ego.

White men don't have a problem with ego because it's everywhere around them. Those of us women who are battling in these places really have to *convince* ourselves to act in this way. So the problem is that it's a beautiful trait. I tell my students, my young students of color, my women students of color, "You better be walking into that room like you own shit. That's how I need you walking into the room."

The problem is that you have to know that you can't be the person you are at work every day with your family. And I happen to have a family that doesn't take any shit. They put me through a lot of trial and tribulations. But I need to not think I'm all that. I need to know I can't walk around in the world like I'm all that, because that doesn't serve. So I am in a constant battle with that, but the good news is, again, that I have a family that really loves me, so they're incredibly patient. In many ways, I have a lot to be thankful for, because it's the kind of learning that you can't really do from books. And it's the thing that is the most challenging, but I'm here for it.

Do you have a message for younger women reading your story here?

The truth is that I have always been inspired by the women I saw before me and the women around me. Women have this mutual-inspiration society, and it's powerful. And for that reason, we are all part of this endless inspiration loop for each other.

I think a lot about the meditation I'm doing right now, which is on the very important art of loving oneself. And that means I'm going to feed myself better, I'm going to make sure I sleep, I'm going to give myself the little baths that I need. Whatever it is that I need, I'm going to make sure I have that. And so, in that sense, it really is about constantly taking care of ourselves and inspiring each other. Because we show each other how to take care of ourselves and how to show up for each other and how to lead.

Sandra Okuma

and

Jamie Okuma

LA JOLLA BAND OF LUISENO INDIANS RESERVATION, CA

Sandra Okuma and her daughter, Jamie Okuma, are both widely respected and celebrated artists from the Luiseño and Shoshone-Bannock Tribes. Having lived on and off the La Jolla Reservation in California, both Sandra and Jamie have supported each other in their creative work and often share booths at art fairs where they each sell their work. Sandra started painting at an early age and went on to design iconic album covers for bands like Lynyrd Skynyrd and the Who. She also worked as a graphic designer at Universal Studios and MCA Records, discovering a love of traditional beadwork later in life. Jamie is a self-taught designer who has gone on to produce one of the most sought-after fashion lines. Now Jamie and Sandra live next door to each other and have found a new form of connection and support on top of their close family connection.

Where did you grow up, and where do you live now?

SANDRA: I was born in Fallbrook, California. I grew up partially on the La Jolla Reservation and then moved to Los Angeles, California, for a while. Then I moved back to the reservation, where I live now.

JAMIE: I was born in Glendale, California, and then my parents moved us back to the reservation, where we live next door to each other now.

What did you want to be when you were younger?

S: I wanted to be a horse.

J: You wanted to *be* a horse?

S: I loved horses. They were my life. I was one of those little kids that just loved horses. I loved the smell of them. I loved to be around them and their different personalities. And I loved to ride them, obviously. But beyond that, I wanted to be different things at different times in my life. I wanted to be a vet because I love animals. I wanted to be a hairdresser at one time, but I was always an artist because I drew my whole life, basically since I could pick up a crayon. My mom was an artist and a very good painter, and she made sure I always had everything I needed to draw.

J: The first thing I remember wanting to be was an astronaut. People would always tell me, "You're going to be an artist. That's what you're going to be." But I was always rebellious. I would say, "No, I'm not. I don't want to be an artist. That's not what I'm going to do." But then I would start making things to sell. As a little tiny kid in grade school, I'd make friendship bracelets and sell them for a dollar. So I was always doing it, even though I didn't want to. Then in high school, I started doing beadwork for other powwow dancers and it just snowballed, and now here we are.

What role do you feel your ancestors, or the women in your family who came before you, play in your lives?

J: I look to them when things are really tough. They went through so much, and they still created the most beautiful things. Our ancestors were hunted down by the US Army. My grandmother was sent off to boarding school as a child, not by choice, but she was always the happiest person. She never once complained about it. So I always think, They went through all of this, so what do I have to complain about? I don't have it rough at all.

S: I always think about the same thing. I mean, listening to my mom—she was born in a time when she saw the real deal on her reservation. My grandfather didn't speak English, and she remembers him wondering where all the kids went. Because in his time, the US government came and took the kids and put them in boarding schools. So she tells me those stories.

I think about that still today. That makes us who we are. Those stories I'm hearing were so close to our Elders' time, and we carry that forward today. We've got different problems and totally different issues today, but you can still get strength from the older generations. Whenever my mom was having problems, she would talk to her grandparents, even though they were gone. She had a picture of my great-grandfather that she carried with her, and she would get her strength from them, and we get our strength from her and from them.

What advice are you trying to instill in younger generations today?

J: I think it's hard because younger people can be entitled about things. I remember before social media, I was working and had a career before all of that, and it was hard. You had to work hard to get where you were without all that. My kids have seen me work *hard*, and I've seen my mom work hard. So I want the younger generation to see that and know that's what you need to do to get anywhere. You need to really put in the work.

S: You have to put in the work. It's really hard work, but if you love it and if it's your passion, it's not *all* work. We all work hard, but I enjoy every single day, and I can't wait to get to it so I can finish it and start on something new. I want young people to know that if you find passion and work hard, you'll be successful.

What are you most proud of in your life so far?

S: Mine is obvious. I raised my daughter, and she's very successful and she's always a really good person. So that's my greatest accomplishment.

J: Hopefully I can say that, but we won't know for another thirty years or so. My boys are still so young. But the fact that my two boys are happy and healthy—that's important. I'm proud that I've been able to support myself and my kids with my talents. That's a big deal.

How has your sense of self-confidence or self-acceptance evolved over time?

S: When you get older, you just don't care. The more you mature and the more you've lived life and seen things and done things, you figure it out. You've been there and done that, and it gives you confidence you don't have when you're younger. I think young people care so much about what other people think about them, and that holds you back. But as you get older, you can see that as long as you're true to yourself, what other people think doesn't really matter.

J: I was actually always that way. Other people's opinions, for the most part, have never bothered me. I've never followed the crowd. And now that I'm getting older, I care even less. I'm not going to let the negative or the ugly thoughts affect me. Obviously I want people to like what I make—otherwise I won't have a job—but just overall, I don't let it affect me personally.

S: I didn't analyze things when I was younger. I was a really happy kid, as long as I had a horse around. I grew up on the reservation, and back in those days, we didn't have paved roads, water, or electricity. We had outhouses, and we didn't have a car. We bathed in the creek. I was happy when my mom was with us, and I never felt unconfident. I think that has passed down to Jamie. We focused more on having fun and making art. We would sit at the table and just draw all day.

J: So much of what we grew up doing was art-oriented. And I'm doing the same with my kids. They're both so creative, and in that way, they're like my mom and me. There's such a strong creative streak in our family.

S: It's funny because the people from my grandma's tribe are very well known for their beadwork, but my grandma never beaded. She was outdoorsy like me and wanted to play outside and ride horses. It was too sedentary for her to sit and do beadwork. So it skipped a generation and went down to Jamie in terms of beadwork. My great-grandma is probably so happy that her great-granddaughter is doing it.

AS YOU GET OLDER, YOU CAN SEE THAT AS LONG AS YOU'RE TRUE TO YOURSELF, WHAT OTHER PEOPLE THINK DOESN'T REALLY MATTER.

How have you influenced each other's views of the world?

S: Jamie is very fearless, and I've always been more introverted. So she's inspired me take more chances. Jamie is not afraid of anything. She wouldn't be where she's at without that ability to gamble and take a risk. She's *all in*. I've learned that from her.

J: My mom's ability to rein things in, for good reasons, was hard for me. But she's helped me slow down and double-check things, which is important. I was very lucky to have both my parents growing up and still have both of them in my life. I could count on them for anything. And that's probably why I could take bigger gambles—I knew if I messed up, they would be there to help me.

Were you two always close?

J: Yes, but what was good was that when I was younger, she was never the type to be my best friend. I knew she'd kick my ass if I messed up. Not literally, of course. But I was lucky I had a mom who would set boundaries and keep me in line. When I was a kid, I couldn't do a lot of stuff my friends could do, but now I see why.

When did you start building a friendship in addition to your family connection?

S: It changed when we started going to powwows as a family unit. Jamie was a powwow dancer, and as a family, we went all over. We were heavy into the powwow scene. And you do everything together: You make your outfits together, and you travel together. And as you get older and more mature, it turns into a friendship, but it was always there.
J: It's funny, because as a teenager, you don't want to be seen with your family. But in the powwow scene, *everyone's* together with their family. It's multigenerational. And because everybody's parents are there with them, too, you don't have that chasm between parents and kids that you might have otherwise.

What are some of your most fun memories together?

J: Everything. Honestly. But also going to the art shows. Traveling and doing the shows together was so much fun. Even though our work is so different, we would share a booth and do everything together.
S: Those days on the powwow scene were fun. Friday night, my husband would get off work, we'd get in our truck, and we'd get to follow a trail, and it was great. That transitioned into doing what we do now professionally, which then led into our shows, like the Santa Fe Indian Market and the Heard Indian. We have such a great time together there.

Can you remember a tough time you got through with each other's support?

S: There have been times when we didn't sell a thing at the market. We'd put a lot into those shows (booth costs, gas, motels), and then we wouldn't sell a single thing. And she saw that happen. So we'd say, "Are we going to eat at Black Angus or are we going to McDonald's?" And we had a lot of McDonald's together. But you know your family's there for you and you're in it together.

J: Living in a tribe, and living in a tribal way, you go through hard things all the time. But you go through them together.

What are some of the most meaningful lessons you've learned from each other?

J: I mean, to never take shit from anybody. That's a big one. That's hard to answer because she never did.

S: I've learned so much from watching everything that Jamie's become. It was an amazing thing to watch, because I knew from when she was very young how talented she was. I admire and have learned from her bravery and her ability to just go out and get what she wants. I can be sort of the opposite way. She brought me out of my shell.

When do you feel your most powerful?

J: When we're creating.

S: Yes, when we're creating something.

J: Both of us, whenever we have a really great idea, that to me is like my most powerful feeling.

S: It's hard to explain. You might have to be an artist and create to know what that feeling is. And I suppose it's the same for a writer if you get a really good idea, or a musician when you hear a new song or a new tune—it just makes you feel really, really happy.

J: It's the best adrenaline rush. I can't think of anything that would feel better, honestly.

Jamie, what makes you proud to call Sandra your mom?

J: Everything. I mean, I thank God I was born to her and nobody else. The way she's lived her life is really inspiring. She takes it one day at a time and lives as honestly and authentically as she can.

Sandra, what makes you proud to call Jamie your daughter?

S: The person she's become. Besides being so creative, she's extremely generous, and I'm really proud of that. She's just a really good, kind person. She's bringing beauty into the world, which we need desperately right now.

What does your current age feel like for you?

J: I feel like I'm finally getting to that stage where I can be like this [wags finger] to the younger ones. I feel like no one can say really anything to me now, because I know I've been there.

S: I feel comfortable, confident. I'm not as stressed out about things as I used to be. I don't have to be. I've made it this far. I'm doing well with my work. I'm still able to do it, and as long as I can keep doing it all, I'm really happy. As long as I can physically and mentally keep doing it, I'm in a really good place.

Julia Alvarez

WEYBRIDGE, VT

Julia Alvarez, 71, is a Dominican American poet and author whose work is known for its compassionate and skillful examination of the cultural expectations of women. Julia was awarded the National Medal of Arts by President Barack Obama and has won numerous literary awards for her work, including the PEN Oakland-Josephine Miles Literary Award and the F. Scott Fitzgerald Award for Outstanding Achievement in American Literature. Julia has written over fifteen books, most recently *Afterlife*, published in April 2020.

Where did you grow up, and where do you live now?

I grew up in the Dominican Republic for the first ten years of my life, under the dictatorship of Rafael Trujillo. For thirty-one years, he had been the dictator. My father was in the underground movement there. And his cell was discovered by the secret police, so we had to leave in a hurry. We landed in New York. As you can imagine, going from this little island no one had ever heard of to New York City was a huge change for me. Now I live in Vermont, where I've lived for the past thirty-three years.

I came here for a one-year job at Middlebury College. It turned into a tenure track, and I met and married my husband, Bill, here—I've been here ever since.

What did you want to be when you were younger?

Oh, I had no options. I was growing up as a girl in the 1950s in a very traditional Catholic culture. Women had no public face or life. This is not to say that the women who surrounded me—my abuela, my tías, my mother—weren't powerful, strong women, and great storytellers. But they didn't have a public life. My paternal grandmother didn't

go past fourth grade. I didn't grow up with the idea that I was going to have a life. You have your quinceañera at 15, and then you're on the marriage market. Because my family believed in education, we girls were expected to get through high school, but that was enough. So I just thought I'd grow up to be like my aunts and my mother, somebody's wife and a mother. I was also a really poor student. I flunked every grade through fifth grade because I was bored in school. It was a dictatorship school. Learning by rote—I hated it.

I was not well-behaved. And it worried my mother, because I was not measuring up to be a nice girl who would make a good match. The teachers would send home notes saying I didn't pay attention. But you know what? I'd get home, and one of my aunties or my grandmother would say, "Hey, come here, let me tell you a story," or they would start in on the story, and I'd be riveted. I'd sit there. And once they were done, I'd say, "Tell it again." I had no problem paying attention. So part of it tells me that I've always loved stories. And maybe I would've ended up being one of those grandmothers who tells stories to her grandkids and the kids around. So I know that the seed was in me, but I wouldn't have had the opportunity that happened without our immigration.

I often say that immigration, and the disruption and loss that came with it, was the worst moment in my life, and also the best moment in my life. Because it allowed me other options and allowed me the possibility of developing what was in me.

What role do you feel your ancestors, or the women in your family who came before you, play in your life?

I think about them so much. It's almost like I'm in conversation with them. I feel their presence in me so much. Sometimes when I'm not feeling what I think of as my best self, I think of women in my family who had that particular quality of patience, or kindness, or presence. And I try to embody it. I feel that I'm a bead in the necklace of the generations. I know that those who lived before me are a part of me. I'm not just myself. I'm now preparing myself to be the answer for those I'm leaving behind. What can I do before I go? How can I share myself? Maybe just through being a

I FEEL THAT I'M A BEAD IN THE NECKLACE OF THE GENERATIONS.

supportive person in a younger person's life, but I, too, am preparing to be an ancestor.

Some of the things that we bring with us from other cultures or other origin countries are encoded in our cells and in our bodies in ways that we knew for many generations. Like ways to take care of each other and ourselves. And those have to be translated into, "What does that mean now where I'm living?" But that instinct or that embodied knowledge is there in us. The thing is, too many times we have dismissed it or felt ashamed of it, because when you come to this country, that's thought of as old-world stuff. Those are old people, and they're embarrassing. The older you get, the more you reach back there and realize you were being given a gift. But it's still in you. It's always in you.

What does your current age feel like for you?

I have to laugh, because when I turned 50, that's supposed to be a big age for a woman—you've crossed over. And I remember walking into my closet and seeing outfits that I'd kept from college. I ran my hand through all of them with deep appreciation and gratitude for having survived and become the next outfit, and the next outfit. But also, I thought, What a relief. I now am going to be the woman that the men look over, perhaps. But what a relief. I can be myself rather than perform myself in order to make it in the world. So I feel that very much now—relief.

I'm much slower at doing some things now, and I don't have the energy resources I had before, but I also feel like I can avail myself of all the layers. And with that, having survived so many selves, I also feel great tolerance, and kindness, and forgiveness, because there's so much to forgive of how dumb you sometimes were. But it also gives you a sense of perspective and kindness toward yourself—and also toward others. A tolerance when you allow not just diversity out there, but diversity in yourself. You begin to open yourself up: Whereas before maybe you were editing out the parts that you thought wouldn't work out there, now you go at things with all those layers in yourself. I think it brings a generosity toward yourself and others. So that's why I feel a kind of appreciation for my age.

One wonderful story that I've heard comes from Native American culture. It's about an old lady who has been reaching up to touch the stars since she was a young girl. And finally, when she's a very old woman, she manages to finally touch a star. And Father Sky looks down at her and says, "How did you get to be so tall?" And she says, "I'm standing on a lot of shoulders." Sometimes I feel like I can't carry another weight, but I think, Hey, it's your turn to offer those shoulders.

What misconceptions about aging would you like to dispel?

Being female, we are raised to always think about what we look like, and our youthful attractiveness and appeal. But I love looking at us old people. I think we're beautiful. It's like seeing a life in a body and face. And it shows—it embodies what that life has been like. And so I think a misconception is about the beauty of that lived-in body and self.

How has your sense of self-confidence or self-acceptance evolved over time?

I still think of myself as a person who second-guesses myself a lot. I think it may be part of my nature. It's also curiosity, and not ever thinking or assuming I've got the answers—it's more that I need to live out the questions. And so the older I get, my self-confidence is qualified by a real sense of "Is this going to contradict what I said before?" But life is so mysterious! And I know how little I know. The arrogance of being young sometimes is thinking you have all the answers. But now that's gone. There's a certain self-confidence that comes from knowing you *don't* have to have the answer, that, in fact, you will never have the answer. You have a variety of answers. And you're more astonished being surrounded by the mystery of this experience of being alive. And how interesting, curious, and diverse other people are. All those things—that's the confidence that comes with aging.

What are you most proud of about yourself?

My first novel didn't get published until I was 41, and I'd already been writing for twenty-five years. And nobody was publishing what was called "sociology of ethnicity" back then. Even though there were so many naysayers, I kept at the thing that I thought was in me to do. And maybe that's one quality: my persistence. My staying with what I thought was important, even though in so many ways it was battered and challenged and felt like it was never going to happen.

There's a passage from the Gnostic Gospels that I would quote to students, and it was something like, "If you bring forth what is within you, what you bring forth will save you. If you do not bring forth what is within you, what is within you will destroy you." I held on to that.

The other quality I would say I'm proud of is my curiosity, but it gets me in trouble. I've never been a successful member of a clique, because if you're in a clique, you have to dismiss all the people who aren't as cool as you. But I was always curious about who the others were. I think I have an openness to life. And it's a good quality to have as a writer.

We don't write because we know things. We write because we want to find things out. You're not the one with the answers. You're the one with the questions. That curiosity leads also to compassion, I think. Because when you're curious, you connect with the other and you feel compassion. You understand. You feel and acknowledge what it's like to be the other.

When do you feel your most powerful?

I was going to say when I'm writing, but that's not true. I am constantly doubting and thinking that what I've written is no good. That it wants one more draft than I want to give it. But I think when I lose myself in the craft, I feel empowered by not *having* to be in power. I'm empowered by being lost, given, surrendered to something that is beautiful or something that I'm trying to create that is beautiful.

The other times I feel empowered are what I call sacramental moments, and they don't happen in the church. They're moments—it could be at a dinner party, it could be while you're walking in the woods—where you feel this thrilling, stirring mystery in what is happening, and you feel lost in it and connected. And it just feels like it expands you. I guess those moments when I feel like I've gone beyond the borders of being a single self are when I feel most empowered. But in a sense, that's giving up power, not having to claim it and pushing it forward.

Who or what has influenced your life the most?

Definitely some of the tías in my life. So many of them have given me the gift of loving me unconditionally. And you can't fake that, especially to a kid.

Also my sisters. Growing up in a family of all girls, who survived so much and moved to such a different place—we all had each other. And we were each, in different ways, combinations of all kinds of cultural messages and things we were experiencing. And I would've been lost without them to help me process those. So the sisterhood was so important. We would call each other even after we grew up and left home. I remember so many midnight calls, just talking things over. And when we came back to our parents' for a vacation, we would have what we'd call "lemon squeezes." Everybody would air out all their issues, and we would help each other. It was so important to have this sisterhood, because I didn't know that many other Latinas or immigrants when we first came to America.

At this point in your life, what have you made peace with that used to be a struggle for you?

Not being a domestic type of woman. I was raised to learn to be one. I was taught household arts, to take care of a house, to feed people, the conventional life. And I always felt like that wasn't in me. But I hid that. I hid it because I was ashamed that it made me less of a woman. As if there was only one kind of woman. But now I've made peace with that.

The other thing is, when you're young and full of curiosity, you have so many dreams for yourself. But you know what? I'm never going to be a graceful dancer. I'm never going to be able to sing opera. I'm never going to be able to do any of those things. And one of the ways I make peace with that is that I can write about a character who does those things. And so I get to live that life.

If you could go back in your life, what would you like to do over—and what would you never do again?

In order to fulfill those conventional roles, I made some choices that were huge mistakes, because they were a violation of who I was. I thought I had to have a man and a marriage. It was fulfilling the romantic paradigm. I don't want to renege on any part of my life, but it brought a lot of heartache and it took a while to recover from those mistakes. And I'm not sure I would do it over, except that I feel great tenderness, and forgiveness, and sadness for the young woman who didn't know any better, who felt like she had to do this to make herself a viable person in her family, in her culture, and even here in America, as a woman.

Knowing what you know now, what would you go back and tell your younger self?

I would just be kinder to myself. And say, "This, too, shall pass." I would say to let go of the shame about not fulfilling some role that others handed me. I remember as an immigrant thinking, Well, are you an American or a Dominican? And it was always either/or. But it didn't have to be. I could be both. I could be complex, and that's okay.

Elizabeth Brim

PENLAND, NC

Blacksmith and artist Elizabeth Brim, 69, has lived in the small town of Penland, North Carolina, for over two decades. In her studio, she makes breathtaking works of art from metal, with a focus on highlighting the contrast between the strength and structure of the material and the objects—like high heels with ribbons, a ballerina tutu, or a pillow with ruffles—she creates. Her pieces have been showcased in the United States, Canada, and Germany. Easily recognized in the studio by her trademark strand of pearls, Elizabeth has forged an important role in the blacksmith community and has become an inspiration to many, regardless of age.

Where did you grow up, and where do you live now?

I grew up in Columbus, Georgia, and I live now in Penland, North Carolina. I ended up in Penland because my marriage went south and I was left in a tight spot. I had been brought up to think that when I grew up, I would have a man to take care of me and that I wouldn't need to make any money because he would be able to provide everything I needed. And also check the oil in my car and do all the things that men supposedly do. But my husband was not that kind of person. We ended up having to declare bankruptcy. I had bought this house up here in Penland thinking that there was enough money that I could have this home here and still live in our nice house in Columbus, Georgia. But after the bankruptcy, I moved here full-time. And it ended up being the greatest thing ever because this is where I needed to be.

What's the biggest risk you've taken in your life, and how has it shaped you?

The biggest risk I've ever taken is what I do now. I had been teaching in Columbus, Georgia, but I quit that job and decided to stop teaching and be a full-time blacksmith. That was one of the riskiest things I ever did, but I'm so glad I did. At the time, I had been doing everything from ceramics to teaching the creative use of fiber and jewelry making. But I thought, If I'm going to get really good at something, I've got to focus on one thing. And I decided it was going to be blacksmithing.

What did you want to be when you were younger?

I wanted to teach art at a college. I thought that would be the perfect job for me. The man who was my teacher, Jamie Howard, at the school where I got my undergraduate degree told me to go to Penland and study ceramics. He would hire me to teach ceramics, and I would have my dream. But going to Penland is what really changed my life. I taught at that school for eleven years but would always go to Penland whenever I could.

What does your current age feel like for you?

Well, before the pandemic hit, I did not feel like my age. I felt probably thirty years younger than I actually am. But now I have started to feel a lot more vulnerable, and I worry about minor aches and pains—wondering if they might be something serious. But I think that is just the pandemic. I really do not feel like I'm as old as I am in numbers. And that's probably because most of my friends are a lot younger than I am. I have friends who are my age, but I think it's really cool that I have a lot of friends of all different ages. We are all just trying to learn and help each other.

In the dining hall at Penland, we have these round tables, and everybody sits around them together. You might end up sitting next to a famous glassblower, and it's like, "Would you pass the mustard, please?" Everybody is treated the same. Some people are super famous, and some are just at the beginning of their career. And it's a great thing to give yourself confidence to hang out with people like that.

How has your sense of self-confidence or self-acceptance evolved over time?

Well, I still don't think I'm as confident as I ought to be because I still compare myself to other people too much. And that's something I really need to work on—not comparing myself to other friends who are artists.

To whom do you turn when you need someone to lift you up?

My sister is the main person I talk to. She's a dancer and choreographer. But you know, family love you no matter what—if you're lucky.

When do you feel your most powerful?

When I'm in my studio, standing at that forge with my anvil. That's when I feel like I know what I'm doing and I can do it. Just being able to make that metal move with the hammer and make it do what I want. But sometimes I have to feel like it's a partnership with the metal. It has a little bit of a say-so, too, but we have a pretty good relationship.

What are you most proud of about yourself?

I am most proud that I have made a name for myself in blacksmithing. I was supposed to be Master Blacksmith at this year's Fire on the Mountain blacksmithing festival, but everything was canceled because of the pandemic. So they asked me to write a script and do an online presentation instead. I thought, Well, okay; at least this is something I can do and concentrate on to take my mind off everything I'm not able to do.

When I googled blacksmithing for inspiration, I found my own name in that Wikipedia listing! There were some famous old blacksmiths and contemporary blacksmiths, and then my name was right there. It made me feel super proud.

I'm also proud that I facilitated the first Penland Iron Symposium in 1989: Expressive Design in Iron. It was the first time that blacksmiths got together formally in the United States to talk about ideas and art in ironworking. And I was pretty much the perfect person to facilitate that because I had been formally trained in art. I was passionate about blacksmithing, and I was also passionate about revitalizing that studio where I learned and worked. So we had a hundred people come to that symposium, and it was electric. You could feel the excitement in the air. That conference saved the program at Penland, and people started coming from all over.

Who or what has influenced your life the most?

The Penland School. It just gave me confidence to be myself. It's also where I learned everything I know about blacksmithing. It gave me a sense of importance and validation. When they asked me to teach at Penland, it was a big deal.

I never really felt like I was a person of consequence, because of the way I was raised to think. The model that I had was, you were subservient to your husband and you had to be because he was going to take care of you and you couldn't take care of yourself. And I think one of the proudest times that I've had is when I paid my first electric bill with my own money that I'd made. And my father never thought I was going to be able to take care of myself, and I think he finally thought maybe I would be okay when I sold the very first apron that I made. And I think maybe my first pair of high-heeled shoes I sold was what allowed me to buy myself a four-wheel drive pickup. It was something that I needed—because I impressed myself.

What misconceptions about aging would you like to dispel?

People seem to think that you don't do stuff anymore as you get older. Recently, a young woman asked me, "Are you still making art?" I felt like she had just thrown a bucket of ice water on my face. And I just said, "What else am I going to do"? People might be asking me that because of the way I look— my hair is turning gray, and my face is sagging—but that doesn't mean I'm going to quit making art.

So one day I called up my friend Cynthia Bringle, who is a ceramicist, and I said, "Do people ask you if you're still making art?" And she went, "Oh yeah, all the time." I said, "What do you tell them?" She said, "I tell them, 'Why don't you just come to my studio and look?'" So I've got to think up something clever to say about that because people are asking me that more and more.

Knowing what you know now, what would you go back and tell your younger self?

I would tell my younger self to always remember that I am the most important person in the world. I've been much happier since I started making decisions based on what I want out of my life. Like the house I have here—it's so empowering to know that I bought this place myself with money that I made from teaching, blacksmithing, and selling my artwork and running the Penland iron studio. I did it all by myself. Sometimes I'll be up in my studio looking out over all this property and I'll see my house and say, "This is mine. And I got it for myself, and I got this new roof put on this place. I'm doing it, and I've got a car and a truck." They were both paid off, and I'm just very proud of that.

Do you have a message for younger women reading your story here?

They need to know that they can do anything they want to. Try to find your strength and know yourself and know what makes you happy and what makes you feel powerful. It's a short run we have here on this earth.

How have your ideas of success and happiness changed over time?

I guess early on I thought I was going to be a wealthy woman of leisure, like a hobbyist artist. But that's not what happened. And it's funny because I have this one friend I grew up with who does live in a damn *mansion*. I went to visit her, and while I was there, surrounded by all this fancy antique furniture, I realized, All of this stuff probably would not have made me a happy person. Living in my modest house in Penland is good for me.

Dr. Dorothy Carter-Anthony

and

Erika Goodwin

WASHINGTON, DC

Dr. Dorothy Carter-Anthony, 87, and Erika Goodwin, 45, became friends after connecting through the Washington, DC, chapter of their sorority, Alpha Kappa Alpha. Dorothy worked as a beloved public school teacher and assistant principal at Robert Gould Shaw Junior High School for over twenty years. Now retired, she is always learning and trying new things, along with her good friend Erika. Erika is a conference planner and project manager and runs Creations by EME, a business that makes small-batch cotton masks. During the COVID-19 pandemic, Erika partnered with other sewers in DC to donate masks to frontline workers. Erika and Dorothy's friendship has taught them both that you're never too mature to seek out new friends.

How did you first meet?

ERIKA: We are both members of Alpha Kappa Alpha in Washington, DC, the Rho Mu Omega Chapter. One of the programs our sorority offers is a mentorship program. I was paired with Dorothy as her mentee in the first cycle of the mentor program.

What were your first impressions of each other?

E: I thought that Dorothy was stately, graceful. She was very poised and well put together and, I thought, very serious.

DOROTHY: I am very serious.

E: That was my first impression, and I don't know how long it took for me to realize that she was a hoot. We had about six meetings, one a month, in our first mentoring cycle.

D: During that first meeting, we clicked. That was it for me. I thought that she was smart, and from what I had heard from the different committees she was on, I knew she was capable. I just fell in love with her.

E: We would have assignments that we had to work through, and she has this quiet way of telling me what to do. We had to fill out mentor forms, and she is very much about the business of crossing *t*'s and dotting *i*'s. She'd say, "Write this down. Are you writing this down?" So I didn't really have a choice but to fall in line. And then it was some of the under-her-breath comments that let me know who she really was.

Can you describe a moment when you realized your friendship was going to be a significant one in your lives?

E: I think for me, it happened over time. I don't think there was one moment when I knew, but there were little moments that add up to an intimate relationship, where it transitioned from the time we had scheduled to be together for our mentorship to something more.

We saw each other twice a month because we would also have a sorority meeting, and in sorority meetings you can sometimes end up sitting with people you volunteer with or maybe people you have a longstanding relationship with. But all my other relationships fell away and I was Dorothy's seat buddy.

D: I was looking for you, and you were always looking for me.

E: We started looking for each other at the meetings. Kind of checking on each other. In a larger organization, it's good to have somebody to check in with you. But she would spot me as soon as I hit the door. "Hey you. Come here. Sit down. What are you doing?" So that was our way of playing with each other and greeting each other. And you could see that the people around us didn't really get it. They thought I was in trouble.

D: But they soon found out that that was not the case. Somebody asked me one time, "What did she do?" I said, "She didn't do anything." That was just our way. But then other people could see that we were melding together, because they would say, "Where's Erika?" And I would say, "Oh well, she'll be here." And they had us looking forward to the fact that we were together.

E: We shared vulnerable things with one another. Those start to build up into a positive bank account. We shared sisterhood and laughter and secrets and adversity and struggle, too. As you share all those things together, you start to lean on each other, and all those connections are saved in a repository. You get to withdraw from them. I will call her because I'm still working and looking to her for encouragement because I still have twenty years until I retire like her.

When we're together, I'm intentional and mindful. I love to soak up all the time I can with Dorothy, and with her friends, too.

Was there anything you were surprised to learn you have in common?

D: We didn't know that we both liked crab cakes so much.

E: Being native Washingtonians, we don't play with our Maryland crabs. I mentioned wanting some crabs, and Dorothy said, "Well, let's go get them." I think that was one of the first times we got together outside of formal activities at our sorority. Her spontaneity in suggesting we do something that I had just mentioned in passing was surprising to me. She was serious, so she was interested in being spontaneous like that. And our love for crabs just sealed the deal—I think we bonded elbow-deep in Maryland crabs.

I was also surprised to find out we were both watching *Game of Thrones*. I was totally surprised that you would watch that show. You watched all of *Game of Thrones*.

D: I look forward to it. I wonder who's going to do what.

What are some of your most fun memories together?

D: Well, after one of our Saturday meetings, there was a sorority sister who was having a birthday party and she invited all of us, and it was at this nightclub during the day. And I said, "Erika, let's go." And Erika said, "Yeah, let's go." And so when we got there, I told her that I had never been in a nightclub in the sixty years I've lived in DC. She thought that was so strange, and she broadcast it just like she was on a megaphone, so the people fell out. They were as surprised as Erika was about the fact that I had never been.

When my nephew heard about it—his aunt in a nightclub—he almost had a stroke. I said, "But it was during the day." He's not a prude. He just wanted to have fun with Erika and me about something that *he* had not taken me to.

E: I think that is one of my favorite memories of the things we've done together. The expressions on people's faces when I walked into the nightclub with you was even better.

D: It has been a hoot, though. I have enjoyed every moment that I've spent with you. Every moment. And when I don't hear from you, I get a feeling that something is not quite right, and then I have to try to email you, or what is that thing?

E: Texting.

D: I will text you or call you if I get a feeling that something isn't right.

How has your friendship helped you through tough times?

E: I'm the mom of an adult child with a mental health disability, and it has ebbs and flows. Throughout all those moments, Dorothy says she gets a feeling when she doesn't hear from me. I think it's probably usually because she's worried that I'm tending to my son. And those are really the moments I couldn't survive without her. Even if it's just the laughs we have together.

D: We're good at laughing. I try to keep things positive. Always try to be positive.

E: Even in tears. Remember what you said about tears?

D: One time when Erika was in such a low, dark place and crying, I told her what they used to tell me when I was a child: "The more you cry, the less you pee." That always makes us laugh. The whole point is to be supportive when people need support. And that's what I like to be for Erika. I want her to know that I'm here for her.

E: I am the daughter she never birthed.

D: That's right. She brings out the mother in me. And another thing—when we first met, she had so much on her plate, I had to constantly tell her, "You must learn to say no." She was bursting at the seams with activities, and I had to tell her, "You can't do all of these things. You have a family and you have a husband. You have a son and you have a job. You're trying to honor all of these commitments. You can't do that." So I think eventually she learned that she couldn't have all those irons in the fire and then take care of herself, too.

E: She used to literally make me practice saying no.

D: I'd tell her, "You can't say yes to everything, even though your heart may want to do it. Physically, you just can't. Mentally, you just can't do it." I learned to say no maybe about fifty years ago. Most people who know me know that I kind of mean what I say, and I try not to overburden and overload myself in doing things. If I can't do it, I'll tell you, and if I say, "Yes, I'm going to do it," you can carry it to the bank. But you see young people, and they don't know. They have to learn that they can't do everything for everybody.

E: That was a special part about Dorothy and our relationship—she will notice things about me that I don't. I think that's when you know that somebody really knows you, when they really see you and get you. And because of her, I know nobody can mess with me.

D: That's for sure.

E: Everybody knows that now. And I think that was a special moment, too, when others start to pay attention and say, "Oh no, you better not mess with Erika, or Dorothy will get you."

D: Yeah. That might not be a good thing, but it's all right with us.

E: The feeling is definitely mutual.

Can you share something meaningful you've learned from each other?

D: I'll say this. I have learned to talk less and listen more. When I say something, I want to be able to know that it has enough meaning to do some good. I don't want to be talking at Erika or about Erika. I want to be able to listen, and that's something I've been trying to practice. Sometimes we're driving right along in the car and we're not saying anything, but we're there.

E: I've learned that there are people who are worthy of your love and your trust. She restored my faith in friendship.

A lot of times, as you mature, you think that your friend card is full. I never shopped around for more friends. But she helped me realize that it's possible to let new people in and that there are people who are trustworthy who you haven't known your whole life. And that, I think, especially helped me to grow other relationships that are beneficial in different ways. Dorothy is where I come for nurturing and wisdom and a kick in the pants if I need it. Or a good laugh, of course. She's part of my squad, and I introduce her as my good, good girlfriend. She's my homegirl. We could go out and kick it.

What makes you proud to call each other friends?

E: Dorothy is so accomplished. This is *Dr.* Dorothy Carter-Anthony. She's no slouch. She means business. She is discerning about her company, and if she lets me in the door, that means the world to me. It gives me something to aspire to, but I know that I must not be so bad if she let me in.

D: I just want the best for Erika. I want her to know that I have her back anytime and that she can always depend on me. I know I can depend on her. I know she will pick up the phone or text me. I think we have that in common. We know we have each other's back.

And the fact of the matter is, there has been a noticeable change in the two of us, so I'm told. People admire the way we react to each other, the way we are protective of each other.

E: I think they see us and consider some other friendships that they might have dismissed. Because you have your affinities within the sorority: people who went to the same school, people who grew up in the same hometown, and people who may practice the same discipline. You kind of stick

SHE IS DISCERNING ABOUT HER COMPANY, AND IF SHE LETS ME IN THE DOOR, THAT MEANS THE WORLD TO ME.

to those groups and don't even think about having friendships with other people. You don't even think about having fun together.

D: My friends in the sorority have become Erika's friends, too. My friends who are my age also look out for Erika.

E: They are the funniest women in the chapter.

D: If you sit with us, you get in trouble.

E: Oh, you get in so much trouble. They're so confident in what they will do and what they won't do. Even if it's something as small as they can't see the screen up front, but they refuse to move from the back.

D: You know the reason why we sit in the back? I sit in the back because when I get tired, I leave.

E: With maturity comes wisdom, right?

D: That's what they say.

E: They sit by the door, and they have a whole pot of wisdom back there. But the presence they command, the resolve they have, the confidence her peers have—I hope that rubs off on me.

What advice do you have for people who want to find a friendship like yours?

D: My mother had a friend who used to say she liked to stay with the young people who came around with her son. She said being with the young people kept her young. She knew what was going on. She liked the music. She could learn the slang and now is learning the technology, and that's important to me because what I *can't* do, Erika can. I can call her and she can help me, walk me through it or come around and do it for me. That's a good thing to have. And on the other hand, my mother said she never wanted to go to the old folks' home or the senior citizens' home because all they talk about is pain and medicine and doctors. So I'd rather be on Erika's end, where I can be with the young people and laugh with them. Listen to their music and eat the same food they all eat. Now I eat pizza! I never cared that much for pizza, but now I do. So I would advise people to split their time, if they can, with younger folks and older folks.

E: I always tell people to look for the person. Look for people who have similar interests. Have a conversation. Make a friend. You never know who you could be friends with among the people who

are all around you. I think in our community, we've always protected our elders, and a lot of the focus is sometimes on protecting them and not just hanging with them. You never know where you might find your next friend.

What do you each hope your friendship brings or gives to the other person?

E: I hope that Dorothy never feels alone. That she always feels loved, wanted, and protected. I keep telling her she's fun to be with, because I think sometimes she may think we're here out of obligation. I'm here for the good times. I may check on a few things while I'm here, but I'm here to hang out and be with my friend.

D: If I hadn't had Erika and my nephew during this past year of the pandemic, it would have been horrible to be in this house for a whole year. But I haven't missed a beat. I'm enjoying life.

What does your current age feel like for you?

D: I feel 40, and she keeps me young mentally, physically, and spiritually.

E: We're the same age, Dorothy. We're the same age. For me, it depends on the time of day. In the morning right after I leave the gym, I probably feel like I'm in my thirties. I feel like a superhero. But later that night? Not so much. I'll be 45 this year.

D: Just a babe.

E: I think I feel about my age. I mean, at 45 you know enough to not go out and do foolish stuff. You know enough to ask for advice or ask for help. Your knees don't creak that much. Well, maybe just a little bit. I think it's a sweet spot. Now I'm looking forward, as Dorothy encourages me, as I consider what I want the next twenty years of my career to look like. I could have a second career.

D: I wish I had not *retired* retired. I know I retired from my job, but I wish I had taken up something else. And then, of course, my nephew would say, "And what would that be?"

E: It could be anything. It could be anything, Dorothy. I love that you're a lifelong learner.

D: I learn my Spanish once a week. I've been taking this Spanish course for two years now, but I'm going to continue on it. I try to do it more than once a week, because you're supposed to do it every day. I don't do it every day.

E: Because you're retired. You could do what you want to do. She knows more than me about some things. She learned how to code! She's just a great partner. She keeps me where I'm supposed to be, at the right time at the right place, doing things with decency and order. My life was really chaotic, and she is almost like a good meditation.

Bobbi Brown

MONTCLAIR, NJ

Makeup artist, entrepreneur, and author Bobbi Brown began her career with just ten lipsticks. Over the following three decades, she grew her eponymous makeup line into an international empire and went on to found new beauty and wellness brands and become a certified health coach. Not content to rest on her laurels, Bobbi, 64, cofounded 18 Label Studios, a film and television studio; launched an editorial website, JustBobbi.com; and redesigned a boutique hotel in Montclair, New Jersey.

Bobbi has been honored with the Glamour Woman of the Year Award and the Jackie Robinson Foundation's ROBIE Humanitarian Award, among many others. In addition to being inducted into her home state of New Jersey's hall of fame, she was appointed to President Obama's Advisory Committee for Trade Policy and Negotiations.

Where did you grow up, and where do you live now?

I was born and raised in Chicago, went to Emerson College in Boston, lived in New York City, and have now lived in Montclair, New Jersey, for more than thirty years.

What did you want to be when you were younger?

I always wanted to be a mother and a teacher, and luckily, I'm both.

What does your current age feel like for you?

Definitely not 64. I love to move my body; it makes such a difference in how I feel—I don't have an age when I'm in the middle of exercising. Moving to hip-hop or disco, kickboxing, boot camp—whatever it is, if I'm moving: no age.

What misconceptions about aging would you like to dispel?

That it's not okay to have lines on your face. I don't shoot things into my skin—I'm not saying my way is for everybody, but I look in the mirror, see my lines, and go, "Okay, those are my lines." Then I put on some moisturizer and that's that. You can't fight aging. Instead, keep your skin as radiant as possible by eating tons of fruits and vegetables, drinking lots of water, and staying active. A little bit of blush helps, too.

What are you most proud of about yourself?

The three boys I managed to create.

How has your sense of self-confidence or self-acceptance evolved over time?

Confidence comes with age. The older I get, the more comfortable I am in my own skin—I know who I am, what I like, and how I want to spend my time. I don't bog myself down with things that can't change or don't matter.

What role do you feel your ancestors, or the women in your family who came before you, play in your life?

I've learned how to be a good person and a mother from the women in my family. My mother taught me to be nice, say "thank you," and always put family first. Being a working mom, I always prioritized my kids' events: pickups, drop-offs, soccer games, school performances—I was always there.

What message do you have for women reading your story here, and what impact do you hope your life and story have on those around you?

My advice is to never give up. If I had given up, I wouldn't be where I am today—or on this page, for that matter. Remember that women are the ultimate multitaskers, and we are capable of anything, no matter how hard it seems. It took me a while to speak up in a conference room of all men. Ask yourself "what if" to the things that seem

WHEN ONE DOOR CLOSES, ANOTHER OPENS—AND IF IT DOESN'T, BUILD ONE YOURSELF.

impossible. What if I state my opinion? What's the worst that will really happen? Or what's the best-case scenario? I hope my story reminds women how amazing we are, and that the best-case scenario isn't as far-fetched as it seems.

Can you describe a turning point in your life, and how it changed things for you?

A major turning point in my life was leaving my namesake brand. I had no idea what I wanted to do next, so I just said yes to everything. Now, four years later, I'm the boss of my dream brands, and I wouldn't want it any other way. As clichéd as it sounds, when one door closes, another opens—and if it doesn't, build one yourself.

What is a lesson you're still learning or need to learn?

I'm learning to take things down a notch and keep my focus on the present moment. Life is too short to be stressed and to think ahead *and* behind like crazy. I'm working on enjoying quiet time, taking breaks, and living intuitively.

Who or what has influenced your life the most?

My husband, Steven. I couldn't have done it without him—he made my magic happen. He's brilliant, caring, and thoughtful, and he knows what to do in every situation.

What's the biggest risk you've taken in your life, and how has it shaped you?

I've taken many risks, from starting my own cosmetics company to selling it, leaving it, and starting over. Sometimes it's important to press the reset button—to look at what's working and what's not, and make changes. As you rebuild, don't be afraid to try something new. Each risk I've taken has made me more fearless, and led me to the next.

How have your ideas of success and happiness changed over time?

When I was younger, I thought success depended on my job and salary. Now I've learned it's much simpler than that—it's about quality time with people you love, doing what you love, and finding a balance. Success and happiness are nothing if you can't enjoy them with other people.

At this point in your life, what have you made peace with that used to be a struggle for you?

That I'll never be tall and lengthy. I'm five feet tall and happier wearing sneakers than high heels.

Knowing what you know now, what would you go back and tell your younger self?

I would tell myself to not be so hard on myself and that it will all work out. You're not like everyone else—stay curious and see what grabs you. Once you find that thing, move forward with confidence and drive. Take other people's success as encouragement, and never take no for an answer.

Ysaÿe Barnwell

WASHINGTON, DC

Singer and teacher Ysaÿe Barnwell, 75, has devoted her life to the joy of music. In addition to working as a professor at Howard University, she has been the composer for numerous choral, film, video, dance, and theatrical projects. She earned bachelor's and master's degrees in speech pathology from the State University of New York College at Geneseo, and a PhD in speech pathology from the University of Pittsburgh. She also earned a Master of Science in public health from Howard University. She has performed and taught around the world and inspired countless generations to lift their voices in the power of song.

Where did you grow up, and where do you live now?

I grew up in New York City, first in Harlem and then in Jamaica, Queens, and lived there until I graduated from high school. I decided to go to college in upstate New York, in Geneseo, and I lived there five years. SUNY Geneseo was nearly all white students then, back in 1968, so I decided I really needed to be in an all-Black environment after that. So I applied to teach at Howard University. They accepted me, and I've been in Washington, DC, ever since.

What did you want to be when you were younger?

I wanted to be a violinist because my father started teaching me when I was two and a half. My father had been a concert violinist, and had taught violin in our home. Then when I was about 12, I saw *The Miracle Worker* on Broadway. I wanted to teach kids who were like Helen Keller. That's why I went into speech pathology and then actually worked with deaf people after. I discovered Gallaudet University here in Washington, DC, and I started taking sign language classes and making some deaf acquaintances. I learned quite a lot from them. And I hope they learned from me, too.

When I joined the singing group Sweet Honey in the Rock, it was because Bernice Johnson Reagon had seen me signing music. She said she had never seen a Black sign language interpreter. And we had a long conversation about it. And so when I first joined Sweet Honey in the Rock, I joined as the interpreter. Then she found out that I could sing, so I made a decision to sing, and they brought in Shirley Childress Saxton, who was the group's interpreter for about thirty years.

What does your current age feel like for you?

It feels odd to me. Because, with the exception of some memory issues, I feel like I felt when I was 50. I don't feel like I have any physical limitations. I feel like I can do all the things that I have been doing. I'm blessed with good health. And if I, like I said, could handle forgetting things, I would feel like I did when I was 50. My movements are good. I love to dance, although I haven't done it recently. But when something I like comes on the radio, I can still move. And I can still bend over and touch my toes. So I sort of feel like I always did.

How has your sense of self-confidence or self-acceptance evolved over time?

I have never had anyone I respected tell me I *couldn't* do what I said I wanted to do. Dr. Marilyn Yvonne Rosedale, a professor of mine, was the only white person I ever heard say, "If you want to do it, you can do it." She was the best teacher I ever had. And we became friends, and we had amazing conversations.

What are you most proud of about yourself?

I have a PhD in speech pathology because I saw *The Miracle Worker* on Broadway and had a hard time emotionally understanding the experience of people who couldn't hear, because music was my whole life until then. So when I went to college, I wanted to figure out how people who couldn't hear could experience the world of music.

Through all the things I wound up doing, deafness never left me, which is why Sweet Honey in the Rock has, even to this day, had a sign language interpreter. When I came into the group, I talked to them about deafness and the fact that because Sweet Honey was an a cappella group, it would make a lot of sense for there to be an interpreter. From that point on, we have always had an interpreter for the group. My interest in and exploration of deafness and of interpreting gave me a sense of self-confidence because I was proud of what I was able to learn and how I used it to translate the experience of music.

What's the biggest risk you've taken in your life, and how has it shaped you?

Well, I think the biggest risk early in my life was deciding I was going to go to this college where there were only seven Black folks and I made the eighth. That was a huge risk. And what I commonly have said about being there was that there were white folks and there was snow. And both were these experiences that I just can't even imagine having anywhere else.

So what I learned about myself from being one of a very small group of Black people, I think, was eye-opening, and liberating in some ways. It made me comfortable with being unusual. I was unusual there because I was Black. But I had some skills that people would never have expected, like being a violinist. And so I played in a string quartet there, and in an orchestra.

When do you feel your most powerful?

I have felt the most powerful when I was singing songs from the civil rights movement. It felt amazing, because there was rhythm that you could show and get other people to join in. There would always be a clap. It was so visceral, those sounds.

Who or what has influenced your life the most?

The two greatest influences in my life are opposites: hearing and deafness. Who would have thought that? But they are. They both came into my life before I was 13, and they've been such foundational aspects of my work, and have influenced my communication. I wanted to find a way to help all people experience music and, like my mother used to say, "All things are possible."

How have your ideas of success and happiness changed over time?

I don't know that I ever had a definition or a criteria for either that was set or determined by other people. I was always told by my parents to be the best that I could be in whatever I decided to do. I've always had to have my own internal "Am I doing my best?" question for determining how I feel. I just do what I want to do. And if I want to do it, I will do my best. So I don't know that I listen to other people's criteria.

How has not raising children affected your life? Do you feel like you've played the role of a parent for other people?

I don't have biological children, but I think I have children in a lot of places. There are just people you latch on to, or who latch on to you. And one of those "children" was just at my house several days ago. I met her when she was a student at Gallaudet. She is very confident, and she knows who she is. And that, for me, is an accomplishment.

I don't know, if I had been married or had had a child, or both, how I would have turned out. I don't know that I would have had the time and the freedom to kind of develop myself and have the experiences that I had. I have no regrets about it. If I'm lacking in one area, well, that's fine. It gave me more time to exercise the other areas.

I do really feel the lack of a relationship, though. It's not that I haven't had them. They just haven't turned out the way most do. So I have to say that I think I've lived a very free kind of life, walking through the world, going where I want to go, doing what I want to do.

But there is still time, and there are some interesting people out there. And I'm an interesting person. It just might take a while to find that person. What that means to me is that you have to be special to be with the kind of interesting person that I am.

I HAVE NEVER
HAD ANYONE I
RESPECTED TELL
ME I *COULDN'T*
DO WHAT I SAID
I WANTED TO DO.

Stacy London

and

Amanda Slavin

BROOKLYN, NY, AND NEW YORK, NY

Stacy London, 52, and Amanda Slavin, 35, are two friends who constantly explore what it means to show up for each other in different ways. Stacy is a stylist, fashion consultant, and author, as well as the beloved cohost of *What Not to Wear*, which ran for ten seasons on TLC. Stacy has written two books about fashion and style, co-owns Style for Hire, and is the creative director of Westfield Style. Amanda is the founder and CEO of the award-winning brand consulting firm CatalystCreativ. She's worked with brands like Coca-Cola and Google, and has spoken at SXSW and TED, in addition to writing her 2019 business book, *Seventh Level*. After meeting through mutual friends, Stacy and Amanda formed a fast and deep bond while supporting each other through a difficult time. Their dedication to each other's constant growth and evolution is one of the reasons they feel they'll be in each other's lives for many years to come.

How did you first meet?

AMANDA: We had a lot of mutual friends and ended up meeting because one of those friends was getting married.

STACY: It's worth noting that most of my friends are younger than me. One of the things that has always sort of informed my friendships with younger people is that a lot of people my own age started to get married and have kids when I was at the height of my career. And those were just not things that I wanted. So my friends have gotten younger over the years, and I have a lot more in common with them.

Amanda and I bonded at our mutual friend's bachelorette party in Palm Springs. I just remember feeling this incredible affinity for Amanda. She was warm, and I found her personality so incredibly charming. I didn't even know her age. It didn't even occur to me to ask. I felt like she was a real kindred spirit.

Can you describe the moment when you realized that your friendship was going to be a significant one in your lives?

S: At our mutual friend's wedding, the couple wrote their own vows. They were so in sync with each other; it was beautiful to see them recite what they had written. If you see something like that and you're in a *good* place in your life, you relate to it. But at that time, I had been in a series of bad relationships, and it just made me feel unmoored.

After the ceremony, we were sitting at the restaurant, and I remember feeling like I was wearing way too tight a dress—like I was in a straitjacket. I went to get a cocktail, and I started to feel shaky, like I was going to get sick.

Amanda was getting ready to give a speech, and I ran outside to get as far away from the area as I could. I bent over this trash can thinking I was going to throw up. But when I leaned over, all that came out was a wail—this insane emotional wail that brought me to my knees.

I remember looking up and being like, Okay, universe. Help me out here. I don't know what to do. I turned around, and there was Amanda walking up to me. I had tears in my eyes, and she just said, "Okay. You need to take a breath, and we're going to sit and we're going to talk." And I said, "You have to give a speech! You have to go on!"

But she was so calm and so cool and so collected. I cried and said, "I'm never going to find a love like that. I don't feel seen." And she said, "You know how you and I have talked about how we don't eat gluten?" And I said, "Yeah." She was like, "You need to think of these people you keep bringing into your life as gluten. You need protein." And then it quickly turned into "soul-tein." And that was when, in my mind, I solidified that Amanda was never going to leave my life.

A: Stacy has always felt like family to me. And people say that a lot, but I mean it in all the ways. It felt like our souls met at our friend's wedding. And then that was it, and there's never been a time since then that has even shaken that connection between us, that relationship between us, that dynamic between us.

S: I think back now and realize that the overwhelming sense of love and connection that was being shown to us through this married couple was actually being offered to me at the same time in the form of friendship. I really believe people come into your life for a reason, a season, or a lifetime. And with Amanda, I was like, Here's a lifer.

We're living through this tectonic shift in the idea of what friendship means and what mentorship means. I still believe that the more years, days, minutes you have on this planet, the more experience you have to offer someone else. But at the same time, we live in a world that is so radically different than it was ten years ago, and if we don't have that kind of intergenerational mentorship, we're missing out, certainly as an older generation, on what's possible for us.

For someone to be twenty years younger than me and able to give me insight without me feeling like it's condescending, that idea is very exciting to me. You don't know what you don't know until you realize that you don't know it and somebody teaches you to know it. And that's how I see Amanda. Amanda is a conduit for me in a lot of ways.

Can you share something meaningful you've learned from each other?

S: When Amanda decided she was going to get married, she took a trip to Australia, where she found her "perfect" wedding dress. The dress was almost twelve sizes too big for her. We could have made four dresses for Amanda out of this dress. But she kept telling me that the dress had "good bones." And I was like, "There are a million dresses with good bones in your size." But she insisted that we remake this dress. So this took a lot of visits to the tailor.

A: I was the most high-maintenance low-maintenance bride. We ended up doing at least nine or ten fittings to get it right, and every time, Stacy would come from Brooklyn to the Lower East Side to oversee it all. She oversaw the tailoring and all the changes and found all my accessories, every bit of the outfit. Stacy was dropping things during fashion week to come make this dress happen. It wasn't even "something borrowed, something new"—it was just "something Stacy." It turns out the reason I was low-maintenance is I didn't even know what "maintenance" meant. I didn't know what I needed. She told me I deserved more than I thought I did, and then helped make it happen. I wouldn't have been able to do any of it without Stacy. She just shows up for people, that's who she is. She helped me be my best self on one of the most important days of my entire life. The bottom line is that she could have just said, "No, this dress doesn't fit you; we can't make this work." But she said, "I'm going to make it work because that's what matters to you." And I think that's the difference between Stacy and a lot of people. She always says, "Even if I don't understand it, even if I don't really agree with it, if it matters to you, I'm going to make it matter to me." And she makes me feel seen in a way that not many other people can.

Is there anything you were surprised to learn you have in common?

S: Our love of Trolls. I love Trolls in general, like the dolls, but the movie *Trolls* changed my life. I loved it so much. It brought me so much joy.

A: Stacy was recovering from spinal surgery and I slept over and all we did was just watch *Trolls*. It reminded me of a friendship you would have when you're a little kid at a sleepover party. Like when you're 13 with your best friend and you look at each other and say, "This is our favorite movie!"

S: After that really pivotal bonding experience with *Trolls*, Amanda found this woman on Etsy who knits cat hair and she made me a Troll hat.

What do you each hope your friendship brings or gives to the other person?

S: Solace and the idea of safety. I want Amanda to know there is somebody she can count on who, again, doesn't judge, and that friendship, very much like any serious relationship in your life, has the ability to evolve with you. I don't expect Amanda to be the same Amanda that I'm talking to today a year from now. I want to see her grow. I want the best for her, and I want to be able to enjoy that evolution with her. So I want our future to be about the excitement of what is to come for her, for us as friends, as her family grows. Friendship is about being malleable. It's about bending, not breaking.

A: I would say support, sustainable support. I want her to know I am always going to be here to say, "How can I show up for you?" and then I will be there. What I want for this friendship in the future is to constantly remind you how powerful you are and constantly be this mirror for you to say, "Look at what you've been able to create. Look at what you've been able to do."

S: And Amanda has been one of those people who has reminded me of how much power we all have, and certainly that I have the power to do whatever I want to do next. And it's easy to lose sight of that if you don't have people who truly do see you for who you are.

Has your age difference ever been something you noticed or that has affected your relationship?

S: I'm 52. Amanda is 35. But in some ways, because I didn't grow up at the same pace as the women in my age group, I really feel like I'm constantly learning from people who are much younger than me. That is a great gift, and also a huge surprise. There was always this understanding for me as I was growing up that you got older and then you became wiser and you were the one to impart information. I think that may have been the case between sort of the industrial revolution and the technological revolution, but certainly now all those rules are gone.

Cheryl Strayed

PORTLAND, OR

Award-winning author Cheryl Strayed, 53, turned one of the most difficult times of her life, a daunting hike along the Pacific Crest Trail, into the bestselling book *Wild*. Her story of loss, grief, and self-discovery was adapted into a movie and has inspired countless others to turn to nature in times of personal struggle, not just to find their voices but also to touch base with who they really are and what matters most to them. Through her writing for countless magazines and as a host of the podcast *Dear Sugars*, Cheryl continues to look at the way we can find greater empathy for each other on our complicated paths in life.

Where did you grow up, and where do you live now?

I was born in Appalachia, in a small town called Spangler in Cambria County, Pennsylvania, where my father grew up and where his side of the family—all of the men coal miners—had lived since the early 1900s after emigrating from Scotland, Sweden, and Finland. When I was six, my family moved to Minnesota, and that's the state I think of as my childhood home; it's where I say I grew up when people ask. My family and I lived in a town called Chaska for several years, and when I was 13, we moved to the woods of northern Minnesota on forty acres of land about twenty miles away from the town of McGregor. I now live in Portland, Oregon, where I've lived since 1995, aside from a few years when I was in graduate school in Syracuse, New York.

What did you want to be when you were younger, and what do you do now?

I wanted to be a writer, and I am a writer, though the truth is more complicated than that. I felt called to write as a child, but it wasn't until I was 18 and in college that I understood that people like me could be writers. I grew up poor and working-class. It wasn't until I was in college that I actually met people who wrote and published books. Until then, the notion of being a writer seemed incredibly vague and far-fetched.

What does your current age feel like for you?

I'm 53. It feels to me exactly like what we call it—middle age. My youth is over, but old age has not yet begun. Both are distant and yet somehow also within reach. I feel more emotionally steady in this era of my life than in any other, more at peace with who I am, and less worried about pleasing others.

What misconceptions about aging would you like to dispel?

That we should be ashamed of it. That our age somehow conveys our worth or our relevancy. My small contribution to combating age shame is that all my life, I've disregarded the ridiculous idea that it's rude to ask someone, especially a woman, how old they are. I go out of my way to state my age in conversation often, and I don't hesitate to ask others how old they are, too. Normalizing transparency about age is my way of attempting to eradicate a stigma that shouldn't exist.

What are you most proud of about yourself?

How hard I work, and how hard I have always worked. Because I grew up poor, as soon as I was old enough to start earning money, I did. I worked full-time through every summer of high school and college, and during the school year, I always had at least one part-time job, and usually a few. I put myself through college without any assistance from family. But my hard work hasn't been limited to earning money and paying the bills. Anyone who wants to be a writer has to be disciplined, and I've stuck with it for decades now, even though writing has seldom come easy to me. Now that I have more financial security because of the success I've had

as a writer, I still work my tail off all the same. I've come to accept that the poor kid who had to hustle and scrape to get by is who I'll always be at my core.

How has your sense of self-confidence evolved over time?

Slowly but surely over the course of my lifetime, I've come to understand that true self-confidence must come from within. Of course it feels wonderful to be validated by others and to hear good things about ourselves—we all need that, and I think that's perfectly fine. But it can't be the thing by which you gauge your self-worth. Real self-confidence rises from that deep place of truth that lives within each of us.

What role do you feel your ancestors, or the women in your family who came before you, play in your life?

I'm obsessed with researching my family tree. One of my favorite things to do is spend hours on Ancestry.com finding every bit of information I can about the people in my family who came before me. While doing this, I've thought a lot about the lives of the women in my family. So many of them were poor. Many had very hard lives. When I bought the house that my family and I live in, paid for entirely with money I earned from the book sales of *Wild*, the pride I felt was connected to my awareness of all the women who came before me who'd worked incredibly hard but never gained financial independence. I'm constantly aware that I stand on their shoulders.

Do you have a message for younger women reading your story here?

I think the most powerful thing we can do for each other is show the truest versions of ourselves as boldly and bravely as possible, to reveal our struggles, our triumphs, our fears, and our courage. When we do that, we remind each other that we're connected by common experience that cuts across every real and imagined divide. My mission as a writer has always been to make others feel less alone, and I've learned that the way we do that is to tell the truth about who we are.

Can you describe a turning point in your life, and how it changed things for you?

My beloved mother died of cancer at the tragically young age of 45, when I was 22. In the aftermath of her death, my once-close family fell apart. I'd married young, and in my grief, I wrecked my marriage. I started using drugs and making a lot of decisions that only brought me deeper into sorrow. By the time I was 26, I'd reached a point where it felt like it could not get worse, and while I was down there in that darkness, down there in the deepest despair, I had what can only be called an awakening. I realized, quite simply, that I had to save myself. My mother had loved me too well for me to ruin my life. I came to understand that I'd been doing all this destructive stuff to show the world how much I loved my mother, to honor her by refusing to thrive without her. In my awakening, the opposite thought came to me, and I realized that the only way I could honor my mom was to become the woman she had raised me to be. To make good on my dreams and ambitions. To live the life she didn't get to live. It was shortly after I had this revelation that I decided to go on a long hike on the Pacific Crest Trail, a journey that I wrote about years later in my book *Wild*.

Who or what has influenced your life the most?

My mother is a tremendous influence on me. She's been dead in my life longer than she was alive in it, but I feel her love with me every day. She taught me so much about persisting through difficult times, erring on the side of kindness, believing in our capacity to do good, and seeking beauty every day.

What is the biggest risk you've taken in your life, and how did it shape you?

At a few important points in my twenties and thirties, I had to make a choice between taking jobs that would provide me with financial security and declining them so I could focus more fully on my writing. At every turn, I chose the more dangerous route, opting for freelance work rather than full-time jobs with regular pay and benefits. I did this because I knew my writing would suffer if I had a full-time job while also being a mother. I knew I couldn't somehow also wedge my writing in there between those two demands. So I found a way to patch together an income while also still preserving some time to write. I gambled on myself. I made a leap of faith. There were some very hard years, lots of stress, and also some serious credit card debt, but in the end, it was a risk that paid off.

If you could go back in your life, what would you like to do over—and what would you never do again?

When I was a teenager, I had a serious boyfriend, and though he was a nice enough young man, I wish I'd spent less time focused on pleasing him and more on pleasing myself. I wish I'd had the confidence in my teens to resist feeling like I needed affirmation from him and other boys. The choices I made as a teenager make me cringe. I was so smart and ambitious, but I buried it so I would be liked and accepted. This do-over wish is also the thing I'd never want to do over again.

How have your ideas of success and happiness changed over time?

They've gotten more real, more grounded, and less dependent on external definitions of what those things are and far more dependent on my own internal measurements.

How has raising children affected your life?

In every way. It's so enormous I can't even exactly answer this question. Once I became a mother, every choice I made about my work, my life, my days, and my nights had to take my children into deep consideration.

What would you like to learn or experience at this stage in your life?

There are so many things I want to do, and so little time to do them all. My latest idea is to develop a one-woman show and perform it at the Edinburgh Festival Fringe, which I attended for the first time in 2019. I was so taken by the storytellers and comedians I saw during the festival. As I watched them, it occurred to me that I'd like to try doing it myself, even though the idea terrifies me. I mean, what am I thinking? I'm not an actor or a comedian. And yet I'm thinking of doing it. I have in my mind that it's something I'd like to do by the time I turn 60.

What is a lesson you're still learning or need to learn?

Saying no. And not just saying no, but saying no and feeling okay with the fact that I've disappointed someone. I'm a people-pleaser to my bones, so it's hard for me.

Knowing what you know now, what would you go back and tell your younger self?

It's going to be okay. Even if it's not okay right now or tomorrow or for some time to come. There are hard times and easy times and sad times and happy times, and they will all pass. Just hold on. You got this.

Mahboubeh Abbasgholizadeh

BROOKLYN, NY

Mahboubeh Abbasgholizadeh, 63, is an Iranian journalist, documentary filmmaker, and women's rights activist. She was the editor in chief of the feminist journal *Farzaneh* and, after being arrested several times for organizing peaceful protests in Iran, moved to Europe, where she continued to write, educate, and work as a pivotal member of the movement for women's rights. In the mid-2000s, she moved to the United States, where she managed the nonprofit organization Zanan TV and taught at the University of Connecticut and Rutgers University. Mahboubeh was awarded the 2010 Johann Philipp Palm Award for freedom of speech and the press. Mahboubeh now lives in Brooklyn, New York, where she continues to work as an educator in schools and also teaches Persian cooking classes with the League of Nations.

Where did you grow up, and where do you live now?

I grew up in southern Iran, in Khorramshahr. It used to be a port and a connection between Iran and the Middle East and other countries. Then the war happened, and now it's destroyed. There is no city like that there now. When I was a kid, I moved to the capital, Tehran. I grew up with a huge urban life in Tehran.

My parents' roots are in Azerbaijan, north of Iran. When I was growing up in southern Iran, on the border between Iran and Iraq, the area was a mix of Arab, Persian, and Turkish people. We were considered Turks. My language was different from Persian. My culture was different from Persian people's.

Now I live in New York, in Brooklyn, so it's very diverse. I don't think I'll ever finish my experience of living in this city. But I'm kind of like a bird—I need to keep moving on. I enjoy being in one place for a while, but I can't live there forever. I think New York's mission for me was making me tough, making me diverse, making me have confidence about being in America, and being powerful enough to deal with all of this stuff in a new country. Now I am ready to move to Los Angeles to live with my family. I want to join my daughter. I am done with single life. I want to be in a real family. I was never in a real family all my life, and I want to have that now.

What did you want to be when you were younger?

When I was 16, we were in pre-revolutionary times in Iran. The revolution happened in 1978. Even in America, that was a very interesting time for political and social justice movements—and we had the same thing in Iran. I was involved in political movements, but the biggest thing for me was becoming independent from colonialism. We didn't want direct or indirect colonialism. We wanted to be independent. That was what I wanted to work for and bring about.

All my passion was, at that time, dedicated to changing the world and bringing justice to my country, my people, and my life. I was a revolutionary girl with anti-imperialist and anti-colonial attitudes. I identified with revolutionary women in Islamic history like Fāṭimah, the daughter of Prophet Muhammad. We were all very idealistic.

At that time, I moved with my husband to Egypt to study Islamic literature because after the Iranian Revolution, we wanted to bring the culture, the real culture of political Islam, from the Middle East to Iran. We had a revolutionary marriage. Revolutionary

CONSCIOUSLY CHANGING GENERATIONAL LABELS AND IDENTITIES IS VERY REVOLUTIONARY.

marriage is when you choose someone to be in revolution with and you say, "We are stronger together than we are alone." It was not traditional. It was not legal. It was just pure revolutionary. We shared the same idealistic work, attitude, values, and vision.

My dream then was to be a revolutionary girl who could fight, who had self-defense skills, who could sleep in the mountains with no blanket, and who could also be very knowledgeable about the philosophy of Islam and could teach and write and be an advocate for an independent country. You have to make your own country after a revolution, so we needed to know what the ideological framework behind our political movement was.

But now? Who am I now? I am just me now. I am a spiritual feminist with ecofeminist approaches. I like to use my body for cooking and gardening and to have nice sex. Life is about good food, good sex, good thinking, and enjoying the day—all these things. I want to just enjoy life.

What does your current age feel like for you?

I used to carry so much baggage on my back. Now it's not on my back; it's in my living room. Every day, I meditate and open up the bags and go through everything and let myself cry and say, "Okay, I've made peace with you." I don't want to carry this much anymore. So this is me now. I think I've had five different lives. I've died from one life and been born into another life in the same body.

I feel like there is a table, and there are five different Mahboubehs around that table. One of them is a young revolutionary woman, one of them is an immigrant woman, one of them is a feminist, one of them is a mother, and one of them is spiritual and just wants to relax and enjoy nature. I think, What do I do with all of you? They sometimes start arguing with one another.

I feel that as I age, I make peace between all these Mahboubehs around the table. They live together, and they have peace.

I think every decade, we have this crisis. And for me, my sixties were about facing death and not shying away from that. I used to avoid talking about death. It was a huge phobia for me. But turning 60 can make us brave enough to face our lives, our deaths, and who we are at this age.

I had to ask myself if I wanted to keep my hair silver or dye it brown. I worried that younger people would think I was too old or wouldn't want to work with me for certain jobs. But consciously changing generational labels and identities is very revolutionary. It reconnected me with my revolutionary roots.

At 60, I started to read psychology and do mindfulness meditation. I started to practice self-therapy, and now I am working on so many things inside of me. My sixties are my renaissance. I just want to be light. Now my internal journey is more active than my external journey. At this age, it's more about spiritual adventure.

What misconceptions about aging would you like to dispel?

There are so many. Especially about what we won't be able to do. I think that if we didn't have numbers and ages, we wouldn't feel age as much. Instead of working with the calendar and with the number of years, it would be better to work with the concept of evolution.

What are you most proud of about yourself?

This is very difficult because there are so many Mahboubehs around the table. Every part of my life was different. I've had to make so many difficult choices in my life, as a feminist in Iran, as a broadcaster in political exile, and here in America. And with all of these difficult choices, I have always chosen with my heart, not my brain. I try to always choose truth so that the little candle inside me that is my power will stay lit.

How has your sense of self-confidence or self-acceptance evolved over time?

Who said that I have self-confidence? That is a big problem for me. I'm in a different period of my life now where I am losing people and I'm having a problem with belonging. I struggled when I was younger and felt like I didn't belong when I realized I was a lesbian. It felt like a crisis. There is a lot of homophobia in Iran. And now, as an immigrant and a middle-aged woman in New York, it can all feel scary. So now I feel like my focus has been to *give* myself self-confidence, rather than already having it. I'm learning to take care of myself like a baby. All the time, I am working on giving myself self-confidence. Because this can be a scary life.

What role do you feel your ancestors, or the women in your family who came before you, play in your life?

When I was a kid, the women around me were independent and powerful. My grandma on my dad's side was in charge of both families. She was like a single mother working very hard to help her family grow up. Several times in my childhood, I was bullied in school, and she came and fought for me. My aunts are doctors and are very progressive. So I think it's about all of these independent women and that strength that runs in my family.

I started to nurture another connection with my ancestors during my immigrant life here in New York. I may not have known these people, or only for a few years when I was younger, but I connect with them when I'm cooking. I started cooking in 2016, and it was a healing process for me. The kitchen was a safe refuge for me. It felt like my hand was not my hand. It was my grandmother's, and she was doing the cooking. She was telling me what to do—she was all around me. I felt her support and like we were in the same space. The smell of that food helped me remember my childhood. Cooking was an instrument to help me connect with my ancestors in a spiritual and healing way.

My grandmothers had difficult lives—they lost many children—and when they cooked, they made a lot of smoke so they could hide their tears. My father's mother used her kitchen smoke to cry for her lost children. When my mom started crying in the kitchen, it was because she missed her family and was homesick for them. For all of these women, the kitchen was a place to grieve and heal.

So now when I cook with them in my kitchen, I want to help rid them of this pain. I want them to just enjoy the smell and eat together. I heal them, and they heal me.

When do you feel your most powerful?

It depends on which of the many different Mahboubehs we are talking about. In one of my lives, I felt powerful when I had my babies in the hospital during the beginning of the Iran-Iraq War. We didn't have much food—or much nutritional food. I had a coupon for food, and we got some eggs and ghee for strength. So it was really difficult being pregnant at that time. When I started to go into labor at midnight, I had to wait until morning to go to the hospital. We didn't have breathing practices and the tradition of husbands coming to the hospital to support their wives. So it was all very hard. But when the nurses placed my daughter on my stomach and I felt her warm energy, it made me feel so powerful. This was my baby, and I had made her. It was one of the most powerful moments of my life.

When I escaped from Iran in January 2010, that was another time that made me feel powerful. I went from border to border and had to be faster than the political police, who were after me. I knew that if I were arrested, they would torture me to admit that I was a lesbian. And at the time, it would have been a big deal for a women's leader to be a lesbian. They would have said I had no morality. It was a crime at that time, punishable by hanging.

So the moment I put my feet on the other side of the door at the border of Georgia and I felt freedom with my feet, I jumped and I hugged the air and screamed, "Oh my God. I am free. I am free!" That joy of being free was so, so powerful. That was the biggest risk, to leave my home country in one night, but when I found freedom, it felt incredible.

I also felt powerful when I was able to kiss my girlfriend, in public, in front of the Flatiron Building at the Dyke March in New York City. I still have a lot of sad feelings about being born a lesbian in Iran. I didn't have the experience of love earlier in my life. Then when I walked in the Dyke March, I looked around me and everywhere were so many beautiful couples. I met my girlfriend one month before the march, and when I kissed her there, it felt like such a powerful moment. I finally chose not to be scared of being a lesbian.

What's the biggest risk you've taken in your life, and how has it shaped you?

I have moved from so many parts of my life to new ones, and I think it was the biggest risk to break with my belief system. I was a part of the Iranian Revolution, and everything was about how revolutionary we could be. So that meant not getting into pop culture and music because that was seen as wasting time. There were so many rules, mostly based around being anti-bourgeois. We were anti-imperialist, and it was a mix of communism and religion, somewhere in between. It was a whole system—a value system and set of beliefs. You removed your individual personality and became a part of the collective.

But then I broke with this belief system when I realized that Ayatollah Khomeini was making mistakes. He was a fundamentalist. He was actually destroying women's rights.

So I took a risk and organized a group of revolutionary women. We would talk about what kind of life we wanted after the revolution. We started to review the Quran. I had a great mentor— she was a leader in the Islamic movement. I started to realize that this utopia they were telling us about was not true. They were making so many mistakes. So this group of women, as friends, we started to discover a new life. It was so hard to take this risk because it was leaving everything we had believed behind. But we were ready to move on.

To take a risk, you need courage. To have courage, you need to believe in your truth. To find belief in your truth, you have to be honest with yourself.

When you learn to take a risk, you get familiar and comfortable with it enough to do it again. Every time you move from one identity to another, you risk feeling lots of pain, shame, and self-judgment.

The collective I had with Muslim feminists in Iran led us to create the first school of critical Muslim feminism. I am still well known for that, but after a few years, I knew it was not my life anymore.

When I got divorced, I had to go in front of a judge, who questioned whether I should have custody of my children. He said that God wanted me to be a wife and a mother, that it was my duty. But I realized that that wasn't the truth to me. My truth was that I didn't care what they said God said. I didn't care what Sharia said. I don't care what *they* said. I felt in my body that I had the right as a mother to have my kids. I went home, with my children, and realized that motherhood had changed my perspective and philosophical discourse. I had moved from duty to God to the individual rights of women.

Do you have a message for younger women reading your story here?

One of the most amazing things in our lives, regardless of how we describe our sexuality or gender identity, is the power of motherhood. And by that, I mean the power of *nurturing*: nurturing other humans. I think everyone has the ability to do this in some form, and it can be so empowering. To care for others and use our strength to lift up others.

Dr. Jasmine Eugenio

and

Malaka Gharib

LOS ANGELES, CA, AND NASHVILLE, TN

Dr. Jasmine Eugenio, 63, is a beloved pediatrician in Los Angeles—and is also Malaka Gharib's aunt. Jasmine moved to America to help raise her. Malaka, 30, is the deputy editor and digital strategist for NPR's global health and development team. In addition to covering issues like refugee crises around the world, gender equality, and women's health, Malaka is a cartoonist and the author of *I Was Their American Dream*, an award-winning graphic memoir about being a Filipino-Egyptian American. She has also worked at the Malala Fund, a global education charity founded by Malala Yousafzai. Jasmine and Malaka's relationship has been a foundational part of their lives and has helped shape how each woman sees the world.

You have been in each other's lives for a very long time, but what were your first impressions of each other?

JASMINE: I came to the United States from the Philippines to take care of Malaka. I was a young doctor. I had just graduated. My sister needed someone to help her take care of her new baby in Texas. I remember when I first met Malaka as a baby, I thought, Oh my gosh. She stinks! Apparently, my sister hadn't given her a bath, because she didn't know how to give her a bath. So the first thing I did when I came was I gave her a bath, and I cuddled her. I cried when I had to leave her.

MALAKA: My first real impression of Jasmine—I call her Tita Pinky—was when I was a little older. I loved that she was so crafty. She had this box of stamps, embossing powder, glue guns, pearls, and ribbons. She was making her own invitations for family parties or painting ornaments for Christmas or making Halloween decorations. We would always play together and make things with our hands. It was so much fun. It always surprises me now that as a doctor, she also has this incredible creative streak. She showed me from an early age that you can be a very multifaceted person. You could be somebody who was really, really good at school and science, but you could also be really interested in making your own Christmas wreath.

When did your relationship transition from a familial relationship into more of an adult friendship?

M: We are a Filipino family, and Tita Pinky is the matriarch. She is the person who hosts holiday parties, who brings people together if somebody is sick, and we defer to her in what to do. So when I was getting ready to leave California for college in New York, my mom really wanted Tita Pinky to impart some wisdom and advice to me before I left.

So we took a trip together to New York for a few days where we just got to hang out, eat at restaurants, and spend really good quality time together. We went out one night and accidentally ended up at a gay bar, where we had this amazing adventure. She told me, "The world is your oyster. You can do anything you want. You can have it all if

you really want to, and you can dream big. Do what you love, and success will follow." That trip and her words left me with such confidence that I could do anything I wanted.

When I started drawing more and made my first zine to sell at the LA Zine Fest, my whole family came. Tita Pinky was there with my grandpa, and they all helped me set up my booth. She has been there for me as I figured things out and became more of an adult.

J: I didn't get to see Malaka as much after she graduated from high school. But when she started off into her own world and I would get to see her once she was out of college, I realized that she was really out there doing her own thing. I was so proud of her and so impressed.

What do you have in common now as adults that surprises you?

M: Tita Pinky wears many hats. She is a doctor, first of all, and she has a really important position at the hospital where she works. But she's also a wedding florist and somehow finds time to do that almost full-time. Once when I worked for NPR and was covering news in Puerto Rico, I ran into Tita Pinky there! I said, "Why are you here?" and she said, "I'm giving water to people who have been hurt by the hurricane." She does it all.

So when I think of how I work and how I like to do it all, I think I have the same work ethic as Tita Pinky. I work hard during the day and I work hard during the night, because it's what I like to do. I just think, Look at Tita Pinky. She's doing it all, and she is loving it! It's hard work, but it's also really rewarding.

Can you share the importance of what you have passed down about your cultural heritage?

J: I think this is the most important thing, and it's made Malaka what she is today. We come from a very close-knit village, and we take care of our children. So with Malaka, she has so many moms, and so many dads, and so many cousins and sisters. I always instill in her that she will never be alone or feel alone, because she knows that right behind her, there is a village. We take care of each other. In every

Filipino home, if you go on a Saturday, everybody is there. If somebody has a problem, it's everybody's problem. If somebody needs money, everybody pitches in. So it's always a village taking care of the village.

M: That value system is one of the most important things she's handed down to me. Filipinos are probably the most collectivistic society in Asian culture. The clan is everything. She's also imparted so much to me about Filipino food and clothing and music.

My grandfather passed away last year, and it was Tita Pinky's idea to do everything traditionally. The women wore cloth fabric skirts, and the men wore white barongs. It was such a beautiful display of traditional dress in the Philippine culture to celebrate our grandfather.

J: I want to make sure we are enforcing our culture at every turn. When Malaka told me she was having her first Filipino Christmas at her house, I said, "Can I send you some traditional Filipino decorations?" So I sent her a huge, huge box.

M: These were all signals to me that you can't fake being Filipino in your life or in your home. And she's helping me to celebrate our culture authentically.

What are some of the most significant things you've learned from each other?

J: Malaka was the first one to leave the nest, and that was very hard on everyone. And when my daughters finally left the nest, it reminded me of when we were at the door watching Malaka, and it became a learning experience for me. Going through what we did with Malaka reminded me that just because children leave doesn't mean that they're gone. They will always come back. Just because they're physically far away doesn't mean the village is not intact.

M: I feel like the biggest thing I learned from Tita Pinky is that you can literally do anything you want and you do not have to conform to any type of box that people will put you in. She's an inspiration not just to me but to so many people. I've told so many people about her and all she does. When people ask me how I find the time to work as much as I do, I think about Tita Pinky and her flowers on the weekends. You have to make the time and do the work you love. That's what I learned from her.

What do you each hope your relationship brings or gives to the other person?

J: We planted the seeds early and tried to instill the Philippine culture in Malaka, and I hope that she can continue to pass it on for my dear children and that she can build her own village and do the same things.

M: Tita Pinky taught me to be really brave. I've trusted her advice all my life, and she's never steered me wrong. So I hope I can do the same for her. Encourage her to be brave.

How have you influenced each other's sense of self-confidence?

M: I saw Tita Pinky's transformation in waves. She started a nonprofit organization later in life. I saw that you can have many, many iterations of yourself as a woman. You can be a mother, you can be a doctor and a career person, then you can transform yourself at the drop of a hat—it's possible. And now I see many transformations in my own life, too. And I know it's possible to do and to be okay doing because she's shown me how.

J: I've seen Malaka persevere. She's always afraid in the beginning, but I think that perseverance came from being exposed to our family and seeing the hardships we've been through. And that's something that not everybody can get or be exposed to. And her perseverance has made *me* more confident now that I'm mentoring young medical students, and sometimes residents. Seeing how confident you are made me more confident that I didn't go wrong in guiding you, and that I can replicate and continue doing the same for other young people. You are my success story. I am so proud of you.

M: I'm proud of you, too! You're the coolest woman I know!

What role do you feel your ancestors, or the women in your family who came before you, play in your lives?

M: My nainai (grandmother) is an incredible woman. She is a college professor, she wrote a book in the Philippines, and she is also very crafty. Just like I'm crafty, just like Tita Pinky's crafty—NaiNai's crafty. All the women in our family are very good at making things beautiful. That's something that I think I learned from NaiNai, who cares a lot about aesthetics, and beauty and presentation. She is a professional woman and also somebody who cares about crafts and making things. That is a strong part of our line of women.

J: It's so interesting. My mom, your grandmother, was very cool. She was way ahead of her time. She pushed me out of the house, and she let me go where I wanted to go. She was very strict with Malaka's mom, but with me, I could go everywhere, I could do anything, and she never stopped me. It was unheard of at the time. That definitely inspired me to be who I am.

What advice do you each have for people who would like to be closer to the women in their family?

M: I'm a big fan of more frequent, small interactions throughout the year. I don't have long conversations with Tita Pinky every week. I'll send her a funny picture or text her and say, "I'm having a crisis. I need to call and talk to you for five minutes." I think it's a lot more doable to stay close when people don't worry that keeping in touch means hours of long calls. That can be stressful, so instead I try to keep things short and fun and frequent—because it's a gift to have people right in front of you. I want to be direct and get to the point.

J: I think I get closer to people because I tell good stories; and they're honest stories. To me, that's the secret of being friends and your friends being confident in you: to tell each other honest, good stories, and to listen to theirs, too.

What is your favorite thing about your relationship?

J: That I may not see Malaka for a long time, sometimes months, but when we see each other, it's like we never parted. We stay connected even when we are apart. When I go somewhere in the world, I find myself thinking, Malaka's going to like this. And I bring her a small gift from everywhere I go. There's a whole bag of these little things that I have for her, and she appreciates them.

M: She knows I like small things, and she never forgets me. She always makes me feel very much like I'm still there at home with her when I'm not. I'm so grateful that our connection spans those distances.

Ngoc Minh Ngo

BROOKLYN, NY

Ngoc Minh Ngo, 58, is a Brooklyn-based photographer whose work takes its inspiration from the beauty of nature. Born in Vietnam, Ngoc grew up in a small seaside town, where she discovered her love of the colors found in the ocean, trees, and the sky. Ngoc has published two books, *In Bloom: Creating and Living with Flowers* and *Bringing Nature Home: Floral Arrangements Inspired by Nature*, both of which celebrate the changing seasons and their impact on flora.

Where did you grow up, and where do you live now?

I was born in Vietnam and lived there until I was 12. I spent my teenage years in Northern California and lived in Paris and Tokyo before settling in Brooklyn, New York.

What did you want to be when you were younger, and what do you do now?

I couldn't figure out what I wanted to be when I was growing up, even though I was curious about many things. I enjoyed many subjects in school and was a good student, but I never felt that I was exceptionally good at anything. In college, a teacher tried to convince me to major in math, but I knew I wasn't good enough to be a mathematician. I came to New York with the intention of studying painting restoration, but I was told that I needed to take two years of chemistry before I could even apply to the program. I discovered photography while working on a feature film, and decided to pursue it professionally.

What does your current age feel like for you?

I like the metaphor of the seasons to describe the different ages of our lives. I am in the autumn of my life. Just as autumn has its beauty, this stage of my life has its own rewards. I feel far more confident in myself than I was at 20. I am more accepting of life and less impatient with it. The autumn is also a time of winding down, and I am aware that there is more time behind me than there is in front of me. It is a fact of life, and it forces me to weigh every decision I make more carefully. I am more conscious of the here and now, and I am more mindful of my intentions. Decades' worth of experiences and memories have made my life infinitely richer than it ever was.

What misconceptions about aging would you like to dispel?

I used to think that as one ages, life narrows down and the paths start closing in until the inevitable end. Yet as we age, we also accumulate knowledge and hopefully acquire wisdom, and that in itself opens up different avenues. I've learned that we have to leave ourselves open to new experiences and keep learning, at any age.

What are you most proud of about yourself?

I think I've been blessed with a strong sense of empathy. I always try to put myself in another person's place in order to understand where they are coming from. To be able to see the world from another person's perspective is one of the most important things we can do to foster understanding and compassion, something we sorely need at the moment.

How has your sense of self-confidence or self-acceptance evolved over time?

When I was young, I was always looking outward, toward other people, for validation or approval. Over time, I realized that I just have to be the best version of myself, to draw whatever I have from within myself. My self-confidence comes from knowing my strengths as well as my weaknesses. I am much more comfortable in my own skin than I was in my twenties.

What role do you feel your ancestors, or the women in your family who came before you, play in your life?

There were very different women role models in my family when I was growing up in Vietnam, and three of them had the most impact on me.

My paternal grandmother was the kindest woman I know. When I was about 4, I was sent to live with her for a few months, and I still retain the feeling of being around her even though I don't have any visual memory of that time. I can still recall the sense of peace and calmness that she seemed to carry within her. She was a very quiet and self-contained person and taught me to be the same. She died a few years after that, but she left an indelible mark on me.

My beautiful mother taught me a great deal about resilience and self-determination. She has had the most remarkable life. Orphaned at 13, she became a revolutionary at 17 when she joined my father to fight against the French colonial regime. Having borne nine children, she started a business with friends to supplement my father's income. At 42, she lost all her fortune and became a refugee in the United States. She learned a new language and worked alongside my father as they operated a grocery store. Three years later, she took an exam that qualified her for a job as a nurse's aide, embarking on a career that lasted for twenty years and gave her a whole new circle of lifelong friends. Since my father's death thirteen years ago, she has been the happy matriarch of a large family, with eleven adoring grandchildren.

The woman who had the most profound effect on me, however, is my father's cousin Mu Huong, who came to live with us when I was around 9 years old, when my father was transferred to another city. My parents moved there with my two youngest sisters and asked Mu Huong to come and run our household, where the rest of my siblings and I remained, along with a small staff—a driver, a housekeeper, and a cook. Unlike my mother, whose intelligence and determination were well hidden behind her beauty, which dazzled men and reassured them at the same time, Mu Huong wore her plainness with her force of character. Yet she schooled my mother in her dress, advising her on the latest fashions. She could cook both Vietnamese and French food better than anyone I knew. Most of all, she was resourceful, independent, and highly capable. When my father's transfer turned out to be more permanent and the rest of us joined him, she decamped to a small town in the highland, where my parents had bought a coffee plantation years before as an investment. Without any farming experience, she made the plantation productive for the first time. She spent the rest of her life there. In the short time that she was in my life, she taught me to be strong, to be fearless, and to believe myself capable of whatever I choose to do.

What message do you have for women reading your story here, and what impact do you hope your life and story have on those around you?

I believe that the difficult events of my life have made me a stronger person, and that every experience, good or bad, is a learning opportunity. Life does not proceed in a straight projection of uninterrupted progress. There's bound to be setbacks and challenges along the way. Who you are is the sum of all your experiences and what you make of them. Lastly, your life is immeasurably enriched by those around you, so you must take care of them.

When do you feel your most powerful?

I have given a lot of thought to the dynamic of power. To have power means to have dominance over something or someone, something I don't wish to have. It is desirable to have the power to do good, but often power becomes an end in itself for those who seek it. I don't think I have ever felt powerful, but I have felt strong at certain times in my life. My strength comes as much from inner resources as from the support of my family, friends, and community.

Can you describe a turning point in your life, and how it changed things for you?

When I was 12, our country, South Vietnam, lost the war to Communist North Vietnam. From one day to the next, my life changed beyond recognition. My family and I had to leave everything and everyone we loved behind. We forged a new life in the United States as refugees. At an age when most kids just want to fit in, I found myself in an unfamiliar place where I was conspicuously foreign. My parents had more than their share of struggles to keep us sheltered, clothed, and fed, so I learned to be self-sufficient. I learned to speak English by watching TV. Later on, I applied to college on my own and only told my parents that I would be leaving home to attend UC Berkeley once I had made all the arrangements. I often think that I would have been a very different person had we not been forced to leave Vietnam.

How has parenting affected your life?

For the first five years of my daughter's life, I shifted my focus from my career to being a mother. Even though I continued to work, having as much time as possible with her was my priority. I loved being with her and watching her discover the world. In the process, she taught me to look at the world differently. As she grew older, I became more conscious of setting a good example for her in my work and my life in general. I also tried to be a gentle guiding force intellectually whenever she needed it. Now that she is in college, I love discussing everything with her, from books and movies to issues of social justice and racial and economic inequality. She always broadens my viewpoint.

What is a lesson you're still learning or need to learn?

I need to learn to be more disciplined with my time. Like everyone else, I have given too much of my time to the digital rabbit hole. I need to learn how to reclaim some of that time and put it to more productive use.

What would you like to learn or experience at this stage in your life?

There is so much that I still would like to learn—the history of women painters in European art, the history of roses in China, the history of Japanese painting and literature, the poetry of Emily Dickinson, botany. I would like to learn how to paint. I would like to make a garden and watch it grow and mature. I would like to fill my days with art, literature, film, and nature. And I want to experience all of this with my family and friends.

Diana Nyad

LOS ANGELES, CA

Diana Nyad, 72, is one of the toughest athletes in the world. At 64 years old, she realized her dream of being the first person to swim from Cuba to Florida without the use of a shark cage for protection. Diana has never let sharks, jellyfish, or expectations of what she should do get in her way. She was inducted into the US National Women's Sports Hall of Fame in 1986 and is also an award-winning author, journalist, and motivational speaker who has inspired people around the globe to always keep pushing to achieve their goals.

Where did you grow up, and where do you live now?

I was born in New York City, but I had a French mother. I was lucky, during my first seven years, to be in Paris half the year with my mother. French was my first language. That's proven to be a fortuitous thing my whole life—languages and foreign cultures in general. Then, when my mother divorced my father for the second time, she had some French friends down in Florida near Miami, so we moved there. So, starting in second grade, I was in Florida. We'd go to New York for vacations. Manhattan was our place to escape to. I had New York in my blood, and Paris in my blood, but really the love of the ocean and the great outdoors and warm weather all year round.

Then, by age 9, once I started swimming very seriously, I didn't want to go to New York, Paris, anywhere. My mom would say, "Well, of course you're going to go with me and your brother and sister. We're a family, and you're 9 years old, and you're not staying by yourself in Fort Lauderdale." I said, "Yes, I am," so I did. I sort of just became a swimmer and was very, shall we say, fanatical with it from early on. That's kind of the geographic big background of my childhood.

Now I live in Los Angeles. I moved here with my partner many years ago. I said I never would. I said I'd go to Antarctica before I'd go to Los Angeles. I thought nobody here reads and the museums are horrible. But that's just not true. There are great people everywhere.

What did you want to be when you were younger?

My fifth-grade teacher kept all of her students' essays. One essay we had to write was about what we wanted to do for the rest of our lives. All the boys wrote that they wanted to be policemen and firemen. All the girls wanted to be nurses and teachers. I wrote an essay that she sent to me many years later, when I swam around Manhattan and had a little bit of renown from that. It says something like, "I didn't know any of my grandparents. But I found out that mostly they lived to be from their early to their mid-eighties, so probably by genetics, that's what I'm going to live to. That means I have only seventy-two to seventy-five years to go. Time is running out! I've got to sleep less. I've got to study more. I want to speak all the languages in the world." It was a ridiculous essay. "I want to be a great athlete. I want to be a doctor, a physician. I want to help people." It was the overblown-ego letter, but the whole point of it was, I was worried about time passing. Most kids, when they're that age, they don't even know where they're going to be on their next birthday. It's too far away. But I've always been worried that I would close my eyes on the final day of my life and look back with regret. I do have regrets. We can only learn what we learn. But I think what I wanted to do more than anything was not waste any time in this precious life.

I do believe that the thrust of it for me, always, is about recognizing that you never get to do this day over again. You never get to do this year over again. You'd better make your choices, and you'd better make them the best you can.

How has your sense of self-confidence or self-acceptance evolved over time?

You might make an assumption that one's confidence grows as you get older, but I'm not 100 percent sure that's true. I think, from the outside, I appear to be somebody who's strong and

145

confident. But I can be just pathetically junior high insecure. For instance, I've taken up tennis in a ferocious way over the last two years. I'm a real student of the game. I'll walk by a court and say, "Hey, why don't those ladies ever ask me to play? I'm just as good as they are. Why am I being shut out from their game?" The truth is, there's no shutting out at all. If I asked them, if I went to them and said, "Hey, you guys, can I play with you sometime?" they'd say, "Sure. How about Saturday?" But I take on the insecurity, and think, I'm not good enough. I've got to get better, I've got to prove myself, instead of just being a student of the game, enjoying it and working every time I get on the court. I definitely have insecurities about feeling left out or feeling disrespected, so I work hard to be respected.

What are you most proud of about yourself?

I think I'm a compassionate person. As much as I have been very single-minded and driven toward certain goals that haven't left much time or space for anybody or anything else, I think I've always been a person who cares. If I see someone who's left out in a group, I'm the one who goes over and makes sure they're included. I'm proud of myself for being that person.

Who or what has influenced your life the most?

I love stories of resilience. I'll never forget reading the story of Ernest Shackleton's trip to Antarctica. I remember thinking, Who would have that kind of guts, to sleep out, with all his men, on an iceberg, and be willing to be the first one to die? I've always loved those stories of ultimate physical adventures, like climbs to the top of Annapurna and Mount Everest.

I had a friend who died young of cancer. She had kids, and she was tough. She was full of "never say die." She said, "Not me. I'm not going down." Then she did go down, and maybe even more impressive than her battling was her grace in saying goodbye. She had to say goodbye to all of us, and to her kids, and she didn't cry. She cried alone, and she cried with her husband, but she didn't cry in front of her kids. She didn't want to scare them. She just said to them, "You all are going to live beautiful lives."

I've watched the way people have gone through life, and I've always been inspired by the kind of people who live with great bravery.

What's the biggest risk you've taken in your life, and how has it shaped you?

On a very concrete level, that's a dangerous vast wilderness out there, that ocean between Cuba and Florida. There are the sharks of the tropics, and box jellyfish, and that's the most potent venom on planet Earth, so you are definitely in a risky situation when you're out there just swimming with your little body on the surface. No matter what safety protocols you take, there is risk. My two best friends, every time I would go to make another attempt to swim across, would say, "Is this the time? Is this the time you're going to die out there?"

But one thing I am proud about is that I've had the courage to fail. I think it takes courage to fail. I'm willing to shoot high. I'm willing to give up the PhD program and pursue swimming around Manhattan Island and then becoming a sports broadcaster, which I didn't know was coming.

I'm willing to chase big dreams and be inspired and learn who I am, discover who I am, and make everybody around me who's on that trip with me discover who they are, rather than settle for a mediocre dream where I won't get to know myself at all.

How have your ideas of success and happiness changed over time?

Oh, definitely less ego. I take my dog to the beach at sunrise. He's old now, so we're not going anywhere fast. We slowly stroll, and not only do I see how happy he is, I'm contemplating myself, too. There's nothing like looking out at the horizon to extend your imagination, and then there's just the ocean in general. I wouldn't have taken that kind of time when I was younger. In my twenties and thirties, I was like, "Get out of my way!" If we were walking down the sidewalk in New York, I'd give you a little elbow if you were slowing me down, wouldn't care if I pushed you out into the street. I used to keep Spanish and other language vocabulary cards hung up on a clothesline in the bathroom, because I couldn't imagine taking the time to brush my teeth or to piddle, just standing there, just sitting there doing that.

I'm just not like that anymore. I now value things in life that are slower, like a conversation with a friend who needs it. If you'd known me when I was 25, you might have found me entertaining or impressive. But you would have said, "Jesus, there's no give-and-take. There's no soft exchange of human being here." Now I can be just as energetic and inspired by walking along the shore with my dog in the morning.

At this point in your life, what have you made peace with that used to be a struggle for you?

If I've been rejected for a project or even something as simple as a tennis match, instead of spiraling down, instead of beating myself up, as a general rule I've gotten better at catching myself quickly and saying, "Wait a second. Did you do the best you could? Were you very happy with that proposal you sent in, and don't think you could have massaged it better for a couple of weeks?" Then I let go of it. There were probably a dozen different reasons for that decision, and it could be that none of them had to do with me. They had to do with other things—timing, quotas people have to fill, other people's proposals that matched just what they had in mind at that moment.

What would you like to learn or experience at this stage in your life?

I've been in love twice. And I've been in two long-term relationships, but both when I was much younger. Sometimes I look at myself and say, "Isn't it the human condition, isn't it the human way to couple and make a home and make a nest together?"

Most of the people I know—men, women, straight, gay—when they're single, their first goal before a job or before cleaning their home or whatever it is, is to get hooked up. They want to live this life with somebody and share it with somebody, and I'm just not feeling it. I don't think I'm scared. I don't think I'm keeping myself from a full life. But I have to admit that I miss slow dancing. I miss holding hands in the movies or on the couch. It's just that closeness a couple has. I guess it's something I'm taking a longer look at. Am I really going to go to the end of my life without another real romance, a real intimate relationship? I ask myself that.

What misconceptions about aging would you like to dispel?

Well, all of them. I have to be real: I'm different. My body is different at 72 than it was at 21, but honestly, except for the cosmetic end of it, it's not *that*

different. I'm playing a fierce game of tennis. I did that swim that nobody's ever been able to do, man, woman, young, strong, when I was 64 years old.

My mom was a ballroom dancer. She was lean. She was beautiful. She barely aged. Alzheimer's is what got her. But her physical level of vitality and all that barely changed. She was told 60 was old age. Now we, the people, have changed that. Now we talk more about 80 being old age. I mean, look, we recently had two guys in their seventies running for president, so we must have believed that for four to eight years, they'd have the physical stamina and mental acumen to be able to do the most important job, ostensibly, in the world.

So why should we put restrictions on anybody? You're never too old to chase your dreams. You're never too old *or* too young. Age should just barely be a factor in anything we do.

What impact do you hope your life and your story will have on those around you?

I don't have to worry if people are going to remember me as a superior athlete. But I want to be remembered as a great friend. I think it's most important to dedicate yourself to being a great friend to the people in your life.

Erin Zimmer Strenio

and

Jeanette Bell

NEW ORLEANS, LA

Erin Zimmer Strenio, 35, and Jeanette Bell, 77, became friends while working on the Garden on Mars project in New Orleans. Jeanette is an expert gardener who's been growing flowers, vegetables, and fruits on vacant lots in New Orleans for over twenty-five years. She was named a 2015 People's Health Champion for her urban gardens. Erin was the managing editor of the James Beard Award–winning website Serious Eats and has written for *Saveur*, *Bon Appétit*, Food Network, and the *Washington Post*. Erin led the local marketing for Good Eggs, a farm-to-fridge delivery service, in New Orleans when she first met Jeanette. Erin has helped Jeanette with her goals of fund-raising and bringing fresh food to her community, and the two formed a bond through their work together in the garden.

How did you first meet?

ERIN: I met Jeanette in 2015, when I moved down to New Orleans from Brooklyn. Jeanette would drop off her beautiful bouquets and fresh herb bundles at Good Eggs, where I was working at the time. She'd stroll in wearing a fabulous hat, and she always made everyone smile. I was immediately charmed by her spirit. I remember thinking, Wow, I hope I have half as much energy and gumption as this woman when I'm her age. I really wanted to be her friend.

So I called her up and said, "Hey, I know nothing about gardening, but I want to help you. And something I can help you with is getting the word out and organizing workshops for the local community to learn how to grow things." I could just sense that she had so much to give and so much to teach people, and I knew that one thing I could bring to the table was finding ways to connect her with more people. She's such a treasure, and I wanted to share her with more people. We've been friends ever since.

Can you describe a moment when you realized that your friendship was going to be a significant one?

JEANETTE: Erin organized a workshop, and we were at the garden in the Lower Ninth. She showed up with some home-baked goodies for us to snack on. I thought, Now, *this* is the kind of person I really need to be working with, because if somebody takes the time to make something at home and bring it, you know that person is invested in what you're doing.
E: There was a moment where Jeanette gave me a key to her garden, a literal key to her garden, and I knew that meant we were entering a new level of our friendship. So, I would say that was very special, and I still have it on my key chain.

What is your favorite thing to do together?

J: We've had some really good times that you wouldn't normally have with a person if you didn't have a good relationship with them.
E: Like when the Ace Hotel opened in New Orleans, they were looking for a local florist to provide big bunches of magnolias for their entryway. Jeanette has a beautiful magnolia tree outside her house, so we were out there scrubbing those leaves because they wanted them shiny and perfect looking. We brought them to the hotel and they were like, "Oh, we wanted *Japanese* magnolias, not Southern magnolias."

We were like, "Um, excuse me?" But I think we were both exhausted from this day of being out in the heat and scrubbing them and also just couldn't help but laugh it off together. Yeah, I'll never forget scrubbing the magnolia leaves with you, Jeanette.

I also love spending time in the car with Jeanette. We used to just ride around the neighborhood. Once, we drove by a garden lot and a woman was gardening, and we pulled over and started chatting with her and talking to her about what she was growing and her family connections to growing food. Just being able to spontaneously have these engaging conversations with people in the community is one of Jeanette's superpowers. And being a part of that, and being open to whatever might happen when you're driving around with Jeanette, is one of my favorite ways to spend time with her. We have a good time together.

What are some of the most meaningful lessons you've learned from each other?

E: I think her resilience is so inspiring. She'll be out gardening late at night and back up and at 'em the next morning. I get so energized seeing her in action and knowing that she makes aging look beautiful. The way she is still out and about, turning these overgrown abandoned lots into beautiful gardens and teaching people and inspiring them to do the same and try growing something for the first time. She makes me excited to get older and to be able to share wisdom with people of all ages in the community. Knowing that she still has that energy and spark in her after all she's been through in her life—that resilience is really incredible to watch.
J: One of the things I have learned from Erin is how to connect with younger people. I've learned from how she just walks up and starts talking. These are young people I probably wouldn't approach because I would expect them to not be receptive. But Erin doesn't see it that way; she just moves forward. That's the thing I find so amazing about her, that she just moves forward. She has changed the way I approach young people about gardening.

What do you each hope your friendship brings or gives to the other person?

J: I'm hoping that Erin will look at what I've done and say, "Jeanette did that as a senior. I've got my youth, and I've got knowledge, and I've got techniques to bring people together. I can contribute." And I think she already knows she has the ability to contribute because of her work with Garden on Mars. So, at some point I expect her to take the initiative to start something, some project, that involves younger people, people her own age. Because this is where we are headed right now—toward having more young people be involved in food access.

E: I hope our friendship reminds her of all these gifts she has and is able to give. I want to show Jeanette what a rock star she is. I hope that having me and my peers looking up to her and looking to her with admiration . . . I hope she knows that we all want to be learning from her.

Do you feel like gardening keeps you young?

J: It prevents me from feeling like, There is a good reason you can't do this. There's no good reason I can't do this. If I want to do this, and I have the energy, I actually believe that oxygen is sweeter in a garden than it is in an office. I know that gardening keeps me healthy. And that's one of the things I want so much to pass on to young gardeners: You can be healthier if you will take gardening seriously.

Why is it so important to pass down gardening knowledge to the next generation?

J: I believe that climate change is going to change all our lives and we need to get to the point that we are not expecting other countries to feed the world. So, in order for the next generation to make the changes that are necessary, they need to know more about the actual growing process. And you can't do that in a classroom. You can talk about it in a classroom, but that's why I want a university out in the gardens teaching. Because once those students have an opportunity to work in the garden and accidentally taste a string bean and realize that that string bean has a really different taste—that's when they really start to learn and understand. And *that's* what we need this next generation to do.

How has spending time in the garden changed you?

J: Spending time in the garden has not changed me. What it has done is kept me from being changed by the pressures of being a person of color in this society. It has prevented me from being hardened by the challenges that I cannot overcome because I can't change the color of my skin. But I can still be positive and pick myself up when I get knocked down. Those are the kinds of fortifications that you need in this society, that a person of color needs in this society.

What impact do you hope your life and your work will have on those around you?

J: I have the benefit of knowing the impact my gardens have on the people around me. For seventeen years, I've had people coming by, stopping and talking to me, telling me how great it is to have this blighted lot turned into a garden. Neighbors tell me how wonderful it is to have beautiful roses blooming twelve months of the year. I have tour buses stop and people on the tour bus wave at me and tell me how great the garden looks. So I recognize what a benefit these gardens are to the people who live around them right now.

Michele Saunders

CATSKILL, NY

Michele Saunders, 78, has always followed where music has led her. Growing up in France, she listened to jazz and rock 'n' roll, but it wasn't until she moved to New York City in her twenties that she found her place in the worlds of art and style, where she was one of the undeniable queens of NYC nightlife in the 1970s, '80s, and '90s. Having worked as an agent, a stylist, and now a location scout, Michele is beloved for her great eye and inimitable style. She sat down with writer Miss Rosen to talk about her life and work so far.

Where did you grow up, and where do you live now?

I was born in Paris after the Second World War. My parents had a country house in Normandy, where my father was from, so I was a city girl and a country girl. These are my roots.

Now I live in upstate New York. Michael de Benedictus was the reason I came to Catskill. My son Zach's father was adopted by Michael and his partner and grew up here. After Zach was born, I used to come up here to ski at Hunter and visit in Catskill, which was nearby. Michael was producer and keyboard player for Larry Levan, the DJ at Paradise Garage, which was my "church." I was fascinated by Michael's music, especially his song "Make It Last Forever," one of the last songs he and Larry wrote together.

Being upstate reminds me of how I lived as a little girl in Normandy. New York City is nearby, and I'm in the countryside—so it feels like nothing really has changed in about seventy-five years.

What did you want to be when you were younger, and what do you do now?

Music has always been the common denominator in my life. When I was 3 years old, my father used to play jazz records, and I would dance to them. When I was a child, I wanted to be a ballerina and a ski champion. I followed my dreams and became a ski instructor, and I danced every week at the Garage.

I went to a strict Catholic boarding school, where I had to be very well behaved, but at the time I was fascinated by rock 'n' roll music, and no one else in my school was interested in that. I knew I would never be free to express myself in Paris at that time. I had to come to America.

I wanted to be a journalist, studied political science, and received a Fulbright scholarship to attend Mount Holyoke College in Massachusetts. Every Wednesday, I took a five-hour bus trip to see Amateur Night at the Apollo in Harlem in the 1960s. No one at school could understand this. I never became a journalist, but I later worked as a photographer's agent and house music manager. Now I do real estate upstate, so I'm a very well-behaved person [*laughs*].

What does your current age feel like for you?

In my late thirties, I lied about my age because I didn't like it. By my early forties, I had given up the lies, and I decided to get into really good shape, which is the best way for me to fight age. Then I had my son at 45. Things became different. Age didn't even matter. My mother used to say, "Stand up straight and walk young." I'm like my mother. I have her genes. I'm lucky, but not everybody is.

What misconceptions about aging would you like to dispel?

I've recently modeled for Birkenstock and Brooklyn Industries. In the same week, I did stories for *AARP The Magazine* and *The FADER*. Hello! You have to be totally comfortable with yourself to do this.

What are you most proud of about yourself?

I have a few things I am proud of right now. The most recent thing was performing *UnderScored* with Ephrat Asherie Dance at Works & Process at the Guggenheim and the Lincoln Center Out of Doors

I FOLLOW THE MUSIC TO WHERE IT TAKES ME.

festival, and a residency at Kaatsbaan Cultural Park. It was beautiful and emotional—a new family for me. We also called ourselves a family at the Garage. The soul is similar. It is a little thread that goes back to my childhood: I follow the music to where it takes me.

I'm proud to be a dot-connector with real estate these days. I have helped build a community in Catskill over the years. In the '80s, I was one of the few people in South Beach trying to bring it to life with my friend Patricia Field, when nobody thought of going there. I'm proud to have been upstate before the crowds came. I'm proud to have represented artists such as Art Kane and Steve Hiett. I'm proud of being independent, never being bored, being happy alone, and being current, and that young people like me. I'm proud of my roots and the continuity in my life, of different chapters with similar ingredients.

How has your sense of self-confidence or self-acceptance evolved over time?

Today, I am more confident than I ever was, but that doesn't mean I don't doubt myself. Performing *UnderScored* at the Guggenheim in January 2020, I had an amazing moment. After the opening act, it was my turn to speak. The music stopped, and there was a roar of applause. I thought the place was on fire. It was an incredible feeling.

What role do you feel your ancestors, or the women in your family who came before you, play in your life?

My mother is present with me all the time. What I regret the most is not talking to her enough. You forget how precious time can be. My mother was a character. She taught me to never be bored, to be fine by myself, to respect my health but not be obsessed with age. She was five foot one, and she walked tall. She was funny, too. She used to say, "A lunch without wine is a breakfast."

When do you feel your most powerful?

I am an epicurean, and I love to indulge my senses—but in a simple way. Whether that means cooking, dancing, dressing, decorating, skiing, or being in nature, it's a high that I've been looking for all my life. I feel powerful when I am working with young people and telling stories from the past but bringing them to the present. I'm excited about the future.

Can you describe a turning point in your life, and how it changed things for you?

It was when I had a child. I was 45, and I thought I was not interested, but my gynecologist said, "You know what? It's the last call." They told me everything was okay and he was a healthy boy, so I said, "Let's do this!"

Having my son taught me how to be a much better person—more giving, more caring, more everything. Parenthood, motherhood, is the biggest adventure. I'm glad I did it.

How has raising a child affected your life?

This is one of the reasons I'm staying current. My son's life with his friends is very similar to my life with my friends. As a matter of fact, some of his friends are my friends. I met them because I am in various worlds of fashion, music, and art. I feel related to him on that level as well. The fact that I'm in the world of young people is a continuation of my relationship with my son.

What would you like to learn or experience at this stage in your life?

I want to finish projects I've started. I have an incredible archive of photographs made throughout my life: me and James Baldwin hanging out in the South of France, Diana Ross and me working on her Central Park concert, my dance group at the Garage, and more. I have a lot of material here.

Calypso Rose

QUEENS, NY

Calypso Rose, or Linda McCartha Monica Sandy-Lewis, is the mother of calypso music. She started writing her own songs as a teenager and, despite protests that women did not belong in calypso, was able to rise to the top of the calypso charts. She has composed more than a thousand songs and recorded more than twenty albums. In 1978, she was the first woman to win the Calypso King competition, a win that inspired the competition to change its name to Calypso Monarch. At 81 years old, Rose is still working as hard as ever. She came out as a member of the LGBTQIA+ community in 2012 and has never been afraid to tell people exactly what is on her mind.

Where did you grow up, and where do you live now?

I grew up in Trinidad. I was born in Tobago, but I was adopted by my uncle's good friend in Trinidad. I used to travel a lot for work, and that took me to Puerto Rico and then the Virgin Islands, and then I moved to Jamaica, Queens, where I live now.

Do you remember the first time you sang? How did it make you feel?

I was 13, and it made me feel great. I started composing at that age, too.

How does it feel to be such a pioneer in what you do?

It makes me feel great to know that I could do something for other people, especially women, because somebody has to stand up for them.

PUT YOUR POWER
IN YOUR MIND
AND GO FORWARD.
JUST SAY,
"I WILL. I WILL.
I MUST. I MUST."

You've always addressed political and social justice issues in your music, and that takes a lot of bravery. Why is that important to you?

It's very important for me to do, to be a woman and to stand up, because male calypsonians used to say, "Why are you singing calypso? Calypso belongs to a man. It's a man's world." I'd say, "No. The good Lord has given me the inspiration to create, and I have to put my music out there to the world for them to know."

What does your current age feel like for you?

I am 81 and feeling great. I know I'm going to live until I'm 100. I know this because the Lord creates us, and he brought us to earth to do things. And when you do these things you're supposed to do, he compensates you. And as long as you take care of yourself, you will go until you're 100.

Do you have a message for younger women reading your story here?

They must trust in themselves. Anything you want to go for—go for it. Put your power in your mind and go forward. Just say, "I will. I will. I must. I must." And that will take you through. Trust in yourself.

What role do you feel your ancestors, or the women in your family who came before you, play in your life?

My great-grandmother was from Guinea; she was enslaved. She used to take care of me when I was very small. I remember it well. She used to put me on her lap while she smoked a jackal pipe. One day, she shook her head as she watched the sea. She said, "No man knows their burial ground." And I never knew what she meant until I grew older. What she meant was that no one knows where they will be when they die. She never went back to Guinea, so I always remember that and try to be grateful for where I am.

On my father's side, my great-great-grandfather was from Liberia. He was bought and sold and ended up in South Africa and then in Scotland. From Scotland, he ended up in Tobago. There is a building in Tobago called Sandy Hall in commemoration of my great-great-grandfather, my ancestor. He burned down the governor general's house to free the slaves.

So do you see where I came from? We are great fighters. I fight very hard for what I want.

How have your ideas of success and happiness changed over time?

When I'm onstage and I see old people jumping and laughing and dancing and stretching their hands out to me, oh my God, it makes me feel great and happy. I bring joy and love to the people all over the world. That is happiness and success to me.

What impact do you hope your life and your music will have on those around you?

By the age of 18, I knew I could get on a stage and bring joy, peace, love, and happiness to the world. That's the impact I hope to have. I have to have a knee replacement this year, and I know as soon as it's finished, I am going back out there to complete my job—to make people laugh. To bring joy, love, happiness, and peace as long as I am alive.

What brings you joy?

When I see the little ones running behind me calling my name: "Mama! Mama Rose! Mama Rose!" It makes me so happy. I never had any kids of my own. But now I have children all over the world. To see them with their hands stretched out calling out to me—that brings me joy and happiness.

Is there anything that used to be difficult for you that you've now made peace with?

No, because I made up my mind a long time ago that what I want to be will be. I want to be like a tree. When you plant a tree, you give the tree water and the tree grows and flowers and bears fruits, and then you can give, give, give away to the world.

What are you most looking forward to?

I am most excited to be back on the stage. And I know I will be on the stage until the Lord says it's time to come home.

The Resistance Revival Chorus

NEW YORK

The Resistance Revival Chorus is a collective of over sixty women and nonbinary singers whose shared goal is to uplift women's voices and raise them to sing both joy and awareness into resistance and protest. Founded in 2017, the collective has connected women of all ages and created meaningful bonds throughout the chorus. Four of those friends, Zakiyah Ansari, Nara Garber, Paula Henderson, and Brooke Williams, sat down to talk about what their friendships have meant to one another and brought to their lives. Zakiyah, 54, is the advocacy director of the New York State Alliance for Quality Education. She's the mother of eight children and a 2020 Atlantic Fellow. Nara, 51, is a documentary director and cinematographer who specializes in observational social impact films. Paula, 58, is a New York City–based saxophonist, DJ, and astrologer. Known as "Moist Paula" for her rock band, Moisturizer, she has toured internationally and is now the DJ at Hotel Delmano in Williamsburg, Brooklyn. Brooke, 55, is a mother, activist, musician, and blogger living and working in Brooklyn, New York. She helps run the Demo Crew, a group that reaches out to voters to give them the information they need to ensure that their voices are heard.

How did you all meet and get started with the Resistance Revival Chorus?

BROOKE: I met everybody through the chorus. And I started in the chorus at the very beginning. I was there at the first meeting. It was formed by a number of women who were organizers in the Women's March. The national Women's March, the first big one. I was one of those organizers. We got a bunch of people together who were either musicians exploring activism or activists exploring musicianship, and the goal was to focus on how we keep having the strength and energy to keep fighting. The idea was to bring that sense of joy to the movement, because joy is really what gives you power. Joy is a really powerful thing. Each iteration of the chorus has just been more full of amazing and incredible—and inspirational—women. There are a million leaders in this chorus. And yet, somehow, everyone is really generous. Everyone leads with love.

NARA: I had seen Paula before, but everyone else I met through the chorus. I just couldn't get over how many amazing, interesting, beautiful people were in the chorus. I had wanted to join for so long, but I was nervous and couldn't figure out how to go about doing that. But there was this palpable empathy among the members, and it made me feel so welcome. There is a sense of shared values, even if we represent a wide spectrum of political beliefs.

ZAKIYAH: I've been with the chorus since the beginning. A Muslim woman I worked with told me about the chorus, but I missed the first rehearsal and assumed I couldn't participate. But they said I could still come, and when I got there, I just faked it until I made it. I thought I would be in the back of the group, but I was right up in front in the middle of Times Square. This was before the official launch, and there were fifty of us dressed in white. The chorus organizers told us to tell anyone who asked that we were working on a commercial and selling mayonnaise. We all laughed, but sure enough, as we were lining up to perform, someone asked us what we were doing, and I told them we were shooting a mayonnaise commercial.

As much as I'm an introvert, I'm very much a people person. And I like connecting with folks. To be in a space with so many women was really

COLLECT THE WISDOM OF YOUR ELDERS WHILE THEY'RE STILL AROUND.

refreshing. It was an amazing combination of all of those beautiful, diverse things: experiences, class, religion, bodies, worldviews. We have a single chain that we use for everything, from families that need our support to mutual aid that lets us connect with the whole city. It really is a loving space.

PAULA: The four of us are part of a small group of singers over 50. I think I'm the oldest, unless someone's not fessing up. But our group includes people as young as 18. And to connect with someone that young through singing was new to me. It's an amazing mix of women of all different ages. But I don't really care how old or young people are. It's more about who you end up sitting next to. Nara, Brooke, and I sing tenor. So we're always standing together.

What do your current ages feel like for you?

N: I turned 50 last year. My father died in 2017, and my mom died about nineteen years ago. Losing both parents made a much bigger difference to me than turning 50 did. It's just a very unique place in life where you realize that all of your elders are gone. Life feels really midway to me. My family doesn't have a great track record for longevity, so I don't think I'll live to be 100, but it feels very in the middle.

I've been spending a lot of time, recently, with significantly older friends, a generation older. Some are friends of my parents, whom I reconnected with after my parents died. I met this wonderful 88-year-old woman. She told me that, for her, 50 to 65 was her golden period. She was incredibly productive and at the height of her power at that point in time. And I have actually looked forward to this period in life since I was in my thirties and felt my friends were wrapped up with a lot of concerns that didn't seem relevant to me.

But I would do work, particularly, in Alaska with this group of women who were in their fifties, and I thought, I don't know if it's Alaska or if it's women in their fifties, but if I can have friendships like that when I'm in my fifties, where the little stuff can sort of be shoved to the side and you just focus on the things that are more important, then I'm fine with aging. I'm pretty happy to be where I am. Do I wish there were more time? Yes, of course. But yeah, I'm content being in between.

B: I just turned 55. I feel very much like it's a transition moment in my life. Similarly to the way I felt when I was 30, I feel I'm entering a new phase. And so I'm feeling partly really excited and partly kind of nervous. For the first time in my life, I've had to pay a lot more attention to my physical self. I have MS, so I've had to pay a certain amount of attention to that all along, but all of a sudden now, my energy matters. It's this combination of some changes feeling like a bummer and some feeling totally fine. And that reflects what life is in general. I think it feels more relaxing, actually, to be 55 years old. I feel like there's a lot of stuff I just don't care about anymore. I still love clothes and love getting dressed up, but it doesn't have the same outsize importance that it did when I was in my twenties and even in my thirties. So I feel like it's more fun and self-expression as opposed to trying to figure out what type of person I am.

Z: I just turned 54, and I've just started to embrace my ability to connect with folks and to sit in my experience and share that in a comfortable way. I'm not trying to share from a place of "I know it all" or "I've got the answer," but just sharing what's worked for me or my relationships. I think I'm just now at this age starting to sit in the understanding that to be able to do that, and share that way, is a gift. Just to be able to be there, to hear and listen to folks, and to ask if I can offer something to the conversation is amazing. Also, the reality is that many times it *is* helpful, and that's something else that I'm realizing I like to do: help people.

I'm a mom to eight kids, and I have four grandchildren. Everybody here knows that that's my joyous place. I've embraced that. But I used to be embarrassed to share how many children I had or that I don't have a college degree. Part of this age is really coming into myself and owning that my experience is my experience. No one can take it away from me. It matters. I have a lot to offer. I'm going to do that and excel. And understand that that makes me an expert in me. And so, that's enough. That's enough.

P: Unlike Zakiyah, Nara, and Brooke, I'm single. So, I think that's a different part of the experience of aging as well. I started feeling stressed about getting older when I got to about 46. And then lo and behold, I became involved with someone who was thirty years older than me and suddenly I was like, Oh, I'm so young and cute. It was an immediate fix for that.

That gave me a lot of confidence in those really difficult perimenopausal years, which can affect women adversely when we start acknowledging that our bodies are changing and that depending on our role in society, that that could be construed as a loss or a setback.

I was single, and I was playing in rock bands. Most people in the bands I play in are younger. So I feel like I lucked out in averting that crisis earlier on. Then menopause came. And when I first thought I was entering menopause, I told these older women I know, "I think I'm going into menopause." And they both cackled and said, "Men are on pause." They just threw back their heads with laughter.

But I was like, "I don't want men on pause." But once I got used to it all, I realized that menopause was the greatest tool. Why does anyone ever suggest that it's anything other than a reward? For me, it was so good, and has been ever since.

I *love* growing older. There are so many rewards and so many things that I thought I wouldn't like about it that I actually love. It's banal, but I love staying home and going to bed early. My idea of what's exciting on a Friday night has really changed, and it's no great loss.

What misconceptions about aging would you like to dispel?

P: Yeah, that at some point I would be too old to keep playing in rock bands or go on tour. But I cannot wait to get back on the road. To me, *not* being on the road is much more difficult. I worked with an author who was writing a biography of this woman who had been married to Merle Haggard and was his backup singer. She was still on the tour bus in her eighties. This was like twenty years ago. I was like, "She's still on the bus, and she's in her eighties. So I can still do it." I can imagine that some bands might have a reservation about bringing me on tour because I'm an older lady. But the people who take me know that if they want to go out to a club after a gig, I'll just go sleep in the van until they're done.

I'm like, "Knock yourselves out." I make myself a cup of tea and kick back, have the van to myself, and it's just fine.

N: I've been fortunate not to grow up with many misconceptions because both of my parents modeled intergenerational relationships for me. And I've done a lot of filming in Indigenous cultures where elders are so respected and so revered that I've sometimes questioned why Western culture in general tends to be so afraid of aging.

But the second you put it in a *professional* context, I get it. I love directing. I make most of my income from shooting and editing, and shooting is just hauling really heavy crap from point A to point B much of the time. The shooting itself is exciting, but you expend so much energy just carrying things. I used to be interviewed for projects, and interviewers would say, "Do you think you can hold the camera that long?" And I'd think, I just biked fifteen miles to this interview, and it's 90 degrees outside. Yes, I think I can hold the camera. We'd be carrying heavy gear around and someone would say, "Oh my God, I can't carry this upstairs. I'm 37! I can't do this anymore." And I'd be thinking, We can either talk about this all the time or we can just carry it upstairs. So, I ended up hauling all the stuff up, which embarrassed the rest of the crew because they were all guys. But I carried the stuff. Once I got it all up, I said, "And by the way, I'm 50." There was this collective "*No.*" It's fun to be able to drop your age, because that in and of itself dispels the myth.

How has your sense of self-confidence or self-acceptance evolved over time?

Z: I struggled for a long time with self-confidence. I grew up in an abusive home, where my father beat my mom. And I didn't realize until I was an adult that that's where my lack of self-confidence stemmed from. Having eight kids while having low self-esteem, you can get lost in your children. But I didn't want to be that parent that was like, "You can't leave and go away to school. All that I've done for you and you're leaving me?" So I got involved in education advocacy. Fast-forward to now, and I still struggle with self-confidence, but I am definitely more confident than I was before. I have found my voice in advocacy. I put myself in situations that challenge me, like speaking to a mayor or speaking to a secretary of education or speaking to someone in power, generally a white man, not knowing what his preconceived notions and stereotypes of a Black Muslim woman might be. That can be tough if you experience low self-esteem. But I was fortunate enough in 2016 to participate in training that really helped me center myself. Now I don't ever walk in feeling like I am not worthy to be in a space. I think a combination of my training, age, and being able to see all the ways I've made a difference has led to me being more confident.

B: I would say I went from low self-confidence to *less* low. I went from being paralyzed by these internal voices that told me to be quiet to just deciding that I was not giving those voices any kind of power anymore. I don't know if that is self-confidence or if it's just not caring as much anymore. Or just deciding that I don't have enough time to worry about it like I used to. But the more you open up and expose your vulnerability and realize that that is actually a source of power, the more you realize that, wait, this is actually the way to go, that being more vulnerable and leading from a place of love rather than being afraid is actually powerful and, as far as I'm concerned, the best way to go through life.

N: I'll say that those voices can still be deafening for me. I don't think that's changed at all with age. Recently, I participated in a panel on arts and activism moderated by sixth graders at my old school. I saw former teachers of mine logging on. After the panel was over, a group of us stayed online to chat and everyone said to me, "You never used to talk!" So while I can still struggle to speak up, that event was a reminder that I used to never speak, and I've found more confidence.

P: I have those voices, but I don't think the voices are age-related. And even though I'm extroverted and appear confident in a group setting or a performative setting, I don't speak up, really. I don't have a tertiary education. I just finished high school. That's it. That's something that, particularly since moving to this country from Australia, I'm aware is a *thing*. I usually don't tell people because there's this assumption that everybody has a

formal education, but I didn't. And as a musician, I'm self-taught, and I have amazing insecurity about it. But the age thing comes into it in a way that's helpful for me. Because there are all these younger musicians in their twenties and thirties who think I'm not doing something right because of the way they learned something in school. But in my head, I'm like, I've been doing this since before you were born. It's a feeling of indignation, and their voices sometimes still win out, but I know that I don't want to bring any of that doubt into the next chapter of my life. I will not bring that shit into whatever's next for me.

When do you feel your most powerful?

B: Onstage. I wouldn't have necessarily thought that would be what I would say, but there's something about being in a situation with the chorus that makes me feel safe. You have people's attention, and you really do have this opportunity to influence people in whatever way it is that you want to, whether it's sharing your music or delivering a message.

In the late 1990s, I sang onstage with the Beastie Boys. I wrote a song with them, and they called me to see if I wanted to come sing with them. I was the only person onstage who didn't have an instrument. I thought, All right, I'm onstage at Madison Square Garden, and I'm the only one who can run around! So I put my hands up, and everybody in the audience put their hands up, and I thought, Oh, my God. I just made 18,000 people put their hands up! And actually, it worried me about rock stars and how much power they have and their egos and then all of a sudden, it was this whole moment. But the thing I took from that was that you really do have both this power and this responsibility.

Z: My answer is the same: onstage. But not performing so much as speaking at a rally and talking about things we're demanding. To be able to hold attention while also having people actually hear and understand what you're saying—and motivating them to action—is really when I feel most empowered.

N: I had two immediate reactions that were not antithetical, but very different. On a powerful level, my immediate response was about physicality. My work when I'm filming is actually very physical. I work mostly in observational documentaries, and they're very personal, and they're very intimate. I almost never have a crew bigger than three people, and I like to film for myself on my projects when possible. And so there's the need to maintain an intimate relationship with your subject and let them know that they're being seen and heard. And then there's the whole technical apparatus of making sure that everything is correct in an uncontrolled situation. And there are days when you just *know* you're at the top of your game. When you're relating to people correctly, everybody feels comfortable, and somehow, you're also nailing things technically. Those moments are magical, and they carry me through the days when nothing goes right.

P: I feel most powerful onstage, and I feel super-duper powerful when I have my saxophone. It's really big. It's like a chalice. I learned really early when I played that instrument that it gave me this magic feeling. But I also feel powerful as part of a group. When I'm with a band or when I'm with the chorus and we're united in this thing, I think that's when I feel most powerful.

What are some of the most meaningful things you've learned from one another?

P: I find Zakiyah very motivating in a march. Marching, chanting—those things are new to me, and I would say those are the times where I feel shy. I wouldn't initiate that. But when Zakiyah is there, I feel really motivated and I can get behind it and be lifted up by her power in that situation. Nara and Brooke have taught me how to be nice and interesting and just awesome.

B: I've learned a lot about astrology from Paula, and through that, I've learned a lot about myself. Her sense of adventure, and that *life* is an adventure, is really inspiring. Nara is so considerate and kind and sweet and never forgets a detail. She

examines everything and has really taught me to pay attention to what I communicate in the world. Zakiyah has shown us how to be a leader (and how to apply lipstick) and inspires us with her seemingly endless supply of energy.

Z: Age has allowed me to receive kind words like these much differently than I would have a few years ago. So I'm receiving all of this with deep appreciation. This group has helped me better understand how important it is to be vulnerable and open. I've been dealing with depression over the past few months, and to feel the arms of these women around me while I'm going through this difficult time has been so powerful. Feeling them love on you so deeply—and at the same time to be able to laugh with them. It's just really beautiful.

Do you have any advice for people who would like to join a group but might be a little hesitant to do so?

Z: Regardless of whether it's a singing group, don't compromise, and don't get discouraged. If it doesn't work out the first time, keep trying. Sometimes when people have bad experiences, it's like, "I am not going to try this again." Trust me, you will find that group, but don't compromise what makes you comfortable. Trust your gut. Trust your instincts.

Knowing what you know now, is there anything you would go back and tell your younger self?

N: My advice to my younger self would be ask questions of your elders before they die. I live in the world of stories. I love personal stories and personal histories, and I failed to do that myself. And as a documentary filmmaker, I tell people all the time. If somebody says, "Oh, I love my grandmother," I say, "Ask her to tell you her stories now." I was actually about to make a film about my father, but he died about a month before we were to start filming. Collect the wisdom of your elders while they're still around.

I *LOVE* GROWING OLDER. THERE ARE SO MANY REWARDS AND SO MANY THINGS THAT I THOUGHT I WOULDN'T LIKE ABOUT IT THAT I ACTUALLY LOVE.

Lujira Cooper

NEW YORK, NY

Brooklyn-born activist and author Lujira Cooper, 74, has lived as an openly gay woman since the Stonewall uprising in New York City in 1969 and has been fighting for LGBTQIA+ rights ever since. Lujira's work in supporting the rights of LGBTQIA+ people has focused on the intersection of sexuality and race, highlighting the increased discrimination LGBTQIA+ people of color experience every day. Lujira has dedicated her life and time to activism, volunteering with SAGE (a group focused on supporting LGBTQIA+ elders and connecting them with younger LGBTQIA+ people). She is also an author, focusing on Afrofuturist work.

Where did you grow up, and where do you live now?

I grew up in Rockaway, Brooklyn, and then moved to Jamaica, Queens. Now I live on the Upper West Side of Manhattan.

What did you want to be when you were younger?

I wanted to be a teacher. I loved all my teachers. Well, most of them. And now, since I run a writing group, I guess I am a teacher.

What does your current age feel like for you?

Sometimes I feel like I'm 12 going on 2. And other times I feel like I'm 74 going on 174. It depends upon the day. It depends upon how my body decides it wants to react. But mentally, most of the time I feel like I'm about 12, because I feel like I'm exploring stuff. The one thing I believe in very strongly is to keep learning.

How has your sense of self-confidence or self-acceptance evolved over time?

Let me give you something I heard. When Oprah Winfrey turned 50, Maya Angelou was on her show. Maya Angelou said that when you turn 50, you don't give a damn. When you turn 70, you definitely don't give a damn. I said, "No, Maya, you got that wrong. I *never* gave a damn." I have been a rebel with or without a cause all my life. I was raised to be a very independent child, independent and also accountable.

What are you most proud of in your life so far?

Going back to school in 2016 and getting a BA and an MA in English and creative writing. I got a Bachelor of Science degree in criminal justice in four years. I'm proud that I was part of "50 Years of Pride" and of speaking at the opening ceremony of Pride in 2019. Of course, I'm proud of being a part of *Not Another Second*, a documentary project that tells the untold stories of twelve LGBTQIA+ seniors.

What role do you feel your ancestors, or the women in your family who came before you, play in your life?

I remember my aunt who went back to school at 69. It's funny, because when I went back to school, I was about the same age. We even had the same birthdate. She was just forty-four years older than I am. That was the kind of thing that I learned at an early age: to watch people and listen to people. I trusted the ancestors.

I'm working on a futuristic book right now, and there are a lot of ancestor stories in it. The main character is always talking about her ancestors. So I think I stand on the shoulders of the people who've come before me and who have made life possible for me at this time.

When do you feel your most powerful?

When I'm writing. Because I can just get out of myself and just *be*.

Who or what has influenced your life the most?

My aunt Kelsey and my mother, who taught me when I was 9 years old that you're accountable for your actions. Also women like Shirley Chisholm,

I HAVE BEEN A REBEL WITH OR WITHOUT A CAUSE ALL MY LIFE.

Barbara Jordan, and Maya Angelou. Those are the people that I've tried to be like.

How have your ideas of success and happiness changed over time?

I don't think I *had* any ideas of what success was. Happiness may be finding the right person, being with them. But success in and of itself? No. I think for me, now, success is the completion of projects. It's not so much about getting a book *published* (although I do wish to do that), but completing the damn thing so that I can get on to book three. I also think of success as really being able to help other people.

If you could go back in your life, what would you like to do over—and what would you never do again?

I don't think I'd change anything in my life. I think I am the person I am because of the experiences I've had. I think it all finds a way into my writing. Everything's research.

At this point in your life, what have you made peace with that used to be a struggle for you?

The one challenge I still have is my intolerance for stupidity. Sorry. I'm very honest about that. People who act stupidly get on my last nerve. That has not changed. I sometimes wish I could be more compassionate, more understanding, but I usually just have to take a deep breath.

What is a lesson you're still learning or need to learn?

I'm sure there are a few. One of them is to be a little more patient. I think also just to relax more.

Knowing what you know now—and you know a lot—what would you go back and tell your younger self?

Be brave. Study your history, because things have a way of repeating.

What are your hopes for the future of the LGBTQIA+ community?

My hopes for the future of the LGBTQIA+ are the same hopes I have for people of color: that those issues will no longer be issues. I would love to see us get to a place where the color of your skin and whom you sleep with and all that sort of stuff really does not matter. I don't see it, which is why I say we've got to continue fighting. One of the things I really would like to see is more laws passed—not acts, because the acts always have to be renewed. Executive orders are wonderful, but they can always be overturned. So I'm very much into having the laws on the books; then you have something to fight with.

What misconceptions about aging would you like to dispel?

The misconception that older people know everything. Each group of people has something to give, and just because a person's older does not necessarily make them wiser. And just because a person's younger does not make them less wise. But I try to be a wise person, at least once a week.

Sonoko Sakai

LOS ANGELES, CA

Sonoko Sakai, 66, is a Los Angeles–based writer, teacher, and cook whose cookbook *Japanese Home Cooking: Simple Meals, Authentic Flavors* has brought the joy of Japanese food and traditional cooking to countless homes around the world. Sonoko grew up in various cities around the world. Her love of storytelling has taken her from an early career in film to a life now filled with students to whom she imparts her core beliefs: freshness, seasonality, simplicity, beauty, and economy. Her love of nature has inspired her to slow down and take a closer look at the world around her. From what she grows in her backyard garden to what she teaches her cooking students, Sonoko is able to find beauty in small things everywhere.

Where did you grow up, and where do you live now?

I grew up in many places. I was born in New York and raised in Tokyo, San Francisco, Los Angeles, Kamakura, and Mexico City. My father worked for Japan Airlines. He was the first generation of employees to be transferred overseas, to open offices after the war. My father was also a soldier, so for him to be able to come to the United States and then raise a family was really something. I was the first American-born child of four siblings. But we moved back and forth every time my father got an assignment.

My father's last assignment was in Los Angeles. And I was at the age where I was getting ready for college, but I wasn't ready to go back to Japan. Boys at the time were raised to be leaders of the future, but girls were not. We were called "boxed girls." Daughters were put, figuratively, into a box and raised to become good housewives. But I didn't want that, so I rebelled and stayed in LA and finished college. I decided I would make LA my home, and I have been here ever since.

What did you want to be when you were younger?

I wanted to be a shop owner. There were these beautiful family-owned artisanal shops in my neighborhood in Kamakura during the sixties, and I loved every single one. I walked by them on my way to school every day and would imagine being in their shoes. So one day, I would imagine I was the fishmonger who sold the fresh seafood brought in from the local fishermen, or that I was the lantern shop owner. He would wash his dentures in a fountain by the bus stop, then go inside, sit on his tatami mat, and draw these beautiful landscapes on the paper lanterns. Then he'd hang them up to dry, and I was just mesmerized by that.

There was one general store that attracted all the children in the neighborhood. It sold origami and colorful strings and paper bags and erasers and firecrackers. All the items were placed at a height so that children could reach for them. The shop owner made us feel important. There were so many amazing shops. There was even a rice miller, who milled rice fresh. And every time he milled the grains, you could smell the bran. It was like fresh toast. He had this ritual of writing haiku, too. So every time I passed by him, I would see the haiku of the day and recite it to myself.

These are the people who inspired me every day. So I wanted to be one of those shop owners. They provided us with culture, a sense of community, and artisanship. So when I talk about artisanship today, and why it's so important in cooking, that's where it comes from.

What does your current age feel like for you?

Sixty-six going on 40. I think I'm starting to dress a little younger, too. My students are all millennials. They're fun and funky; they have tattoos, or they bleach their hair and dye it purple. They make scarves for me. I feel a bit ageless, but I also don't want to look like mutton dressed as lamb. But I feel pretty young. And I usually have more energy than

I'M HAPPIEST WHEN I'M SHARING SOMETHING WITH PEOPLE, WHEN IT'S NOT JUST FOR MYSELF.

most of my assistants. I don't know why, but if I get enough rest, I recover pretty well and I work hard.

What misconceptions about aging would you like to dispel?

I'm the Medicare age, and these institutions put you in that category of old people and then assume that you're going to experience all these symptoms of old age. When I was in my thirties, nobody ever asked me these types of questions. You know, "Are you going to the bathroom a lot? Are you having back issues?" It's all these horrifying questions. And I was always in denial. I didn't even like people at the supermarket when they said, "I think you're qualified for Senior Citizens Day."

I guess it's that people seem to think that when you get older, you deteriorate and you lose your senses and you just become a dull human being. But I'm finding the opposite to be true. You have to respect your age and feel good and beautiful, and in order to do that, it has to come from within. Nobody can tell you—you have to feel it.

I like to remember my grandmother, because she lived to the age of 102. When I was in my teens, she always looked old to me. And I said, "Grandma, do you feel old?" And she said, "No, I don't." She said, "I am so wrinkled, but I don't feel old." And I never asked her that question again. And she never changed; she was young until she was 100, she was baking bread until she was 100. She died at 102, but she was charged until the day she died.

If people could regard aging with dignity, with respect, with positivity, I think it would make our lives much easier and brighter. It's not the end of the world; it's not retiring into darkness. I think I'm just starting. At 60, you are reborn. I had lived five cycles, according to the Chinese calendar. That's a lot. And I get to relive again. You just have to tell yourself, "Okay, you have this clock; now you've reset it. And you can reinvent yourself if you want to." There are just so many options.

How has your sense of self-confidence or self-acceptance evolved over time?

I'm nowhere near perfect. Like everybody else, I've had my ups and downs. I had a pretty good career in film as a buyer, but I always straddled my interests in two areas: storytelling and cooking. I always wanted to go into cooking, but because my husband is an artist, one of us had to have a stable job. So I stayed in film.

I was a pretty good film buyer, but I made some bad judgments. I've produced films that came out at a bad time and completely collapsed. And I also suffered from poor health because I had breast cancer. But it was detected early on, and I survived. These things can really shrink your confidence. You *think* you're confident, you think you're not going to ever fail, but when you suffer from poor health, it can feel like a failure.

But I just decided that I had to deal with it. You know what helps? Keeping a Daruma [a small wooden doll modeled after the founder of the Zen branch of Mahayana Buddhism]. It tips and rolls over but always pops right back up. It's a symbol of overcoming adversity and that whatever you lose will one day come back to you. So for me and the issue of self-confidence, maybe I'll lose it for a while, but it will come back. You could gain your confidence back over time if you keep working at it.

What role do you feel your ancestors, or the women in your family who came before you, play in your life?

I think about them every day. It makes me cry when I think about my grandmothers. And my mother—she just died two years ago, which was really hard. My mother and my grandmother were two great women. They're my role models in life. It's just wonderful that I got to see two generations of strong women who lived through wars, major earthquakes, and hunger.

They would always talk about how they survived. They had to go to the ocean with buckets and boil the water down to get just a pinch of salt. They were hungry all the time. But they survived, and they both loved food and loved cooking so much. My grandmother and my mother both grew their own food and made miso and all kinds of fermented foods.

I think it's because they had so little, because they had to live through scarcity, that they became really strong women. They didn't want us to take anything for granted. So it's about not being wasteful and making the best of what you have. Every meal seemed to be like a ritual. You appreciated the person who made it, and you didn't waste even a grain of rice in the bowl, because the farmers grew it. It was a lesson every time. I really thank my mother and grandmother for who they were; they were good teachers.

What are you most proud of about yourself?

It's very simple. I'm happiest when I'm sharing something with people, when it's not just for myself. I feel that when I'm teaching. There's a lot of reflection that happens, when I teach, but I feel like every time I have the opportunity to share what I know with people, I gain a little bit more confidence. It drives my engine.

How has parenting affected your life?

I love being a mom. Parenting has been probably the most important thing for me as a woman—learning how to give unconditional love to a child. We're very close as a family, and I think being a mom really gave me an opportunity to be selfless, to give.

How have your ideas of success and happiness changed over time?

Small victories are what I really like. Happiness is not huge. And if happiness doesn't have to be huge, it can be small pieces combined over time that turn into the happiness you want.

What's the biggest risk you've taken in your life, and how has it shaped you?

I have best friends from junior high school, and they always say that if there was a wave, they would take a little float and hang out by the shore, but I would go for the strongest wave and dive in headfirst. I guess my life has always been about taking risks.

When my parents told me I had to come back to Japan and enter into an arranged marriage, I said no. I stayed in LA. That was a huge risk, because they cut off my finances. There was no trust fund. So I went into film school and met a wonderful professor who opened me up to the world of films and photography. I learned to take care of myself

and learned more about storytelling. And I was just his backroom assistant, but I said, "This is fascinating. This is storytelling." And he actually helped me write my first cookbook, called *The Political Pursuit of Food*, because I used to cook for him. He said, "You cook so well, you should find your English voice through the kitchen." And he helped me put the book together, and I wrote it on a manual typewriter thirty-five years ago.

It was a risk to go into film, but I did it anyway. They wanted me to keep it only as a hobby. But it must have been inside me, because my father was an avid filmgoer, too. Just before the war and before censorship came in, he went and watched two hundred films in one year in every theater he could. He skipped school to see American films. He would go into the theater with his Leica camera, photograph the scenes from these movies, and then put the photos in an album. He had all this storytelling. So I was interested in film because my father loved film, too. It was all a big risk, one risk after the other. Sometimes I failed, but I don't regret it.

I've taken personal risks as well. My husband and I took a break for a while, which was a huge risk, but now we've come back together and are husband and wife on different terms. A little bit more forgiving, mature, and older. Older is wiser, too. After thirty-nine years together, we learned to set certain respectful distances so that we don't kill each other. But it's wonderful that we have been able to reframe our marriage in a way that feels right for us.

He lives out in our ranch house in the desert and works on his art and does anything he wants. I visit him once a month. It works out perfectly. Then he comes back to the city and stays here and fixes my plumbing and complains about my disorganized house and tells me to make miso soup, and becomes the typical Japanese husband again. But it's good. It works out better this way.

At this point in your life, what have you made peace with that used to be a struggle for you?

Language. I grew up in three cultures: Spanish, English, and Japanese. My parents pulled me out of the school system before I even had a chance to build a foundation. So I would be in an English school for one year, then I would be in a Spanish convent school for three or four years, in complete immersion. It was a sink-or-swim situation. Then I moved back to Japan and was in a Japanese school, totally Japanese. It was so hard for me.

So language has always been a challenge for me, and it still is, but I've overcome it by saying, "Somebody will just help me fix it. If it's a grammar mistake, the editor will help me correct it." And my husband—he's also native Japanese—says, "Don't be afraid." His English is terrible, but he says, "As long as people understand what you're saying, you don't have to be so eloquent. You don't have to use difficult words; just be who you are."

What would you like to learn or experience at this stage in your life?

I'd like to get better at baking bread, and I'd like to learn how to garden better, using the scraps to compost. I am always in the garden. I'm bringing things out of the garden, milling it, making food, and putting it back into the garden. So basically, I just want to do what I'm doing right now, but better.

I don't need to change anything else. I just want to go deeper and better, and if you didn't give me anything else to do, I'm still very happy, because I know the garden alone has huge possibilities. It's a huge place to learn about nature and food. So I'm pretty set, I think.

Knowing what you know now, what would you go back and tell your younger self?

I should have listened to my parents more. I was a rebel. I could have been kinder to my sisters or brothers. I have too many areas that I could have been better in, but I don't know. I am who I am, so I don't like to look back. I like to look into the future.

What message do you have for women reading your story here?

Whatever you do, just pay attention. Paying attention is giving a little bit more time to the activities that you do. It could be mundane, it's like your everyday thing, or it could be paying attention to your loved ones or to a plant or to an animal or to your cooking—it could be anything. But I think if we pay a little bit more attention, you see better, you taste more, and you learn something from it. I just think that you're always observing, always looking. And I think we need to learn how to observe closer.

So I wish everybody good luck. Remember there are always opportunities to reinvent yourself over and over again at any age.

Dea Sasso
and
Rachel Prouty

ASHEVILLE, NC

Dea Sasso, 72, and Rachel Prouty, 33, have known each other since the beginning. Well, Rachel's beginning. Dea met and befriended Rachel's mother through their shared work in public health. Rachel got to meet Dea as a newborn and now, as an adult, she shares a deep adult friendship with Dea that also includes a lifetime of family memories. Dea and Rachel share a love of bookbinding and have worked together off and on from Dea's studio in Asheville, North Carolina. They've seen each other through loss, grief, and illness, allowing for ebbs and flows in their relationship over time. The COVID-19 pandemic has renewed their closeness and reminded them again that meaningful friendships can stand the test of time.

How did you first meet?

DEA: I've known Rachel's mom for so long, since we worked together in public health. So I met Rachel when she was in utero.

RACHEL: Dea was sort of there for some of the initial drama of my parents getting together. There was a band that was broken up because of it. There was a drummer. My dad was the guitarist. It was a whole *thing*.

D: It was a bumpy ride. But I initially became close with Rachel's parents because my ex-husband, Chris, is one of Rachel's father's closest friends. They were thick as thieves. So we were friends and did couple stuff together. The guys did things together. The gals were already doing stuff together. It was just really, really nice.

R: My parents are notorious for the depth and width of their friend groups. And so my family sort of always had really rich relationships with neighbors and friends.

My most concrete early memory of Dea's first bookbinding studio was this sort of freestanding structure in her backyard. And I don't even know what the context of it was, but occasionally, Mom would drop me off there. I remember I would hang out in the studio with Dea and we'd maybe make a miniature book or cut up some marbled paper. It was something that was just part of our family, and we'd go celebrate or go have dinners or evenings together. My parents created this friend group so there were always other caring adults in my life.

D: We were planting seeds, little did you know.

When did your relationship evolve from being family friends to an independent adult friendship? What was that like for each of you?

D: I had been in Massachusetts caring for my mother, who had had a stroke. But I had so many commitments down here in Asheville already. I had a house and was trying to make the change to live here permanently. There are a lot of bookbinders in Massachusetts, but there were next to none here in Asheville. I was like a fish out of the pond. And I had a lot of responsibility. So there was a period of time where I was mostly hearing about Rachel through her mom and dad rather than actually being there for some of the things she was going through.

My taffy just got pulled a little too thin. But then she came to visit Asheville and we got to reconnect.

R: I was in art school, and a professor named Cig Harvey taught me how to bookbind. By the end of my time there, I was making artists' books and really pushing boundaries, but still learning bookbinding techniques. And I thought about Dea's work as a bookbinder. I didn't know what I wanted to do with my work and life at that point. Then about two years after graduation, I went to a New Year's Eve party at Dea's ex-husband's house, and she was there and she said, "Come visit. We've got a room for you; come check it out." So I went down to Asheville for a weekend, and Dea and her partner Marianne picked me up.

I knew I needed to leave Boston and that I didn't want to move home to western Massachusetts. It just so happened that my friend Maggie, who I call my "creative wife," visited Asheville separately and was like, "I don't have a plan. I like your plan; let's go." So Maggie and I both took the leap and moved to Asheville together.

Maggie apprenticed with Dea first, before I did. Then I spent probably a solid two or three years doing the multi-job hustle in order to make things work. I made time to be at the bindery to learn.

Dea made this deep investment in helping Maggie and me try to figure out how to build a creative life. Dea was such a grounding force when we didn't really know that many people in this town and were both single. At that point, I had no idea how to date or what I was doing, and Dea saw me through the relationship that I'm in now. I feel like we just had a lot of really important conversations while we were working in that bindery at this really formative transition period. And she was a really big part of that.

D: I've always thought of Rachel as a surrogate daughter. I told her parents when she moved here that I got her now. I always saw this area as perfect for a person who wants to do something artistic. Anything you're into, somebody is into it here. And for book artists, the demand was high. I always thought that for young women, especially those who are going to have a baby and want to be home, earning money while the nap is happening or the child is in day care or in preschool, it's a perfect way to tap into the demand and also keep bread and butter in your own house, from your own work bench.

R: Being in Dea's studio was such a crucible. It gave me the full picture of what running your own business is like. There were definitely days when you could see just how big the pile of things to do was and you'd have to try to dig out from underneath it.

More important, I watched Dea run her business while also providing her mother the utmost level of care. She would go in and kiss her mother hello and see her before she went down into the studio, and it was just kind of all in the mix together. The fact that she already felt like family left a deep imprint and eased my transition into forming this adult friendship. We both got to do what we loved to do and figure out how to try to make it all work together.

Was there anything you were surprised to learn you have in common?

D: Politics. A lot of politics.

R: I would say food. It doesn't surprise me that Dea's politics are as radical as mine, because she's friends with my mom.

D: We also have a shared love of beer.

R: I don't think I appreciated, as a kid, all the small, radical ways that Dea bucks convention. It seems to come really naturally to her. And I think that is something I have always gravitated toward but not always been able to fully lean into.

D: I love our relationship. I think we will always remain connected, some way or somehow, as our paths go forward. I'm really close to Rachel's parents. So I want that to continue, too. I don't close many doors in my life; I just kind of add them. I was married to Chris for twenty years. Then I had a partnership with Marianne for twenty-five years. Now everything just keeps evolving.

R: I think Dea's sense of comfort in allowing the ebb and flow of life was really freeing to be around. Dea saw me at a point of exhaustion when I was trying to work five jobs and keep things afloat. I bumped up against a lot of financial strain, but our connection has been able to evolve even as I shifted away from her studio and toward teaching. I needed the stability and I needed weekends off.

I know with Dea that the door is always open. And knowing that our relationship can have its ups

I DON'T CLOSE MANY DOORS IN MY LIFE; I JUST KIND OF ADD THEM.

and downs and that it's okay has been a powerful thing to see. Since the pandemic hit, I feel like we've really deepened our connection again.

D: Bookbinders are like that. Almost every bookbinder I've ever known will give you the shirt off their back. Rachel doesn't know it, but I'm trying to get her to think about coming to teach at the folk school where I work. She's the hope of the future—she's the very person who needs to be coming in to teach these classes, and I'm the person who wants to get her there.

R: I feel like we've gotten to this point where it feels like a completely nourishing friendship. Dea is always telling me I am the hope of the future or telling me, "Oh man, when I hit the lottery, it is coming your way." She's always saying she can't wait to pay off my student loans if she wins the lottery. It's this incredibly supportive connection that is strengthened by feeling like we're family and also friends. It's been so cool to have in my life, and it feels like something I don't think many of my friends have.

What are some of your most fun memories together?

R: I have visions of drinking limoncello in Dea's kitchen. I came over for dinner, and friends of hers had a bottle they had brought back from Italy, and it was one of those wonderful nights where nobody is in a rush. Dea knows how to make the most *incredible* salads, so you feel like you eat your vegetables but you *also* eat a pile of bread at the same time. You know what I mean? It's the best.

But I also have fond memories of taking marbling class intensives where we learned from two master marblers. I was a rookie, and then I got to watch Dea bust out her marbling skills, which I don't see on a daily basis. Seeing her do what she does best is one of the really fond memories I have of days we've spent together.

D: It's just really nice, Rachel's transition into adulthood so that we have a peer relationship now. It was a long time ago, but I have a distinct memory of us from my fortieth birthday party where I wore a lime-green bodysuit and a lime-green Mohawk. I have the picture of Rachel there as a little girl, and it's just wonderful that we can share that deep connection over time. My husband and I didn't want to have children, so Rachel has always been a

surrogate daughter, someone whose life I could be a part of through her parents. I just think we're going to be connected for the rest of my life, and our lives. There's always more to be discovered.

R: I have to add to our funny memories: I'll never forget our two quarantine meals together. Dea has been really safe, so our main time seeing each other has been me buying bread at our favorite bakery and dropping it off at her house outside. But I've had two meals with her, one of which was in a homemade dining area separated by plastic shower curtains.

D: Mylar. It was archival Mylar.

R: I walked down her path to where I knew we were going to sit, but there was music playing and food already out. There was this *ambience*. It was amazing. The second time we ate together, it was cold, so we couldn't sit outside. It was after Thanksgiving, so I ate my post-Thanksgiving leftovers in my car with a space heater next to me. And Dea was in her RV right above me with the window open, so we were distanced but both warm. I texted my mom afterward and said, "I don't even know what just happened. I ate at Dea's house, and she was in the RV. I ate mashed sweet potato in my car and it was the best thing ever."

D: Public health was my first career, so building this place out back was second nature. I went to all these Johns Hopkins trainings, and I'm up to date on every aerosolized droplet that could possibly become a problem. So I made this roll-down Mylar wall, and then I just disinfect it, roll it back up, and bring it back down when we're going to have another meal, but two tables, 12 feet apart. And it was great—we had a fabulous meal, and we didn't have to be worried.

How has your friendship helped you through tough times?

R: There was a time when we were trying to figure out if we could make it work for me to work at Dea's studio with her. We were in this tough place of bumping up against the differences in my needs and the capacity of what people could pay. And it was a pretty fraught thing. I just remember that even though we navigated our way through it, that moment was emotional, and it was pretty tough to try to figure out what the right thing to do was.

D: That was the hardest time I can remember. Because it doesn't matter what I wanted for Rachel, or even what she wanted—we both had constraints within what we were doing and in our own businesses. And that was difficult.

R: And Dea was exhausted. The bindery had its own demands, life had its own demands, and then the level of elder care she was providing for her mother was intense. Care work is *work*, and the level of labor she had been sustaining for thirteen years before her mother passed was a lot.

D: It was heartbreaking not to be able to be there for Rachel in the way she needed, to help with that transition in her life. It felt like I was in such a caregiver mode that I was completely abandoning myself in many ways. I'm not sure that I was thinking straight all the time at that point. I was up all night, and I had two elders, my mother and my father's sister, to care for. They both passed peacefully at 95. I'm glad I had them in my house for the last period of time in their lives. It was a lot to handle, but I was very fortunate to have that.

The thing is, we are all on borrowed time. So what are we going to manifest here? I don't waste a lot of time in trying to worry about things I can't control, not that I don't want to do it, I just have to fight that tendency, and I end up with more energy to do other things. I love all the jobs I've had in my life—they're all my passions. It's a form of wealth, even though I won't be wealthy.

R: Dea is a really incredible model for breaking all the molds we have in life. Just because you don't have kids or don't have a traditional family structure doesn't mean there can't be so much love and richness in your life.

I think that's what's helped me lean into being really comfortable with the unknowns in my life. Some of my ability to make the choices I've made so far is because I've had people like Dea in my life. She demonstrates through her lived experience that there's no shortage of love or connection or support to be had.

I think it's good to break down and spread out the idea of all the labor involved in having only a nuclear family. Spreading that work out among a larger network of people is so helpful, and both my mother and Dea have been a huge part of modeling that in my life.

D: I have total confidence in Rachel. I might bite my nails about my nephews sometimes, but *never* about Rachel.

What do you each hope your friendship brings or gives to the other person?

R: I love being able to offer Dea moments of celebration. She is a great person to go to for celebrating and savoring those wins in life. I hope I can offer that—that influx of fresh energy, fresh eyes, and some tech support.

I'm just excited to be able to continue to do things that she gets excited about. Even small things like, "Hey, our friends just came out with a new dark stout beer. I'm bringing it over!"

D: I want to be there for Rachel, and I think she knows I always will be. For anything. Whether it's her creative life or her personal life or navigating new chapters with the adults in her life, I want to be there for her.

THAT'S THE BEAUTY OF A RELATIONSHIP— IF YOU'RE OPEN TO BEING CHANGED BY WHAT YOU LEARN, IT WILL ALWAYS BE SOMETHING MORE THAN YOU IMAGINED. TWO PLUS TWO EQUALS SIX.

What advice do you have for people who would like to find a friendship like yours?

R: Look for a shared interest or passion. Dea and I have the benefit of a long history, but there still is that part of the Venn diagram that is a shared passion and skill for books and bookbinding. When you're thinking across generations and you're really passionate about something and keep your mind open in those spaces, you can connect through those passions and across age divides.

D: Open yourself up and be willing to be changed by the person you are in the relationship with. That's the beauty of a relationship—if you're open to being changed by what you learn, it will always be something more than you imagined. Two plus two equals six.

What does your current age feel like for you?

R: I turned 33 this year. And I was born on May 11, 1988, so double digits are like, kind of a thing. I will be the same age my mom was when she had me. So I'm entering that interesting era. I've been doing a lot of internal work, and there's been a lot of studying and thinking that hasn't necessarily led to outward change in terms of work, or what I do, or how I spend my time. But I feel like I am very close to the next door opening and the next big change.

D: I would say almost the exact same thing. I'm on the cusp of something big. I'm planning a trip across the country with a man I adore, who I've known and loved for fifty-two years. We've always had a connection. I saw him through his first two marriages. He's seen me through a marriage and a partnership of twenty-five years. We're planning this month on the road, and I'm really excited about it. I hosted his seventieth birthday party on Zoom, and I know that 70 was a big change for me and it feels like a lot of possibility. Stay tuned . . .

Can you share something meaningful you've learned from each other?

R: Seeing a model of a passionate life and getting to be in it, and see it up close, and see all the ways that openness and creativity and enthusiasm can infuse friendships, activities, hobbies, your core craft, and the thing you make and do, has meant the world to me. And Dea has taught me that. Being able to see her passion and energy and devotion in real time has been amazing.

I think in our culture we can be good at tearing traditional systems down, but not as good at demonstrating what the alternative could look like. Dea has taught me to be curious about that, and to ask questions like, "What parts of this would I take? What parts would I do differently?"

D: I get a lot of hope from Rachel. I feel like our friendship is a source of hope. I feel invited in with Rachel, and I think I've learned more about what it was like to be a parent figure and a peer—because a lot of the best parent figures become peers as you get older.

I don't have another person like Rachel in my life. I have *Rachel* in my life. I don't have other people in my life like Rachel that I have this kind of sharing with. And I hope without expectation that she's in my life for the rest of my life.

Natalie Rogers-Cropper

ROCHESTER, NY

Dancer, speaker, and instructor Natalie Rogers-Cropper, 59, has movement in her DNA. From an early age, Natalie knew she wanted to dance, and at the age of 18, she bought a one-way ticket from Trinidad to New York City, where she auditioned for and was admitted to the prestigious Juilliard School. After seeing legendary dancer and choreographer Garth Fagan perform, Natalie moved to Rochester, New York, where she became a principal dancer with his company. She has won a prestigious Bessie Award and was voted one of the top three female modern dancers in the world by *Dance Magazine*. After dancing at the 66th Annual Academy Awards, Natalie assisted Fagan with his Tony Award–winning choreography for *The Lion King* on Broadway. After giving birth to her daughter in her early forties, Natalie returned to the stage, where she has danced and taught the Fagan Technique as the company's director for over twenty years.

Where did you grow up, and where do you live now?

I grew up in Trinidad and Tobago, and I live in Rochester, New York, now. The last place I lived before that was Houston, Texas. I ended up in Rochester because of Garth Fagan.

Garth came to Houston to perform. And that's when I saw the company for the first time. I saw them perform, and that was it for me. I was in. I packed everything up and moved. Within a week, I had quit my job and gone to Rochester to dance with the company.

What did you want to be when you were younger?

At 7 years old, I told my mother I wanted to move out of the house and be an artist with my own studio. She was like, "Well, how are you going to support yourself?" And I said, "Well, you're going to support me." She didn't laugh at me; she took me seriously and said, "No, you have to make a living when you're on your own." And that kind of shut me up for the moment.

When I was 15, I wanted to do interior design, and I was seriously pursuing that. I went to London with my family on a holiday and we were looking at schools for interior design, and then I saw a Broadway show, *Bubbling Brown Sugar*, and it was an all-Black cast. I'd never seen anything like that before. And that's when I knew I wanted to be onstage. It was a complete flip. And that same trip, we went from looking at art schools to looking for dance schools, too.

But I couldn't leave Trinidad without pursuing a degree—that just wasn't done in my family. The United States Information Agency had an office in Trinidad, so I went there to look up all the schools that did dance. I picked fifteen schools and sent requests for information. When the package from Juilliard came, I knew that was the one for me.

I had no idea how hard it was to get into Juilliard. Each year, almost three thousand people apply, and only thirty get in. I didn't know any of that. No clue. I had purchased a one-way ticket. I was *so* sure that I was going to do this. They had to take me. Three months later, I auditioned at the Juilliard School and got in. I came to New York, stayed, and that was it. I went straight into school a month later.

How has your sense of self-confidence or self-acceptance evolved over time?

I grew up as the youngest in a family that was very joyous and festive. We had a love of music, dance, and talking, and definitely a love of education. So my confidence came from my parents to start, of course. I didn't notice this until later in life, but my

WE ARE ALL LIMITLESSNESS. BUT LIMITLESSNESS HAS TO BE LEARNED. YOU HAVE TO PRACTICE IT.

parents never emphasized that I was a girl. They never said, "Girls do this," or "That's not what girls do." I didn't hear any of that. I was just doing my thing, and I had no real idea of needing to be limited because of what girls were "supposed" to do. When you grow up kind of with that grace, it's not very hard to see yourself as anything. So I've always had that level of confidence that says, "I really don't care what you think. I'm going to do it."

What are you most proud of about yourself?

The ability to remove "can't do" from my life. We all grow up with limitations. We think, I don't know if I can do that. And you don't do it. Because you think, That's out of my reach; I can't do it. Or you try to do it and it doesn't work, so you just give up. I did that. All young people do. But I eventually learned that "can't" is a word that shouldn't exist. And that nothing is impossible.

As children of creation, we are all limitlessness. But limitlessness has to be learned. You have to practice it. So that's what I feel I've been doing all along. And if you tell me I can't do something, I would be happy to prove you wrong. I fight like a mother and I will get it. And now that I'm older, I know what's worth fighting for.

What does your current age feel like for you?

My age feels like heightened awareness, knowledge, wisdom, common sense, more quiet, and more harmony. When I say more quiet and more harmony, I mean *internally*. The internal struggles are not there anymore. That's really what's so amazing to me and what drives me so much—that I kind of know my shit. There's a path I'm following that's very clear to me, and I'm not deviating from it at all.

And I have a greater acceptance of what is the *now*. This moment is what I have. And this is what I'm going to enjoy or celebrate or mourn. Whatever I'm doing, it's for now. And that's not going to drag on to our next day. It's just what is. Every day, I live like that. My long-range plan is to live every day fully.

But the physical stuff can be tough. Sometimes you just have to say, "*Okay*, I can't bend over and pick up anything easily. I'm having trouble with my socks today." And that's hard. But I prefer for the intellect and spirit to be nourished, way more than the body. I'm not that concerned with the body anymore.

What misconceptions about aging would you like to dispel?

That we become tired and lazy. That we are disconnected from the times we are in. That's what I hear from my daughter, and I say, "No, I disagree with you. I choose not to tell you, but I'm learning from what I'm seeing and from talking to you." Because I want to know what is happening in the world. I want to know what the youth are feeling and experiencing. This is what I'm into because I want to be into it. You can't be a dancer and artist or anything without understanding what's happening in the right now. I have to remind myself sometimes, how would I react to what's happening in the world right now if I didn't have my experience? How would I be experiencing this?

Those myths, that we have disconnected and that we will not fight anymore, I don't believe them, because most of the people I know who are my age and up, they're still out there fighting. They're making sure *their* children are out there, too.

I think as a dancer and an artist, you have to tap into all your selves, the one you were at 5, the one you were at 15, the one you were at 23, the one you were at 40, 50, and up. The way you perform is to be vulnerable like that, to be open, because that's when your spirit comes through. More opening, less ego. That's the spirit of a real artist—to give of yourself. If you are not generous, inherently, you're going to have a very hard time as an artist.

What role do you feel your ancestors, or the women in your family who came before you, play in your life?

My family, we're very social people. There were a lot of these gatherings, three times a week, with friends and family. It was constant. They would gather, and the women and the men would be talking. I was little and would watch and listen to the women have a voice and an opinion and stick to it and argue. Nobody was limited by being male or female. It was just, "What nonsense are you talking? Back that up. That's rubbish!" So, I just saw people. Once I saw people who were women like me acting just like the men, I felt empowered.

I had two great-aunts who never married. And back in those days, around 1902, not being married was *a thing*. One was the first Black head of nursing at the hospital in Tobago. She broke records. And my other aunt was very happily living her life and died single. I could see the joy they felt in their lives. Nobody was lonely. You know what I'm saying? And as a child growing up watching this, I'm going, "So . . . it's okay to be alone. That's great!" They were a constant reminder to do exactly what I wanted to do. The main influence of my ancestral women has to do with independence without bitterness. They really taught me how you can *not* have what everybody has and still be happy. You can still be totally at peace with yourself.

When do you feel your most powerful?

Onstage. That's why I chose this career. The power is not the kind of power that I can describe as the young version of power, which is "I have control over you." It's not that. It's the power that I am reaching others and that I can sense your soul, the audience, the spirit of people needing some kind of spiritual nutrition, and the power I have to be able to give that. Much like a priest would. And I don't see very much difference between churches and performing, quite frankly. That ability to inspire and to get people to make their lives better and to feel good about anything, that power is very important to me.

We are put here to create. I believe that's our purpose in life. And it can't happen without love. You have to be able to love.

Having had the kind of upbringing I had, the love that I have can be tapped very easily. That's what makes me perform, the love for human beings and other people. All of that, *plus* love for myself. I want to be a powerhouse, I want to share all of this for my growth, I want to be able to be a priestess. That's what I want to do, and that's what I feel is my goal in life, so let's see if I achieve it. We'll see.

Who or what has influenced your life the most?

So far, Garth Fagan is number one on that list in terms of influencing. There are lots of other people: parents, sister, brothers, that kind of thing. But overwhelmingly, he has been all those things: both mother and father, boss, mentor, and artist.

How has parenting affected your life?

In 2003, I told Garth that I was leaving the stage because I wanted to have a child and needed some help, fertility-wise. So I stopped dancing for eight years, had my daughter, and said, "Well, I'm not coming back."

But when my daughter was 8 years old, I was watching the dancers in the company and realized there was a lack of maturity among them. And that's when I went, "Wait, wait, wait. Let's work on this." I felt something *ping* inside me, like it always has, and I knew it was that time again. It was time to go back to dancing and teaching. Garth was thrilled.

But I didn't know if I could do it. I was approaching 50 and would have to get back into shape, but lo and behold, it all came back like it had never left. It was so powerful to be dancing again—in a new way. I've danced for years and years and years. But now it felt so different. Because I met every gesture and move without fear, and I think when you're a parent and you have a responsibility to another life, you have to start to lose some of those other fears. That new sense of responsibility added new dimensions to me. Parenthood didn't take anything away; it *added* to me. There's so much more to me after becoming a parent—it's like I have a whole new range now.

At this point in your life, what have you made peace with that used to be a struggle for you?

I was raised not to accept mistakes. And that made me really stressed out, because when I did make mistakes, it became really traumatic for me. But once you understand that you are *human*—that everything is not going to be perfect—you can actually feel better. Once I let all that crap go, that's when dancing became a lot easier and more fun. I kept thinking, Darn it, if I only thought like this ten years ago. . . .

Knowing what you know now, is there anything you would go back and tell your younger self?

No, because I needed to go through that journey. I need to go through the journey of the mistakes and the stupid decisions. I like who I am. So I wouldn't tell my younger self a thing, because it would have changed the course of my life. I embrace all the pain that can come with life—I don't mind being hurt. I don't have a problem with pain anymore. So if I have to go through that, then it means I'm alive. I'm human.

What is a lesson you're still learning or need to learn?

I'd like to learn peace and a full understanding of how *all* life is connected. How I am an essential and necessary part of a bigger whole. Until the day we die, we're learning what we are doing here. The more I work on that, the calmer I feel.

What impact do you hope your life and story will have on those around you?

Garth brings in all sorts of different dancers to the company, younger and older. Some of the younger dancers can do *anything*. But he also brings in older dancers. And the older people in the audience are like, "My goodness!" Their understanding of what he's saying with these dances to people of my generation and older is clear. I cannot tell you the number of older people who have come up to me, tears in their eyes, to say, "Thank you so much. I understood *exactly* what you were doing up there."

That is so good to hear. That really is where I need to be. That's what I want to leave: a positive impact. It's not about me or what kind of dancer I am. I just want to leave people with that feeling of change and affect people in such a way that they can renew their own lives. I've chosen the nonverbal way of getting that across, because that appeals to me. I want to be physical in that message, and I know now how to do that.

What would you never do again?

On a superficial level—amusement park rides. Never again. It so doesn't make sense to me to have a desire to feel like you are at risk, like you're about to die. People say it's about the adrenaline, but I'm a dancer, so adrenaline is already part of my life all the time.

What's the biggest risk you've taken in your life, and how has it shaped you?

I don't consider most things a risk, but the biggest risk to me was to marry and have a family. Because I had so believed that that was not for me, and I was very happy with that. Two of my aunts were fine. I was certainly fine. There was no problem. I thought marriage wasn't aligned with my performing career. But I was wrong. Then I thought having a kid didn't align with my plan, but she also proved me wrong, and I became a stronger dancer because of it.

Elizabeth Gilbert

NEW YORK, NY

Journalist and author Elizabeth Gilbert is perhaps best known for her 2006 memoir, *Eat Pray Love*. The book that inspired a blockbuster movie and launched countless trips around the world in search of self-discovery also marked a time of great change in Elizabeth's life. Her writing has followed moments of triumph as well as loss, as she has navigated the death of her partner, Rayya, and found her way in the world again at the age of 52. Elizabeth's honesty and openness about living with fear and self-doubt, and how to embrace joy along the way, has made her one of the most beloved voices of her generation.

Where did you grow up, and where do you live now?

I grew up on my family's small Christmas tree farm in northwestern Connecticut. Now I live in New York City and rural New Jersey.

What did you want to be when you were younger, and what do you do now?

When I was younger, I wanted to be a writer. Now I am a writer. And in between then and now, all I ever wanted was to be a writer. I have been incredibly fortunate.

What does your current age feel like for you?

I'm 52 years old, and it feels like absolute liberation.

What misconceptions about aging would you like to dispel?

Let me put it this way: I'm a twice-divorced, once-widowed, childless, middle-aged woman, living all by herself. With nobody to love! And nobody to love me! On paper, I'm a cautionary tale—something you might warn a young girl she must never become. But in reality, I'm very likely the freest and happiest woman you'll ever meet. All I do is lark about, doing whatever I like, checking in with nobody. It's glorious. Most days, I feel like Tom Sawyer. So make of that what you will.

What are you most proud of about yourself?

My proudest accomplishment is having befriended my own mind.

How has your sense of self-confidence evolved over time?

I think I always telegraphed self-confidence, but some of it was an act, and it took a lot of energy to play that part. Now I'm just relaxed, almost everywhere I go. I'm at ease because I know that I've got myself. I know that I will never roll Liz under the bus, and that brings a certain sense of freedom.

What role do you feel your ancestors, or the women in your family who came before you, play in your life?

Living or dead, they never stop inspiring me with their resourcefulness, resilience, and creativity. They were all women who figured out how to make things work. They imbue me with that spirit of self-reliance, still.

Do you have a message for younger women reading your story here?

Simply this: It is better to live your own life imperfectly than to live a perfect imitation of anyone else's life.

When do you feel the most powerful?

When I am at my most relaxed. The most relaxed person in the room is the one who holds all the power.

Who or what has influenced your life the most?

My former partner and best friend, Rayya Elias. She was foundational, transformative, strong, inspiring, and damn near fearless. On the topographical map of my life, she was Mount Everest. She taught me how to always tell the truth, with both fierceness and compassion. Before she died, she told me, "I won't rest until I see you standing on your own two feet in every circumstance in your life." I like to think I carry some of her power inside me.

What is the biggest risk you've taken in your life, and how did it shape you?

Leaving my first marriage, and deciding not to have children. Up until that point, I was still trying to live my life according to the very narrow template that had been offered to me by my family and my culture. After that, all bets were off.

If you could go back in your life, what would you like to do over—and what would you never do again?

I'd love to float in the warm seas of Fiji again. And I'd be very happy to never again set foot in divorce court.

How have your ideas of success and happiness changed over time?

The only thing that matters now is serenity. Because without that, accomplishments don't really mean anything. If you have all the success in the world but are still at war with your own mind, you will just be a miserable person living in a much nicer house. It's very hard to force me to do things that disrupt my serenity these days. I just won't have it.

How has choosing not to be a parent affected your life?

I think that choosing not to have children was one of the most important decisions I ever made—if not *the* most. I struggled with the question in my twenties, because I felt like I was supposed to want kids. But the truth was, I didn't want them. And I have never missed them. I don't think I would've been able to become myself if I'd had children. So it worked out best for everybody!

At this point in your life, what have you made peace with that used to be a struggle for you?

I used to be quite viciously unforgiving toward myself. I could take myself out of commission for years by shaming myself and blaming myself until

I was battered and shattered. I am a much kinder person to myself now that I am older. I have learned how to be my own unconditionally loving mother/partner/sister. Whenever I make a mistake now, I have a little voice inside my head that says, "Don't worry, angel. We won't throw you away for it!" That friendly kindness has changed everything.

What would you like to learn or experience at this stage in your life?

I've been doing a lot of meditation and breath work in the last few years. I tried for decades to have a steady meditation practice, but my interior voice was too restless and cruel to allow it. Now that I've laid down arms against myself, it's a lot more peaceful to sit still. I'd like to deepen those practices even more, until one day I just vibrate right on out of here.

What is a lesson you're still learning or need to learn?

This most beautiful and compassionate definition of LOVE—Let Others Voluntarily Evolve. I can still get impatient and judgmental when I feel like other people aren't growing and evolving according to my ridiculous standards.

Knowing what you know now, what would you go back and tell your younger self?

Don't entangle, don't enmesh. You can share your heart with people, but don't give your spirit away to anybody or anything. Keep that spirit as a private conversation —just between you and the God of your understanding. Everyone will be happier that way.

IT IS BETTER TO LIVE YOUR OWN LIFE IMPERFECTLY THAN TO LIVE A PERFECT IMITATION OF ANYONE ELSE'S LIFE.

Gail Marquis

JERSEY CITY, NJ

Gail Marquis, 66, was named to the USA Basketball National Team to represent the United States at the 1976 Olympics, the first year that women's basketball was featured in the games. Following her basketball career, Gail earned a business degree and found success as an executive on Wall Street. She is now the director of development at New Jersey City University. Gail and her wife, Audrey Smaltz, live and work from their home in Jersey City, New Jersey.

Where did you grow up, and where do you live now?

I grew up in Queens, New York. I stayed there most of my growing-up years, until about age 21, and then I started to travel and move around a lot. Now I live in Jersey City, New Jersey.

How has your sense of self-confidence or self-acceptance evolved over time?

I think growing up before, I was *kind of* confident, but nothing like I am now. I think the confidence built. It came after being on the Olympic team. I think living on my own in Europe for four years when I played professionally helped, too. I came back and started making decisions for myself, and the confidence kept building. Probably later into the '90s, I got a big boost of confidence when I started to be a broadcaster for the American Basketball League. And I remember having to speak up because if you're going to broadcast, you have to be able to hear yourself talk. I put those headphones on and I was talking to the crowd or my cohost and I could hear *my* voice.

I think that was one of the turning points where I started to become more confident and able to speak up. I pride myself on having the courage to speak to people I don't know or people who are well-known. I don't have a problem going up to them and introducing myself and getting to know them.

How have your ideas of success and happiness changed over time?

At one time, I thought happiness was to have enough money. I thought happiness was a nice house. But as I've gotten older, happiness has shifted to mean being fulfilled and healthy. Around 1999, there was a year or two when I was sick. Not bedridden sick, but very uncomfortable, and I'd always been healthy before. I was having problems breathing, and I just wasn't myself. They were giving me steroids, my weight was up and down, my hair was in and out, and I realized what a blessing it is when you do have good health. So I see that as such a value now. And I pride myself on not only being healthy but remaining healthy, being able to move, and keeping my mind sharp.

I work at keeping that stability, keeping a good head on my shoulders, and that makes me feel content.

When do you feel your most powerful?

I feel powerful after I've exercised and gotten through a difficult task. We do boot camp here on Saturdays, and I don't *like* to go, but I go every Saturday. I finish those workouts, and I can feel my body, my bones, my legs, my back. I can feel my feet. I can feel myself. I feel pretty powerful.

I work at a local university, where I handle development, which is fund-raising specifically for the arts and sciences. I feel powerful when I'm able to connect with people and get a conversation going. Whether I get a gift or not, I know there'll be a follow-up conversation because this one went so well. And believe it or not, I feel powerful in that sense because one, not everyone could do some of the cold calls that I have to do, and two, I can put the people on the other side of the phone at ease.

What misconceptions about aging would you like to dispel?

To me, age is just a number. It's all about how you feel. It's about how you take care of yourself and what goes in your body. It's also about how you are treated and how people treat you.

It's a big misconception when people say, "It's all downhill from here." That's not true. It is really what you make of it. I thought I was close to retirement, and then I got a promotion. I am the type of person who when you give me a challenge, I am going to take it head-on.

To me, one of the misconceptions is that at a certain age, someone has no purpose, or that you're already done. You want and need to be able to keep giving and helping. And you don't want to be a burden on someone else. So that means strong mind, strong body, and strong ideas, so you're not just waiting for someone to come and take care of you.

What role do you feel your ancestors, or the women in your family who came before you, play in your life?

There have always been strong women throughout my life. All three of my father's sisters went to college. They were nurses, surgical nurses, lab nurses. On my mother's side, one or two went to college. And all of them always instilled in all of us kids that being good—not being *well-behaved*, but being good—and being out there was the way to be. I think about how forceful they were, how sure, how adamant that each generation kept pushing the next generation. So I take my ancestors with me everywhere I go.

One time, I was receiving an award at the New York Athletic Club. I remembered that Jesse Owens, the four-time gold medalist, was invited to the New York Athletic Club to receive an award the year he won at the Olympics, and he and his wife had to walk in through the kitchen. They could not come through the front door; they had to go through the back door.

So when I went into the New York Athletic Club, I would step in the front door and holler out my father's name or my uncle's name and think, Can you believe I'm walking through the front door of that same place Jesse Owens was? Daddy, look where I am!

What's the biggest risk you've taken in your life, and how has it shaped you?

I went to France to play professional basketball. In those days, after college you were pretty much done

playing basketball. But I had negotiated a contract with a team in France. They paid for my flight, room and board, and even a car. I went with a friend who wanted to go at the same time. But the second year, she didn't want to go back. I could easily have said, "Well, I don't want to go by myself." But I remember leaving to fly back to France and everybody's hugging and kissing and saying goodbye and I had to say to myself, Don't turn around. Don't look back. Just go forward. That taught me to figure things out on my own and be courageous.

Eventually, I was able to get an entry-level job with a brokerage firm on Wall Street. It was a risk because I didn't have a degree in business, but I knew I liked the competitive nature of it. And that's why I was able to make that pivot. I enjoyed it. I loved the tempo. I wanted to learn more about what a stock was, what a bond was. I took a chance going to Wall Street and standing up for myself—because there weren't many people there that looked like me. There weren't many women. But I wanted to keep going forward.

I wanted to be in sales, but they wouldn't let me. I wanted to be in management, but they ended up having me train some young, blond-haired, blue-eyed guy who just waltzed right in there. I was kind of mad, and I took a day off and wrote a complaint letter. I came back and trained him for over a week, and then I said, "I'm getting out of here." I found another place to transfer and move to and I kept moving—always moving. I eventually was able to manage my own department and rose up the ladder until I got to the point where I could get into sales. To me, those were big risks worth taking because I easily could have, again, been the director of the local recreation center a couple of blocks from the house. I could have chilled. I wouldn't have had to take a subway or a bus because it was just "ride your bicycle down the street," but to me it was a risk to swing out there.

And what I enjoy about it is that after you've been through some of those wars and some of those battles and you've had to speak up for yourself, then you're always able to do it. When I do speaking engagements, I don't have a care in the world outside of what I've prepared. All of that has added to my confidence level. I've always been

I'M NOT GOING TO BE SMALL SO THAT YOU CAN BE BIG.

STRONG MIND, STRONG BODY, AND STRONG IDEAS.

able to get people who are nervous or intimidated by me to calm down. I can't help it that I'm six feet tall and that I'm African American and that I'm so accomplished. And I'm not going to be small so that you can be big.

Knowing what you know now, what would you go back and tell your younger self?

I would tell my younger self: Don't be scared. Swing out there. Go ahead out there. Stand proudly, even if it's solo. Somebody will join you. It's going to be okay. You're a leader. And the things you want, you want them because nobody else has done them. To be the first at so much that you want to do, or to walk that road that nobody else has traveled, might be uncomfortable, but there's a reason it's uncomfortable. Nobody else has done it.

What would you like to learn or experience at this stage in your life?

If money were no object, which is the way I look at a lot of things, I probably would run for political office. It's not too late. But the only thing I don't like about political office is having to raise money. So what am I doing now? I'm raising money for a university. What did I do before? I was asking people for money to put in their retirement fund or life insurance policy. I've been asking for money for like, twenty years, but that's what's in my head about running for office.

How has not raising children affected your life? Do you feel like you've played the role of a parent for other people?

I don't have any kids, but when I think about parenting and I think about the village that we live in, I think, Look at all these children I have! Which is what keeps me at my role of fund-raising and continually asking for money for scholarships and for programs to advance students, especially those who are socioeconomically challenged or go through food insecurities or housing challenges.

I met one young lady in her senior year of college who, three months before graduation, was going to drop out. I said, "Wait, wait, wait." She and her mother had been evicted. I told her to wait and I found a way to get a foundation to pay for her to stay in the dorm. I mean, isn't that what we're raising money for? So that this child doesn't have to drop out with three months to go? We can't let her lose all that. Then, at the end of the year, she needed help to buy shoes and a graduation dress. I said, "I've got one of my gift cards. Go to the mall, buy the shoes, buy whatever you want; it's from your godmother Gail." So I hear from her still. And these are the children you have to help.

Do you have a message for younger women reading your story here?

I hope you'll read my story and feel empowered. Tell our stories; tell your stories. Don't just sit on them, because they can help so many others. Our stories are life. We made it through. Give yourself a pat on the back.

Pauline Sanchez

and

April SunShine Sanchez

MESA, AZ

Pauline Sanchez, 68, and April SunShine Sanchez, 40, are a mother and daughter from Mesa, Arizona, who have found strength in not just their bond but also their Diné (Navajo) culture's matriarchal traditions. Both women have weathered difficult times together, including serious health challenges, and found faith in a mixture of Indigenous traditions and worldviews in which they were raised. April and Pauline see it as a part of their legacy to think forward about the generations to come after them, and to look backward to honor those who came before and all they've made possible for today's generations. They sat down in their home in Mesa to talk about their early lives, their family's mix of Native American and Indigenous Mexican traditions, and how both have shaped the way they see the world and their missions in life.

Where did you grow up, and where do you live now?

PAULINE: I was born on the Navajo reservation. It was in January, so it was a cold time, and when my mother went into labor, my father carried her from their tent on a little knoll down to my grandmother's hogan so my mother wouldn't fall. So I was born in my grandmother's hogan. Traditionally, when our umbilical cord comes off, the place they bury the umbilical cord is in the hogan. And so I'm assuming that's where I left my umbilical cord, in my grandmother's hogan, just north of Flagstaff, beyond a small trading post, over some hills, and down a little knoll.

That's where I was born, and I spent my childhood in that area. We had horses, cows, and sheep. And my father worked really hard to take care of our animals there.

APRIL: I was born in Provo, Utah, in the Wasatch valley. My parents had three children already—all boys. When I was born, they didn't have money to go to the doctor to get an ultrasound. So they didn't know I was a girl. My dad tells me the story of my birth and that during that time, not only were they struggling financially but he was surrounded by spiritual darkness because, he says, "I didn't know how I was going to feed another small mouth."

He says that it started out as a cloudy day and then when the nurses placed me in his arms, the sun broke through the clouds. And it was in the month of April, so he named me April SunShine. So I was born on the Wasatch Front in Provo, Utah, with both of my parents bringing me into the world. Now we both call Mesa, Arizona, home.

P: But we're still tied to our people on the reservation, and I still speak Navajo—that's my first language. I'm grateful for it; it helps me to see life from a different paradigm and a different point of view than English.

The beauty of the language is that it doesn't change—what is sacred is sacred. And I really like that foundation that was situated for us, that we're so tied to our Creator. Our language is one of relationship and kinship.

A: My parents started a wilderness therapy program, so we spent most of our youth hiking and living our ancestral way in the Sonoran Desert

IN OUR DINÉ CULTURE, DECISIONS ARE MADE TEN GENERATIONS IN ADVANCE. I OWE MY EXISTENCE TO THEM.

and Tonto National Forest. My mom kept us tightly connected to our Diné culture, and my dad kept us connected to his Mexican culture. So I grew up in this really beautifully harmonized, multicultural, multitribal culture.

What did you want to be when you were younger?

P: Honestly, I just thought I'd live on the reservation. I didn't have any dreams of, you know, anything. I would come to the trading post, and I went to the hospitals often enough, but I apparently didn't like the hospital enough to dream of being anything medical. I knew the Navajo reservation, and I knew the way we lived there, so I just thought I'd always be like that and just be that way.

A: When I was younger, I wanted to explore. I would climb trees to see what was above the houses. I was always curious about what else was out there. There was a time when I wanted to be an astronaut, but I don't think that lasted very long. I think it was just the idea of exploring and having adventures and new knowledge. Adventure was always fun for me. And learning to write now has been an adventure, but it hasn't been without challenges.

I had a stroke back in 2014. It was a little crazy—it was a *lot* crazy, actually. It left me with an inability to use my hand and the loss of some motor skills, and also affected my speaking, vocabulary, and memory. So it has taken me a few years to come back from that.

Two of the things I loved before all that happened was writing and reading—those were part of my soul. So when I knew I was supposed to be a writer, it was quite a difficult journey because I had to face my disabilities. So being able to coauthor a book recently was a huge step forward for me. My goal now is to be a writer. It's a struggle with my brain, so I just keep going because I love it.

What role do you feel your ancestors, as well as the Elders in your community, play in your life?

P: Their spirit, their songs, their prayers, I carry them all with me. They had this belief that you needed to carry love for your family and really hug and press that into them. My mom would say, "You are sacred. You are my heart. You walk in my heart." That was pressed into her, and then she pressed it into us. So that they could live simply and be happy. That kinship between us and our community is something I get from my ancestors.

Their stories and the way they spoke, it wasn't loud, but it was deeply felt. I don't have words in English to describe the way their voices changed to take on this deep, purposeful spirit, I think. They would tell you to remember to carry their lessons with you. To pray in the morning, to get up and greet the sun, to be alive in that day, to get things done, to work on all the different kinships, to care for everything and make sure everything is okay in that day. They are all still with me.

A: I was taught from a young age that in our Diné culture, decisions are made ten generations in advance. So when they make decisions, they think of the tenth one to be born from the person who's making the decision. That was something that my masune, my maternal grandmother, taught me growing up: Someone made a decision a long time ago to survive and to keep going, and that is why you are here. And so we live in this multifaceted reality, if you could say that, where we are constantly remembering the past and honoring it, and making decisions for the future by what we're doing now. So I know I owe my life to someone who decided they were going to make it through the long walk, or they were going to make it through the Mexican Indian Wars. So I know I literally owe my existence to them, but that also helps me remember that my existence is not solely my own. That my personal survival enables the existence of future generations.

I know personally that through some of my hard struggles in my own life, my ancestors have walked with me and have helped me through those experiences.

How has your sense of self-confidence or self-acceptance evolved over time?

A: I'm the first generation to be born off the reservation, to live off the reservation, and also to speak English as my first language. My parents learned English as a second language, and I grew up doing all these firsts. I didn't realize that that's what I was doing. It was a struggle growing up, because I had this very different family. Very multicultural and multilingual. And where I grew up, there weren't a lot of other brown people. And I had this family that was Native American and also Indigenous Mexican. That made me different because I was not white, but also not 100 percent Mexican or Navajo. So I grew up not feeling like I really belonged, and that was hard. I had this experience where I had to figure out where I belonged at all these junctions of my life, when people would ask me where I was from or who I was or who I identified with. For a long time, that was really hard, because we speak Navalish and Spanglish in my home; I spoke at least five different dialects. But I finally realized that all of that was exactly how it needed to be for me, and that I was, in fact, a bridge between two countries, two groups of people, and two different cultures and languages. I realized that at least at our family table, all those Mexican traditional foods are in harmony with the Navajo fry bread and the mutton. I finally realized how valuable that was and how uniquely different it was, and that it was okay to just be me. It was okay to just talk about the family that I grew up in, that I didn't have to make a distinction of being only Navajo or only Mexican, that it was okay that I didn't speak my Indigenous languages fluently. And I think the big turning point for me was realizing that my speaking English was actually a gift, because I could now read everything that was written about my people, all of the treaties, our histories, and actually reply from our perspective, describe who we were and correct some of those things and protect us.

In my home, I can walk from one room where there's Spanish being spoken into the next room, where my mom is on the telephone with her sister speaking Athabaskan. And then go into another room where people are speaking English. And I know that all those things are not negatives. They all have immeasurable worth. And I am just one generation and five hours away from my people, and still able to live a successful life in the city.

Were you two always close?

P: My shout of joy when she was born, it rang through the heavens. The joy of carrying her and taking care of her when she was tiny, it was such a delight. Our relationship started to morph and change as she got older. She learned how to cook and how to sew. She became very creative. I taught myself how to sew and cook, how to bake bread and to collect skills and things that she could learn from me. But she has also taught me so much. She taught me to be more patient, more loving, and to hold your tongue sometimes.

A: Our relationship has definitely changed as I've gotten older. I moved in with my parents because of my health problems, and because of that, I got to see my parents as adults. And that's really different from when you're a child, because then their world pretty much revolves around you.

I remember it slowly transitioned into where we started to just enjoy each other's company as adults. We could just talk about parts of their lives that they never shared with us as children and things that they wanted to do with their lives. And part of that was a shock to me—they would share things that I had never heard before. But we could understand those things now, because we're adults and have experienced different things. And so I think our relationship became stronger, and it evolved into this new place.

Now that I've been dealing with a lot of health troubles, my appreciation of my relationship with my parents has changed again. It's been eleven years now, dealing with health issues, and I've almost died several times. They've helped me so much during my recoveries. And as an adult, you realize how much they did for you when you were little. Helping me learn those small things *again*, especially right after my stroke, made me realize how much they had done for me as a child. They're really the reason I'm alive now.

For a lot of families and also different cultures, once you're 18, you leave. But that's different for matriarchal societies and also in Mexican culture. I was really grateful that my parents held their doors open for me to stay as long as I needed to.

P: People ask us, "How does it feel to be empty nesters?" and my husband and I say, "We're not empty. We don't live that way. That's English culture." It's our culture and happiness to have adult children in our home.

What is a meaningful lesson you've learned from each other?

A: I think one of the most meaningful lessons is this idea of pressing love into people. It was something that my grandmother said to my mom and taught her growing up. When children would come to you, you wouldn't just embrace them and let them go. You would take them and you would press them into you gently and really hold them. So they could feel the familiarity of your body, you know, and recognize that that is a safe place.

In Navajo they say life is sacred. And that's part of that teaching—you hold it sacredly. When you hold children, that's what you do—when they're busy running around and they come to you, you hold them. So that there's just this quiet moment of love passing between you before you put them down and they run off again. All those little collections of moments that change you and keep you tied to the people who taught you that—that's what helps you remember where you come from.

Knowing what you know now, what would you go back and tell your younger self?

A: I really believe in the power of women, and especially the responsibility we have to turn around and teach the younger women in our lives. This is something I actually think a lot about because my five nieces range from ages 5 to 16.

One of my nieces recently asked me, "Why do we have to share?" And I think in these moments, it is so important to set such a clear and solid foundation. Because whatever answer I give her is going to affect her relationship with her family and with the world around her. I think about the power that is within her tiny little body and the fact that she will affect generations to come with her decisions and what she thinks and what she shares with the world. And so for myself, one of the things that I hope to continue telling my younger nieces— and maybe someday I'll be able to travel back and tell my younger self—is to keep moving forward and don't give up. Keep your eyes looking up, keep fighting by looking up.

I say this because I was a victim of sexual abuse and assault. At one point I was so lost, I could only look down. I threw myself into service and sports and all of these outside activities, but they weren't soothing any of the wounds that had been inflicted upon me against my will.

I prayed to the Creator and said, "I need an answer. And I need you to tell me what to do, and I'm not getting up until you do." When I received the answer, it was to remember that I have to keep moving forward and to keep looking up. I can only keep fighting if my eyes face upward. That's how I can see where I'm going.

P: I would choose to go back and encourage and counsel myself in a moment of doubt. I would just say, "You're worth it, you're worth it, you've got it. You're strong, you're smart, you have everything inside. Just water it, nurture it, and let it bloom. Be loving and kind and patient with yourself and with others, and be full of gratitude. Your future is going to be good."

And I would say to anyone else, or everyone else who might read this, please remember you are of immeasurable worth to others. What you do and say and bring to the world matters, and our love, our generosity, our kindness does an amazing thing for people. The world needs us. The world would not be what it is without the women.

Kate Pierson

WOODSTOCK, NY

Kate Pierson's red beehive hairdo may be one of the most iconic looks in rock music, but it is her voice (both onstage and off) that has made her a legend in her field. As one of the founding members of the B-52's, Kate, 73, has won countless awards for her music and has produced two solo records, as well as collaborating with musicians like the Ramones, Iggy Pop, and R.E.M. In addition to singing, Kate plays the guitar, bass, and keyboards and is constantly pushing herself to learn new music and recording skills. From her home in Woodstock, New York, she sat down to talk about how growing up in a musical family shaped her ambitions, and how traveling the world inspired her to grow her own roots and find a balance between her creative and personal lives.

Where did you grow up, and where do you live now?

I grew up in Weehawken, New Jersey. We lived in my grandmother's house with her. We lived on the ground floor, and she lived upstairs. It was right by a reservoir, and you could walk to the park where Alexander Hamilton and Aaron Burr had their duel. Growing up there was fun—it was kind of like *Little Rascals*. All the kids played together all the time. Then we moved to Rutherford, New Jersey, when I was 8 years old. I've lived all over the place, but now my wife, Monica, and I live in beautiful Woodstock, New York.

What did you want to be when you were younger?

I wanted to be what I am. I always wanted to be a singer. My father was a professional guitar player when he was younger. Then he got a job when he got married and worked in this plant called the Curtiss-Wright Corporation. But he played guitar all the time at home. And my grandmother played piano. My mother was not musical, but my grandmother always played "Mockingbird Hill" on the piano. My brother was musical, too. So I grew up to be exactly what I wanted to be. I always knew I wanted to be a singer.

Do you remember the first time you sang onstage?

Oh, yes. It was not on a stage, exactly, but in church. The Presbyterian church. I don't remember what it was, but it was just a choral piece. I had a solo part, and when it came, no words or song or melodies came out of my mouth. Everyone was gesticulating wildly to get the rest of the choir to join in and cover up the gaff. I remembered, years later, that the choir director had told my parents, "She doesn't have a very pretty voice, but it's loud." That must have become embedded in my mind, and I just choked. So, that was my first experience. But I got over it pretty quickly.

What does your current age feel like for you?

Hitting 70 was not pleasant. I just felt like, Oh, I can do 60; oh, 65 is great. Oh yeah, life begins at 60. And then 70 started feeling like . . . well, mainly so many people in my family died in their seventies, and I don't have a longevity kind of gene pool. But there were some people in my family who did last longer. But my state of consciousness, I feel great. I feel like I'm in the right place; this age feels really good. I feel fine, I feel healthy. But when I think about it, I don't like that over-70 feeling. The way that age is viewed, although things have changed in terms of what people think—it's still an ageist society. So I still feel like people kind of gasp, like, "Oh, you don't look that old!" Or you get comments like, "You look great for that age."

What misconceptions about aging would you like to dispel?

I think the main thing is that you will *feel* old. But you just don't feel older at all. Inside you feel young. People who are older, we often feel like we're still in our twenties in our heads. And I can do all this stuff. And I think that's the main myth—that you're going to feel like this big change is going to come over you. And maybe it will one day, but not in the way you expect. In this country, there's this constant improvement trajectory—like you could always get better in the gym. But people realize that at some point, you might level off in a sort of state of contentment and acceptance.

How has your sense of identity or understanding of yourself changed over time?

Well, oddly enough, my wife says I'm so extroverted, but I don't think I'm a big extrovert. Within the band, Fred and I are the extroverts. But when I was in grade school, and high school even, I was very shy. I didn't have a lot of self-confidence when I was younger. But I grew out of that.

I think being away from home after high school and having independence helped. My mother was not one of those "You can do anything" people. It was basically "You can't do anything. I'm afraid." I came to understand why she felt that way much later, but she was very fearful. Once I got out of that environment, I felt like I was going to do everything I wanted to do. Break the rules, take acid, go to Europe, have sex, just do it all.

How has that breakout period affected your self-confidence as you've gotten older?

When I was in junior high and high school, I had a band called the Sun Doughnuts. It was a folk protest band, and we wrote our own songs. And I had no shyness about singing or singing out. And then when the B-52's formed, I felt like I *couldn't* write outside of that. We wrote a lot of stuff, most things collectively by jamming, which was a really amazing experience. To be in a band together for over forty years, it's kind of like a family. We share all the profits equally and it's a democracy, but I felt I couldn't leave or do anything outside or I would be ostracized or punished. And I felt that very strongly. And part of that is true—that's how bands break up. Someone does their solo thing.

But I wanted to write a solo record. And finally this opportunity came up to write with these Japanese friends, and to go to Japan and work there. Making that record was a great experience.

We toured; we ate fabulously. And then I realized that I could easily collaborate with people. And my self-confidence grew, and I started doing more solo things, and then I felt free.

What are you most proud of about yourself?

What I'm most proud of is that I'm still learning. And I'm still really excited about learning. When I talked about aging, and how there's a point where you feel like, well, you level off, as far as learning and curiosity, I feel that it's endless.

I'm taking guitar lessons; I'm a pretty good guitar player, but I'm getting better. I'm learning this recording system called Logic Pro that I thought was going to be way too complicated, but it actually turned out to be not that hard at all, and I'm really rocking it. And so I think that's what I'm most proud of, that I still am so excited about learning.

When do you feel your most powerful?

Well, definitely when I'm onstage and performing, I feel alive. I feel like I'm very much in the moment, living in the moment, because I'm looking at the audience. Some people don't look at the audience when they perform, but I very much look at people. I feel like I'm performing *with* them. And I see them dancing and how happy they are. And that's a really kind of ecstatic moment when I feel like these people are here, and they're all so happy. We're giving them happiness, and they're giving us happiness. And it's a wonderful sort of exchange of you feeling that you're all one.

How does it feel when a song you've written resonates with people?

It feels amazing. Mostly it's been with songs I've written collectively with the B-52's, like "Love Shack" or "Rock Lobster," and everyone's doing this down, down, down dance part of it or some ritual thing that everyone does. And that feels so good. But when I did my solo record, *Guitars and Microphones*, even though it's a smaller group of people that it resonates with, maybe, it still feels great to have written something much more personal. And seeing people relate and singing, and being able to express a much more personal song, it's incredible.

WHEN I'M ONSTAGE AND PERFORMING, I FEEL ALIVE. BECAUSE I'M LOOKING AT THE AUDIENCE. I FEEL LIKE I'M PERFORMING *WITH* THEM. I SEE THEM DANCING AND HOW HAPPY THEY ARE. WE'RE GIVING THEM HAPPINESS, AND THEY'RE GIVING US HAPPINESS.

What's the biggest risk you've taken in your life, and how has it shaped you?

Well, I guess when I first left college. And then Kent State happened. I had been so involved in protesting and the civil rights movement and the anti-Vietnam movement, and when Kent State happened, I just felt like, It's over. The revolution, it's not going to happen now. So a friend and I took off and hitchhiked through Europe. Then she went home, and I continued to travel through Europe for almost a year. And that was a big adventure. That experience was very empowering and educational, but it also threw me off track in a way. When I went to Europe, I met my future ex-husband. He was English, from Manchester. We had this vision to do a "back to the land" thing. And we wound up, through the hand of fate, back in Athens, Georgia.

I had resigned myself to the idea that me singing and being in a band was never going to happen. But then there was this psychic who was a waiter at a vegetarian restaurant in town, and he said, "Come over to my house and I'll give you a reading." He put a literal *bear's head* on his head. And he said to me, "You're going to be famous for something." And he said to Brian, "And you will have facilitated it somehow." And I was like, How? But then shortly after, I met the rest of the band that would become the B-52's, and we started jamming.

Looking back on it, what that taught me is that you don't always get to your goal in a straight line. You can't force it to happen how or when you want it to happen. You have to accept that it's a long and winding path. It goes round and round and up and down.

What role do you feel your ancestors, or the women in your family who came before you, play in your life?

I could write a book about that. I've always been fascinated with ancestry for some reason, and could spend hours on Ancestry.com. What I found was that all the women who came before me had this pioneering, adventurous spirit because they immigrated to America. All of them were poor. And they struggled. But my mother's side of the family had a great sense of humor. All the women had a really hilarious sense of humor. It wasn't an easy life for any of them, but I feel like that gave me some sort of feeling of strength through sense of humor.

Knowing what you know now, what would you go back and tell your younger self?

Just don't be afraid. I would tell my younger self not to be afraid to run away from home, or go directly from high school to New York City and get on the folk music circuit. Or join a rock band. Why didn't I just move to San Francisco and get into a psychedelic band? I just kind of went into that "fall back on it, go to college" thing. I don't regret going to college, but I guess all those experiences led to where I am now. I would go back and tell myself to banish fear.

What would you like to learn or experience at this stage in your life?

Well, I want to have another solo record. And I want to do some more shows—solo shows. The last solo record I did, I just did a few shows, but this time I'd like to do more live. And I love livestreaming stuff. I'm loving that. I'd also like to write. I'd like to write a book.

For all of us in the B-52s, the band was our mother ship. It was our rock. Sure, we did some solo stuff, but we kept coming back to the band. And some people do *so* much—they write a play and they've written a book and they start a charity. And it's like, how do they do all that? It's like some people just have this drive.

But I think everyone in the band, including me, has this other life at home. Lives that we all really cherish. And sometimes I think, Why didn't I just push myself more and do more music? But I love gardening. I love being with my wife. I love being with the dogs. I love being in nature and just chilling out at home. I've done touring all my adult life and been away from home a lot. So I think now I appreciate just living.

How has not raising a child affected your life?

My wife and I have three friends who are in same-sex couples. And each friend has a younger partner who just had a baby. So my three friends are hovering in their sixties and just had babies. So we're loving being around all these babies. When I am around children, I become like a child. I love to play with little kids, and I love being around young people. But there is a time—and I've seen this in other friends—when your biological alarm clock goes off, and all of a sudden you feel like, *I* want to have a baby. And that time passes if you don't move on it.

I tried, sort of, but I didn't want to go overboard. It didn't happen organically. And once I got over that, the hormones of it, then it was like, Wait a minute. I'm fine not having a baby. So I'm just happy to see my friends' children, and I'm pretty content with the way things are with our dogs.

What impact do you hope your life and your story will have on those around you?

I hope people who read my story see that it's very possible to achieve things in an organic way. If you follow what you love and you follow your instincts, you might wind up in a perfect place that you may not have even known was there.

Cara Reedy

NEW YORK, NY

Writer, comedian, actress, and journalist Cara Reedy, 46, is a strong and determined activist working for the rights of disabled Americans. In her role as program manager for Disability Rights Education & Defense Fund's Disability Media Alliance Project, Cara works to make space for disabled media professionals. After working at CNN for ten years, Cara coproduced a documentary, *Dwarfism and Me*, and has continued to use her voice and her platform to advocate for the right of disabled people to control their own narratives.

Where did you grow up, and where do you live now?

I grew up in St. Louis, Missouri, in a little town called University City. It was full of hippies. And now I live in New York City, in Washington Heights. I've always wanted to live here in New York—honestly, because of *Sesame Street*. By the time I was 4, I was like, "*That's* where I'm going to live." And it never wavered. I didn't come here until I was in my mid-twenties, but I'm so glad I did, because it's the right place.

What did you want to be when you were younger?

An actor. It just felt natural. I'm a performer. There's no way around that, even with the way I write—it's written for performance. Performing was always the thing I wanted to do.

What do you think your younger self would think of what you do now?

I think she would be proud. But I think she'd be a little confused. Because little Cara just thought you go to school to be an actor, and then you just do it.

And when you're young, there's no way to predict all the roadblocks that are going to be put in front of you. So my life in advocacy would be strange to her, I think, because she'd say, "Why are you doing that? Why don't you just go act?"

What brought you to advocacy work?

My friend Becca always says that activists are traumatized people, because trauma brings you to advocacy, and that's what makes you fight. And then once you're in advocacy, you're retraumatized. And so I would say trauma brought me here. A lot of it.

Which is why I'm so militant about fixing the problem, because it was so bad for me. And I endured so much that I'm just like, "No, no. No one's ever going to live that experience ever again if I can help it." I'm in therapy now, and I'm unpacking a lot of things that happened over the years, and you don't realize how bad it is until you look back and you're like, "Whoa, that was a *lot*."

I had a really hard time in art school. I actually *don't* have a degree in theater because I quit when I was three classes away from finishing my major. I went to art school for photography and I had some great teachers there. I can't say that about the theater program, but I did have some great teachers in the photography program. But I had one that had an outsize influence on me. He targeted me the entire time I was in school, screaming at me, telling me to quit, saying I was never going to be a photographer. He would do it in front of other people. I wasn't even allowed to have a full portfolio show. That was where a cloud of "maybe I'm not as good as everyone else" started.

I spent ten years at CNN. That was also not a great place to be. It was horrible. I'm only now starting to unpack it all. I read a tweet about trauma that said, "It takes a couple years for the trauma to run through your body and then destroy it." And that feels accurate to me.

Coping with trauma is different for everyone. I watch *Sesame Street*. The other day I was watching season 1 of *Sesame Street* because I had had a particularly heavy day, and that just made everything feel a little bit better. Gordon read a book and Big Bird came out to talk, and it just felt like I could breathe a little more easily.

People ask me why I went into these jobs if they were traumatizing, but I didn't know they would be at the time. I always expect a certain amount of ableism. I expect a certain amount of racism. I live with it every day. And misogyny, too. But added up all together, it's a lot to deal with.

What does your current age feel like for you?

My current age feels like I'm working on caring less about what other people think of me. I'm still working on that, and I'll catch myself and have to talk myself out of caring. But I'm much more equipped to walk away from this stuff now. Dropping the rope is my new favorite thing. When people won't let go of something, I just drop the rope and let it go. They're still off fighting, expending energy, and I've moved on.

What misconceptions about aging would you like to dispel?

I think one of the biggest misconceptions is that life's *boring* when you get older. I find it *much* more exciting. This part of my life, I'm getting to do all the things I ever wanted to do, and people are looking at me and saying, "She's the one you should go to for that."

I feel vindicated. But it also has freed me up to be really creative. And all the things I wanted to do in my younger years, I'm doing now. And all the things I thought I forgot from theater school, from photography school, all of that stuff that I thought I forgot or that I didn't learn—I'm surprised by how much I remember and how successful I can be with what I know.

How has your sense of self-confidence or self-acceptance evolved over time?

It's much better now than it ever has been. When I was at CNN, there seemed to be an opinion that I should just accept being an assistant for the rest of my life. They were really confused by my need and wanting to do more. And so they spent a lot of time telling me I *couldn't* and that I wasn't qualified for it. It takes a minute to recognize that you're qualified for it, because there's been years of people telling you you aren't. So I'm talking about this all more openly now because I can't be quiet anymore. It's a big part of why I'm starting a disabled journalist association.

When do you feel the most empowered?

When I'm using all the skills I've learned over the years *through* the trauma *for* other people who have experienced trauma. Because it feels like it was worth it. I don't feel like trauma is ever worth it, really, but at least there's some use to it. I'm working on a bunch of projects with all disabled women of color right now, and it's been so fun. I have a production company on the side of my advocacy work, and we did a social justice game show. So we may not be able to forget our trauma, but we can use it for our work. You can use it in positive ways that make you feel better and don't make it feel so deadly.

What role do you feel the women who came before you, in your family or in the communities to which you belong, play in your life?

So many. The Black family is really an underrated institution that people on the outside don't really understand. And I think part of being Black is protecting that space and not revealing too much about how we work. But other Black people, when we see it, we know. First of all, Black mothers are so powerful in our lives. Grandmas, aunts, everyone. My aunts call me all the time to yell at me and tell me whatever. But there's this deep connection through the female line, and I think that gives me so much strength and support.

I think in Black families, or at least in mine, you're responsible for other people. Not that you sacrifice yourself, but you have to be responsible for other people. You've got to look out for them. There's something that glues us together through this matriarchal line. Even on my dad's side, I didn't know my paternal grandma, but I still feel connected to her. She got her PhD when Black women weren't doing that. Or *couldn't* do that. It's a strong lineage of women I come from.

At this point in your life, what have you made peace with that used to be a struggle for you?

I've really made peace with people not being comfortable with my body. People don't love a little person. They love it if you dress like a clown. They love that. But they don't love a little person who's attached to a militant brain. And so I've made peace with people treating me poorly for my body. I don't mean that I *let* people treat me poorly, but I have made peace with the fact that it's going to happen for the rest of my life. I'm going to try to change it, I'm working to change that perception, but I don't harbor any illusions that I'm going to get rid of all that. And this doesn't mean that when someone says something on the street, I don't clap back, but I do know it's coming. It's more their problem than mine, because when my mouth gets going, you're going to be embarrassed, not me.

What impact do you hope your life and your story will have on those around you?

I hope that people will start to understand how intersectionality is a real thing. And I hope that people will really start looking at how intersectionality can cause you to experience things in a deeper and more traumatic way. I really hope people hear what I've been through and start to understand that business as usual actually doesn't work. It traumatizes a lot of people and leaves a lot of people behind.

Everyone has to look at the way they're interacting with other people and their preconceptions about any group and challenge themselves. Challenge yourself on this. If someone is telling you something and you're saying, "I don't think that's happening to you," you should listen to them.

And I have to investigate myself. People don't even realize that disability is a spectrum. Because I grew up in this society, I've got ideas that are bad, and ableist and racist and all those things, and I have to constantly look around and check myself. I'm not saying I'm perfect, because I'm not. But I do know I have to check myself, and that when someone's trying to tell me something, I have to shut up. I just hope people will listen more.

Susan Falkowski and Vivian Howard

KINSTON, NC

Susan Falkowski, 63, is the front-of-house manager at Chef & the Farmer, a destination restaurant in Kinston, North Carolina, run by chef, restaurateur, cookbook author, and star of PBS's *A Chef's Life* Vivian Howard, 43. Vivian was the first woman since Julia Child to win a Peabody Award for a cooking program, and her debut cookbook memoir, *Deep Run Roots*, was a *New York Times* bestseller. Along with her husband, Ben Knight, Vivian moved back to her hometown of Kinston from New York City in 2006 and found herself struggling to adjust and find the right support at her restaurant until she met Susan, who would end up becoming a close friend and confidant. Years later, both Susan and Vivian realize that they've had a profound impact on each other's lives and how they view the world.

How did you first meet?

SUSAN: I first heard of Vivian back in 2006, when she left New York to come home to open Chef & the Farmer. And I thought, My goodness, what is this young girl thinking? Why would she leave New York and all she has going on there to come home to this rural part of the country where nobody appreciates fine dining? But she did, thankfully. I had been in the restaurant business for years, and I had left for two years to spend some time on my farm.

Everybody kept saying, "You've got to go check out this new chef; she's just wonderful." I gave it a year and I said, "Okay, I'm going to go." And when I did, I walked into Chef & the Farmer in 2007 and had dinner. I was quite impressed with this young woman and applied for a job two weeks later.

VIVIAN: One of our biggest struggles at Chef & the Farmer has always been finding talented people who really love this kind of work. And Susan was legendary in this area for being the best at what she did. I remember I didn't understand why it took her so long to come work with us. And I just remember her first day. I was at the pass, and she was sitting at the bar, which is all the way across the restaurant. And I remember her needing a little bit of time to get into the culture of the restaurant. I remember looking at her at the bar and thinking, Oh, I feel sorry for her.

S: I never really knew that you caught on to that. But it was tough. I would come home and cry. I think at one point I wasn't sure I was going to stay, but then I thought, You know what? That's silly. You're a big girl. So we worked through all that.

Can you describe a moment when you realized that you were going from being coworkers to being more meaningful friends?

S: I remember one of the first conversations we had was about pimento cheese, of all things, and I had your pimento cheese and sausage dip at the restaurant, and I thought it was just fabulous. And we talked about pimento cheese and I thought, We have a lot in common. I remember thinking, You know, I like this girl. This is going to be okay.

V: The early days at Chef & the Farmer were really stressful, and my husband and I waged our wars in front of everyone. And so Susan and everybody that worked at the restaurant were privy to that. And I cried a lot. I cried at the pass, which is where I worked. And I just remember one of my first real conversations with Susan being about how hard it was to work with your husband, and she let me know that she was watching and paying attention, and that she cared about me, and that it bothered her. And so that was, for me, when I started to think of her as a friend and not just a server who came up to the pass asking for their food when it wasn't ready.

S: You were so young and so ambitious, and you had so many things going on, but that was a part that was affecting you, and it just made me want to protect you. I wanted everything to be perfect. We struggled a lot, we had our moments, but to me, you were invincible. And then when I would see that part of you, that vulnerable part of you, and say, "It's okay, we'll get through this. We'll be okay."

What are some of the most meaningful lessons you've learned from each other?

V: From Susan I have learned what it means to be great at what you do and to love it, and to set a standard that other people want to achieve. Watching Susan read a table and identify the person who needs to be made to feel comfortable, I have seen what it means to be a master of your craft. And I think you can only do that when you really love something. Next to my dad, she's the most pure example of someone who loves what they do.

S: It's a joy to watch Vivian create, to be a part of all these wonderful things she has done. It's heartwarming to see how she interacts with people who really want to be a part of her life. It's wonderful to watch her be compassionate with people.

Can you remember a tough time you got through with each other's support?

S: When we had a fire at the restaurant in 2012, which was devastating to all of us, like our own personal home burning, that was very tough. It was hard to figure out how we were going to come back from that, because I think at that point, being in business, we had just turned the corner of really starting to be successful, and then we got that huge

setback for five to six months. But we came in as a team every week and cleaned what we could clean, and salvaged what we could salvage ourselves before the professionals came in. That really brought us closer together; it made us depend on each other and know that we needed each other. It was a time for all of us to put everything aside and just work to bring the restaurant back. And the same thing with the hurricanes; we've had to close for several storms. And when you have to go through that and your livelihood is affected, you learn to depend on each other and know that you can't get through this by yourself, that you need your restaurant family to help. And I certainly looked to Vivian for her leadership with all of that, because we couldn't have done it had she not been at the helm.

V: There have been a lot of experiences over the years when I look at the restaurant and realize that Susan is just my person. I think in part because she's older and in part because she's been in this business longer than I have, and she's seen a lot of seasons come and go, and the rise of success and the slow trickle of a restaurant's death. I feel like she has wisdom that I don't, and I trust her in a way that I don't automatically trust other people.

As you have gotten to know each other better over the years, is there anything you were surprised to learn you have in common?

S: I think we have a tremendous amount of things in common, especially the way we were brought up. We were both farm girls, and we both wanted to escape that in our younger lives. I wanted to get away from my family farm when I was growing up—I think I may have been a little bit ashamed of it at that point. And I tried to go as far away from my farm as I could, and I think Vivian did that as well, on a much grander scale than I.

And then somewhere in our lives, we realized that family and your upbringing are very important. I wanted to come back here, and I think she wanted to come back to her roots. And I think being raised to value family and food is something we have in common.

V: We've always talked about our weight. At the beginning of service every night, Susan would come up to the pass and we'd chat for a few minutes, and she'd always talk about how fat she thought she was. And I would do the same, as I stuffed my face with potato chips.

One of the moments that is tattooed on my brain was a few years ago, after our TV show was out and my cookbook was out and everything was butterflies and rainbows in my world from the outside. And Susan and I were in the server station and she was saying how proud she was of me and how she never could have imagined ten years ago that all this would have happened. And I said something so stupid, but it was what I was thinking at the moment. I said, "It would all be great if I were skinny."

And I don't think I would have said that to anybody else, but it's something that we had talked about personally for years. And she pulled back from me and was like, "Oh my gosh, I'm so disappointed in you now." And I really couldn't stop thinking about that, because I thought Susan would understand why I couldn't really feel like I've accomplished all these things because I still didn't like the way I looked. But she didn't, and that's something I have pondered, and I think it helped me reshape the way I see myself.

S: You look fabulous. But it's a battle we fight every day, isn't it? I think the majority of us do not see ourselves the way other people do; there's always something wrong, there's always something we want to improve. But we're sounding boards for each other, we've been there for support, and I would like to just continue to be able to do what I do on a daily basis.

What makes you proud to call each other friends?

S: It's been wonderful to watch all that she has created and dreamed up. It's more than I ever thought I would get to experience at this stage in my life; it's just wonderful to be a part of that. It's tremendous for me, it really is.

V: I'm proud to call Susan a friend because Susan is a good person with a lot of compassion, and she's been in my life since way before anybody cared about me publicly. So I'm proud of all of my long-term friendships, because I think that says something about those individuals and the degree to which you care about them.

What do you each hope your friendship brings or gives to the other person?

V: I hope Susan sees herself in me and sees that rural country girls can do whatever they want to do, as well as or better than anyone else. I think she's done the same thing I have in a lot of ways, which is really tackle something and become great at it, and give your whole self to it as a means to overcome that little bit of shame you have for being from a rural, country-bumpkin background. I mean, maybe that's a strange hurdle to overcome, but I think it's one we share.

S: There have been times at the restaurant when things were not going so well for me, and all I had to do was reach out to her and she was right there standing by me. I hope she will realize that she has a lot ahead of her still. I'm 63, and she's barely 43. I hope she will continue to develop and grow and expand, and carry this journey that she's on as far as she can. That she'll realize that age is just a number. There's so much that I hope she knows she has ahead of her, because it's going to be a wonderful trip for her.

What advice do you have for someone who is curious about or interested in making new friends of different ages?

V: I think you get so much from people who don't necessarily have the same life experiences as you do. And as I said before, I see wisdom in Susan, and that's something I value. We all lean on our friends for different things. And when all your friends are from basically your same walk of life, it's hard to glean other perspectives. And someone who's lived more life than I have has a perspective that I find really valuable and helpful, and is a good person to have in my friend group.

S: I find that having younger people in my life keeps me current and keeps me learning. You never stop learning, no matter how old you are. We all learn from each other every day.

Herreast Harrison

NEW ORLEANS, LA

Born and raised in Louisiana, Herreast Harrison, 83, has led a life dedicated to learning, teaching, and reading. After the devastation of Hurricane Katrina, she launched a program to bring books to the children of New Orleans, distributing over twenty-three thousand books. Her dedication to the children of New Orleans continued with the establishment of Guardians Institute, founded in honor of her late husband, Donald Harrison Sr., Big Chief of the Guardians of the Flame Mardi Gras Indians. Guardians Institute is dedicated to the development of youth through literacy, New Orleans's indigenous cultural arts, and West African and new-world oral traditions. A quilter since childhood, Herreast has used her sewing skills to create exquisitely beaded and embroidered Mardi Gras suits as well as quilts that have been exhibited in museums across the country. Now she runs Guardians Institute and continues to sew for her daughter, Cherice Harrison-Nelson, the Big Queen of the Guardians of the Flame.

Where did you grow up, and where do you live now?

I was born in a little town in Louisiana by the name of Lecompte. We moved to New Orleans when I was about 6 or 7. I've been here ever since. I'm now 83 years old, so I've been here for quite some time. I went to grade school here, high school, and college. And then I married my husband here. I've worked and operated several businesses here in New Orleans for most of my life.

I love it here because the cultural traditions practiced by people of African descent in New Orleans are really the most wonderful thing to have been connected to. They're the source of who I am. Learning new-world versions of rituals traditionally practiced in Africa has been one of the most profound things that New Orleans has had to offer. Had I been anywhere else, I don't think I would have come into the knowledge of that, or had the understanding or the appreciation of what was happening here.

What did you want to be when you were younger?

My sister and I both wanted to be seamstresses. My sister is two years and seven months older than I am. We are very, very close. We did a lot of mischievous things together. We made a lot of playthings: dolls out of bottles, with straw for hair. We were creative and very inventive. That's when I learned to do design and do our own things as opposed to just following a straight pattern.

My mother did alterations and made all of her own patterns, out of either newspaper or brown paper. So my sister and I learned to make clothes out of scraps for our dolls. Later on, I would make my own prom gowns and embellish them with beads. My sister is still a tailor; she does wedding gowns and fine sewing.

What role do you feel your ancestors, or the women in your family who came before you, play in your life?

I think they've affected me a great deal, because of the things they taught me about how to treat people. Especially people in the community—they taught me how to be helpful and to be a good neighbor if someone was ill. To always make sure you would check on your neighbors, to find out if they needed anything.

Some of those lessons they taught me were sayings that I didn't understand as a child. My mother used to have a saying about how you can take a pitcher to a well only so many times before it gets broken. For the life of me, I couldn't figure out what that meant. But I think it's all starting to come full circle now, and I'm starting to understand

DO EVERYTHING YOU POSSIBLY CAN TO MAKE THE PEOPLE YOU LOVE FEEL COMFORTABLE IN THEIR OWN SKIN. NEVER FORGET TO SAY YOU LOVE THEM.

what some of those sayings meant. I think with the pitcher, it meant that if you have a bad habit, and you keep doing it, at some point it might wreck you and cause you trauma and heartache.

Sometimes when I hear my daughter, who is now in her fifties, passing down some of the things I've taught her to *her* children, it brings me to tears. Just thinking about the depth of what my ancestors taught me that I have passed on to her, that she is now passing on to her children. It was not traditional education, but it was an education that was so rich in depth. This type of ancestral education is so profound that it can shape lives and personalities. This type of wisdom has the ability to endure for all time. To me, that's wonderful. I really am appreciative of what I learned, what they taught me, and what I was able to pass on.

What does your current age feel like for you?

Great. It's great, except my body is not complying as well as I would want it to. Otherwise, it's just great. I wouldn't want to do anything but to change out my body. The wisdom and the knowledge I've gained are priceless. And that gives me the sort of confidence that allows me to never let someone dictate how I should think, what I feel, or what is fact or fiction.

What misconceptions about aging would you like to dispel?

You can and *should* do anything you want to, and really go for it. Ageism can't stop your desire to do or want. You see a lot of people who have put things on their bucket list they want to do, like jumping out of airplanes at 95, and even at 100. I say go and do it—do it all.

What are you most proud of about yourself?

The four children my husband and I brought up. That's our greatest production. I just love the people they turned out to be.

How has your sense of self-confidence or self-acceptance evolved over time?

I don't know how I developed such a strong concept of who I am, but I definitely did. I have one theory that I was always someone who *tried*, not someone who did everything right. So I'm not suggesting

that I didn't have some missteps, because we all do. None of us are perfect. We have done things that other people have been not pleased with. And we've had things done to us that we were not happy about, either. But I have always tried to not let that faze me or bother me. I think I've just always had this level of self-confidence about myself, who I am, and what I am.

Some of that confidence might have come from the fact that I was a great student. Not perfect, but I worked hard. Some of it might have come from my husband, too. If my head had gotten any bigger with every compliment he gave me, I wouldn't have been able to get through the door. He would always say the kindest things. He adored me so much.

When do you feel your most powerful?

When I'm talking to children. It's not so much that I feel powerful in that moment. I just want to give them everything they need to navigate this systematically unjust world. This world can be so cruel to people of African descent—it hurts my soul. It hurts my heart. The criminal justice system as it's practiced is unfair. So many people who are incarcerated are innocent. The unjust distribution of wealth according to race hurts my soul.

I guess I feel more empowered when I'm talking to children because I want to show them how to navigate all these complicated issues. You have to try to be your best, and do your best, and treat others the best. Because you've been conditioned to hate each other and to use all kinds of colorism against each other.

What message do you have for women reading your story here?

Love yourself, always. Give yourself unconditional love. Assess all the things that are happening around you. Listen to the voices of the people who came before you.

Do everything you possibly can to make the people you love feel comfortable in their own skin. Never forget to say you love them.

Mimi Pond

LOS ANGELES, CA

Cartoonist Mimi Pond, 65, is an icon in the art world. She has written for television and countless periodicals, including *National Lampoon*, *The Village Voice*, the *New York Times*, and *Adweek*. She has written and illustrated five books and currently contributes to the *Los Angeles Times*. She won the PEN Center USA Literary Award for Graphic Literature Outstanding Body of Work. Her graphic memoir *Over Easy* was on the *New York Times* bestseller list and won an Inkpot Award from Comic-Con International in San Diego. Mimi now works from her home in Los Angeles, where she lives with her husband (and fellow artist), Wayne White, and their dog, Mabel Brown.

Where did you grow up, and where do you live now?

I grew up in San Diego, California. I went to art school in Oakland, and then I worked there for four years. Then I moved to New York City to pursue my career as a cartoonist and illustrator. That's where I met my husband, Wayne. He was getting more work out here in Los Angeles; we wanted to have a family, and LA was closer to my parents, so that's how we ended up in LA.

What did you want to be when you were younger?

I wanted to be a cartoonist. My dad was an amateur cartoonist, and my parents kept saying, "Oh, she's going to be a cartoonist when she grows up." I thought, Yeah, that sounds good.

What role do you feel your ancestors, or the women in your family who came before you, play in your life?

My mother was always very outspoken and was the dominant one in the relationship with my father. She had a very strong personality and taught me not to be afraid to speak up. But at the same time, she was a product of her background. She was raised in the South and fought her own battles with kowtowing to male authority and then finding herself completely disgusted by it. And I could see that was maddening for her. But it was something I couldn't do.

I remember having this fight with my brother. At one point, he said, "I'm funnier than you are." And I said, "Yeah, but I make money doing it."

So I had this contentious relationship with men from an early age. I watched a lot of women in the humor and comedy business in meetings laughing at guys' jokes even though they weren't funny, and I could see exactly what was going on, but I could never bring myself to laugh at a guy's joke that wasn't funny. It was good for me but bad for my career.

How has your sense of self-confidence or self-acceptance evolved over time?

Well, I tell you, getting older has been the biggest boost to my self-confidence. It was like I woke up at 50 and thought, I'm not putting up with this anymore. I know better than these other people. Why do I think I don't?

I'm really sorry it took me so long to stop second-guessing myself. I always had confidence, but I didn't give myself permission to be that really confident person until I was over 50.

What does your current age feel like for you?

I feel like I'm doing my best work, and I feel like I have the experience of sixty-five years. I have the virtue of all that experience that I can call on. So I don't envy younger people. But at the same time, I'm breaking down physically. Every day, I get creakier, and I've got an arthritic hip, and I just physically can't do as much as I used to be able to do. I don't have that energy I had, so that's a drag. At the same time, I have way more discipline than I

GETTING OLDER HAS BEEN THE BIGGEST BOOST TO MY SELF-CONFIDENCE. IT WAS LIKE I WOKE UP AT 50 AND THOUGHT, I'M NOT PUTTING UP WITH THIS ANYMORE. I KNOW BETTER THAN THESE OTHER PEOPLE. WHY DO I THINK I DON'T?

used to, and, thank God, now I have more time. The kids are grown and out of the house, so I might have more time for my work.

What misconceptions about aging would you like to dispel?

Our generation has started to change a lot of perceptions about what it means to be old. There's so much baked-in ageism in popular culture and movies. It's as if suddenly people are old, infirm, feebleminded, and weak—especially women. It's as if they are completely useless. But our generation is changing that idea, because it's just not true.

How have your ideas of success and happiness changed over time?

I'm pretty happy. I have a husband who loves me, and I have two fabulous children, and I have a beautiful home, and I'm doing exactly what I want to do. At one point, I would have said I would have been happier as a screenwriter, writing for television, but that's another thing that never really panned out—again, because of men. I didn't want it that badly, and my comfort zone is making comics and making stories. I always had total control over my work, and film and television is definitely a collaborative medium that I never learned to work within. My sixth-grade teacher wrote on my report card that I didn't relate well to my peer group.

When do you feel your most powerful?

When I'm working and I manage to make my work look the way I've seen it in my head. And then when other people respond to it in a way that I want them to, that's very gratifying.

At this point in your life, what have you made peace with that used to be a struggle for you?

You have to make peace with feeling uncomfortable. This is the most important thing. Because every day, there's that feeling that I've got a demon and an angel on each shoulder and the demon's saying to me, "What makes you think you can draw? That's disgusting. Look how stupid that is." And the angel's saying, "No, it's good! Keep drawing!" You have to

listen a little bit to both of them and push through that feeling. And when you do, that's the best. I feel like it takes a lifetime to learn that lesson fully.

Who or what has influenced your life the most?

My parents were both good influences on my life. My mother was kind of a loudmouth who stood up for herself and for her kids. She and my father were both very supportive of what I did. I was given a good childhood. I didn't have any horrible things happen except two horrible brothers who were never told to stop torturing me. They would say things like, "You're just a girl!" and you can really internalize that stuff. But my reaction was, "Oh yeah? Well, watch me." So I guess that's a good thing, you know?

Knowing what you know now, what would you go back and tell your younger self?

Have more confidence. Stop second-guessing yourself as much. Assert yourself more. You have as much right as anyone to have an opinion, and your opinion matters.

What impact do you hope your life and your work will have on those around you?

I hope that I make my family proud with what I've done, that they can see me as a role model for getting things done and doing creative work and not taking any shit.

Do you have a message for younger women reading your story here?

Trust yourself; listen to your inner voice. Trust your instincts. They're usually right. Don't let people tell you what to do. Do what you want to do. Figure out what makes you happy, and find a way to do it.

Yunghi Kim

BROOKLYN, NY

Yunghi Kim, 59, is an award-winning photojournalist who has fearlessly covered stories of conflict worldwide, from Rwanda and Iraq to Afghanistan and Kosovo. An immigrant from Korea, Yunghi has bravely told stories of war, protest, and change through her lens—which served as a bridge to communication for her as a child when learning English was a challenge. Yunghi was taken hostage in Somalia during her reporting, only to return and finish her coverage of the Somali famine, which made her a finalist for the Pulitzer Prize. She has received some of her field's biggest awards, including Magazine Photographer of the Year from Pictures of the Year International (POYi), one of only two women to ever receive it; the Olivier Rebbot and John Faber Awards from the Overseas Press Club; the Visa d'or for News from Visa pour l'image in France; and the White House News Photographers Award. Her dedication to her life's work and what she has learned from that work contain a multitude of wisdoms.

Where did you grow up, and where do you live now?

I was born in South Korea, and I came to America when I was 10 years old. I came in 1972 on my birthday. I grew up in the New York City area, but I left at 18 after high school. I lived all over the place, and then I came back in about 2005, and I now live in Brooklyn.

What did you want to be when you were younger?

I was a lost child. I was very shy, which is common for photographers. Because I came here at 10, I had to learn English, and I had a really hard time learning. Language is a really hard thing for me. So I think one of the reasons I became a photographer was because of my hardship with languages. Photography can be a sort of a universal language. I discovered it early, in high school, and it became my passion.

How has being an immigrant shaped your life?

I've also always had great street-smart instincts. My parents left to go to America when I was 2. This is common with immigrants of my generation— they leave the children behind to be raised by the extended families until they're settled in a new country and then they go back and bring the children. So I was raised by my grandmother until I was 10. I didn't see my mother again until I was 10.

When I came to this country, it was the first time I really saw my mother. I had never *seen* her. Korea was on the other side of the earth, and traveling there was very expensive, so she never came to visit us in Korea. I always knew that I was going to America any day now, always. But the waiting was hard. My childhood was about waiting—waiting to go to America. I was always in limbo.

What drew you to the type of photojournalism you do?

Photojournalists have a sense of history. Every event we cover, we do so with an awareness of history, and we take risks to do that. It's part of who I am now. When the COVID-19 pandemic hit, I couldn't stay home and not cover it. And when history is happening, like with the George Floyd protests and Black Lives Matter, I always take that calculated risk to cover it. It's a higher mission; it's not a job. It's not a nine-to-five. I look at it as bearing witness to what's going on in my generation, in our time.

How has deciding not to raise children affected your life?

That's a conscious decision I made early on in my career. In my thirties, my career was peaking, but I could also feel my biological clock ticking. I made the choice to focus on my career because I didn't think it was fair to a child for me to be doing what I'm doing and trying to juggle both. I *couldn't* juggle both.

I think to be a mother, you have to have a commitment, and I wasn't ready for that kind of commitment. I'm very close to my nieces and nephew, and I'm kind of a second mother to them, which has actually been more rewarding for me.

What role do you feel your ancestors, or the women in your family who came before you, play in your life?

I'm Korean, and Korea is a very patriarchal society. But in my family, the men weren't there for the women. And if they were, they weren't helpful. My grandmother had to raise seven children by herself, and my mother was a single mother who raised three kids. My father wasn't any help, and she actually did better without him. He was stuck in the idea of patriarchal Korean society where men are honored by women, and I don't think he adjusted to the shift here.

My mother was a woman ahead of her time. She went into medicine in the late '50s, when women culturally were not encouraged to have a career. But she had one. I come from a long line of very independent, self-sufficient women who had to survive because the men just weren't there.

What does your current age feel like for you?

I don't think about it much. I forget how old I am sometimes. I mean, who counts when you get to your fifties? But I'm still outside taking pictures and running around. It just feels like I'm me. I don't feel 59, and I don't think I look 59, either. But I do feel my body getting slower. When you go to protests to cover them, you've got to run around. I can't run as fast as I used to. I fall a lot. But with age, I still think things are better. I think we have the experience, we have the knowledge, we're disciplined. We have the confidence, and we know how to prioritize.

Older women are a force to be reckoned with—especially minority women, because we were the underdogs. That means we're tougher and grittier. We try harder, and that's always been my philosophy.

What's the biggest risk you've taken in your life, and how has it shaped you?

The biggest risk I took in my life was going into photojournalism, because in Asian families back then, you just didn't do that. You'd go into engineering or you'd go into medicine, and I went into photojournalism. My family was like, "What the hell is that?" I went into photojournalism when it was largely men, certainly not Asian women.

But the reason I got away with not going into medicine or engineering was because my mother was a single mom, and she had to work a lot. She was working three jobs to support her kids. She was working all the time. And my two siblings and I kind of raised ourselves. We never had a babysitter because she didn't have the money. So while she was working, I escaped her attention, and I was able to sneak out and do photography. And she didn't have any say in it.

She basically ignored my career until 1992, when I was sent to Somalia and was held hostage. I got evacuated, but I went back to finish my job because I knew some guy back at the office would say, "Oh, she couldn't cut it." So I went back to Somalia to get the photographs I was originally sent for, and for that harrowing experience and body of photographs, I was a finalist for the Pulitzer Prize. And when I was a finalist, then, in a very Korean way, I finally registered with my mom. I went through a period where I got a lot of recognition and she would come with me to award ceremonies and she was very proud. After that (and her getting to meet Barbara Walters and Peter Jennings), she took a keen interest in my career. There was finally no more, "Do you want to go to med school?"

Where do your inner strength and determination come from?

I get it from my mother. She was spunky. She was four foot eleven. She had a thick Korean accent, but her written English was perfect. She was very smart. When she would go out to department stores with her thick accent, people would treat her badly because she was an immigrant. But I saw her move mountains. If she put her mind to something, she'd just do it. My mother was my role model, but she wasn't a typical nurturing mother. I didn't have the

OLDER WOMEN ARE A FORCE TO BE RECKONED WITH—ESPECIALLY MINORITY WOMEN, BECAUSE WE WERE THE UNDERDOGS. THAT MEANS WE'RE TOUGHER AND GRITTIER. WE TRY HARDER.

mother-daughter bonding that other people have—but I respected her. She wasn't always there for me emotionally, but she did the best she could. And if you look at what she did—put three kids through college by herself—it's noble. I have no baggage about that.

How has your sense of self-confidence or self-acceptance evolved over time?

It was all because of photography. It's something that came naturally to me. Once during the Iraq War in 2003, I was on assignment for *Time* magazine and I was in Iraq near the border of Turkey. The border was closing, and I worried I wasn't going to be able to get into Iraq from Turkey to cover the war. So I walked into Iraq. Tell me, what guy does that?

I literally walked into Iraq with what I could carry—which was two cameras, two lenses, and a satellite phone, no clothes—and with one colleague and a guide. I walked in monsoon rain into Iraq, and it took four nights. And then I couldn't talk about it for ten years because it was an illegal border crossing. So on the tenth anniversary of the Iraq War, in 2013, I wrote a piece for *National Geographic*, from memory, about what I had gone through. Now, with social media, you'd be tweeting everything. I'd be like a rock star. But back then, you just didn't do that. You just went, just went quietly. And so that inner strength and confidence I have is real. And it comes from my mother.

What are you most proud of about yourself?

My photographs. My photographs are a testament to my accomplishments, and nobody can take that away from me. I earned it. I risked my life for it. And they're a record of history. So that's how I look at it.

I'm specifically proud of the series I did on Korean comfort women [women and girls forced into sexual slavery by the Japanese army before and during World War II]. I helped introduce that issue to America in the '90s. It was an intensely personal project. It wasn't an assignment. I thought it was an important thing to do because as a Korean American, the issue of comfort women affects all families. Because it's about their daughters, or it *could* be about their daughters.

When do you feel your most powerful?

When I'm taking pictures. Because I have the ability to capture images that impact people. My photographs are emotional and intimate, and I think those are important things about them. My job is to inform, but also to provoke thinking. When viewers see a photograph, they can relate to it. Even if it's just a half second that you look at—it should evoke curiosity. A picture should make you say, "Wow." And I think that's the power of photojournalism.

Knowing what you know now, what would you go back and tell your younger self?

I would tell myself to not be so hard on myself. But also, why look back? I look forward. What's the point of obsessing over something you did? I take a long time to make a decision, but once I make it, I don't waste time looking back—I only look forward.

What do you see when you look forward? What do you imagine your future looks like?

I am still shooting. I'm in the process of organizing my archive. I'd like to do a book. The thing is, as you get older, you have tons of ideas. That's the beautiful thing about getting old. I didn't have so many ideas in my twenties and thirties. I was just trying to fit in, to prove myself. Now I don't feel like I have to prove myself. I have ideas, and I can make a statement with them, lead the way. I started a grant, so I give back to photojournalism. I've been advocating for copyrights for photographers, to educate them about copyrights. I think getting older, you're more focused, and you see the picture of what needs to be done with your ideas and figure out how to do it.

The older I get, I realize the variety of situations I've been exposed to. That includes being on the streets photographing Black Lives Matter events and seeing all these emotions and all the anger and hurt. You feel it when you're out. I'm richer because I've seen all that.

Is there anything about your work that people should know that they don't?

That it's physically and mentally very tough. The situations you're exposed to are fluid. Writers can do an interview after the fact. Photojournalists can't; they have to be on the ground as it happens. And you have to position yourself early.

When I went into Somalia in 1992, I had to be in position in Mogadishu on the beach before the marines came and landed. So I flew in a little bush plane, which was terrifying, but we had to get in. So I did it. I was in position on the beach when the first Special Forces landed in the middle of the night. It takes a lot of resources and physical and mental strength to be a photojournalist.

What misconceptions about aging would you like to dispel?

I think it was Paulina Porizkova who said that at age 55, you're dismissed from the table and from the conversation. There's truth to that. But personally, I have a lot of stuff I want to do, so I don't know what anyone's talking about in terms of being dismissed. I was out during COVID-19 taking pictures. Who else does that at this age?

I would say that I am more selective with my time as I get older. I think you do everything and make your choices with a little bit more grace. You don't feel like you have to do everything—you can do things in a way that is enjoyable to you. And then you do them in a way that helps you take care of your community. And for me, that's photojournalists. Giving back becomes important. You look at it differently. It's beyond yourself. It's taking care of your people.

At this point in your life, what have you made peace with that used to be a struggle for you?

I wish I were a better speaker. But I don't think I'm going to be a better speaker because it's just not the way my thought process works. But I learned to compensate with my photography, because I think if you look at my photographs, they have depth and layers of emotions. But if you talk to me, I may not be able to articulate that same thing.

How have your ideas of success and happiness changed over time?

When I was younger, it was about getting validation and recognition. But as I get older, that's not as important. Now it's more about doing projects where you're giving back to the community.

Do you have a message for younger women reading your story here?

You will meet doubters in your journey; let that motivate you to prove them wrong. Persevere. Have faith in yourself, but also know it takes time and patience to cultivate any talent and understanding of the industry surrounding the craft you choose. So do your homework and look at the long game, the craft you choose as your life's journey. My motto is "Doubt my ability, and I will prove you wrong."

What impact do you hope your life and your work will have on those around you?

I want people to remember that I was tough, but that I cared about those around me and I showed it not in words but in actions. My photographs speak for me; they're a record of what I witnessed, and they're a record of history.

Mickey Thoman

and

Mary Thoman

SWEETWATER COUNTY, WY

Cowgirl Mickey Thoman lives and breathes life on the ranch. As the matriarch of a large ranching family in Sweetwater County, Wyoming, Mickey has raised and cared for her seven children and countless animals on her family's property near the Green River. She oversaw the construction of a one-room schoolhouse on her family's land so her children (and grandchildren) could stay, learn, and work on the ranch for years to come. Now, at the age of 92, Mickey still works around the ranch, cares for her horses, and serves as an election overseer in her county. She sat down to talk with one of her daughters, Mary, 72, now town commissioner, about their work on the ranch, and what their intergenerational connection has taught them about life.

Where did you grow up, and where do you live now?

MICKEY: I was born and raised on a ranch north of Kemmerer, Wyoming. I lived there until I got married, and now I live here on our family ranch in Sweetwater County.

MARY: I was born in Kemmerer, where Mom and Dad were living at the time. Then they bought a ranch on the Green River, so I spent the rest of my life at the ranch on the Green River. I went to the one-room ranch school on our property, and so did my kids. I went to Green River for high school and then on to college.

Do you remember what you wanted to be when you were little girls?

MICKEY: I just wanted to always live on a ranch and ride a horse.

MARY: My grandma used to say my mother would walk five miles to catch a horse so she didn't have to walk.

What role do your ancestors, or the women in your family who came before you, play in your lives?

MICKEY: We lived on the ranch all our life and did ranch work. Worked with livestock. Just like all the women that came before me.

MARY: There were seven of us children, and we had the one-room school here on the ranch. So Mom always took the lead in taking care of the cattle, and my dad and the boys took the lead in taking care of the sheep. She was always outdoors and had all of us with her, helped each of us train our own horse. My grandmother was more of an indoor person, a really good cook. But she would go out and help, too.

MICKEY: The women in our family are no strangers to hard work.

Can you share some of your most fun memories together?

MARY: I think one of the best memories I have with Mom is her taking me to the corral every day to train my first horse by myself. Well, with her help, of course. It took all summer. Mom has a patient way with horses. She gets them; she spent all her free time at the corral going around, bonding with

THE WOMEN IN OUR FAMILY ARE NO STRANGERS TO HARD WORK.

the new calves and the horses and getting them to trust her. They bond with her really fast because she's patient with them.

MICKEY: Mary was a big help to me. I always did the ranch chores, and Mary would look after the little ones. She was very good with them. She was like a grown-up mother, even though she was just a kid. But she also liked to be outside and ride. I actually raised the kids in a sheep camp. When I got married, I took the kids with me after they were born.

MARY: Every summer, she went to the mountain with the kids—until there were four kids. It was taking three camps to house us for the summer. So we had our sheep wagons that we lived in during the summer and then we lived in the ranch on the river in the winter.

Mickey, were you always close with your children or was that something that happened as they all grew up?

MICKEY: When I was younger, I had to go to boarding school when it came time for high school because we got snowed in too often here to commute. I swore that I was going to raise my own kids—somebody else wasn't going to raise them. So it was quite a lot of work to get a school on the ranch. But we finally did. We found a good teacher and had school in the front room until Christmas. Then we got a one-room schoolhouse built for them. We've had that up and running on our ranch for fifty-nine years now. I wanted us to be close, so we built the school here so the kids could always be at home on the ranch with us.

What is your favorite part about ranch life?

MICKEY: Having your family together and working together. And being around the animals.

MARY: The peace and the quiet. We're fifty miles from town here at the ranch, so I've never really had a community. I've always enjoyed going to town, going to my meetings or going shopping—but then coming home, it was just absolute peace and quiet.

Mary, you were recently elected county commissioner. Are you the first person in the family to hold public office?

MARY: I've been a conservation district supervisor and chairman for twenty-one years. My father was on the school board for seventeen years. He spent seventeen years doing all the difficult reorganization when the counties were combining districts. He went through lawsuits and all sorts of meetings. Our family has always been in public service. We belong to Farm Bureau stock boards, all the organizations that affect our business.

Mary, what's one of the most meaningful things you've learned from your mom?

MARY: To just have patience. She's always the one, the go-to one. If we can't find something, Mom will always say, "I'll get it. I can do it." That's probably the most valuable thing we have with our mother. She's the peacemaker. Sometimes I try to get all the kids in the same room, and she doesn't want them to argue, so she'll go from kid to kid and try to talk them through something, when I just think, Get them together and get it over with.

Mickey, what's one of the most meaningful things you've learned from Mary?

MICKEY: I guess just being able to work with my daughter and my family as a group here on the ranch. It taught me that we always come home to each other.

MARY: Being together is important to our family. My mom has lost two children. She's raised all of us without drinking, drugs, cigarettes, or any bad habits. But she lost my sister in a drowning accident when my sister was 22. Five years later, my brother, who had two little kids and a wife living with him on the ranch, was killed in a truck accident. So she's had to go through some pretty grueling tragedies. And then my father, he died twenty-two years ago.

What got you through those tough times?

MICKEY: Just going out and doing chores. Keeping busy with the animals and talking to them helped. I didn't have the time to feel sorry for myself—I just kept busy. That was the best cure.

MARY: Mom's personality changed after we lost my dad because she was always the stay-at-home mom, quiet. Dad always took the lead with the business and everything. After Dad died, boy, she got out, wanted to go to all the meetings, all the dances, and all the conventions, and she took a more active role.

Mickey, what did it feel like to have that change in your life after your husband died?

MICKEY: I don't think I changed all that much, but my daughter says I did. I guess I just tried to get out there and do more and do what he did. My husband took me around the desert and told me all the places that we had sheep and what they did. He kept a diary, so I would go back and look through the diary, day by day, and see what we did on certain times and try to keep that up. Now I write in a book, too, important things that come up that I think the kids should know.

MARY: Well, she has over twenty grandkids now, and she has all their birthdays written down so she can remember to call them, which is better than I can do. She will have a lot of help at the ranch when she wants it.

Knowing what you know now, is there anything you would go back and tell your younger self?

MICKEY: Not really. I think that's part of the way I was raised and the way I was . . . the way I've been up until now. I wouldn't change my life that much. I'm happy with how I grew up and what my life has been.

MARY: Well, I guess I would say it's funny what you wish for, because sometimes it comes about in a different way than you expect or plan. Because I've been through so many different occupations, actually, besides being tied to the ranch all the time. When I was a kid, I always wanted to be a veterinarian, but I thought, I can't do that because I can't stand the sight of blood, even though I had to see blood caring for the animals. So as it turns out, I became a schoolteacher and taught business. And then I won two fellowships, so I went back to Colorado State University, got my master's and my PhD. So I did become a doctor, just an education doctor instead of a blood doctor.

MICKEY: Then she learned to fly, and eventually she ended up with her own airplane. She'd fly around and check on the livestock.

MARY: Well, I sold the airplane, but I still love to fly. Every time a neighbor goes, I try to jump a ride.

What's the biggest lesson you have learned from your animals?

MICKEY: Patience.

MARY: Yeah, patience, definitely. And that everybody says sheep are dumb, but I've been outsmarted by them quite a few times.

Mary, what makes you most proud to call Mickey your mom?

MARY: The way she was able to raise all of us and have a healthy, happy family that had good values and worked hard.

Mickey, what would you like people to know about life on a ranch?

MICKEY: I guess I'd like them to know how our kids grew up and how responsible they were and how hard they wanted to work. I think if more people knew about our life on the ranch, they might be jealous, because it helped us keep our family together and teach them good things. Because to get kids to do something, you got to work *with* them. If you want them to do something, go help them.

What does your current age feel like for you?

MICKEY: I kind of hate it, because I go down and see things that need doing, and I can't move fast enough to get them done. But I'm lucky to be able to move around, I guess.

MARY: But she stays out there all day and does it anyway. She just has more aches and pains. I try not to think about my age. I don't feel like I'm as old as I am; I feel like I'm still really active and excited about my new role in life as commissioner. I can't be held back by my age. And my mother certainly hasn't been held back by hers.

What keeps you going, Mickey? What makes you excited looking forward?

MICKEY: To just get up and move. To do things I want to do.

MARY: Mom got run down by a cow two years ago. She cracked some ribs. It's slowed her down for a while. But the doctor said, "You need to get out there and you swing your arms and you get down to the barn every day. Keep moving."

MICKEY: You find yourself having a harder time picking up your feet, but I'm lucky I haven't fallen.

How has your family shaped your life?

MICKEY: I raised seven good kids. And they have their kids. None of them drink or smoke or get in trouble. So I'm thankful for all the well-being our family has and how that's let us live the life we do.

MARY: My family instilled that work ethic and that love of the land in me. It's a deep love of the animals and the ranch, too. A lot of kids can't wait to get away from the farm or the ranch. They want to get out and explore the world. All of us, even the grandkids, are buying ranches and farms and staying in agriculture. It's just amazing, during these times when it's so costly and the return is so poor, that they are excited to be doing that and trying to find ways to survive and keep in it.

Elaine Denniston

DORCHESTER, MA

Elaine Denniston, 82, started her career as a data keypuncher and "rope mother" for NASA's Apollo Program in 1966. Though she was an invaluable part of the project (often alerting coders to their mistakes), there was no opportunity for her at the lab, so she enrolled in Radcliffe College (now part of Harvard University) the following year. After graduation, Elaine attended Boston University School of Law and practiced law, after which she moved on to administrative work until her retirement. Having played a part in so many crucial projects, both Earth- and Moon-based, Elaine is now happy to play an important role at her church, where she is on the vestry.

Where did you grow up, and where do you live now?

I grew up in Roxbury, Massachusetts, in a housing project with my mother, who was a teacher. I went to Boston public schools, and now I live in Dorchester, Massachusetts. In the intervening years, I lived in Allston, which is another part of Boston, and in Cambridge when my children were growing up.

What did you want to be when you were younger?

I wanted to be a pharmacist. I was born in 1939, so I grew up in the '40s and '50s. Women's roles were very, very different then. I figured a pharmacist would be a nice job. I didn't want to be a nurse, and I definitely didn't want to be a teacher.

I ended up going to college and then law school, which I chose because I still didn't want to be a teacher. I had two children. My husband was a doctor, and I didn't want to compete with him. I figured that if I went to law school, I'd be done in three years, so that's not too many years, because remember, I had children when I went to college. I would do my studying during reading periods while they were in school. When I went to law school, I would study in the evening. My children were home. They had simple TV dinners.

I used to worry that I was getting educated on the backs of my children and that they were being left out because I wasn't there to be the at-home mother. But my children were made of better stuff than I gave them credit for. They've all shined their lights in their own ways.

What does your current age feel like for you?

In my head, I know I'm 82. But I don't look 82, even with gray hair. I'm sprightly and always on the go, but my body lets me know I'm not the young chicken I used to be. I used to do a whole lot of things that I can't do now. If I go to the museum and walk and stand for two or three hours, I feel the effects for the rest of the day, but I go anyway.

I've had two knee replacements. My back hurts a lot. I have arthritis in my back, in my hands, in my ankles, in my knees. You name a joint, I've got arthritis in it. I've had cataract surgery for both eyes, and I wear trifocals. I definitely can't stand or walk for long amounts of time, but I do all right.

I don't know what 82 is *supposed* to feel like. I know a lot of people who are younger than I am who look as old or older. So I'll take what I can.

How has your sense of self-confidence or self-acceptance evolved over time?

Well, I went to Girls' Latin, which is a competitive academic high school here in Boston. There were all these very smart people there, and I was just this kid. I was one of six Black students in a class of 125. I kind of was in the middle of the class. But I remember we had this one exam in chemistry. It was given to everybody who took chemistry—I think maybe even in the city? And at my school, I had the highest score.

I've had bumps along the way, but I've felt better about myself as time has gone on.

What are you most proud of about yourself?

I think I'm most proud of my children. I'm very proud of what they did under the circumstances because I thought I was depriving them. In reality, I was probably giving them space to grow on their own.

What misconceptions about aging would you like to dispel?

Even though it's trite, age *really* is just a number. I think people expect old ladies to sit and knit. And I can't knit because of my arthritis. But I can do a lot of other things. I like to have dinners with my friends, but if I don't take a nap, I will be toast before the end of the meal, so I always take a nap, even if it's only an hour. That's something I never used to have to do. But you know, you can still do things; you just have to plan them better.

What's the biggest risk you've taken in your life, and how has it shaped you?

Going to college was my biggest risk, and it turned my life around totally. Prior to that, I had been working at keypunching. My supervisor left to have a baby, and they brought in this guy. They had me showing him how to do what I did. So they organized a department around him and boom, he's my boss now. They told me he was chosen over me because I wasn't going to be able to fix the computer if it crashed, which is *kind* of legitimate, but they could have easily made a plan in that case since there were plenty of other people around. The man who took that job said he was going to Northeastern University, so I thought, Hmm, I'll show them.

I went home and talked to my husband. I said, "Well, I guess I'll apply to Northeastern, BU, and Suffolk." He said, "Well, why don't you apply to that school across the river?" I said, "Harvard?" He said, "Yeah, that one."

I requested an application. The school called me and said, "We want to interview you first." I went in for the interview, and they asked me all the usual questions. They asked, "Why do you want to go to Harvard?" And I said, "Well, I know I'll get a good education, and besides, it's the closest."

I walked home, not knowing how the interview had gone. I called my husband to say, "Is there anything you need from Harvard Square while I walk home?" And he said, "No, but Radcliffe just called. Your application's in the mail." I never thought in a million years that I would go to Harvard, but I did.

Knowing what you know now, what would you go back and tell your younger self?

I would tell myself that others' opinions of who I am do not matter, and that goes for my mother, too. My mother told me I couldn't sing. And, well, I *can* sing. You have to learn to stand on your own feet and realize that your value is your value, and nobody can take it from you.

When do you feel your most powerful?

In the morning of a bright and sunny day, I get up, and by the time I finish doing my morning exercises, singing, I'm ready to hit the day.

Do you have a message for younger women reading your story here?

Don't let yourself be guided by and think your value depends on other people's expectations or negative opinions.

What impact do you hope your life and your story will have on those around you?

I hope the biggest thing you can take from my life is that things don't have to go the way you plan them. Your path may be totally changed by circumstances that you have no idea about right now. Sometimes a disappointment can be the opening for a wonderful opportunity.

YOU HAVE TO LEARN TO STAND ON YOUR OWN FEET AND REALIZE THAT YOUR VALUE IS YOUR VALUE, AND NOBODY CAN TAKE IT FROM YOU.

Joan E. Biren

and

Amelie Zurn-Galinsky

SILVER SPRING, MD

Joan E. Biren, 77, and Amelie Zurn-Galinsky, 57, have been friends for over thirty years. Joan (also known as JEB) is a groundbreaking filmmaker and internationally recognized documentary artist whose work has honored and documented the LGBTQIA+ community for decades. Amelie is a talented clinical social worker and queer health activist who lives next door to Joan. Their friendship explores the boundaries of how we consider platonic relationships, deep connection, and chosen family.

How did you first meet?

AMELIE: I don't actually remember the first time we met, because I think we saw each other out and about at a lot of AIDS and LGBTQIA+ actions in the late '80s and early '90s. But my first memory of a long talk with you was when we were trying to get Whitman-Walker, the local lesbian and gay health clinic, to return to its commitment to lesbian health. You came by to get some pictures of the health conference, and we ended up talking about the movement, AIDS organizing, and losing so many of our loves.

JOAN: I, who remember very little, remember that conversation quite clearly. I remember saying to myself, Oh, this is a really smart person. I think I need to get to know her better. I enjoy talking to this Amelie.

How has your relationship evolved from your initial impression of each other?

A: From that first moment, I always felt like I was curious about what Joan would think. How would she see it? And will I see her at X, Y, and Z action or meeting? The next time we ran into each other was when the Mary-Helen Mautner Project for Lesbians with Cancer was founded in the spring of 1990. We were at the early organizing meetings in Susan Hester's house on Capitol Hill. I was most definitely one of the younger people there by at least twenty years, because there are exactly twenty years between Joan and me. I remember thinking, I want to be a part of all these things. I just remember having really beautiful conversations, even at a time when we were discussing these really difficult things.

Then I moved to Silver Spring with my lover at the time. We started doing Jewish stuff together with Joan because we had a kiddo who was 12 and we started having Shabbats. You would come over, and we started making it a ritual. I became curious about how we could make family time together and how we could have that family time that infused kind of a combination of pagan, radical witchiness with a Jewish thread. I loved doing all those Jewish rituals with you and making family with you.

From there it's evolved into our art and activism, and now that we're in this later part of our lives, we're starting to ask ourselves, What do we still want to do? I love that question that keeps being asked between us about "What have we done that's good and that we want to leave for other folks to know about, and what do we want to keep doing?" That's a vital part of what's meaningful in our friendship.

How do you describe your relationship?

J: We used to go places together, and sometimes I would have to introduce Amelie, and I would say things like, "Amelie is my sister/comrade/neighbor." And then we would see the confusion waft over the face of whomever we were speaking to. I wanted better language to tell people how special you were to me, so I think for at least a month we worked on that, and we settled on saying we were nonromantic life partners. And we were so excited because it seemed like a big advance over sister/comrade/neighbor.

But these days, I'm thinking that description is not as good. I'm thinking that nonromantic is not the right word, because I think our relationship has a lot of romance in it. You bring me flowers, you send me sweet texts, you cook me soup. We don't have a sexual relationship, but to me, we do have a romantic relationship, so we're going to have to go back and work on the naming again.

But I think that the name doesn't matter as much as the fact that we want people to acknowledge and respect that we have a relationship that is both intimate and committed. And a lot of people have these sorts of relationships. And I think it's popping up more and more. People like Mia Mingus and Mia Birdsong have been talking a lot about how we should have celebrations for falling in friendship love. And that's a way to acknowledge it.

I like what Alok Vaid-Menon posted on Instagram. They said, "I want a world where friendship is appreciated as a form of romance. I want a world that doesn't require us to be in a sexual romantic partnership to be seen as complete. I want a movement that fights for all forms of relationship. I want a world where our security isn't linked to our monogamy."

Your relationship is so significant. Can you describe a moment when you realized that it would last for a lifetime?

J: Well, it's a problem that relationships like ours don't get the same social recognition and legal protections that come with marriage. Everybody deserves these benefits. And the truth is, less than half the people in this country live in nuclear families, but nuclear families are still upheld as the ideal and presented as the norm, even when they don't work.

So, this summer, Amelie and I worked very hard with the other people in our chosen family to finalize all the documents that I needed to make sure that my wishes would be recognized in this messed-up legal system. So that the people I wanted to take care of me could take care of me. That took a lot of work, and it was very expensive. But when it was over, it brought me a lot of peace, and everybody deserves this. And my very smart friend Nancy Polikoff, who is a family lawyer, has proposed a registration system called a designated family relationship, where anyone married or not could just choose the person they wanted to make decisions about their health care, and financial guardianship, and inheritance, and burial, and all those things.

A: There are two moments that I think about that are super significant in our relationship around this issue of claiming family and saying you'll show up for the other person. One was when Joan was diagnosed with cancer in December 2010, and I said, "We gotta shop around. We gotta figure out what you want to do, but know that I'll be at every appointment as much as I can be there." And one of the things that I loved about that framework and that gift to Joan, and to myself, was the steadiness that it provided her at that time.

I said to my co-parents, Licia and Tamara, who were helping me raise my kids, "I need your help and support. What I need from you is to watch the kids, do school lunches, do pickups, so that I can be at chemo appointments, surgery appointments, consultations, and follow-ups—no matter how long this takes."

WE SHOULD HAVE CELEBRATIONS FOR FALLING IN FRIENDSHIP LOVE.

On chemo days, I would dress up and bring Joan our ceremonial coffee and breakfast, and we'd drive down to get chemo. It made me feel like we were bringing all the energy and love from the place we live and the community we live in. We were bringing that all with us. It just made it so clear that it's a team, and that the team is someone showing up. And I remember how much surprise and joy it gave to the nursing staff.

J: The other significant moment was when you brought up the possibility of making a retirement fund for me. And I rejected it. I think it was partly because I think of myself as someone who likes to think she can be self-sufficient and self-reliant. I was also afraid it would mess up our relationship, because I had seen other relationships where money got in the way of things. But fortunately, the opposite has been the case. Accepting your offer, your generous offer of financial help, has taken away a huge fear. You don't even know how big the fear is until you can let go of it. It has allowed me all kinds of freedom and ways to think that I hadn't been able to think or act before, and I'm so grateful.

What are some of the most meaningful lessons you've learned from each other?

J: Amelie has taught me to be more generous by example, because she is one of the most generous people I know. She is a wonderful mother and an incredible social worker and therapist. Every day, she is managing a household and being with family and running a business on her own, but then she finds time to do things like deliver food to immigrant families every week during the summer, donate plasma and platelets once a month during the pandemic, volunteer as an election judge, be part of the sign building for actions like Black Lives Matter. All of this in addition to being so attentive to the many beloveds she has in her life. So I know I can't keep up, but I do my best.

Amelie also taught me to be less jealous, because in the course of my long life, I have had a lot of relationships. Long-term relationships, short-term relationships, monogamous relationships, polyamorous relationships, but I never did very well with the polyamorous ones because I was always very jealous. Amelie is the least jealous person I

have ever known, met, or heard of, hands down. I'm not jealous of the many other people in her life whom she loves and cares for. I don't feel like I'm in any kind of competition with them, because I want her happiness, and that's what makes me happy. So I'm thankful to Amelie for teaching me that so I can really believe it. You can't do it in theory, you know; you have to do it in your heart.

Amelie also pushes me all the time to do more to help others and work harder for a just world and to deal with my own racism. Because we're Jewish, we talk a lot about the meaning of tikkun olam. What does it mean to repair the world? How do we apply that to reparations for Black people, restoring land to Indigenous people, defunding unjust systems in our society? These are the things we talk about all the time. As an older person, it keeps me moving in a good direction.

A: I think that a gift Joan has given me is perspective. The dialogue that we've had has always been so vibrant because she does not talk down to me. Joan never said, "Why are you, this young person, in the middle of this cancer movement with a bunch of gray-haired people?" She always honored and respected that I had something to say and something to bring.

I always feel a mutual trust that we'll figure things out, that even if we misstep in our words, or our thinking, or our hearts, we will find a way to understand each other and hear each other. That is just such a valuable piece of our friendship, and it started for me on that first day and has been true throughout.

Is there anything you were surprised to learn you have in common?

A: Yes. I was a reluctant dog mom at first. When we started living next door to each other, our dogs, Sadie and Cory, would just basically hang out at each other's house all day long. It created such a beautiful friendship between the two dogs, and so many of my conversations with Joan were over the fence, talking about the dogs, or collecting the dogs, or being together with the dogs. So our shared love of these two dogs, that neither of us realized we would fall in love with, was a total surprise. That it brought us together was a total surprise in our friendship because I don't think I would have guessed that.

J: Well, we've both had issues with boundaries. We both love this quote from Prentis Hemphill: "Boundaries are the distance at which I can love you and me simultaneously." I used to jump very quickly to try to solve every problem that came up. I wanted to have all the answers, but I had to learn that I am not Amelie's problem solver. Now I try to be the person who will listen attentively until the end and see if you ask for any help or if just listening was the help. So I think the surprising thing is that Amelie believes me now more when I say that certain things (like listening) are not a burden. I think you believe me when I say that it's an honor, because it brings us closer and it increases our trust and lets me give something back to you.

I trust you to set the boundaries that you need. I think you know I will do my best to respect those boundaries and not feel rejected, or like I was overstepping. We do get in trouble sometimes, but we tend to work it out pretty quickly. I know we both get hurt feelings now and then, but we don't hang on to them, and we have lots of conversations about what works and what doesn't work.

Why do you think you came into each other's lives when you did?

J: I am so, so grateful for my relationship with Amelie, but I know that there are so many LGBTQIA+ older adults who are much, much more isolated and lonely than I am, and than their heterosexual counterparts are. My generation was less likely to have children, so we don't have children to help us out, and we're more likely to be estranged from our biological families because biological families were more intolerant in past generations. Professional caregivers are still often prejudiced against LGBTQIA+ people, and rarely get any kind of cultural competency training. So LGBTQIA+ people are reluctant to go into places for assisted living, or senior centers, or nursing homes, or anything like that because they're afraid they're going to be met with hostility and violence.

I don't know why we came into each other's lives at the time we did, but I know I'm very blessed to be in community with Amelie, and that I want to keep working with her to help make the world a place where more people can be held and loved and safe and have friendships like ours.

Rosita Worl

JUNEAU, AK

Rosita Worl, 84, is the president of the Sealaska Heritage Institute in Juneau, Alaska. An Alaska Native, Rosita is a cultural, political, and business leader in her community, working to preserve and celebrate the Tlingit, Haida, and Tsimshian Native cultures of southeast Alaska. Her work has been recognized with countless honors, including the Gloria Steinem Award for Empowerment (1989); Nation Women's Political Caucus Women of Courage Award (2003); National Museum of the American Indian Smithsonian Institution Honor (2006); Lifetime Achievement Award, Central Council of the Tlingit and Haida Indian Tribes of Alaska (2011); and Alaska Federation of Natives Citizen of the Year Award (2011). She holds both a PhD and an MS in anthropology from Harvard University and an honorary Doctor of Science degree from the University of Alaska Anchorage. She now lives, works, and lectures from her home in Juneau, Alaska.

Where did you grow up, and where do you live now?

The first years of my life were spent in Petersburg, Alaska. Our family moved from our homeland in Jilkaat Kwaan to seek employment opportunities. After my biological mother's death, I lived with my grandparents until I was kidnapped at the age of 6 and brought to a Presbyterian mission boarding home, ironically, in our homeland in Haines, Alaska. It took three years for my mom, who was actually my aunt, to get me out of Haines House and take me to Juneau. (In our culture, sisters are recognized as mothers to their collective offspring, and those offspring consider one another brothers and sisters.) I lived in Juneau until I graduated from high school. I returned to Juneau in 1986 to work as the special staff assistant for Alaska Native and Rural Affairs to Governor Cowper and have continued to live here since.

What did you want to be when you were younger?

I loved my life growing up in Juneau, and in the summer months, I was fortunate to go commercial fishing with my aunt and uncle in Kake or work in the salmon canneries. In the winter months, I would travel with my mother to various communities in southeast Alaska. She was the salmon cannery union representative, and I would take minutes of the meetings. I didn't have a specific career objective in mind, but during my travels with my mother, she instilled in me the notion that I had a responsibility to work for our Peoples.

What does your current age feel like for you?

My grandmother would say to me at the age of 96 that her mind was strong and clear, but she said that when she walked, she would stagger as if she were "drunk." She couldn't reconcile her body's age with that of her mind. I visited her when she was dying in the hospital. I walked into her room, and she immediately tried to fix her hair and tidy her hospital gown. I could see that she was embarrassed because of her appearance. I told her I had to run and get something and left the room. I stayed out long enough for her to tidy herself and then returned to the room. I share the same sentiments as my grandmother. I am beginning to feel the constraints of my aging body, which seem to be exacerbated by being quarantined at home during this pandemic, but my mind is still clear, and I continue to work up to ten hours a day and most every weekend.

Additionally, I know that Westerners and Natives have different conceptions of age. Based on our cultural practices, it was common for women to marry men who were either younger or considerably older than them. Even in our contemporary dances, it is common to see younger men dancing with much older women. We don't have the same generational divide that we see in

Western societies. However, in our culture, Elders have a special respected status. I often say, "When I get old . . ." and then I laugh and immediately correct myself and say, "Oh, I am old!" My chronology of years says that I am 84, but I have to say I don't feel like I am yet an Elder. To answer your question, I would say that I feel about the same as I did when I was around 40 or 50.

What misconceptions about aging would you like to dispel?

While I don't like to see older women dressing as if they are teenyboppers, I think Western societies are obsessed with growing old. In our culture, we grow more valuable as we age, and I think that is a good value. Although seniors may not be as physically active and strong as we were in our youth, with the right attitude, we can accept that we have many other strengths.

How has your sense of self-confidence or self-acceptance evolved over time?

Growing up and living in my own Native world, I've never had issues about self-confidence or self-acceptance. However, when I initially started interacting with the non-Native world, I began to realize that we were "poor," although I had never thought about us in those terms. I also began

to see that for the most part, non-Natives, both institutions—schools, churches, movie theaters—and individuals, looked down on us. I remember going to a public library, and the librarian put paper towels on top of her desk as we children approached. I remember her muttering "Snotty Indians!" I was among the first and few Natives to go to the white high school, while other Natives went to the Indian boarding school. I remember a boy spitting down on me as I went up the stairs. I ran up those stairs, grabbed him, and threw him down the stairs, and then I ran down to kick him as he lay on the landing. Another time, while sitting on the benches in the gym for chorus, a student kicked me in the back. I turned around and grabbed him and threw him on the floor and kicked him back. I was all of five foot two and just over a hundred pounds, but I knew how to fight from wrestling with my brothers. The other students didn't bother me too much after that.

I don't think I lacked self-confidence or self-acceptance, as I always had pride in our family; we were a strong family, and I could always manage to care for myself. What I learned is that I didn't have to fight physically—that I could use my mind and words instead. I've taught my children and my grandchildren that the pen is mightier than the sword.

What role do you feel your ancestors, or the women in your family who came before you, play in your life?

They have made me who I am. In our culture, one of our core values is Haa Shuká—we are tied to our ancestors, and we have obligations to our youth and to our future. Our ancestors developed a great culture and world for us. They protected our land ownership and culture against those who would deprive us of our land and heritage. They taught us to adapt but retain our cultural values at the same time. We have been taught to do the same for our children, our grandchildren, and those yet to come.

It seems that whenever I have a problem or am uncertain how to address an issue, my ancestors show me the way. I've experienced this many, many times. Even in this changing world, their wisdom remains applicable.

What are you most proud of about yourself?

That I raised beautiful, well-adjusted, and successful children who are living in both the Native and non-Native worlds, making contributions to our society, and who in turn are raising wonderful children who are on paths to do the same.

Can you describe a turning point in your life, and how it changed things for you?

My mother was a salmon cannery union organizer. When she died, I received her koogeina in a ceremony. This is a sash used in the Alaska Native Sisterhood organization. This practice builds on traditional ceremonies. When I received her koogeina, I thought about the contributions my mother had made and the pride that gave me. I wondered what I would leave my children. This ceremony made me reflect on my life and gave me a sense of purpose, knowing that I had to do something for my children and my Peoples and follow in the footsteps of my mother.

What's the biggest risk you've taken in your life, and how has it shaped you?

I became politically active in the 1960s during the War on Poverty era. It was also a time when Indians were "in." At community meetings, it sometimes seemed to me that non-Native people would listen to me and support my position because I was an Indian. I wondered how long this would last. On the other hand, I was also labeled a "militant." I would say, "If I were white, I would be called a 'concerned citizen.'" While I was confident in my own culture and society, and I could list the litany of oppressive acts against us, I didn't always have the solutions to our situation. I began to realize that I should seek higher education. I wanted people to listen to me because of my knowledge; I didn't want people to listen to me because I was an Indian. I realized that I would have to learn more about their world, their laws, their institutions. I knew I was smart, but I was nervous about my poor education.

I didn't have to go to school regularly until I was kidnapped. I attended Bureau of Indian Affairs schools, which focused on vocational training, and I missed eighth grade because I had rheumatic fever.

However, I was able to read a lot while confined to bed. I read whatever books my mother could buy from the secondhand store. At that time, those attending Catholic school had to take a test to get into the public high school. The nuns prayed over me as I was taking the test. I passed that test and was able to get into high school, but my attendance at school was sporadic. I traveled with my mother to record minutes at her union meetings. We also left school early or before the end of the school year to go out fishing and to work in the canneries, and we started the school year late because of fall fishing.

I made the decision to go to college later, with three children in tow. I would have to read my texts three times: the first time to write the definitions of words I didn't know in the margins of the book, the second time to insert the meaning of those words, and the third time to understand the text. I loved school—or, rather, learning—and when I was ready to graduate from college, I asked, "How can I be given a degree when I know so little?" Someone suggested graduate school. I didn't even know what graduate school was. I went to graduate school, and it was a powerful experience. Although I was majoring in anthropology, I attended classes at the law and business schools. I would tell people that attending school was like a curtain had been opened for me, and I could see a whole new world.

When do you feel your most powerful?

When I know that I am making inroads in changing systemic racist behaviors or institutions that have been adverse to our cultural practices, beliefs, and way of life.

AS I'VE GROWN OLDER,
I'VE LEARNED THAT
SUCCESS IS KNOWING
YOU HAVE DONE YOUR
BEST, AND WITH THAT
COMES HAPPINESS.

Do you have a message for younger women reading your story here?

Know yourself. Have balance in your life—take time for yourself. Always maintain integrity; treat people with fairness and kindness; be generous, and your generosity and kindness will come back and give you greater happiness. Do not live with anger in your heart, as it has a way of ultimately harming you. One of the lasting lessons I learned from my mother was not to think and act as if you were a god standing in judgment of other Peoples.

How have your ideas of success and happiness changed over time?

As I've grown older, I've learned that success is knowing you have done your best, and with that comes happiness.

My idea of success is also related to the work I've done in ensuring the success of my children and grandchildren. I see success as ensuring that they, and our community's youth, have the opportunity to be established in our culture, learn their culture, language, and history, and have pride in themselves as Natives.

How has raising children affected your life?

I may have been too young when I started having children, and with my first child, I would play with her like she was a doll. I had fun making her clothes and dressing her up. I have loved being a parent, and I love my children, and now my grandchildren, more than anything in this world. I had to learn how to transition from just being a parent to being both a parent and friend. I can say that my children and grandchildren are among my closest friends. It has been a joy watching my children grow up, and I have been blessed in watching them again through their children. I've also learned from them, as they introduce me to things that were never part of my life. My children and grandchildren have enriched my life and are the joy of my life.

At this point in your life, what have you made peace with that used to be a struggle for you?

I've been married twice and was dependent on my husbands. After my last divorce, I remember the gas light in my hot water heater went out, and I was angry at myself that I didn't know how to light the heater. I was so proud that I figured out how to light the heater that I called a friend to tell her. At that point, I made a decision to be independent and realized that I didn't have to be married to survive. I had always been a daughter, sister, wife, and mother, but I hadn't learned to be an independent woman.

What would you like to learn or experience at this stage in your life?

I would like to learn how to spend more time doing the things I want to do for myself. My work has always been the priority in my life, and I believe it is critical for the benefit of our community.

I am envious of my colleagues, who are among my best friends. They are scholars who can devote their energies to teaching and researching. I wish I could have done that, but I knew I had a responsibility to work for my Peoples. I sometimes get a little angry at my mother for instilling this sense of responsibility in me.

I would like to finish a number of manuscripts and bring them to publication. I guess I have to learn how to put my other work aside and concentrate on this.

There are two things I've always said that I would like to do or have. I would like to travel on one of those river cruise boats in Europe—it's a dream, but I can live without it. I would also like to be a great-grandmother.

What is a lesson you're still learning or need to learn?

I need to learn how to maintain balance in my life. I work too hard and long each day. I am fortunate that I am in good health, but I know I need to exercise.

What impact do you hope your life and your story will have on those around you?

I hope that people will learn that one can overcome adversity and live a successful and happy life. I would hope that Indigenous people can see that they do not have to abandon their cultural values and practices to be successful in this modern world.

Priya
Krishna

and

Ligaya
Mishan

NEW YORK, NY

Writers Priya Krishna, 30, and Ligaya
Mishan, 51, share a love of food and a
passion for writing, Priya as a writer and
author of the cookbook *Indian-ish* and
Ligaya as a restaurant reviewer and food
writer for the *New York Times*. Priya writes
for the *New York Times* and has appeared
in several YouTube series about food and
cooking. Ligaya is a writer-at-large at
T: The New York Times Style Magazine,
and has written for *The New York Review
of Books* and *The New Yorker*. Their
friendship has spanned many years and
many jobs and continues to provide a
support system for them that inspires them
both in their work.

How did you first meet?

LIGAYA: We met four years ago at a restaurant I was reviewing, the Crabby Shack. It's a Maryland-style crab shack in Brooklyn, and our friend Tejal brought us together.

What were your first impressions of each other?

PRIYA: I distinctly remember that Ligaya spoke so quickly. I was like, Oh, she talks as fast as I do. She thinks really fast and connects dots really fast, in a way that I feel I do, too, and I leave people behind in the conversation. It felt like we were going at the same speed.

L: I definitely felt Priya's energy, which is what I'm always looking for. When I have people come out to eat with me, they have to have lots of ideas and things to say, partly just to keep it interesting, but also because I need insight. I'm always drawing from other people's thoughts. I'm waiting for people to say something I can quote in my review, and Priya is very quotable. It is also the messiest possible way to meet because that was really messy food to eat.

P: I remember I liked you so much, and I wanted to see you again, but it was one of those dating situations where I had to ask our mutual friend, "Can I have Ligaya's email address? I'd like to email her and tell her I want to see her again."

L: I can't imagine a time when we were not friends. I'm so used to going out with younger people because younger people are the only people who are free all the time to go out with me. I'm always asking people to go out at the last minute, and everybody else my age has children and major obligations to their families.

Can you describe a moment when you realized that your friendship was going to be a significant one in your lives?

P: I knew that Ligaya was someone I would do a lot for when I taught a Bollywood dance class to her daughter's Girl Scout troop. I was like, I would do anything for this woman.

When I ran the New York City Marathon, it was mile 22, and I was literally at the point of just wanting to stop. I was thinking, This race needs to end. It's the part where you're rounding Central Park and you think you're almost done, but you actually have four miles left. I was running with my friend

Kate, and we saw Ligaya. She had her big winter parka on in November, and she was yelling at the top of her lungs. I almost started crying when I saw her.

L: I don't know if I can isolate one moment. Priya is the person I go to. My friends and I, we don't text, really. We talk on the phone or do other things, but Priya is one of maybe three people I text when something happens. I also remember being in a subway with Priya one time. I had talked for an hour and a half straight at that point about the piece I was writing, and Priya was still listening with avid attention. She was still helping me talk it out. She's helped me endlessly with every single piece. Even just by telling me, "Ligaya, you've done this before. This is you. You can keep going."

P: In turn, I have literally brought printed drafts of my pieces to dinners with Ligaya. And she will, at the dinner table, read the story and be like, "Okay, I think you can shorten the lede by doing this."

L: This is one of the joys of my life. I've never had the chance to be an editor in a formal way. I love it. You can send me any story any time.

What are some of the most meaningful lessons you've learned from each other?

L: I learn a lot from Priya about reporting. She's really good at getting people to talk to her, and she gathers so much material. You have such wonderful clarity, and you're able to write prose that is beautiful but also direct, and that inspires me. And the way you're constantly open to new ways of thinking; I can see the ways you're approaching certain issues and thinking about the institutions and systems that we're part of and how your thinking is evolving, and that's really exciting to me, and it's helped me to also be open to new ways of thinking.

P: Ligaya taught me how to be a beautiful writer. There was one time where you were complimenting someone's piece and you said something along the lines of, "There was not a word out of place. Every word was incredibly intentional." I feel like when I'm writing, I'm always thinking about that. She has taught me how to be extremely intentional in my writing. I think that is one of the biggest things.

She's just constantly delivering nuggets of wisdom. It could be really minor things. I remember one day we were eating Georgian food, and she was like, "Priya, I don't like one-third of my friends' spouses." She was just like, "You just need to get used to the fact that your friends won't always marry someone that you really love." It's this combination of hilarious and serious at the same time. We can weave so seamlessly between talking about goofy stuff, talking about semicolons, having a deep intellectual conversation about the literary review and the fact that you do this all while being a mom, a writer. I feel like you're presenting the blueprint for how I want to live my life twenty years from now. And it's really exciting.

L: You keep me young, Priya. You just keep me in the here and now. As we get older, inevitably we become more conservative, and I'm fighting that tooth and nail. I'm glad that you're keeping me in the moment and aware of what's been going on in the world.

What do you each hope your friendship brings or gives to the other person?

P: I hope we can always speak freely to each other. I want to be her conversation partner. I can't think of someone who's a better conversation partner than Ligaya. I just hope she always knows that I always want to chat with her. I always want to be the person you can bounce ideas off of, bounce random thoughts off of. I want to be that comparative source of energy for you.

L: I think that, for me, one of the joys in our friendship has been just watching you. You're such a superstar. It's hard for me to remember that you were still maybe at the beginning of that when we first met. You're somebody who's so incredibly capable of doing stuff on your own that if I ever hear of any opportunity or anything in the world where I can say, "Priya should be there," that's what I want to do for you, as a friend who can open those doors.

Why do you think you came into each other's lives when you did?

P: Ligaya came into my life when I had just left my job as marketing manager of *Lucky Peach* magazine. I thought, I'm going to try freelance writing. But the only clips I had at the time were college essays. I was literally sending editors my college essays as writing samples. But Ligaya was my cheerleader and then eventually became the editor who motivated me to pitch the ideas I wanted to pitch. She gave me the confidence to do that and then would talk through ideas I had to help me make them into better ideas. She was the person at every stage of the process. I feel like she came into my life at the time when I needed that the most.

L: You came into my life at a time when I was starting to lag as a food writer. I didn't want to go out to eat. It just wasn't exciting to me anymore. But to be with someone who brings so much energy and enthusiasm and who could transform those nights out into a joy in and of themselves, it meant so much. She helped me look at the subject with new eyes and remember, Oh, this does matter.

P: Ligaya has always treated me like a peer. It has been a real privilege.

What advice do you have for someone who is curious about or interested in making new friends of different ages?

L: I could be Priya's mom. We have twenty years between us. But the structure of our work life helped us come together. I think it helped that we didn't start off only hanging out one-on-one. We'd always be in groups, which can make things a little bit easier. I feel like it's something you can't push and it's something that probably needs to arise naturally.

P: I totally agree. I think it just has to happen organically. For Ligaya and me, it really did feel so organic. We hung out. We hung out again. It felt so automatic at a certain point.

L: When we hang out, I'm not thinking that I'm older than Priya. I know I am, but I'm not thinking that.

P: I feel like if Ligaya and I had been in the same year in college, we would have been soul mates—best friends. You've always felt like a counterpart to me in some interesting way because even though I wouldn't say we are similar on paper, in actuality, I think we are very much alike.

L: You bring out my goofiness, which is something I don't always let people see. You're the metaphorical face paint that helps me be goofy. I think pure intellectualism would just be too much to take. That would be dreary. Goofiness and intellectualism, that's the perfect match.

WHENEVER WE HANG
OUT TOGETHER, I
LEAVE FEELING MORE
CONFIDENT THAT
I AM THE PERSON
I'M SUPPOSED TO BE.

What did it feel like to find that sort of connection with somebody that's not romantic, but is just as deep and meaningful?

P: Ligaya lives on the Upper East Side and has a partner and a daughter. When you meet someone you like so much, you want to immediately spend all your time with them. Then you realize that this person is a member of a different generation. You can't spend all your time with them. I can't just call Ligaya on Saturday night. There are limitations when you have an intergenerational friendship. I appreciate that, but I do get a little bit sad that we are at such different stages in our lives. That's why the dinners are so important, because it's this one setting where we can see each other.

L: I also mourn being older a bit. If I were closer to Priya's age, we would totally go out dancing. We'd go to Basement Bhangra or something. I've actually gone before in my life so many years ago, but yes, I do mourn.

When we go to dinner, for those hours, I live this kind of other life—which my family knows about. Sometimes they scold me a little, but for that length of time, I am a young person again. Priya gives me this ability to be younger. I think that some of this distance between our ages will blur as she gets older and her life changes a little. Then, hopefully, our families can just hang out together.

P: I think there's something very beautiful to our age difference. When we have dinner, we're sort of in this bubble. I feel like I'm always trying to figure out ways to extend that. We will both take the subway in a slightly out-of-the-way direction so that we can hang out a little bit more, or I'll just miss two subway stops because we're in the middle of discussing a sentence. I'm like, Ah, it's fine. I'll just figure out a convoluted way home from here.

The irony of Ligaya's job is that it really requires a lot of people at dinner because there are so many dishes to try. You need a lot of mouths. So it is rare that it's just me and Ligaya alone. But so often, I wish it were just the two of us. Those rare just-the-two-of-us dinners have been so wonderful. Those are probably my favorite moments.

What makes you proud to call each other friends?

L: I definitely feel like, Wow. I must be cool because Priya likes me. I feel like I must have some sort of credibility because she could hang out with other young people and she chooses to hang out with me. I don't know if that's something to be proud of. I'm just in wonder of it all—of how lucky I am.

P: I feel the exact same way. I feel like I must be some level of smart and sophisticated if Ligaya is choosing to have dinner with me. It makes me feel I'm doing something right when we hang out together. Whenever we hang out together, I leave feeling more confident that I am the person I'm supposed to be and that I am in the field I'm supposed to be in.

L: Priya makes me feel relevant. I feel like that sounds silly, but as you grow older, there is a part of you that starts to wonder if what you have to say still matters, if it ever matters. When she gets excited about the ideas I'm excited about, that makes me feel they really are exciting. That helps me keep going.

Carmen Herrera

NEW YORK, NY

Artist Carmen Herrera sold her first piece of artwork at the age of 89. Now, at the age of 106, she has taken the art world by storm with her bold minimalist works. Born in Havana, Carmen trained as an architect before leaving Cuba for New York. Facing rampant sexism in the art world, she was prohibited from entering exhibitions and was frequently rejected from shows because she was a woman. Undeterred by the art world's refusal to acknowledge female artists, Carmen continued to create her singularly colorful abstract work, which was finally appreciated by the broader art community in the early 2000s. Her artwork has been displayed at the Whitney, the Museum of Modern Art, and the Lisson Gallery, among others. She was the subject of a 2016 documentary, *The 100 Years Show*, and now, as she enters a new century of life, she continues to create new work from her home studio.

What misconceptions about aging would you like to dispel?

If 60 makes you a senior citizen, then I have been one for forty-six years. Those categories and age numbers are all nonsense. I have known 40-year-olds who were lifeless and 80-year-olds who were full of vitality. There are so many clichés and misinformed opinions about aging that it is best not to even bring it up in intelligent conversation.

Age should be ignored as much as possible. There is nothing you can do about it. The key is not to be at the mercy of statistics. Find something you love to do, and never retire.

What does your current age feel like for you?

I cannot walk the length of my studio, but my mind can travel far to places I have been and my imagination to some I have not.

I do regret that I have lost so many friends and brothers and sisters.

I am 106. I am in terra incognita. Let's talk about something else—not age, nor the weather.

I remember the "old age poem" by Sappho, in which she writes that "beauty" is short lived, but life can be long: "And Eros has given me beauty not found in the light of the sun: the passion and patience for life that so often is lost on the young."

What are you most proud of about yourself?

I did not climb Everest, nor did I develop a vaccine, but I had a good marriage that lasted a lifetime (sixty-one years). I have made some good art along the way and had, and have, some good friends.

How has your sense of self-confidence or self-acceptance evolved over time?

As time passes and you make pictures and works that hardly anyone notices, then self-confidence kicks in. Being ignored can feel like a form of freedom to do whatever you want. But the thing is to go on doing—do not give up! On the contrary: Do more and enjoy! To hell with fame and acclaim . . . it is fleeting.

What role do you feel your ancestors, or the women in your family who came before you, play in your life?

I have great respect and love for my ancestors. They were courageous and strong (I speak with them occasionally). My father fought in the Cuban War of Independence on the Cuban side, and my grandfather was a colonel on the Spanish side.

My mother was a lion. She was a working journalist in 1900! And in a male-dominated world. Just think of that. . . .

What impact do you hope your life and story will have on those around you?

I hope my art will give some joy or pleasure or spark someone's imagination. I hope that my so-called "discovery" at 89 will encourage others waiting for the bus.

When do you feel your most powerful?

In the mornings, when I am at my drawing table.

Who or what has influenced your life the most?

My mother the lioness, Carmela. She dared to be a feminist at the beginning of the twentieth century. And my husband, Jesse, who never allowed me to "get a job" and who really appreciated my art.

What's the biggest risk you've taken in your life, and how has it shaped you?

Trading the island of Cuba for the island of Manhattan in 1939.

The most rewarding risk was going off to live in Paris from 1948 through 1953. What a thrill! It changed my life, and it changed me as an artist and as a woman.

Knowing what you know now, what would you go back and tell your younger self?

I regret nothing.

AGE SHOULD BE IGNORED AS MUCH AS POSSIBLE. THERE IS NOTHING YOU CAN DO ABOUT IT. THE KEY IS NOT TO BE AT THE MERCY OF STATISTICS. FIND SOMETHING YOU LOVE TO DO, AND NEVER RETIRE.

Alice Wong
and
Sandy Ho

SAN FRANCISCO, CA, AND BOSTON, MA

Alice Wong, 47, and Sandy Ho, 35, have dedicated their lives to supporting, sharing, and speaking up for the rights and stories of disabled people. Alice is the founder and project coordinator of the Disability Visibility Project, a project collecting oral histories of people with disabilities, and the editor of a book of essays titled *Disability Visibility*. In addition to serving as an advisory board member for Asians and Pacific Islanders with Disabilities of California, she was a presidential appointee to the National Council on Disability, and in 2015, she attended the reception at the White House for the twenty-fifth anniversary of the Americans with Disabilities Act via telepresence robot. Sandy is a research associate with the Lurie Institute for Disability Policy and a community organizer focused on disability justice. She is a co-instructor of Disability Studies at Lesley University, and the founder of the Disability & Intersectionality Summit. Alice's work with the Disability Visibility Project is part of what inspired Sandy to reach out to her. Though they share a strong commitment to community and activism, they also bonded over their love of good gossip and great food.

How did you first meet?

SANDY: Around 2012, I was a program manager for a Stride Learning Mentoring Program in Massachusetts. The program was the first of its kind in the state that worked with young women with disabilities between the ages of 14 and 26 who were mentored by older women with disabilities. That was an important difference of that program, because usually mentoring programs for youth with disabilities pair them with nondisabled adults. Out of this program, one of the activities I had the mentees and mentors do was to write letters to their younger selves. During that process, I was googling for other women with disabilities. And this was definitely during a time in my life where I was just trying to come into my identity as well, figuring out what it meant to be a disabled young woman. That was when I came across Alice's work, and I don't even know what pushed me over the edge—but I cold-emailed her. And surprisingly, she responded.

ALICE: I think there's something about being a disabled woman of color where you feel like a unicorn within the broader disability community. I've always felt like I'm still searching for my people. I remember the isolation and not really feeling in solidarity with others. That's what's prompted me to be really receptive when I meet other Asian American disabled people. When I heard about the work Sandy was doing, I was so impressed. She works with a lot of young disabled women, and I was just like, Okay, this is somebody I *know* I'm going to be friends with. I think it was pretty instantaneous.

S: The response to that Stride project, and Alice's letter, was amazing. I did not expect such an outpouring of other submissions from disabled women across the country and around the world. The things that were being written about, including Alice's story, really clued us all in to the fact that we have a community and support and solidarity in each other. I think our friendship started from a sense of community bonding.

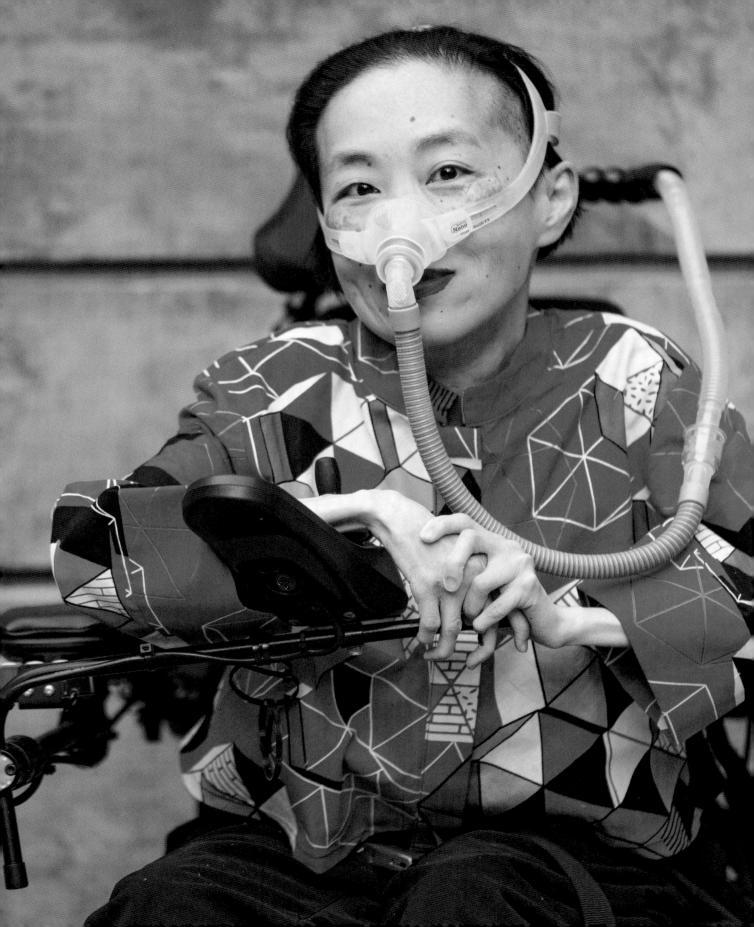

Can you describe a moment when you realized that your friendship was going to be meaningful in your lives?

A: We've been friends for quite a few years, but I feel like this year, with the pandemic, we've really kind of been there for each other through text messages. All the ways we check in with each other and give each other a space to vent and let our hair down—where we don't have to talk about activism or disability, and we can gossip and spill the tea— they've been so important.

S: The moment I realized that Alice was somebody I could call a friend was when she made it clear to me that she's always there to give me answers to the questions that nobody else in our community is talking about. Especially when it comes to what it's like to live on a restrictive income. Being an activist means that you don't have the traditional nine-to-five job, and figuring out what to charge or how to handle doing trainings can be overwhelming. Alice has been one of the people who's constantly reminded me that I have value beyond just being somebody who is there as a diversity token or to give inclusion trainings.

A: I've been on this earth a little bit longer than Sandy, and I have made my mistakes. I've definitely racked up some experiences in terms of intergenerational exchanges, but I didn't see our relationship as a mentor-mentee thing, because it's really about two equals, even though sometimes Sandy refers to me as an older sister. But I see Sandy as absolutely my equal, if not more, because I see her as the future. This is something that's really important: to be utterly sure that the next generation of disabled activists can take on the world. It's not out of obligation. It's about love, the love of our people, and just making sure people feel seen and heard and supported.

What are some of the things you're most proud of for each other?

A: One of the things I'm most proud of, in terms of just seeing Sandy grow in her leadership, is the Disability & Intersectionality Summit (DIS) that she basically organized and created. It's the most amazing event, and a powerful thing to do as an organizer. I respect Sandy so much for her style of leadership.

S: I think one of the most powerful moments for me was at the Disability & Intersectionality Summit when I got to celebrate and honor the first collection of essays that Alice had printed, the *Resistance and Hope* anthology. To be able to celebrate the work of your friends and to uplift and elevate them is a really great feeling. This is why we work together in community and why we see each other as co-schemers in each other's plans.

We started the DIS conference because we were listening to our elders in the community, many of whom are disabled people of color. They told us, "This is not a new thing that's happening, the state-sanctioned violence against Black and brown disabled bodies we're seeing—it's been happening for centuries. For decades, we've been trying to do something about systemic ableism and racism."

At the same time, my friends and I were also noticing a lot of TED Talks circulating focused on disability narratives that we could not relate to. Mainly narratives about "overcoming" or adapting to a disability. So I learned about Disability Justice and the ten principles behind it, and we created an event that centered these principles into not just the content that was being offered at the conference but the way that we would be doing our organizing.

We had barely any budget, and we rented out one conference room the first year, on a Saturday. But hundreds of disabled people showed up. Our youngest presenter was 12, and I think our eldest was in her mid-sixties. That's what the conference is about; it's about meeting our community where they are.

How have you supported each other through big life moments as well as professional ones?

A: I got a chance to profile Sandy for my website, and I did an interview with her. I think that was the first time she identified publicly as a queer disabled woman.

S: Having somebody who is not only going to cheer on your work but also cheer on your personal process is really important, and it's been so key to our friendship as well. That moment of identifying as queer in a disability space and having that be seen as something that I was comfortable to do clearly had a big impact. That type of trust is not stressed enough in friendships, and community organizing work in particular, because without that trust, you don't have activists who are going to be able to take those risks.

A: That, to me, also showed me how our friendship had evolved, in the sense that you felt safe to do that. It wasn't something I asked; I didn't know. I just wanted to interview you. But the fact that you felt comfortable and safe enough to do that—that was incredibly meaningful to me.

What are some of the most meaningful lessons you've learned from each other?

A: I think sometimes I can be more conservative or more cagey in some ways. Sandy's already reminded me several times to just keep pushing my edges. I think it's been so helpful for me to say stuff like, "We've got to hold strong" and to not accept any sort of BS. She helps me feel really invigorated and reminded of why I do what I do. Sandy's there not only as a friend but as somebody who supports me and keeps pushing me in a really good way to keep doing things all the way. It's been great to have a partner in all this.

S: Alice has taught me so much about boundary setting. She constantly reminds me that in the organizing work I do, I shouldn't be afraid to take ownership of the work that is out there. And to not be afraid to put my face and my name to it and to own the work that I've been a part of.

Building relationships has been part of that. I think what a lot of folks probably would recognize Alice for is her work with the Disability Visibility Project and her presence on Twitter. But I think what is not seen, and what I know, is the person behind that Twitter handle. Alice really does take the time to build relationships with folks, and there's intentionality to every single thing she's doing. Alice is the person I feel safe confiding in and asking all kinds of questions; she's also the person I feel safe about celebrating my wins with, big and small.

A: Sandy is someone I can share good news with and not feel like I'm bragging. To be able to have that person who's close enough where she's just as excited for you as you are excited for her—I think these are friendship goals.

What do you each hope your friendship brings or gives to the other person?

S: I hope there is a sense of grounded realness, and just knowing there's somebody who, if you need a reality check, is here to help bounce ideas off of. I want to be a sounding board for things that are happening that I might not even see. I want her work to continue in the best way possible. It sounds so basic, but that really is what it is.

A: Since I am older than Sandy, I think the one thing I really do hope in terms of our continued friendship is that I can help her realize all her dreams and goals and ambitions. I want to see her succeed in whatever she wants to do, and just do whatever I can to support those efforts. That, to me, is one of the things I hope is part of our friendship: the gentle touching of "Apply for this . . . try that . . . go for this."

I'm just ready for Sandy to take over the world. I'd like to lay the groundwork for that.

What is one of your favorite things about your friendship?

A: I would say that it's so much *fun*. I genuinely love spending time with Sandy. I think friendships have this arc or life span, but this feels different. I think that there is unlimited potential for where our friendship will go. That, to me, is really exciting.

Also, I think one misconception people have about intergenerational friendships is the idea that young people are absorbing everything from the older person in the friendship. But younger people also need to come to that mentorship or that friendship with an older person and be prepared to have something that they're going to give back to it. And I always feel that from Sandy.

S: I think sometimes, when they're reflecting on relationships or friendships, people will say, "Oh, I wish I'd met this person earlier or at a different time in my life," but honestly, I have no regrets about when I met Alice—it all happened at the right time, when I was ready and when she clearly had an infinite amount of wisdom to share with me. I think that's something I would wish for others and for disabled people, too: to find your person and your friendship. I do ride or die in community.

I THINK THAT'S SOMETHING I WOULD WISH FOR OTHERS AND FOR DISABLED PEOPLE, TOO: TO FIND YOUR PERSON AND YOUR FRIENDSHIP. I DO RIDE OR DIE IN COMMUNITY.

Emily Meggett

EDISTO ISLAND, SC

Emily Meggett is the beloved Gullah chef and matriarch of Edisto Island, South Carolina. Edisto is one of the barrier islands of the Gullah/Geechee Nation, a community of people descended from West and Central Africans who were enslaved and brought to the lower Atlantic states to work on coastal rice, cotton, and indigo plantations. Born and raised in Edisto, Emily maintains and shares Gullah culinary traditions from her home, where she has lived for over forty years. Family, heritage, and caring for community are at the core of Emily's cooking. While she has cooked for countless members of her community and family (which includes ten children, twenty-three grandchildren, thirty-four great-grandchildren, and four great-great-grandchildren), Emily recently signed her first cookbook deal at the age of 88, and will now be sharing her celebrated recipes with a national audience.

Where did you grow up, and where do you live now?

I grew up on Edisto Island, South Carolina. And I still live here, but three miles from my childhood home.

What did you want to be when you were younger?

There weren't many options back then, so I thought I would be a caretaker. I am now a retired cook of forty-six years and still taking care of people by cooking and taking food all over the island.

What does your current age feel like for you?

Eighty-eight is the new 68. I am still driving. I live alone. I cook for myself, and I'm in good health and still active with the church and gardening.

What misconceptions about aging would you like to dispel?

I am never too old to learn. I have goals. I am about to publish my first cookbook.

What are you most proud of about yourself?

I am proud to say that I was married to my late husband for fifty-five and a half years. We had ten children. By the grace of God, I have twenty-three grandchildren, thirty-four great-grandchildren, and four great-great-grandchildren. I am still able to think for myself, and I am in my right mind. I have a passion for cooking and taking care of people.

What role do you feel your ancestors, or the women in your family who came before you, play in your life?

They play a very important role. My grandmother, who raised me, taught me to always respect my elders, to listen when others are talking, and to always have manners, because manners will take you where money won't.

Who or what has influenced your life the most?

My grandmother Elizabeth Major Hutchinson. She raised me and taught all of us to be mindful of those who are less fortunate than we are. In those days, we couldn't do a whole lot of going out and having a good time. We had to pick a time to do it, because in those days, there was always something that needed to be done. We had to go into the field to feed the pigs. We had to cut wood and bring it inside. We had to start the fire, pump the water, and bring the cattle in. We always had chores to do. In the morning, we had to get up around five and pull two rows of okra or two rows of lima beans—and *then* we'd go to school.

When we came home in the afternoon, we'd change our clothes and get a little something to eat. We'd have a sweet potato or some cornbread and syrup. And then we had to go outside to do our afternoon chores. Then we'd come in, wash up, do our homework, eat dinner, and be in bed by eight thirty.

I raised my children the same way—they always had chores to do. They were taught to have a strong work ethic and to be respectful and do their chores. They are my pride and joy because they never got into trouble.

What's the biggest risk you've taken in your life, and how has it shaped you?

I took a risk and said, "I am going to build this house whether I have a job or not," because I knew God would take care of me. My husband and I bought a piece of property for $75—one acre of land. And we built a four-room house. Altogether it cost us $1,025 to build. There were no bathrooms. There were outhouses. That was in 1960. In 1969, we started another four-room building, which ended up being nine rooms by the time we were done. So we had four rooms in the front, nine rooms in the back. And those nine rooms in the back cost us $28,000 in 1969. In 1981, my daughter helped me with $9,000 to remodel the front and the back of the house. It cost us around $34,000 to remodel it and landscape the yard. But the Lord was so good and blessed me, and we've never had a mortgage.

This house and land was the best thing that could ever have happened, because we have peace. We have love and care and sharing in this home. And the best thing you can ever have in your life is peace.

How has parenting affected your life?

Parenting has had a great impact because I didn't have a choice. It taught me responsibility, morals, value, and respect—and continues to, even at the age of 88.

Not only was I a parent to my children, but to many others. So the appreciation and respect that I get from all of *them* is incredible. Some consider me a matriarch, and I'm proud to be that. And humbled.

If you could go back in your life, what would you like to do over—and what would you never do again?

If I had the opportunity, I would go to college and get a degree, because we didn't have a computer and fancy electronics during my time. I would also never get married. Been there, done that. So my advice to young people would be: Don't be in a hurry to get married; take your time.

When do you feel your most powerful?

When I have peace and a house full of happy people that I have fed a scrumptious meal. And when I can share the goodness of God and his many blessings.

Can you describe a turning point in your life, and how it changed things for you?

In 1967, when I had my last child, she was born with skin the color of a white person. And people, both Black and white, accused me of having a child by a white man. But they didn't know that her great-grandfather was white. That really hurt me so much. It was challenging to get through as a family. But we did. I prayed to the Lord and put my trust in him and had to forget about what people were saying and trust him to bring me through. And he brought me through.

What would you like to learn or experience at this stage in your life?

At this age, I thought I had seen just about everything, until COVID-19 hit. And the leadership didn't do anything to protect the people. I have lived a good life. And if I don't experience anything else, I am satisfied. But I would like to learn how to tweet.

Knowing what you know now, what would you go back and tell your younger self?

Stay single as long as you can. Work hard on yourself and never give up. Anything is possible. Look at me. I am 88 and just landed a cookbook deal!

MY GRANDMOTHER
TAUGHT ME TO ALWAYS
RESPECT MY ELDERS,
TO LISTEN WHEN OTHERS
ARE TALKING, AND TO
ALWAYS HAVE MANNERS,
BECAUSE MANNERS
WILL TAKE YOU WHERE
MONEY WON'T.

Nancy Wilbur

SWINOMISH, WA

Nancy Wilbur, 72, is a teacher, activist, art gallery owner, and commercial fisher from the Swinomish Tribe in Washington State. After a career in education, Nancy, whose Indian name, Saut Sike, means "woman who teaches children," opened a Native American art gallery where she celebrated local Native artists. A former Swinomish Tribal Senate member, Nancy has spent her life fighting for Native rights and lobbying for bills that seek greater land, water, and legal sovereignty for Native people. Nancy now runs a beloved fireworks stand and has worked to support her daughter photographer Matika Wilbur's Project 562, a traveling photography project that documents the 562 currently recognized tribal nations in the United States. She sat down with her daughter, Matika Wilbur, to discuss her life and work.

Where did you grow up, and where do you live now?

I grew up on the Swinomish Reservation, and for the most part I've always lived with my grandmother, Laura Wilbur. She had a beautiful home that borders the Swinomish Slough, and so we grew up close to water. For me, when I get too far away from water, I feel like a fish *out* of water. Water is life. I have to be next to the water; I think that has to do with where we come from. Being Coast Salish people, it's really important that we hang on to our relationship with the water, the rivers, and the oceans. It makes us who we are.

What did you want to be when you were younger, and what do you do now?

When I was in high school, I wanted to be a nurse. I volunteered at a local hospital as a candy striper, and I would visit with the elders, give them back rubs, and bring them lunch. Then one day I was in talking to the nurses and this lady came in and said, "So-and-so expired." I gasped—*What does that mean?* She was talking about him passing away. And she was so matter-of-fact about it. I was devastated. I knew that wasn't the right work for me.

I ended up going to college, and my influence came from my professors at Western: Professor Harris in the education department and Professor Vine Deloria Jr. in the ethnic studies program. I got really involved in Native American history and culture. During my second year of college, my grandmother gave me my Indian name. I was the first person at that time in our family to be given an Indian name because our ceremonies were illegal. It was a huge ceremony, and there was a smokehouse— it was really wonderful. I invited Dr. Harris to come and be a witness. That naming is what changed my interest to education. I taught Native American culture at Skagit Valley College. Then later I went on to own a Native American art gallery and restaurant, and eventually I opened a fireworks stand with my dad; then I started commercial fishing.

What does your current age feel like for you?

I think it's a process. I think it takes a lot of getting used to. It takes a lot of changing my day-to-day. I can't do what I did before. I have to be mindful. I narrow down what's really important to me when I decide what I can do in a day. It's an interesting space to be in. But I'm not sure that I fully like it, because of the physical limitations.

What misconceptions about aging would you like to dispel?

That we're not useful. That we can't do things. I think that when we get to an age like this, I think that we're very valuable because of what we know of the past, what we've experienced, and I think it's that wisdom that can provide a lot of insight into planning for the future. We carry a lot of stories; we have a lot of history. And of course Native American

people recognize that. We're really admired and respected in our culture. So I think that's really nice. I don't think that anyone should have to quit their work because of an age. My grandma worked until she was 92. So I think that the whole country should do that—if they want to keep working, they should keep working.

How has your sense of self-confidence or self-acceptance evolved over time?

I think that as you learn different things, and if you're successful, you become more confident. I have had so many different experiences that have helped me to build confidence. I'd say I feel quite confident now because I was so young and naive. I don't know that everybody feels that way; I have just been lucky to have a variety of experiences.

What are you most proud of about yourself?

I'm most proud of my children. I have amazing children. I'm also proud of something I did a while back. I was at a grocery store, and when I came out, there was a young lady sitting on the sidewalk crying. She said that they wouldn't serve her. I asked her what she wanted, and I went and bought it for her. I started talking to her. She said she didn't have any place to go. I asked her questions about her life and she told me she was an alcoholic. I told her that I knew a place where she could go, at least for a night. I took her there and she went in. I went back to see her, but they wouldn't let me because I wasn't a relative. But I've often thought about her. I think that the entire world would be a better place if we were all kinder to strangers and those in need of help.

What role do you feel your ancestors, or the women in your family who came before you, play in your life?

My ancestors are everything. When I look back at choices I've made, I feel like they have been guiding me. When I started fishing and got out on the water, I felt like a door had been opened for me. Like the clouds had separated. It was this awakening, and I felt so close to the spirit and to all the natural things: the water, and the fish, everything. It was just amazing.

I had one experience on the water that was so powerful. I was coming in from West Beach, going through Deception Pass, which is treacherous, and there was a place where there were riptides and rough waters. It was hard to navigate, and so foggy. I couldn't see in front of me or behind me. I had a GPS, but I don't trust that electronic stuff. When I came up the middle of the pass, the fog suddenly separated—it just opened up, and I went through. When I looked back, the fog closed. I just said thank you, *osium*. I felt like my ancestors were watching over me that day.

What message do you have for women reading your story here, and what impact do you hope your life and story have on those around you?

I'm very proud of the fact that I've been a Native fisherwoman. I started out on an 18-foot skiff and went up to a 70-foot seiner. Fishing is one of the most dangerous fields around. But I think that women can do anything—if you really want to. And the one thing I'd like to say is that I feel like my family, especially my dad, was really at the root of me doing this. I went out on the boats with him when I was little. We lived on the river in a float house. And so I felt like he really nurtured that experience. He applauded and congratulated me.

I hope that young women will recognize their strength and their courage. It takes a lot of courage to do something when you don't know what you're doing or that you've never done before. You have to have faith that you'll figure it out along the way. You don't know what opportunity will come knocking at your door.

Also, I was a teacher and I lobbied against Public Law 280, a law that allowed states to take jurisdiction over reservations. They needed a Native person to lobby against the bill, but I had you [her 2-year-old daughter, Matika] to take care of. I had to find a babysitter, but with support from our community, I had people sign this petition to change Public Law 280. I went to different groups and talked about it—what it would mean for the Tribe. When I went to lobby against the bill, everyone said we'd never get these changes to the bill passed. But I went and talked to some of the people in charge, and they put the bill on the floor for us. It was an amazing experience. So again, if you don't know how to do something, you can learn. People will help you.

Can you describe a turning point in your life, and how it changed things for you?

When I lost my grandmother, and when I lost my brother. There was such a void in my life. I don't think I've been the same since. I used to go to my brother for advice. I'd talk over everything I was going to do. I've really had a big void there. That's where my friend Markus came in. He became like a brother to me. He understood that relationship. He's always been very sensitive to it. And then, of course, my aunt Dot filled in for Grandma. But nobody could ever take Grandma's place. Those are hard shoes to fill.

Can you talk about fishing and the right to go fishing, from then till now?

Native people who fished would take their gill net boats out to the bay or to the river. But white fishermen didn't want them out there. They used to do different things to agitate against us. They would shoot at Native fishermen in the river and try to destroy their nets. They didn't think we deserved to be on the river. So we had to fight for our right to fish. While I was in college, people were fighting at a grassroots level—and getting arrested—for their right to fish.

When I graduated and started teaching, I taught a contemporary issues class. We always talked about the Boldt Decision, which reinstated Native Tribes' right to 50 percent of the fish. It inspired an immediate pushback from non-Native fishermen. It caused so much racism and prejudice. I invited Ramona Bennett, a leader from the Puyallup Tribe who was involved in the fishing wars, to come up to the college to speak with other leaders and politicians.

It was just supposed to be a panel for students, but somebody put it in the newspaper. I came in, and the whole area was filled with angry white fishermen. No students could even get in. Rich Tucker, the coach for Skagit Valley College, stood up, and said, "If you don't sit down and quiet down, I'm calling the police and you'll never be welcome here again." Then we were able to do our presentation. Robert Cumbo talked about the treaty and what was in the treaty. He had all the facts. He said, "Actually, they could have gotten all the fish, so you should feel lucky that you got any at all." Coming from a white man, it had a big impact. So it was a big fight for us. We still can't fish together that often. We had to have separate openings.

Can you share more about what being Swinomish means to you and what sovereignty means to you?

Being Native, for me, is my community and my family. We carry a lot of things from the past in our DNA. I think we are born into it. And as you experience different things, there is a series of awakenings for you. Your spirit and your soul are awakened. They're always there, but you have to awaken them. My grandma taught me a lot. People would come to visit her, and my job was to make lunch—tea, pie, or cookies—and I'd listen to them speak Indian. It was amazing. I feel really fortunate that I had that experience. Just to listen to that language.

Native people need to be sovereign. We shouldn't be asking for anybody's permission. We need to be able to control our environment. I think it's really an exciting time to hear people talking more about the importance of sovereignty.

We are bringing our culture back. We will survive. That's how I feel. We have already. If casinos don't work, we'll make it some other way. If fishing can't endure, we'll make it some other way. We can buy our land back. We can correct that. I think we will. We'll make the adjustments. Being an Indian is in the center of your soul, that inherent, ancestral sense of self—you're born with it, they can't take that away. It's very deep.

How has being a parent and grandparent affected your life?

Being a grandma is awesome. You just get to have fun and love your grandkids. You don't have all the parental responsibilities. But you do have a responsibility to teach them. I think grandmas and grandpas are really important in children's lives. I feel sorry when some cultures don't recognize that, because the children suffer. I think Native people really honor them. I think they really recognize the role of grandmas and grandpas.

I'm so proud of my children. And I love what you [Matika] do with your podcast, *All My Relations*. You work for all Native people. I know we all love one another. We respect each other. But hundreds of years ago, we also used to war with other tribes, so we have to fix that. It's a relationship we need to work on, and you're doing that.

How have your ideas of success and happiness changed over time?

Well, things don't make you happy. Having the best car, or the best house, all of that is not important. I see that. I watch my auntie—she's 90, and she's trying to get *rid* of all her stuff. I think that it's really important to prioritize experiences and relationships. Building and maintaining those is more important. That is the wealth. Family is wealth. Community is wealth. I think that as time went on, as I matured, I learned the importance of that.

FAMILY IS WEALTH. COMMUNITY IS WEALTH.

Niki Russ Federman

and

Rozanne Gold

BROOKLYN, NY

Niki Russ Federman, 43, and Rozanne Gold, 67, have a shared love of food. Rozanne is the legendary four-time James Beard Award–winning chef who consulted for Windows on the World and the Rainbow Room and cooked for Ed Koch when he was mayor of New York City. She is also a journalist, cookbook author, and international restaurant consultant. Rozanne grew up shopping at Russ & Daughters (the iconic purveyor of bagels, lox, caviar, herring, and babka and other traditional baked goods), which was founded by Niki's family over 104 years ago. Along with her cousin, Josh Russ Tupper, Niki owns and runs Russ & Daughters, Russ & Daughters Cafe, Russ & Daughters Bagels & Bakery, Russ & Daughters at the Jewish Museum, and Russ & Daughters at the Brooklyn Navy Yard. Niki and Rozanne's love of and devotion to nourishing people drew them together and has deepened their bond over the years as they've formed an adult friendship and discovered their shared goals of intergenerational connection.

How did you first meet?

NIKI: I inherited Rozanne as a friend. My parents have been friends with her and her husband, Michael, for many years, so I've known Rozanne since I was little. I knew of her as someone my parents really admired and thought so highly of. But it wasn't until I was an adult and working at Russ & Daughters that I realized, Oh, I want Rozanne to be *my* friend, too. And now I'm a grown-up, so I can have that friendship with her.

Rozanne has been such a trailblazer and was a pioneer in the food world before the food world became what it is now. She does so many different things: She's a cookbook writer, a chef, a poet, and an end-of-life doula. I have always struggled with how to attend to all these different sides of myself, but Rozanne is doing it and showing me what can be done.

ROZANNE: One of my talents is seeing other people's greatness, even before they see it for themselves. And I've always felt this a little bit about Niki. I could sense a growing depth. And with depth also comes a kind of forward thinking, and needless to say, I'm a huge fan of that. But I've known Niki since she was so young, and to come in and out of each other's lives the way we have—that's why it's so special to have this time right now.

Can you describe a moment when you realized that your friendship was going to be a significant one in your lives?

N: When my cousin, Josh, and I were building out and creating the Russ & Daughters Cafe, we were trying to keep it under wraps, and we were deeply aware of the fact that we didn't know what we were doing. We were very insecure and scared and self-doubting. A few months before we officially opened, Rozanne and Michael said they were editing a book called *1001 Restaurants You Must Experience Before You Die* and wanted to include Russ & Daughters Cafe. It was this incredible vote of confidence from Rozanne and Michael, two people who know restaurants and know what a worthy restaurant is. And to have her say "I have so much faith in what you're doing that I am going to inscribe you in this book and on this list" was this real turning point for me. I thought, Okay, if Rozanne believes in me and this restaurant this much, I guess we're doing something right. I knew I wanted more Rozanne in my life.

R: There was something about you and Josh bringing your vision into the world. I just remember the pleasure every step of the way when I saw the menu, graphics, the details—every single thing about it was so great. But to acknowledge you on your own, from another generation, is very cool. I mean, it's the first time I really became aware of that.

Niki came on my podcast and talked about her mother, and I talked about my mother and her family's recipes. I always see recipes and cooking as the hand-clasp between generations. It felt like this kind of triangle, a triptych. My relationship with your parents, theirs with you, and now yours with me. And I love it; I value it.

Can you share something meaningful you've learned from each other?

N: What I've learned from Rozanne is that a constant evolution and exploration of all these different sides of yourself is possible. You don't need to stay stagnant, or stay doing one thing. She's been an incredible role model to me in that sense.

R: I don't think she sees herself as this sort of iconic, powerful leader, but she is. She's taken so many big risks, especially with big financial commitments. I never really did these things. But she inspires me to dream a little bigger. To take a bigger bite. And she does it all with humility.

What do you each hope your friendship brings or gives to the other person?

N: I hope it brings Rozanne validation. I think we see a lot of ourselves in each other, and I hope Rozanne can continue to see these qualities that she says belong to me that I see in her. What I have been able to do has been made possible by women like her.

R: I'm on this journey of spiritual nourishment, and looking and seeing what that's all about, and I hope I can share that with Niki, too. I would love to continue to play a mentoring role in Niki's life and help her with what comes in her future.

What advice do you have for someone who is curious about or interested in making new friends of different ages?

N: Let it happen organically. I've been lucky in my life in the sense that Russ & Daughters has given me the chance to be in a space surrounded by multiple generations—whether it's over the counter, with customers, with suppliers, or with my grandparents. I've always lived in this sort of intersection of generations and have seen the energy that comes out of those interactions. So it's very natural for me to have friends from different generations. Sometimes we get very segmented in our spheres of people who are more or less the same age, look like us, act like us. But there's so much to be learned from people who have lived before you.

R: I have no sense of ageism at all, young or old—either way, it just doesn't exist for me. People are people, and I'm meeting them wherever they are in the moment and wherever they're at.

But I do believe that people have to actively and intentionally find mentors and friendships—it's mutually beneficial. And maybe a younger person is a little afraid to ask, but as that older person, I have to tell you, it's an honor.

N: Creating moments and spaces for intergenerational connection has always been a part of my vision. When we were designing the cafe, I told our builders, "I want to create a space where at any given moment you could scan the room and find three or four generations, all in this space. We need a place where you can park a stroller or you could have a wheelchair." Giving these moments of connection through food and space and memory so that the generations can be in conversation with one another is crucial.

What makes you proud to call each other friends?

N: I am proud to call Rozanne my friend because to me, she embodies what a life that is rich and delicious and meaningful can be.

R: Niki embodies what it means to be a whole human being who has the capacity to metaphorically nourish the world. All her qualities make that possible; she also gets to preserve the past and create a new future.

I'VE ALWAYS LIVED IN THIS SORT OF INTERSECTION OF GENERATIONS AND HAVE SEEN THE ENERGY THAT COMES OUT OF THOSE INTERACTIONS.

Carmen Agra Deedy

STONE MOUNTAIN, GA

Lecturer and *New York Times* bestselling author Carmen Agra Deedy, 61, can hold anyone's attention with her words. At the age of 3, Carmen came to America with her family as a refugee from Havana, Cuba. A master storyteller for over twenty years, she has authored twelve children's books and has spoken and told stories to audiences of all ages across the world. Carmen serves on the Smithsonian Libraries Advisory Board from her home in Stone Mountain, Georgia.

Where did you grow up?

I was born in 1960, the year after the Cuban Revolution. Until I was 3 years old, I lived on Santa Emilia Street, in Havana, Cuba. In February 1964, my parents, sister, and I came to the United States as refugees. After a brief stay in Miami, where we were processed, we moved on to Decatur, Georgia, where we joined my mother's family.

What did you want to be when you were younger, and what do you do now?

For reasons known only to the sensibilities of a refugee child, I longed to be a doctor. In preparation for this future career in medicine, I spent countless childhood hours playing "hospital" with my dolls, which were nearly always recovering from some quasi-tragic accident, or were in quarantine after (yet another) outbreak of cholera. Can you just imagine? I must have been a lovely child.

That said, I'm still in awe of the way children find ways to recover from trauma; I liken it to the way a starfish will lose a limb to a predator and then go on to grow another.

I did not become a doctor. I grew up to become a children's author. I suppose I'm still playing make-believe when I dream up stories for children. My vivid memories of childhood certainly inform my writing.

What does your current age feel like for you?

When I turned 60, a strange metamorphosis accompanied that milestone. I found myself changing, slowing down. Not in the physical sense. But in my judgments of, and reactions to, the world around me. I find that I pause more these days, reflect more, before arriving at conclusions. I am less sure of things I once had absolute opinions about. Could it be—dare I hope—a nascent sort of wisdom?

What misconceptions about aging would you like to dispel?

When I was a child, I was drawn to the old. They seemed to me to be in possession of two things that other adults in my sphere seemed to lack: a wealth of stories, and the time to tell them. Oh, how I loved those stories! I think that complete delight in the older people around me helped me grow up with a sense that elders were near-magical people.

If there were one misconception about aging that I would dispel, if I had a magic wand, I'd knock the notion right out of the minds of the young that to be old is to be inherently frail.

My 90-year-old mother lives with me. Her body is small, and when she moves from one place to another, she does it with care. She knows that her once solid and dependable body could now betray her. But she is not frail. She has a spirit that astounds at times. The other night, I was trying to help her get into bed. Her bed is a bit tall for her because it's a special electric one that allows her to raise or lower her head or legs. But this night, she stared it down and said with a sigh, "Everest. The damn thing is Everest." We both laughed, and I started to suggest that she let me lift her onto the bed . . . but before I had uttered more than a few syllables, she charged that bed like a water buffalo and scrambled on top. Once in a sitting position, she looked at me and said, "Never give up."

What are you most proud of about yourself?

My tenacity (not bragging; see above).

How has your sense of self-confidence or self-acceptance evolved over time?

I was much cockier when I was young; cockiness being the exact opposite of self-confidence and self-acceptance. But as I got better at my work, it also became clear to me just how much I didn't know. More than could be learned in a lifetime spent studying the craft of writing. I would never live long enough to read all the books I wanted to, learn all I wished, write all I might. And that, let me tell you, is a lesson in humility.

So, in a sense, knowing who I truly am, and who I am not, what I can do, and what I cannot—this is what allows me to be (mostly) confident. Because I know I'm becoming real. A bit like the Velveteen Rabbit.

Who or what has influenced your life the most?

I think my early years left an indelible impression. I was born into the chaos of a revolution, growing up always on alert, always hungry, always anxious—the firing squads could be heard from our house. And then I (we) had to adapt to a very different culture, climate, language, and all the attendant challenges. My early years were sad ones in many ways. But I learned that there are seasons in life. Some bright, some Stygian. But all—all—eventually pass. It's the notion that things are temporal that has allowed me to live fully. To embrace joy when I have it, and to trust that bad things and wretched days also have their end.

What role do you feel your ancestors, or the women in your family who came before you, play in your life?

We love stories in our family. Love. Them. And so, there is no dearth of lore about the much-loved women (or men) who came before my generation. What role do they play still? Well, I feel that they are never far from me. Not genetically, anyway. I see my mother in me at times and am shocked. Shocked. Every time.

But ancestors also influence me in a less tangible way. Spirits? I don't know that I believe they are near me in that way. But I do believe—I can't help it; this comes from my mother's side—that they may come to me in dreams. Meaning that those dream visitations are more than my highly complex brain hitting "Delete files" at the end of the day.

One dream stands out among the rest. During a very difficult time in my life, my grandmother Graciela came to me in a dream. I was walking along a narrow cobblestoned street lined with houses, much like the streets in Venice. I saw a woman under a stone bridge ahead, and as I neared, I realized that it was my grandmother. And here's the unbelievable thing: In this dream, she realized that it was me in that same oh-my-where-have-you-been way. She looked like she might faint, and I broke into a run. We embraced, and she opened a door under the bridge and said, "Come in, just for a little. I've made something for you to eat." And since in our family, food is love, I knew what she meant. Then I woke up. I tried and tried to fall back asleep and return to that dream, but of course, it was impossible.

When I saw the movie *Coco*, I cried like a teething baby.

When do you feel your most powerful?

When I get a good parking space.

What's the biggest risk you've taken in your life, and how has it shaped you?

Writing. I was not born with a desire to write, or even a gift for writing. I have little doubt of that. I'm dyslexic. Writing is like wrestling the Old Testament angel for a blessing before she has a chance to kill you. But I love stories. And I took the risk of sending a manuscript to a publisher when I was 28 years old. That leap changed the trajectory of my life.

Can you describe a turning point in your life, and how it changed things for you?

When I was in my forties, I was asked to give a TED Talk. Few people had heard of TED at the time. The invitation came on the heels of a speech I had made in Washington at the National Book Festival. Someone had recommended me. Well, the opportunity came too soon. I was nervous; my microphone wouldn't work; I lost precious minutes. I was a wreck, and too inexperienced to know how

IT'S THE NOTION THAT
THINGS ARE TEMPORAL
THAT HAS ALLOWED
ME TO LIVE FULLY.
TO EMBRACE JOY WHEN
I HAVE IT, AND TO TRUST
THAT BAD THINGS AND
WRETCHED DAYS ALSO
HAVE THEIR END.

WHEN SOMEONE OFFERS
TO TEACH YOU A NEW SKILL,
TAKE THEM UP ON IT.
WHETHER IT'S HOW TO
MAKE AN OMELET OR
HOT-WIRE AN ENGINE,
DO IT. LEARN EVERYTHING.
THAT SKILL MAY BE THE
ONE THAT GETS YOU
HIRED, BRINGS YOU LOVE,
OR SAVES YOUR LIFE.

to recover seamlessly. It put me off public speaking for a long time, and nudged me toward writing, where one's mistakes can be corrected in private, before publication. And what I then perceived as a failure became one of life's great gifts.

If you could go back in your life, what would you like to do over—and what would you never do again?

I would go to university. It wasn't an option for me for many reasons, and I am constantly learning, but I would fight harder for that, if I had my life to do over. I have been a writer and an editor, and I serve on the Smithsonian Libraries Advisory Board. But it isn't for the sake of advancement, or even a framed degree, that I would wish for this. I love to learn, and to learn from a great teacher would be one of this life's greatest experiences, I would think.

Oh. As to a "never": I would never (again) hire a contractor named Weezle.

How have your ideas of success and happiness changed over time?

To be surrounded by those I love, to devote myself to work I love, is more success than I believed I ever had a right to.

How has raising children affected your life?

My three daughters have been the greatest source of joy and have brought the greatest purpose to my life—from the moment the first one came howling into the world. They are now grown women and have children of their own, and they are still one of the reasons I get up in the morning with such a positive outlook on life. They are exquisite creatures, every one.

At this point in your life, what have you made peace with that used to be a struggle for you?

Naps. I used to think that succumbing to a nap was a sign of weakness. Now I realize that a good nap is a wellspring of both strength and endurance.

What would you like to learn or experience at this stage in your life?

Travel. All my life, I've wanted to travel to soooo many places. I have a bucket list with no bucket in sight large enough to hold them all. And I would like to learn algebra.

What is a lesson you're still learning or need to learn?

The art of "stillness."

What impact do you hope your life and your story will have on those around you?

Hmm. I don't know that I think of my life in those terms. But to answer the question, I hope that I have eased the passage through this world for those around me, as many of my friends and family have eased mine.

Knowing what you know now, what would you go back and tell your younger self?

Just you wait. There will be dragons, but there will also be lush green and golden lands. Be brave, be bold. *Just you wait.*

Do you have a message for younger women reading your story here?

When someone offers to teach you a new skill, take them up on it. Whether it's how to make an omelet, or shoe a horse, or hot-wire an engine, do it. Learn everything. You have nothing to lose, and that one-off, odd skill may be the one that gets you hired, brings you love, or saves your life.

Last, life is shorter than you can imagine. Why, just yesterday, I was 3 years old. So, live fully, with integrity, and without fear. Be good. Be brave. Be bold.

How has love shaped your life?

It has been the reason for living.

How has loss shaped your life?

It leaves broken places. There is no sidestepping the mucky business of grief. But as Hemingway said about being broken, "That's how the light gets in."

How has friendship shaped your life?

Think "lifeboat."

Wanda Blake

OAKLAND, CA

Wanda Blake, 62, is the queen of chowchow. Her take on the classic pickle relish has become so popular that her Oakland, California, kitchen has been fulfilling more orders than she's ever had before. Wanda's career in food started in her mother's kitchen and continued at the City College of San Francisco, Hotel and Restaurant Management Program. She has traveled around the world, from New Orleans to Brazil, Cuba, and Nigeria, to eat and share her love of food. While she works full-time as an accountant, the success of Wanda's chowchow business is a reminder that it is never too late for a new career chapter if you set your mind and heart to it.

Where did you grow up, and where do you live now?

I grew up in San Francisco, California, and I live in Oakland, California, just across the bridge. I ended up in Oakland because this was the area where they had houses I could afford to buy.

What did you want to be when you were younger?

I remember I just wanted to see the world. I think that's why I decided to become a chef when I was in my early twenties. I thought of it more as a job that would help me go places.

What does your current age feel like for you?

It actually feels pretty good. But I don't think I look my age. So when people say to me, "You're *how* old?" and can't believe it, that feels good.

I remember wanting to be able to retire at 45. But I guess that passed some fifteen years ago. I didn't really have any ideas about what being 60 would be like. But I remember some of my friends, who are a few years older than me, turned 60 and told me, "Not really seeing too much difference here."

This last year, I've really embraced my age. I'm looking at how much experience and exposure I have. I've done a lot. I've been a lot of places. I know quite a bit. I can share and enlighten other people. That's sexy.

What are you most proud of about yourself?

I'm most proud that I have a personality that draws like-minded people to me. You need confirmation and reassurance in your life because sometimes life can be so out there, and you need someone to say they see it, too. But I'm most proud that I know caring and generous people and people who are humble.

What misconceptions about aging would you like to dispel?

I think a lot of aging has to do with your mind. I think you have to have your own mindset. Because I see women in their seventies and eighties and they are *very* comfortable with themselves. And they're living their best lives. But then I have friends whose mothers are in that same age range and they seem much older. So I think the real perception of your age is in your mind.

What role do you feel your ancestors, or the women in your family who came before you, play in your life?

Oh, major. Major. The overall character you have as a woman has a lot to do with what you've learned from the older women in your family. You need to be hardworking and supportive. I did not grow up around any selfish women. I know nothing about that. I was raised up around a lot of queens and very few princesses.

How has your sense of self-confidence or self-acceptance evolved over time?

That's one thing that has definitely grown with age. It's not that I didn't feel confident when I was younger, but I had a gap in self-confidence in my mid-forties. It was a tough time. I felt like I was working harder and struggling more. I felt that gap

I DID NOT GROW UP AROUND ANY SELFISH WOMEN. I KNOW NOTHING ABOUT THAT. I WAS RAISED UP AROUND A LOT OF QUEENS AND VERY FEW PRINCESSES.

again when I was trying to start my food business. It just felt like it was only for young people. I kept saying to myself, You're starting over in your sixties? What the hell are you doing? But then I also told myself, Woman, you've been a late bloomer before. You'll do wonders. And you've got young people riding with you; pull some energy from them.

My friend Thérèse Nelson was listening to me struggle and said, "Why don't you just do a pop-up?" I had no idea that her question would change my life and bring me to where I am today. Because it was that very pop-up that launched my chowchow business.

What's the biggest risk you've taken in your life, and how has it shaped you?

The pop-up idea, for sure. That's where I had the realization that I could do what I loved about catering but without all the headaches. When Thérèse said, "Pop-up," I thought, Wait a minute. I can have the menu I want, do it *when* I want, have complete control over it, and it doesn't have to be seven days a week? That sounds like the perfect food vehicle for me.

When I had the pop-up, I was trying to get to a place where I could do something more on a regular basis, and when the place I wanted fell through, a vision of chowchow came to me, and that was it. Then *Bon Appétit* wrote a piece about my chowchow, and now I'm in the chowchow zone.

The lesson for me now, though, is that I have to keep the passion and the momentum but still take care of myself. So when I speak at my local entrepreneur class, I'm asking people these little things. Like, "Are you resting? Are you eating? Did you drink water today?" I have to remind myself that I'm going to breathe and I can only do what I can do today.

When do you feel your most powerful?

When I went to the post office and delivered the last 157 of my orders, which ended up being 435 jars of chowchow. When I took that last set of boxes to the post office—that was a power moment. I'm having conversations with my team to show them how we are going to keep this up and just feeling the energy of those people and their thoughts and questions about what I was saying—that was powerful. I'm supplying jobs, real work, for four people. That's a big deal.

How have your ideas of success and happiness changed over time?

It's not about money or financial goals for me. My happiest thing is to travel. And to travel with a food connection to it—that is my ultimate thing. I had seven trips planned this year, but I will have to wait until the pandemic is over to travel again. So right now I'm thinking, Okay, so where are you going to go when it's safe to travel? Where are you going to go, Wanda? I want to go to Tasmania next.

I'm also learning how happy it makes me to hear the excitement of my peers about my success. That is the ultimate. To hear them talking about how much they love my chowchow—it doesn't get much better.

Knowing what you know now, what would you go back and tell your younger self?

Don't be so afraid.
And love yourself more.

At this point in your life, what have you made peace with that used to be a struggle for you?

Not having children. It took me a while to make peace with that. But then I started listening to my friends, and their children were driving them wild. I realized that I don't know if I would have the patience for that. I could imagine that maybe my child would be different, but the things I've learned and been able to do would be much harder for people with children to do. The money I've invested in traveling and going to the restaurants I've wanted to try—I don't know that I would have been able to do that.

If you could go back in your life, what would you like to do over?

I think it would be having a child. Because that was a fearful thing for me. One, I never wanted to have children without being married. And I was around a lot of people who didn't have good relationships. Maybe if I would have looked more at the older people who had good relationships, that would have been a better vision for me. But I was raised by a single parent, and I was fearful of having a child and being alone. And then when I finally did get married, it was too late; I couldn't have children.

So if I could go back, I would not be so fearful in relationships with men. Maybe I could have had more of an opportunity to have more of a family and have the support to do that. But I have a huge chosen family of people. I have a lot of people who are closer to me than they are their blood. And it's a good thing that you can still draw the support and love and energy you need from people who are not directly related to you.

What impact do you hope your life and your story will have on those around you?

The first word that comes to my mind is *joy*. I hope people think, Wanda: She had fun. She was funny. She had joy. I hope I have brought that to people.

Do you have a message for younger women reading your story here?

Don't judge your fears or yourself. Don't put judgment on yourself because some person told you you're worthless. Don't let anyone else's judgment block you from doing what you want to do. Just let it out and let it go. The last couple of months, I don't care who sees me cry. I let that shit out.

Rebekah Taussig

and

Bhavna Mehta

KANSAS CITY, KS, AND SAN DIEGO, CA

Writer Rebekah Taussig, 35, and artist Bhavna Mehta, 54, met in a thoroughly modern way: through Instagram. Rebekah shares her life, her work, and her experiences as a disabled person in Kansas City openly and honestly on her social media feed, @sitting_pretty. Her debut memoir, *Sitting Pretty: The View from My Ordinary Resilient Disabled Body*, was published in 2020. Bhavna, a San Diego–based visual artist specializing in cut paper and embroidery, was new to discussing disability openly online when she first discovered Rebekah's writing. Their friendship has grown through deep conversations via email and over the phone, inspiring them both to look at how friendships form and how people can meaningfully connect without seeing one another in person.

How did you first meet?

BHAVNA: We met online, on Instagram.

REBEKAH: I went back to our direct messages to see if I could find our earliest interaction, and it was a drawing you did of me with one of my cats.

B: Your Instagram feed was so real. As soon as I read a couple of posts, I thought, Whoa, who is this woman? And where is she? And I really wanted to get to know you.

R: Because I am oversharing constantly on the internet, I think Bhavna might have known me a little bit more than I knew her initially. I was so curious about her artwork, so I ordered her book. And as I read through it, I thought, Oh, this woman. I want to be in the world with her and talk with her more.

What were your first impressions of each other?

R: I think that the first deep impression I experienced was when I read Bhavna's book project and got to see the way she slowed down and looked at this one letter that her father had written so closely and carefully.

She blew the letter up really big and cut out every word in the letter by hand. And then it became like this big installation, which is still on display. I felt a lot of wonder around the person who would create something like that.

B: In her book, Rebekah mentioned that her brother was asking her what she was writing about and she went on to say she was talking about bunk beds and having a full life as a child. But then as she continued, she said eventually she ended up talking about shame. I must have read that story like fifty times.

I saw several of my friends that week for coffee and I would say, "Okay, before we do anything, I have to read you this post. Let me just read you this post. And then we can talk." Because I think language is so important. And I honestly have shied away so much from talking about disability, not just to family but to friends and even to myself. And you coming up with the language and coming up with something that you were able to share openly—you were able to expose your own vulnerability about how a word like *shame* can open up something that isn't a shameful thing.

In that piece Rebekah wrote, shame became like a door. It was an opening for this amazing flood of ideas and ways to talk about things that are really hard to talk about. I love how things shifted for me just on that one word. And I'm still thinking about it and I'm still trying to figure out how you did that. It was mind-blowing for me.

R: I feel like I am like a tornado of words all the time, and I'm desperately trying to grab on to one. And I feel like, again and again, with Bhavna, she is the person I would look to as someone who is able to quiet that storm and bring us back to the one word.

Is there anything you were surprised to learn you have in common?

R: I remember being surprised to learn that we both have a difficult time with friendship and deep connection. I feel like even with the people I'm closest to in the world, I often feel very different from them in core ways. And so I think I'm often surprised when I'm able to have a space to connect with you in a way that can be difficult to have language for, because I don't have a lot of that in my life.

B: We connect digitally, and somehow we understand each other. I think if we didn't have the literal distance between us, maybe we would be in each other's lives in a much fuller way and more ordinary way. So we really have to be innovative in how we connect with each other.

There are so many representations in popular culture of what women's friendship is, but it's not enough. What's out there isn't giving me an idea of how *my* friendships can be. I think too often we can get too caught up in the idea that getting together for drinks, being in each other's lives in physical ways, is the only way to have a friendship. I feel like so many versions of friendship have been re-created based on the example of *Sex and the City*: four white, able-bodied women who can have any man they want. But we need new models of friendship. We need to figure out how we can show that to the world. I'm deeply interested and invested in that.

How has disability affected the way in which you connect with friends?

B: Even though my husband has a disability, he became disabled at the age of 23, and I became disabled at the age of 7. And I think I have realized just in the past year what a difference that makes and that you've had a whole life before being disabled. But when Rebekah and I talked, we realized that we both were disabled at a very young age, and I think that connection is really strong. It's an inexpressible connection.

I was reading Maggie Nelson's new book, and she talks about how the inexpressible is contained in the expressed. And for me, I think the idea that we are sort of connected because of early disabilities, that's an inexpressible, but there's something there that remains unexpressed, and it's contained in everything we have expressed to each other. So the development of the friendship sort of feels more natural and more beautiful.

R: There's an immediate recognition somehow, even if it hasn't been explicitly stated, but it's like our hearts and our guts feel it right away.

What was it about each other that made you feel safer to take that risk to open up and make a new friend?

B: I was very attracted to what she was doing online—and very curious. I love the idea of curiosity and affection and attractiveness and friendship. On some level of course it's platonic, but on another level, there is an intensity that you don't feel with many people. So I think that was what made me reach out.

And then she made the decision to be photographed in her wheelchair, come rain or shine or snow. And to write about it and show how to do it for other people. I think that was incredible. And something about only being able to have conversation as your form of connection allows you to go very deep, very quickly. There's, like, no small talk, ever.

Has the difference in your ages been something you've noticed or felt in your friendship?

B: I think it's there, but it doesn't feel like a big difference because I feel very naive in certain areas. And Rebekah is extremely mature about certain things. So I feel we meet in the middle that way. And I will say, I feel naive because I honestly haven't talked about disability, ever. I grew up with the idea that you're already drawing so much attention to yourself by your different body, why would you draw even more attention by talking about it? And so I grew up thinking people saw I was different, so I didn't need to talk about it.

So I feel very new to exploring that part of myself. And to find Rebekah, who's been doing it wonderfully for a while now, is something I really appreciate. Her maturity is so informative.

R: The only time I've considered our intergenerational connection was when we talked about accessibility in the world. And you just reminded me that you and your husband both have lived longer, before the ADA was in place, and you know what the world was like before that. And so a lot of ways that you look at the world and accessibility and the direction that we're headed and what it means to live on the planet as it is now has this context and perspective that I don't have. I was 4 when the ADA passed here, and that has shaped my life in ways I know I take for granted. I definitely do. And you can reframe that for me in a way that I think is really important.

What are some of the most meaningful lessons you've learned from each other?

R: When I'm with Bhavna, my breath feels easier. She makes me slow down and breathe and take a beat to look around and notice what is really important. That is the gift of knowing Bhavna over the years.

I can be very hard on myself, and she just always brings it back down to earth with so much grace and kindness and wisdom that I just want to be nearer to her. That is how I feel about Bhavna and her presence in my life.

B: I think the most meaningful thing for me is to have found another person who really responds to my innermost longings, desires, and ideas and is able to innovate in a very physical way. And although we haven't yet seen each other in person, the idea of the body being the connection is also very meaningful.

Also, I feel being older has given me an appreciation for the fact that our time with our friends is so short. But I am trying to make the most of it and be satisfied with that. That's, I think, age. I did not feel this way ten years ago, but in my early fifties now, I feel like I want to use whatever time we have fully. And I'm so proud of that. Like if we don't have any more time together, we used every second we had talking about things that were important, and that was fulfilling. That was beautiful.

WE NEED NEW MODELS OF FRIENDSHIP. WE NEED TO FIGURE OUT HOW WE CAN SHOW THAT TO THE WORLD.

Kat Howkins

and

Susan Pritchett

WINTERVILLE, GA

Kat Howkins, 65, and Susan Pritchett, 66, are partners in life and work. They share a tremendous love of animals and, after finding an old Victorian farmhouse on twenty-two lush acres in rural Georgia, decided to open an animal sanctuary. Sweet Olive Farm cares for both farm and exotic animals, from alpacas to zebu cattle. In addition to their work with animals, Kat is a landscape designer and Susan runs a business selling handmade knitted goods for children with her best friend. Their devotion to their family, kids (both human and animal), and community shines through in their work together. They sat down with their friend Kristen Bach to talk about their life together and the lessons they've learned so far.

Where did you grow up, and where do you live now?

KAT: I was born in Macon, Georgia, and grew up in Atlanta, and now I live in Winterville, Georgia, with Susan.

SUSAN: I was born in Albany, Georgia, and have lived in New York, Sweden, Australia, Atlanta, and here in Winterville.

What did you want to be when you were younger, and what do you do now?

K: When I was younger, I wanted to be a vet, but I couldn't pass Chemistry 101. I graduated from the University of Georgia with a degree in art history, and now I run the animal rescue here at Sweet Olive Farm with Susan.

S: I wanted to be Nancy Drew when I was younger. Now I just read a lot of mystery novels. Twenty years ago, I founded Blabla Kids with my best friend, Flo, and we worked with Peruvian artisans who hand-knit our children's products. We started that company out of my garage in Atlanta, not knowing anything about how to run a business. Now we sell in fifty countries around the world. In the meantime, Kat and I started rescuing dogs in Atlanta. We looked for more space to bring them in on weekends and ended up out in the country in a Victorian house. We moved a barn and built fences, and now we have ten dogs in the house (and yard) and two guardians in the pasture.

What does your current age feel like for you?

K: My current age *feels* like 34.

S: I feel my age. I just lost my mom, which has made me evaluate how short life is and how much more I have to do.

What misconceptions about aging would you like to dispel?

K: I'd like to dispel the idea that you have to do something or be somebody by a certain age. I remember when I was little, my mom told me I would have to wear makeup when I grew up—and that freaked me out!

When I was 30, I wondered if I would still be able to landscape when I was 40; when I turned 40, I wondered if I would still be able to landscape at 50. Now I am 65 and I am running a farm and working harder than ever. There's this idea that you are going to get weaker and do less as you age. But that's not true. Also, you don't have to wear makeup if you don't want to.

S: People seem to think you have to get mentally and physically weaker as you age. But when you stay busy and do things you love, you keep your brain healthy and your body strong.

What are you most proud of about yourself?

K: I'm really proud of the day camps we have been having at the farm and the wonderful interactions the kids have with the animals, the land, themselves, and me.

S: I am so proud of my daughter, May, and the amazing young woman she is. I am proud of Kat and of being the person she loves. I am also so proud of the farm and what we have created here.

How has your sense of self-confidence or self-acceptance evolved over time?

K: I didn't have the best self-confidence when I was a kid. I was a tomboy with a pixie haircut and a gap between my teeth. I used humor to feel confident. Standing up for my kids, John and Kate, was always easy, even standing up to authority figures on their behalf. But now, as I get older, I never think things are impossible. Whether that is saving an animal or trying to do something that seems financially impossible I know it's not.

S: I was really quiet and a bookworm; then I moved to the East Village. Initially, I was nervous about walking to the subway station by myself, but quickly everything changed and it became my stomping ground and I loved it. Those were formative years for my self-confidence.

What role do you feel your ancestors, or the women in your families who came before you, play in your lives?

K: My grandmother and other women in my family were very strong, lived out west and were good salt-of-the-earth people from Swedish and German immigrant families. They worked hard, told stories, and liked to have a good time. When I was young, my dad was very sick, so my mom and I had to take care of the heavy work around the house. I just always chose to do hard physical work, and now my children do that as well.

S: My mother is my inspiration for my visual sensibility. She was known for her flower arrangements and her rose garden, and I'm obsessed with roses because of her. She gave me my passion for antiques, color, and style. I love how she treasured things, placing great importance on tradition and family keepsakes. To this day, I have an intense love affair with color; it totally affects my being.

Do you have a message for younger women reading your story here, and what impact do you hope your lives and your story have on those around you?

K: You can do it! You can help; you can go vegan to help the animals and the world and future generations.

S: I hope people can strive to bring awareness to the incredible sentience of all animals. We have so many stories here at the farm that prove how smart and knowing and connected our animals are to each other and to us. Sometimes an animal arrives and it becomes instant best friends with another, not necessarily in the same species. Once, we reunited a family of cows—mother, sister, brothers—after four years, and they knew each other right away and ran together and licked each other's faces. That was such an incredible moment; it brought tears to everyone watching.

When do you feel your most powerful?

K: When we do a rescue and help save an animal. Or when the vets come out and we do shots. I feel powerful when I am around the energy of animals and the energy of kids. I feel powerful whenever my wife and I are crying or laughing. We have laughed so many times together; it just feels good.

S: I feel powerful when I am with Kat and we acknowledge that we have created a meaningful life together and that we are saving animals' lives.

Can you describe a turning point in your life, and how it changed things for you?

K: When we came to see the old Victorian house that we live in now. I didn't want to see it; I was perfectly happy living in Atlanta. Susan begged me to see it, and we turned down the driveway and I said, "I hate to say it, but I am moving here." It wasn't too long before we had animals coming in and Sweet Olive Farm Animal Rescue was started.

S: A turning point for me was when we said yes to "one" potbellied pig, and we built a pen for him, then Fulton County Animal Services decided to put us on speed dial for every farm animal found wandering around Atlanta. That is how we started the sanctuary.

What's the biggest risk you've taken in your life, and how has it shaped you?

K: In the early '90s, it was not easy to leave a marriage to a man because you were gay. It shaped me into my real self, although it is hard to believe that would have to be a risk. The one thing it didn't change was my relationship with my kids.

S: I agree that this was a difficult time for me as well. My brother called a family meeting for everyone to voice their opinions about how they knew I was gay and didn't think it was appropriate for my daughter to have a gay mother. That was when she was a toddler. And by the time I met Kat, my daughter was in middle school, and my family loved Kat the instant they met her. It was pretty obvious that she was devoted to me, so I guess that meant a lot.

How have your ideas of success and happiness changed over time?

K: I don't think they have changed. As long as my family and animals are happy and healthy, I'm happy. And as long as my Chihuahua, Tex, doesn't wake up at 3:30 in the morning again.

S: My idea of happiness is when a weather event is anticipated (a hurricane or tornadoes, or bitter freezing-cold weather) and we do everything to make sure that all our animals get through okay—and they do!

WHEN YOU STAY BUSY AND DO THINGS YOU LOVE, YOU KEEP YOUR BRAIN HEALTHY AND YOUR BODY STRONG.

How has raising children affected your life?

K: I love being a mom, and it made me understand what pure love feels like. Once I became a parent, I was just John and Kate's mom.

S: Having May was the greatest gift. When she was little, I just loved looking at her face. Now I still love looking at her face, but I really love her mind and how it works. It has brought me so much joy to see her grow into the young woman that she is.

At this point in your life, what have you made peace with that used to be a struggle for you?

K: Coming out to people as being gay—I still don't feel comfortable announcing it to my community in rural Georgia. Maybe it's the rebel flags . . .

S: It is an interesting area of the countryside that we live in. It is progressive in our small town, then a mile down the road there are lots of Confederate flags and a popular gun store.

What would you like to learn or experience at this stage in your life?

K: I would like to go back to Tasmania someday, and I would also like to learn more about medical practices for animals. Just yesterday, I helped a vet friend drain a cyst on Coco, the goat, and it was amazing!

S: I want to get more physically fit and stronger, so that I can make the Stinson Walk, which I've long dreamed of doing. It is a pretty advanced forty-kilometer rain forest hike in the Gold Coast hinterland in Queensland, Australia, down to the site of a plane crash from eighty years ago. The lost aircraft was a real mystery in its time.

What is a lesson you're still learning or need to learn?

K: Patience. And how to say no.

S: Organization. The longer you live, the more things there are to keep organized, especially when you move belongings from city to city, house to house, or move childhood treasures from your childhood home to your current home.

Knowing what you know now, what would you go back and tell your younger self?

K: You are going to get a farm, you will get to work with animals, and you will find that special person you will grow old with.

S: You are going to have the most wonderful relationship with the person you love and who truly sees you.

How has love shaped your life?

K: I've always had a lot of unconditional love from my siblings, parents, and extended family, and it has given me stability. When I told my sister I was gay and I was scared, she just said, "I'm your sister." And that meant everything.

S: Love gives you the foundation to do anything.

How has loss shaped your life?

K: My dad died when I was 40, which made me responsible for my mom. You really just never get over it. We deal with loss at the farm because we have elderly, sick, or neglected animals that have to be cared for, and sometimes they don't make it or they die of old age. I always say I can deal with it, but you never get used to it. The loss hurts, but you gain so much from the love you shared with that animal.

S: There are dogs that I still achingly miss. And I haven't really come to terms with losing my parents. My mother's passing was very recent, and I still think about picking up the phone and calling her.

Lisa Congdon

PORTLAND, OR

Artist Lisa Congdon, 53, didn't discover her passion for illustration until she was in her thirties. Because her career blossomed in her early adulthood, she has been able to connect with and inspire so many others to follow their dreams and remember that it is never too late to try something new. Lisa has written and illustrated nine books, travels internationally to speak about creativity, and was named one of 40 Women to Watch Over 40 in 2015 and featured in *200 Women Who Will Change the Way You See the World*. She lives and works in Portland, Oregon.

Where did you grow up, and where do you live now?

I grew up in a couple of different places. I was born in Niskayuna, New York, which is right outside Schenectady. I lived there until I was 8 years old, and in 1976, my family moved to San Jose, California, where my dad got a new job with General Electric, where he worked all his life.

I went to college at Saint Mary's College of California in Moraga, which is a small liberal arts school. I had a really amazing experience there. Then, the day after I graduated in 1990, I moved to San Francisco, and I lived there all the way until 2015. Now I live in Portland, Oregon.

What did you want to be when you were younger?

I really wanted to be an archaeologist. I've always been obsessed with collecting things, starting when I was a really little kid. I used to love to go to the junkyard with my grandmother and dig for old treasures. It made me excited in a way that nothing else in my childhood made me excited. I think I still have some papers from fourth grade where I talk about how I want to be an archaeologist. Because to me, digging for treasures is the ultimate pastime. And in a way, I still sort of do it when I go to flea markets, or antiques malls or whatever.

How has your sense of self-confidence or self-acceptance evolved over time?

I would say that I'm just starting to come into my sense of confidence and of being at home in my body. I'm just starting to know myself and feel secure in who I am and my ability to say what I mean—even if I think it's going to disrupt or upset someone else. I guess I'm coming into my own ability to have boundaries.

I had a realization when I was 49 that one of the ways in which I show up in the world is through social media. I both love it and wouldn't have a career without it, but I also recognized that there were aspects of my relationship with it that were damaging to me or that I was allowing to influence how I felt on a particular day. So I found myself as this sort of mature, grown woman, old enough to have a teenage daughter, and yet I had a relationship to social media that on the outside probably looked very healthy to others but that I was really struggling with on the inside. So I just did a lot of very intentional work around that, which led to me taking more ownership of what I stood for, being braver about what I talked about on social media, telling more and more real stories about mental health, and protecting vulnerable people. That took a lot of practice. But over time, the more and more I did that, and sort of entered into that relationship with this attitude of ownership, I realized that the world didn't come crashing down. In fact, I felt better about myself.

I was also diagnosed with breast cancer in 2020. I was told very early on, "You're not going to die. We've caught this early." But there is something about having a diagnosis for a disease that kills some people that makes you confront your mortality, and it woke me up to showing up in the world for what I believe in and not worrying so much about how other people would judge me for doing that.

I shared my diagnosis publicly, and the outpouring of support was amazing. There was so much from so many people. It was in that moment where I felt, Everything is okay. I am loved. Sometimes people go through that when they're younger, and sometimes people go through that when they're older. Sometimes people never get to experience that in their lifetime. And I realized that I felt that because I put myself in a vulnerable position by being myself in front of hundreds of thousands of people every day. You can't reap the benefits of love unless you are vulnerable and allow yourself to make connections with other people and give of yourself. That was the greatest lesson of my life, and it freed me in so many other ways.

I got a tattoo during all of this that my friend Adé Hogue designed for me. It's on my leg, and it says "terrible beautiful." I really think that in life, the most profoundly beautiful things often come from the most painful, difficult things.

When do you feel your most powerful?

When I'm on my bicycle. I have discovered over the last few years that I need something outside my work. I need at least one thing outside that part of my life to ground me, to keep me in my body, to separate me from thinking about work all the time. For me, cycling has been this gift.

My partner, Clay, and I joined a cycling team called Sorella Forte in Portland. The name means "strong sister" in Italian. It has been amazing. I found a place where I can move my body, get exhausted, talk with women about things other than art and design and social media. It is the most refreshing, safe place for me.

When I was in my twenties and early thirties, I always felt a lack of confidence. But something happened in my late thirties and in my forties, where I started taking risks and doing the things I always thought were reserved for other people. If you had told me five years ago that I would be riding a hundred miles a week with other 50-something-year-old women who are complete badasses, I would never have believed you. Sometimes I'm on the bike, and we're wearing our matching kits, and we're riding really fast, and we're climbing hills, and I feel so powerful in that moment. I picture the

35-year-old me or the 25-year-old me who always wanted to do that but either didn't necessarily want to put in the work to get there or could never imagine that I could be that person. And I'm like, I am that person now. And that just makes me feel really full and happy.

I feel like one of the greatest things about getting older is that perspective about how all the shit you were scared of and didn't understand becomes your story, and your story is what connects you to other people. What connects you to other people is what helps you be who you are.

What role do you feel your ancestors, or the women in your family who came before you, play in your life?

I was kind of a late bloomer. I was a late arriver to this world I'm in now. My career rests on the backs of the people who came before me. I would not be where I am without their generosity. The relationship I had with my former agent, Lilla Rogers, was formative. She took me on when I barely had three things in my portfolio. She saw something in me that I didn't even see in myself. When I decided I didn't need an agent anymore, she said, "I've been waiting for this day to arrive. I knew you were going to be ready. It doesn't make sense for you to be represented by me anymore, because you've got this." We remain very close. She was an amazing mentor to me; she saw the value in me as an older person starting her career late in life. She said, "You have more wisdom, perspective, and maturity at 41 than people who are 21. You'll make progress on this path more quickly, because you have all of these other skills that you bring to the table." She taught me that my age was actually going to be my power, not something that would be to my detriment. And she was right.

How has not raising children affected your life?

I don't always feel a tremendous amount of privilege being queer, being in the LGBTQIA+ community, except when it comes to this expectation of childbearing. I feel like oftentimes in our community, we get a pass on the "Why haven't you had children?" conversation. Because from the get-go, our lives have always been so unconventional. It's really a strange thing. I have always wanted a fairly traditional relationship. I've always been monogamous. I've always wanted a life partner. I am very domestic. I love being at home. I love everything about being in a relationship, and I'm with somebody who is also like that. But I have never wanted children. And I love kids!

But I have always wanted to travel, and to have comforts that are just for me. I figured out what I was going to do and who I was so much later in life than a lot of people, and I didn't want to give any of that up. I remember when Clay and I were on our third date, we high-fived each other in the middle of dinner when I sort of blurted out that I didn't want children. Both of us love kids. I love being an aunt. But I feel a tremendous amount of freedom not having children. I really do respect, so much, all of my friends who want kids and have kids. It's just not for me, and I feel like I have this really full life.

What misconceptions about aging would you like to dispel?

One of the questions I get asked most often by women is, "Look, I'm 54 or 63 and have just figured out that I'm a really good artist, and I want to put myself out there, but I am terrified of competing with younger women, or even men. How am I going to grow a business? How am I going to do the thing I want to do?"

I also say that as older women, we have more creativity, more perspective, more wisdom, more experience, and hopefully more confidence in our favor. That is such a powerful tool in figuring out what you're going to make art about, how you're going to put it out into the world, how you're going to talk to your audience.

People think older women become invisible or less powerful or irrelevant, or have less to say. But they absolutely do not. I made this book in 2016 called *A Glorious Freedom*. It's about women over 40 who, like me, found their calling later in life. These women have so much energy, so much experience, and so many great ideas, which is why they were successful later. And so I always encourage women to suspend disbelief about what they can accomplish and begin to think about themselves and imagine themselves as more powerful, more creative, and more wise.

What are you most proud of about yourself?

I think it takes a lot of energy and openness for me to show up in the world in the way I do every day. I'm proud of that. Part of my mission is to demystify what it means to get older and be a working artist. And to demystify what it means to be somebody who supports progressive politics and be actively antiracist. To kind of lead by example in a way that isn't "I'm the expert" but "I'm a learner, and I don't know what I'm doing, but I'm going to show up in the world anyway." I'm most proud of myself for trying every day, as hard as I can, to be that person who wants to show up but is also open to learning, and feedback, and growth.

Do you have a message for younger women reading your story here?

Surround yourself with other women who move through the world in a confident way and who don't take anybody's bullshit—but who are still open to growth, to learning and evolving. So much of who we are and how we show up is what we *tell ourselves* about who we are. So much of how I wake up feeling these days, despite feeling like the world is falling apart, is so grounded for me in the messages I tell myself about who I am, versus the messages I told myself three, four, five, ten years ago about who I was.

I understand, on a profound level, that I am worthy of love, and belonging, and connection, and all those things. I didn't necessarily always believe that. The only reason I can wake up feeling that way now is that I did all the work to understand that. I encourage every woman to do the work required to get to that place. Because not feeling that you are worthy of love, belonging, and connection is a terrible way to live. You, like every human being—despite your mistakes, despite your mishaps, despite all the times you fucked up—are worthy. And feeling like we're not is the thing that holds us back. And for me, figuring that out has been transformational.

Blair Braverman

and

Martha Schouweiler

WISCONSIN

Blair Braverman, 32, and Martha Schouweiler, 68, share a deep and devoted love of dogs. As dog mushers in Wisconsin, each running her own team, they have found a way to do what they love while staying true to their core beliefs. Martha has blazed trails and won awards that have inspired mushers like Blair to take on the toughest races, including the Iditarod. Blair has shared her love of dog mushing in her debut memoir, *Welcome to the Goddamn Ice Cube*, and as a journalist for the *New York Times*, *Vogue*, and *This American Life*. Blair and Martha's friendship is a reminder of the important role intergenerational connections play in supporting women in fields that have traditionally been dominated by men.

How did you first meet?

BLAIR: Well, I think I probably heard of Martha first because she is an absolute legend in midwestern mushing. She has won one of the biggest races around, the John Beargrease, six times. I was just getting into racing for the first time in the Midwest and aspiring to do those races, and Martha had these really cool sweaters at musher meetings. She had amazing Norwegian sweaters, and I learned to mush in Norway, so I promptly made a fool of myself and hung around her a lot. I just wanted her to like me.

I have visions of seeing Martha on the trail in her red suit. That's when I think we probably first talked, at a race called the IronLine. It was a really crowded room, and we seemed to seek each other out for some reason. I guess it was just meant to be.

What were your first impressions of each other?

MARTHA: Blair and her husband, Q, came to visit us because they were going to buy three dogs from us. We got to sit and talk a lot in our cabin, and my first impression was that it was so much fun to talk to them. There was definitely a connection. You can't necessarily explain a connection like that, but it seemed like we had so much to talk about besides the dogs. Even just little things, like sweaters or hats or gear or food. There were many, many things to talk about. There was never really enough time to talk about all we wanted to talk about.

B: Martha is among our closest mushing neighbors because she lives an hour and a half away, which is pretty close (most mushers are far-flung). But every race I was in, I was so nervous and intimidated to be out here with all these mushers I admired. Every single race, at some point, Martha passed me going a million miles an hour. I'd start the race, and then it was this comforting thing to know that at some point, she was just going to zoom by, and her dogs would be at a sprint and mine would be at their steady little trot, and she always said, "Hi, Blair!" It became this thing that would give me this little burst of encouragement in these races that felt really daunting at the time. She was just sort of this very fast, but warm, presence on the trail.

I WANT TO BE REINCARNATED AS ONE OF MARTHA'S DOGS. THE COMMITMENT AND THE LOVE AND THE FUN SHE HAS IN HER DOG YARD, IT'S BEAUTIFUL.

Can you describe a moment when you realized that you were going from being colleagues in a particular community to being closer friends?

M: We were fortunate to get together a couple of times outside the races, and I think it was when she was going to be doing the Iditarod that we went to dinner so I could give her a few tidbits of encouragement before the journey. I had this overwhelming desire to support her and felt so proud that she was my friend.

B: I thought of you out there, Martha, because it was a race where you weren't going to pass me and say hi. Subconsciously, I'm always waiting for Martha to come up behind me and say hi.

The other time I knew we were going to be friends was when we bought our lead dog, Pepé, from Martha. We weren't sure if you were going to part with Pepé, because you were so close to her. But we fell in love with her, and you let us bring her home. I remember you walked up to the truck as we were leaving and said, "You just need to know, she really loves me."

And it was so true. We had to make sure Pepé came back for visits, and whenever we were in the same place, Pepé had to see you and you had to see Pepé. And she turned into the dog who's really made our team what it is.

Pepé led our team for all of the Iditarod, most of it in single lead, which is an astonishing accomplishment for any dog. So I always feel like a little bit of you is here with Pepé. She's shaped our team so much as well, and that was another gift we got from you.

M: I can't explain how much I adored this dog. But it was meant to be. Pepé couldn't have been placed in a better home. It's almost like Blair is another me. And it turned out so well. To see how far you took Pepé. You just can't imagine how proud you made us.

As you have gotten to know each other better over the years, is there anything you were surprised to learn you have in common (besides your love of dogs and mushing)?

B: I'd say Norway. Martha, you're pretty Norwegian, right?

M: I'm Swedish and Danish, and there's a little bit of Norwegian. It's all close. Those Scandinavian roots, I think, have been a connection for us, which was fun because I love all things Scandinavian. It turned out that Blair had spent time in Norway, which was evident in little things like clothing from vintage thrift shops.

B: Martha and I would show up to races dressed identically. It wasn't on purpose. It just happened. We have bonded over mushing fashion.

What are some of your most fun memories together?

B: I think that musher campouts with Martha are a blast. Mushers have campouts together where we meet up for fall training and sleep out in the woods and train with our dogs. We got invited to one with Otter Run Kennel, which is Martha and her son Chad and daughter-in-law Erin's kennel. So, we went out for a dog run at 3:00 a.m. with our dogs, and then Chad was running their dogs, and we got back and Martha had this wall tent set up with a beautiful fire in it, because it was raining and it was 35 degrees. In that time, she had made, from scratch somehow, in the woods, cinnamon rolls and this fish fry. She had caught the fish and then fried it over the fire in a cauldron. I did not understand how you had done all that, and there were chairs and drinks, and I did not understand how. Then you told us a story about how you saved someone's life on Lake Superior, and I was like, This person is legendary. And we found out that you and my husband were both on the short list for the first season of *Survivor*.

M: That campout was really memorable, especially because the conditions were awful, and I was trying to make it totally comfortable. But when we all got together, we got to just be ourselves and sit around the fire and chat and eat and then go back out again.

Can you remember a tough time you got through with each other's support?

B: Mushing has ups and downs—whether it's a dog being sick, or a race that's disappointing—and it means a lot to have someone you care about and admire who understands that. It's such an intense lifestyle and experience, so it feels incredible to know other people who have gone through it. I've called Martha for advice about so much, and just knowing that she understands what this lifestyle is like is really meaningful.

What are some of the most meaningful lessons you've learned from each other?

M: From Blair I've learned about being in the moment and embracing and cherishing every second, because those moments are so special. Certain races with Blair have been especially memorable. Like standing outside Beaver Bay, I recall what Blair was wearing and the discussion right before the race. That connection is very special.

B: Martha is so ambitious and so kind at the same time. That combination—it's hard for me to think of a person who shines so much in both of those categories because they're not always things we think of together. She's also taught me so many small but useful things, like putting trail mix in a Gatorade bottle for when we're mushing so that you don't have to use both hands to eat it.

I remember a race you were in, the Gunflint, when you were winning and then the person behind you didn't have a headlamp, so you gave her your headlamp and then she won. You didn't even talk about it much; it was just one of those things you did. It's an example of your character. You're so competitive, but there's no question that your humanity and kindness and care for everyone out there on the trail eclipses that.

Why do you think you came into each other's lives when you did?

B: I got into this sport fourteen years ago, but my husband and I have only had our own dogs for less than half that time. And when you get your own team, your life changes so much and there are so many different ways you can do things. And I am always so grateful that we have you as a role model for the kind of mushers we want to be. You have had such an impact on how we built our team.

I always say I want to be reincarnated as one of Martha's dogs. The commitment and the love and the fun she has in her dog yard, it's beautiful. The dogs are going out in boats in the summer; they just have all these activities. It really models for us, as we are getting into the sport, the kind of life we want to give our sled dogs, and it helps us

understand how to envision that, how to plan for that, how to make that possible. I think Martha represents the future of the sport in so many ways. The way her kennel, Otter Run, does things is the mushing that I hope we have fifty years from now, and a hundred years from now, and a thousand years from now.

M: As I've gotten older, it's so encouraging for me that there are other younger women in the sport. That gives me a lot of hope. I won't always be able to do this. So it just makes my heart sing when I see younger women like Blair getting into the sport and doing really well.

B: A moment that I remember with you, Martha, was a few years ago at Gunflint, which is a two-stage race. It's fifty miles, then a couple hours' break, then another fifty miles, and it's the first big race of the season for most of us in the Midwest. I work full-time as a writer—that's my profession—and one thing I started doing was writing stories about our sled dogs online, and particularly on Twitter, as a way of sharing this thing that I love.

We'd done the first stage of the race, and I was exhausted, and we were hanging out at the Trail Center. I wrote a story for Twitter about the first half of the race, even though I was very tired, because I knew there were people who were following the team. Martha sort of looked over my shoulder and said, "What are you doing?" I handed her my phone, and up until then, I had never felt like there was any overlap between my mushing life and my writing life. Martha said, "Wait. Did you just do this right now? Like right now, after this fifty-mile run?" And it was this story about our blind dog that had gotten stuck out on the trail and had been guided by two other dogs to make it back and I was like, "Yeah, this is what I do." I was so tired, and I was worried that she might think this was foolish or that I was getting distracted. But you were so encouraging. It just felt like you *got it* in that moment, like you were the first musher who understood what I was trying to do on the trail and off the trail through sharing stories of the team, and it meant a lot to me.

What do you each hope your friendship brings or gives to the other person?

M: I want Blair to know that I genuinely care. In this world where people, everything, seem to be so divided, I want you to know that there is someone who really cares about you.

B: On a basic level, I want you to know that Pepé is getting the best life we could possibly give her and we love her so much and we talk all the time about how she's like the third human on the team.

In a bigger way, I want you to know that you're changing the sport and that we're trying to follow in your footsteps.

M: This is such an amazing sport, and that's why only another musher gets it. I mean, most of my children don't get it. But when people like Blair get it, there's something really special about that.

B: I think you're modeling what a small team can do. That's what's going to be sustainable in the long run, and you're still winning everything! I think you're shaping the sport in the Midwest, which has such a healthy mushing community. It's helping to reinforce that people can have small teams and take the best possible care of them. You're modeling that, and so many people look up to you and then try to do those things just like you do.

M: Blair and I treasure our moments together, and I want her to know it's okay to just be yourself. I think part of what we're getting from dogs, the positive thing, the thing we love about dogs, is that they're not critical. They're just love. And that's why we love dogs. We sometimes look for that in friendships, and it's hard to find. You can be completely yourself around dogs. They're not noticing the dirt on your coat or the dirt on your face. They just love you, and they're being in the moment. And that is what I also appreciate in my friendship with Blair—just being able to be ourselves. We always have fun together.

Ceyenne Doroshow

QUEENS, NY

Ceyenne Doroshow is a performer, organizer, community-based researcher, and activist in the trans and sex workers' rights movements. She is the founder and executive director of G.L.I.T.S. (Gays and Lesbians Living in a Transgender Society) and has worked tirelessly to protect and uplift those in her community. Ceyenne recently raised enough money to buy a twelve-unit apartment building in New York City, where she will provide housing for those in need as well as a medical center to provide health care. Her latest book, *Falling into the Fire*, is in the works now. Ceyenne sat down with writer Harron Walker to talk about the lessons she has learned in her life and work.

Where did you grow up, and where do you live now?

I grew up in between Bushwick and Park Slope, Brooklyn. And I live in Ozone Park, Queens, now.

What did you want to be when you were younger, and what do you do now?

When I was younger, I wanted to be just what I am now: a young lady of trans experience.

What does your current age feel like for you?

Fun and exciting. I'm living.

What misconceptions about aging would you like to dispel?

That when you get older, life is over. That you have nothing to look forward to. That it can't get better. It *is* better.

What are you most proud of about yourself?

I'm proud of helping others. Of building and creating community at G.L.I.T.S. I'm proud of having the chance to be like a global parent to so many community members. I'm proud of starting this work of helping asylum seekers in harm's way. I'm proud of being able to bring them to safety, and of continuing this work for almost five years now.

Creating substance and sustainability within housing in New York City is something I am proud of. I am continuing the fight by responding to the need for COVID relief and building, literally *building*, a place for community now. We went from renting Airbnbs for people getting out of jail (helping them to shelter in place for safety) to getting them the necessary tools to survive and *not* go back to jail to now buying a twelve-unit prewar building to house everyone. These apartments hold community and give residents the chance to go to school, to reenter society, and to reinvent themselves through education. We are building leaders to do this work when I'm gone.

How has your sense of self-confidence or self-acceptance evolved over time?

I'm still not confident in a lot of things. It's human to not be that confident. I wouldn't say I'm all that confident in the work that I'm creating. I just have a vision. So my self-confidence is built on rocky ground right now. Because I'm creating from scratch. I'm doing something that none of us have ever seen or done or thought of doing. I'm doing what corporate America, not our government, not our senators, not our mayors, has thought to do for the LGBTQIA+ community.

What advice do you have for others who may not feel confident all the time and want to push through that?

Believe in your dream. Believe in that dream, and focus on it; use that as your target. Use that as your focus point and your vision. Use that insecurity and that lack of confidence, and you'll turn things around in your work. As you create, you get a bigger sense of what your involvement is in society, because you're creating for your own society.

What role do you feel your ancestors, or the women in your family who came before you, play in your life?

I think every woman who's had a major influence on my life has given me a little part of them. My mom taught me a lot about class, respect for myself, and respect for others. Flawless Sabrina taught me patience, and to always have an open door and an open-door heart. She taught me to not be so willing to close the door on people, but also not to take shit. And to sprinkle a little glitter on everything in your life.

Miss Major Griffin-Gracy really gave me the chutzpah. She gave me saltiness and told me it's okay to be mad as hell. She told me it's okay to tell people no. And it's okay to stand up for myself. But it's also okay to say "fuck you." And that is a testament to who she is, and who I've become.

Coco Chanel Rodriguez taught me that love does last forever. Being married for almost fifty years, as a trans woman. My sister taught me resilience. She has suffered and gone through cancer and fought. And now her partner has cancer, and she's fighting that battle. Her mom died of cancer. She is a survivor of survivors.

I think all the women in my life, who are strong women in my life, have left a blueprint, almost stepping on my heart to push into me what they want in the universe. And I think I'm doing it.

Do you have a message for younger women reading your story here?

Never, ever take no as the answer to whatever you want to do. Fight and defend yourself, to the best of your ability, with class and dignity. We don't always have to get down and dirty with the naysayers. I believe in unity. I believe in community. And I think all women should push this out. You should exude whatever is in you that is positive. Because the positivity you put out in the universe is the positivity you'll receive in life. We all have the ability to change society. Use your body and your mind as the vessel to teach someone else the tolerance you've learned.

When do you feel your most powerful?

I don't feel powerful. I feel like the world is sitting on my shoulders, and I don't know how to make it stop. Which makes me feel like my world is spinning. But I think the power is when I help one of these young people with a degree—or two, or three. Picking up the phone and hearing they've achieved, yet again, another milestone in my life, in their lives—that's power. It's also the love and respect I receive from them all that gives me the power to go on. I would say being a sort of parent to many makes me powerful.

Can you describe a turning point in your life, and how it changed things for you?

Oh, a turning point. Discovering that I can live on my own. I can be alone. I don't need a mate. I don't need a man. I don't need anybody. Not in my bed, and not in my life. I can do this, without having to have a partner. And it's okay. It's okay to be alone. I spent half my life having a partner, going through countless episodes of domestic violence. And somehow or another, I managed to sustain. Managed to fight for my life. Managed to still believe in love. My turning point was discovering I didn't need a man to do any of this.

Who or what has influenced your life the most?

My children. That love and dedication from around the world. My kids are awesome. They call me with responses to their successes. And that is the pride that I carry.

What's the biggest risk you've taken in your life, and how has it shaped you?

The biggest risk I've ever taken in my life, I just took recently. Buying a twelve-unit building and trying to build sustainability for community, but also planning to open up a health clinic. And build a skyscraper over it. That's a risk. It's all a risk. It all has the potential to come crumbling down. But I'm taking the risk. I'm jumping into the pool with the sharks, to create this space.

If you could go back in your life, what would you like to do over—and what would you never do again?

Hmm. I would like possibly to change my childhood, but if I changed my childhood, would I still be the person I am today? What would I never want to do again? The domestic violence. The many

I THINK EVERY WOMAN WHO'S HAD A MAJOR INFLUENCE ON MY LIFE HAS GIVEN ME A LITTLE PART OF THEM.

nights of being scared. The many nights I asked for help and no one dared to answer. The many times I had to wipe my own blood off my face or my body. I can do without that. I'm good.

How have your ideas of success and happiness changed over time?

My idea of success is creating, always creating. Ever since I got into this work, I have always been able to create. And everything I create is designed to inspire people to go out there and do what *they* need to be doing.

How has raising children affected your life?

It keeps me on the edge of my seat all the time. It literally is the reason I breathe, and the reason I *can't* breathe. It's always wanting to know that my kids are safe, and that they're eating, and that they're strong. And that they're physically able. And that they're getting all the knowledge out of life that they can get. But I think parenting changed my life more than anything else because it's an undying kind of love. It's the adulation that's most important. It's the notoriety you need and want. It's the very essence of love. It's the core of hellos and goodbyes. Parenting is everlasting. I don't ever want to look at my children and think that I can't love them or won't be able to love them. It is the core of what my days begin and end with. Because I love my children.

At this point in your life, what have you made peace with that used to be a struggle for you?

My anger. My anger at many things: my anger at not being accepted as a child, my anger at not fitting in with the in crowd, my anger at not wanting to be in with the in crowd. And especially my anger against the people who wronged me, who hurt me. Who physically hurt me, who mentally hurt me.

But making peace with your anger and healing yourself pushes you, catapults you to go even farther. When you can let go of that anger, you literally are letting go of anchors on your life. Being big enough to stand and rise above your anger. And that means getting over it through any process you can: Therapy. Talking to your friends. Talking to your family. All of that helps change your direction and helps change your anger into success.

What would you like to learn or experience at this stage in your life?

I want to learn Mandarin. I want to learn French. I want to learn how to cook every meal I can. I want to learn tolerance for people I find annoying and ignorant. And I want to learn how to blend my makeup just a little bit better.

What is a lesson you're still learning or need to learn?

That you can't help everybody. That not everybody is willing or needs to be helped. That I am not everybody's savior. And that I need to be my own savior.

What impact do you hope your life and your story will have on those around you?

I hope my work changes the direction of my community. I hope my impact builds the hope and belief that we can do anything we set our minds to. That a dream is more than a dream; that when you put 100 percent into your dream, it is a reality.

Knowing what you know now, what would you go back and tell your younger self?

Don't be so stressed. Don't be so needy for love. Because it will happen. And don't ever, ever give more of yourself than people are willing to give to you.

How has love shaped your life?

Love has shaped my life in many ways. It has broken my heart. It has lifted my heart. It has changed my heart. Love has given me the ability to do the work I'm doing today. Love is something I'd like to pass out, if it could be bagged and boxed. I think everybody deserves it.

How has loss shaped your life?

It's the worst pain. It's pain that feels not only emotional but also physical. It's stifling. There are moments when you just wish it would all go away. Loss can damn near take your life. I am trying to grapple with this, considering I just lost somebody who was Hindu, and in Hinduism there is a thirteen-day celebration of life that's quite intense. For thirteen days, every day, you're reliving that loss over and over and over and over and over and over again. Till the finale, which doesn't really give you closure; it tells you the ceremonial part is over, but you have to carry that loss with you every day. And there are days you wake up, and you realize that when you go out your door, that person isn't there anymore. Or you know, some of my sisters are gone, and have been gone for years, and a thought will pop into my head or I'll smell something familiar, and I have to feel that loss all over again. Because sometimes it's just that. It's a leaf falling. It's a smell. It's somebody's conversation. It's somebody walking by. It's a face. It's a shadow on a wall.

Loss during COVID is probably one of the most traumatic things I've had to go through. The pandemic took a lot of people I know out of here. I became overwhelmed by the sense of loss, all in a matter of two or three months. Just bombarded by what goodbye looked like through the lens of Zoom funerals. And you can't imagine what it's like to not touch your loved one, or see them face-to-face one last time. So I am still in the primary stages of grieving, because I've had to be on the forefront of grief. And then I rise.

How has friendship shaped your life?

Oh my God. I've got some friendships that I feel like I've had forever. It feels like those friends have always been in my life. And those friends are family. Those friendships are, you know, the be-all and end-all.

How has work shaped your life?

Work has shaped my life 100 percent. Work has become a twenty-four-hour-a-day thing. I wake up working, I go to sleep working. I get phone calls in the middle of the night. I get stress calls in the middle of the night. I get help calls in the middle of the night. But it's made me a first responder. It's made me the type of person who can do this without breaking down. I probably need to break down. I've probably got some real falling apart to do. But this work won't let me. Because it's never ending. Which makes me resilient, by the way.

How has community shaped your life?

Community is hit or miss. Community can pick you up and also can drop you. Community can be your rock, and also the rock that's on top of you. Community can help you rise, and can break your heart at the same time. Everybody has their own flaws. As leaders, we have to know that community can fail. And it's okay.

Grace Lynne Haynes

and

Cheryl R. Riley

NEWARK, NJ, AND JERSEY CITY, NJ

Artists Grace Lynne Haynes, 28, and Cheryl R. Riley, 68, come from different backgrounds and different generations, but they share a desire to live creatively—in and out of the studio. Grace is a visual artist who creates paintings focused on bright textures and patterns. An inaugural member of Kehinde Wiley's Black Rock Senegal residency, Grace was included in the 2020 edition of Forbes 30 Under 30: Art & Style. Cheryl is a visual artist, writer, furniture designer, and art adviser who focuses on artists of the African diaspora. Cheryl and Grace met at a time when they were looking to make intergenerational connections in their community. Cheryl was able to support Grace in her entrance to the art community, and Grace was able to remind Cheryl that you can always ask for help and get what you need from those who care about you. Their friendship has inspired both women to stretch their lives creatively, knowing they have each other's backs.

How did you first meet?

CHERYL: Grace and I met through another artist friend, Adebunmi Gbadebo, when they were residents at Vermont Studio Center together. At the end of their session, a snowstorm arrived and canceled their flights. The VSC kicked them out of their rooms to prepare for the next group. I had been a resident there, and during my time, I took over the basement under the dining hall for raucous dominoes games. So I told them about that space to go be cozy and warm in.

GRACE: When I first met Cheryl, I was astounded by her kindness and generosity toward me, when we barely even knew each other. I also was intrigued by her artistic lifestyle, great fashion sense, expansive art collection, and passion for helping artists of the African diaspora. I knew she was truly one of a kind with a heart of gold. I struggled in the past to find genuine mentors, and she came at the perfect time when I was beginning to think this would be a lone journey. Cheryl immediately saw the potential in me and has been actively supporting me as both an artist, mentor, and friend since then.

Can you describe a moment when you realized that your friendship was a significant one and would have an impact on your lives?

C: I think for me it was after we both did good deeds for each other. I sold some of her artworks early on to important collectors, which not only put a few dollars in her hand but also boosted her confidence, I believe. For me, it was after reading her writing and humbly asking her to edit my artist statement for a grant or residency proposal. It was knowing I had a supportive friend, and she taught me a lot about editing.

G: I was going through a very tough time in my life when I met Cheryl, and she still saw the best in me. Most people will see you down and try to keep you there, but then there are others who remind you of your best self so you can rise to the occasion. I knew ours would be a significant friendship when I visited her apartment for the first time. Cheryl was so welcoming, and I knew she was someone I would want in my life for the long term because she reminded me of what was possible. Growing up in a super-conservative home, it was hard to

ALL GENERATIONS
HAVE STRENGTHS
AND WEAKNESSES,
AND WE BECOME
MORE WELL-ROUNDED
INDIVIDUALS WHEN
WE HUMBLE OURSELVES
TO LEARN FROM
ONE ANOTHER.

visualize a life that was artistic—not just as a career. But Cheryl is living proof that being creative is a lifelong pursuit, and that giving back is the key to fulfillment.

What are some of the most meaningful lessons you've learned from each other?

C: Grace has taught me to ask for and accept help without feeling I need to immediately repay it—that accepting help is a gift in itself.

G: I've learned the importance of giving back to artists in the industry once I get settled in. Cheryl reminds me that not only giving back but giving back passionately and selflessly is the key to advancing our culture. This isn't an individualistic journey; it's an expansive intergenerational journey in which we all can learn from each other.

What have been some surprising things you've learned or experienced in your friendship?

C: I have learned that even though Grace is self-possessed and stoic, she has her fears and insecurities, and that she feels safe exposing that side of herself to me.

G: We have very similar childhood backgrounds, both coming from conservative homes and branching out into a new city to further our identities as artists. I love how we didn't let the circumstances we were born into define who we are.

What advice do you have for someone who is curious about or interested in making new friends of different ages?

G: I would say to both, come in with an open mind. Oftentimes younger people think our elders are outdated, and the elders think the younger generations are naive and don't know any better. There's so much intergenerational knowledge that can be exchanged. All generations have strengths and weaknesses, and we become more well-rounded individuals when we humble ourselves to learn from one another.

What do you each hope your friendship brings or gives to the other person?

C: I hope my friendship with Grace brings her a feeling that she is safe with me, fully accepted and honored. I hope she knows that through all her ups and downs, I will be loyal and loving, a safe haven for her.

G: I hope my friendship with Cheryl is a light in her life. I hope I can be a source of inspiration and positivity!

Elisabeth Plumlee-Watson

and

Jean Loria

CLEVELAND, OH

Gardens are a place of growth and renewal, and in the case of friends Elisabeth Plumlee-Watson, 34, and Jean Loria, 69, a garden was where their friendship developed and bloomed. An avid gardener and reader, Jean was a frequent shopper at Loganberry Books, the independent bookstore in Cleveland, Ohio, where Elisabeth is the manager and buyer. A shared interest in foxglove was the topic of their first conversation in the shop, but it was at an author event that the two realized they were both lesbians and had been in search of more intergenerational connections within their queer community. Both Jean and Elisabeth say they've learned a lot from their friendship, and hope to continue to support each other and their shared love of community, gardening, and expanding their chosen family.

How did you first meet?

ELISABETH: I'm a bookseller at Loganberry Books here in Cleveland. I learned about publishing while doing author events here at the shop, and that led me to New York, where I worked in publishing for eight years, met my wife, and got married.

We knew we wanted to move back to Cleveland, so I called Harriett, the owner of Loganberry Books, and she said, "Why don't you come work for me?" Now I work here in a manager role, and I'm also a book buyer—but I'm also out on the sales floor a lot. And Jean has been a very loyal customer and a longtime shopper at the store. That's how we were first introduced. It's also how I learned she was into horticulture, because she came in to help with a giant sansevieria plant at the shop.

We had the great privilege to get a house with a garden, and I started amassing a collection of digitalis—foxglove—which I had become enchanted by after seeing Beatrix Potter's illustrations of them as a child. I was having trouble raising them from seed, so one day as Jean was checking out at the counter, I asked her if she knew about foxglove.

Jean has this incredibly deep knowledge and long experience with native plants and horticulture. I was sheepish to ask about foxglove, because it is definitely *not* a native species. But she had great advice, and she recommended a variety she had grown before. I found some seeds in the UK and was able to start some plants and shared them with her.

JEAN: I enjoyed calling you Madam President of the Digitalis Society.

Can you describe a moment when you realized your friendship was going to be a significant one in your lives?

E: Jean came to an author event for Casey Cep, who wrote a book about Harper Lee called *Furious Hours*. That was when Jean met my wife, Paige. Casey was there with her wife and was talking about Harper Lee as a lesbian and Lee's friendship with Truman Capote, who was a gay man, and the trauma of queerness at the beginning of the mid-twentieth century and in the white South.

It was a very, very long line for signing, and I was standing in line with Paige talking to Jean all the way up to the table where Casey was going to sign both our books. We were talking about how neither of us knew that Harper Lee was lesbian. That's when I realized that Jean was also and that she had this history with the lesbian community here in Cleveland. From there we were in touch a lot more.

J: Over the last couple of years, I'd been kind of looking around because the lesbian community here had a lending library of books by and for women. We couldn't keep the library where it was anymore, so we dispersed the books to people. And as time went on, some of those people were gone and the books were scattered far and wide. I had kept some of the collection that included issues of *The Ladder* and some *herstorical* things like that. It had been in the back of my mind that I was looking for somebody who was interested in books and feminism and who was a younger lesbian.

That's when I asked Elisabeth to help me find a new home for the collection. I knew of different archives around the country, but she was so wonderful in helping me get my complete collection archived in New York. They're now a part of the Lesbian Herstory Archives in Park Slope.

E: One of my friendships in New York was with a woman, Dianne, who passed away two years ago. She was 82 at the time and was a retired Catholic nun. She was in the original edition of the book *Lesbian Nuns: Breaking Silence*, and she had this incredible archive of papers about being a lesbian Catholic in New York City in the second half of the twentieth century. She had wanted to get that collection archived at the Herstory Archives, and she was the one who connected me with the organization so I could help her get her papers archived. That earlier intergenerational friendship was why I had a connection to the archive and was able to help connect Jean with them, too.

J: I just thought it was all so wonderful. Then after we started to visit each other's gardens more, I found myself thinking, I'm just so lucky Elisabeth invited me to her knitting group.

E: That's right! I helped teach Jean to knit. She'd done such amazing work with just a book from the library. Paige and I had a monthly women's craft and knitting circle for about a year. It's been cut short by the COVID-19 pandemic, but it was really great.

What were your first impressions of each other?

J: I knew she was a book person and very smart. Soon, though, I got an insight into her being someone who had many interests beyond that, including the whole "getting your hands dirty in the garden" thing. She was just very fun to talk to. That doesn't always happen, when you can just have a fun banter conversation while you're in your favorite bookstore getting your favorite things.

E: Whenever Jean came into the bookstore, she always gave the impression of a breath of fresh air. In the winter she would sometimes wear gardening gloves into the store, which I loved because I will sometimes wear garden gloves out and about because they're practical for that. She just seemed like someone who was very connected with the earth and was out there doing things and loving being out in the growing world.

J: I did try to wash my hands up before I came into the store.

E: I think the other thing I remember was how much *fun* she is to talk to and how playful she is—always ready for imagination. I always feel empowered to be more imaginative and more playful when I'm talking to Jean.

Was there anything you were surprised to learn you have in common?

J: I think this is one of the things that's so great about getting a chance to be around younger lesbians. I was an old-school lesbian: feminist, separatist, *blah, blah, blah*, that kind of stuff. So marriage wasn't really one of our political issues. Domestic partnerships, yes, but not so much marriage. I wasn't surprised that Elisabeth was married, but I was a little bit surprised at the knitting circle when she started talking more about going to church. I thought, Okay, here comes another one of my biases going off. Religion. I think one of the really most wonderful things for me, aside from Elisabeth herself, is just that rethinking of issues. I grew up going to church, but had rejected that. But now I can see that things are different, and this seems to be a nice part of their lives. I think it's really helped me grow and sort out and try to rethink some of the ideas I've held.

E: Paige and I talked about being surprised by how much we missed time with our gay elders. I had only ever found that experience of connecting with gay elders with the church in New York where we were married. The only reason I ever ended up going back to church and wrestling with my Christianity again and figuring out a way to be Christian was because of this specific church in the Village, St. Luke in the Fields, which is historically supportive and inclusive of queer people.

There were so many healing things about it, but I think within the context of queerness, there's so much baggage related to family, ancestry, and where we come from. But I think it's so important to remind everyone that it happens every day— this fracture from our genetic families, and being explicitly told, "You're no son of mine, no daughter of mine, no child of mine." It can be both a tacit feeling of not belonging to the chain of people and time, or it can be really explicit. When Paige and I started getting to know Jean more, we would turn to each other and say, "Gosh, I hadn't realized how much it means to talk to queer people of older generations." Even the word "queer" is something my generation has reclaimed as an epithet. I didn't know how Jean would feel about it.

J: It's fine with me. I put myself in that context of the second wave lesbian community. That was a big experience for me—decades of working in community where we built a lot of our own infrastructure and holistic health centers and a library and a newspaper and a gym and a production company that brought in musicians from all over the country. It was a different time. But as we've moved out of that separatism and back into working with others, I've found that all these skills I learned in our collective structures have been so useful. I still identify as lesbian, but queer—I think that's just great. I love the word.

E: The hardest part about leaving New York was leaving that community where we were. There were a couple of other people in their thirties and forties, but, like many churches, this church was made up of people 60 and up, and most of them just happen to be gay. So to move here to Chicago and meet Jean, to become friends with her, has been wonderful. Jean, just by being herself and by talking about her experiences, gives me back a part of *my* story that my biological family is never going to give me. There's nothing like the embodied history that comes from relationships.

What are some of your most fun memories together?

E: Standing in and walking around Jean's garden with her, because she's tended that space for decades. She's taken care of it for over thirty years. Hearing her talk about the arc of the little ecosystem there and what's new and what's old and what used to be and what's coming in to replace it is just so special. Gardening is such a slow-motion art form because you just have stress over years and years. And so to see one woman's relationship with one piece of land that has been so many things over the years just enchants me every time.

J: The first time Elisabeth said I could come over and see the ducks they keep at their house was so much fun. Both Elisabeth and Paige were there, and it was just so much fun watching the ducks and all the things that Elisabeth was doing. Elisabeth was homeschooled, and she just seems to figure out how to do things and then just does them.

How has your friendship helped you through tough times?

J: Duck days have been important for me, because I live alone now and just to be outside during the pandemic was a balm for my soul.

E: There's something so comforting about the clockwork of knowing that every Saturday at noon, Jean will come by for duck eggs, and even if I'm just waving at her through the window, she'll be there. With the loss of so many other routines during the pandemic, just the comfort of a friendly face—or one-third of a friendly face behind a mask—every week at a certain time has been wonderful. I would never have guessed before this how steadying and cheering that could be.

Can you share something meaningful you've learned from each other?

E: Our friendship started because I wanted to learn. And I'm inspired by how gently Jean holds the course of her day-to-day life. Part of that is the way she holds her garden. If you work the earth for forty years, you learn how much is out of your control. I always come away from a conversation with Jean with an awareness that if I just stand in my life and see what comes, it will be okay. It will be good, and there will be wonderful surprises.

J: My friendship with Elisabeth has been a gift. There are a lot of facets and dimensions to Elisabeth, and it gives me a chance to learn. That's very meaningful to me, and it's beneficial to see how flexible she is in the way she thinks about things—particularly in relationship to queer people. That helps me break down some of my stereotypes about things. That's been very meaningful for me. It's pretty easy to sort of sink into your own little dirt pile. But she's shared so much with me and helped me grow.

What do you each hope your friendship brings or gives to the other person?

E: One of the greatest parts of friendship, and one of the wonderful things I've gotten from Jean that I hope I give back to her, is a consistency and presence and that I can look forward to being available to her in big ways and small ways for years to come. I guess constancy is the best way I know to show her how much I look forward to years of both great conversations and learning things, but also of being there for each other.

J: What I would like is for both Elisabeth and Paige to know how much I want them to have a really wonderful life. That they're both such great, great women. I want them to know that there's someone standing by who wants the best for them. I care.

What advice do you have for people who want to find a friendship like yours?

J: Most of the women I know would love to have a friend who's younger. It's huge. If I had a secret formula, would I want to give it away? I don't know. It's an enviable thing to be able to have a friendship with someone who's younger.

E: Since my earliest childhood, I have gravitated to and had the most effortless friendships with women over 60. As much toxicity as the church culture I grew up in gave me, it was also an environment that brought together, in a kind of unusual and very constant way, people of different generations who are not normally connected.

Most young people I know would be equally delighted to have an older friend. I think so often of when I first moved to New York and began my friendship with Dianne, who was in her mid-seventies at the time. I was living in a very small apartment with six other people; there were always lots of people in their twenties around. And I would come back and say, "Oh, Dianne told me the most wonderful story." They were always so envious. They would always say, "That sounds like so much fun. I wish I could meet her. I wish I had that kind of dynamic in my life."

So maybe my advice is the same as Jean's. Age is relative, but I would say to people who are in the first half of their lives, find friends who are in the second half of theirs. There's a generosity and lack of trying to be cool that I never felt in those friendships. They just wanted to be friends with me, and it didn't matter if I was 17. If you want to be a person's friend, they probably want to be your friend, too.

What does your current age feel like for you?

E: I feel incredibly anxious about my mid-thirties because I feel like people have an idea about what they should be doing and what they should have accomplished or what life should be like at that point. I think it's about people having children; so many of my friends are having babies, but so many others are really making it clear that they're deciding *not* to.

I think it has to do with that feeling of family and, after being married for a couple of years, trying to figure out and imagine what family will feel like for decades. Before it was just about making the partnership, and trying to have a relationship with my own family, despite their great devastation that I'm lesbian. There was so much concentrating on my past, my family of origin, and there's a lot of anxiety around thinking about what family will look like, either chosen or created or whatever.

J: I'm 69. I'm twice as old as Elisabeth. I worked in science for a long time and then my sister had a landscape business, so I did that part time with her. I'm not interested in engaging in nostalgia, but now I'm facing the reality that I'm not going to be able to do that much longer. If I can do another season, I'll be surprised, and I'll really enjoy it. And so there are those thoughts, but I recently remembered these T-shirts that were in an Archie comic. They had characters on the front dressed up, and one of them said, "Oh no! I forgot to have kids." It's funny to me, but that's part of what I'm feeling.

I was talking to a woman who lives next door to my sister. She's really nice, and I asked her, "Are you taking applications for an aunt?" And she said yes, she would accept my application. So that was kind of fun. I'm just trying to keep three legs on the stool to keep myself up, because the work thing is going away, and work is a big part of identity for a lot of people.

Eloise Greenfield

WASHINGTON, DC

Author Eloise Greenfield, 92, has been one of the most trusted and beloved voices in children's literature for over fifty years. She published her first book in 1972, and has gone on to publish over forty books since then. Her stories celebrate the warmth and fullness of African American life. She was awarded the Coretta Scott King–Virginia Hamilton Award for Lifetime Achievement by the American Library Association and continues to inspire writers of all ages with her stories of family and friendship.

What is a fear you've overcome or made peace with?

When I was a child, and through much of my adulthood, I was uncomfortable whenever I was alone in even the tiniest spotlight. When I decided to become a writer, I knew I had to conquer this. It took years, but I finally did it. Whenever I had to speak in public, I pretended I was an actress playing a character who was not shy. That little trick worked.

What did you want to be when you were younger?

I have always been a reader but had never thought much of being a writer, like I am now. But when I was in my early twenties, I was desperately bored working as a clerk typist at the US Patent and Trademark Office, typing long letters to applicants. Because of my love for words, I decided to try writing. I began to study books on the craft and write regularly. After several years, I was able to be published.

What role do you feel your ancestors, or the women in your family who came before you, play in your life?

The love of my parents made me feel free to follow my own path. My parents wanted their five children to do well but didn't push us in any specific direction. They spent a lot of time with us. We lived in Washington, DC, so they took us to the Smithsonian museum and the Lincoln Memorial. I also remember my father taking me to the top floor of the Washington Monument. He picked me up so I could look out the window. All the cars going by looked like toys. At home, we played board games and word games, laughed and debated. The house was always filled with music. This nourishment helped me to become a writer.

What are you most proud of about yourself?

My work.

When do you feel your most powerful?

I don't know that I feel powerful. I feel that life sometimes knocks us down, and we stay down for a while. But we do recuperate, get up, and move forward again.

What does your current age feel like for you?

One's age is not something to be ashamed of and lied about. I remember when most offices had no air-conditioning. I remember when long-distance calls were not free and the longer you talked, the more you paid. Living a long life gives us knowledge and perspective.

What impact do you hope your work will have on those around you?

I hope my work will inspire others to follow their dreams and choose the work that is right for them. Writers should never be discouraged by rejections. I still receive them.

Megan Hunt

and

Patty Pansing Brooks

LINCOLN, NE

Megan Hunt, 35, and Patty Pansing Brooks, 63, are both state senators from Nebraska. Megan was the first openly LGBTQIA+ person elected to the state legislature of Nebraska, as well as the first woman to represent the Eighth District. Patty has served since 2014 and also works as an attorney. Megan and Patty became friends while serving in the state senate, finding common ground in their support of progressive causes. Their connection has grown beyond their governmental duties, and they have formed a deep personal friendship that has provided each of them with the inspiration they've needed to do the work they do.

How did you first meet?

MEGAN: I had known of Patty and admired her for a long time. I was very active in the reproductive justice community, and Patty was always speaking at the events, and she was always being honored with awards for her work. She just had this history of advocacy that was so impressive to me as a lawmaker, because you don't see that in a lot of people who are elected. And I was at some rally at the capitol while I was running for office, and Patty was speaking, and I went up to her afterward and said, "I'm Megan." And she said, "Oh, hi, Megan." Then she moved on to the next person and my friend was like, "She's running for legislature!" And then Patty came up to me and she was like, "Well, you should say that!"

I was so intimidated by her, and I didn't want to sound like I was bragging or asking for her endorsement or support. I just wanted to meet her, and I just wanted her to like me. That was my first interaction with her. And then after I got elected, we had a legislative leadership event in Nebraska, and that was when we kind of finally started talking. Patty heard me compliment a Republican colleague—I complimented some work that the colleague and Patty had done together to support public schools in Nebraska—and then Patty came up to me later and she was like, "That was really smart of you to talk to her," and then we hit it off. That's the origin story from my point of view.

PATTY: When Megan won her election, I was so thrilled when we got out to the legislative council meeting. I just really appreciated the way she would talk to everybody. And I knew we were going to hit it off because of Planned Parenthood, because of her willingness to take a stand. Her strength and forthrightness have of course endeared me to her.

Can you describe a moment when you realized that your friendship was going to be more significant than just being colleagues?

P: There are so few people in the legislature, or anywhere in life, who are willing to take a stand and be fearless. Megan does not always make her decisions and act according to what is best for her politically, although she's astute enough to know that. But we both have a knowledge of who we are, and a knowledge that we have to act according to what is best for our constituents, or we can't live with ourselves, basically.

M: I think that's also such a characteristic of women in leadership. Not all women are the same, but my anecdotal experience working with mostly male lawmakers is that the work people like Patty and I do is very strategic, it's very thoughtful, but it's very driven by values. I think it's a little bit less opportunistic than what I see some of our other colleagues do. There are few people like Patty in this line of work, and it *is* work. It's a job. We aren't entitled to be elected. All of this will go away. We're just here for a little while to try to make a difference with the tools we have.

But it's rare to meet people in this field who don't see themselves as better than other people, or aren't always thinking, What's the next best thing for me? What's the next thing for my career? What's the next thing for my next political opportunity? I knew that Patty wasn't one of those people and that we would be not only close allies in the legislature but also close friends in life and friends for life. Because she's such a genuine person. There are people who get term-limited, who leave elective office, who move, who do different things, and you just never talk to them again. It's like, "We got along, but we weren't friends." But then you meet people who are so unique and singular, and Patty is one of those people.

P: Megan is intentional in all she does, and she just cares so much. She's so passionate. I think of her as the adult in the room most of the time, even when I'm there. Half the time I get really fired up on some things and she's really calm. Megan is very good at pulling facts and data, which I think allows her to be steady and to take a breath, because you've got to get the data out and correct. So she does a fabulous job with that. She has counterparts in the legislature, a couple who are about her age, and her abilities to rise up and be steady of spirit but forceful and intentional in her thinking are really remarkable.

M: We all have a podium with a microphone by where we work in the legislative chamber, and Patty has all these little Post-its taped to her podium. One of them is a quote that says, "Never wrestle with pigs. You both get dirty, and the pig likes it."

Another one just says, "Kindness in your voice," and that's something I think about every time I get on the microphone. I haven't written it down on a Post-it note, but I'm not kidding when I say 90, 100 percent of the times I get on the microphone, I think, Kindness in your voice. And that's something from Patty.

Is there anything you were surprised to learn you have in common?

M: Well, we're both former Republicans, and we're both former active Republicans.

P: I was Lancaster County cochair of the party. At that point, I was chair of the Lincoln-Lancaster Commission on the Status of Women, and I was on the Planned Parenthood board. And I was elected to be cochair of the county Republican Party.

M: I was the president of my campus Republican group in college, and like Patty, I wasn't socially conservative, and neither were most of my members, neither were most of my Republican friends. And this would have been in like 2004, so not super long ago. And you can see how fast things have changed in the party. But how I would characterize that surprising similarity, outside of putting it in political terms, is that both Patty and I have this quality of being willing to change our minds when we get different evidence, and staying curious, and wanting to be educated, and wanting to learn, and staying more true to our values than to people's expectations of us.

P: And I think a willingness to listen to others. I think one of the things that drew me to Megan was that we have someone we admire in common, and that's Senator Ernie Chambers, who's the most hated and beloved senator in Nebraska. He's been here for forty years—they created term limits just to stop him from coming back. He was outspoken. This is his last year in the legislature, and we don't know if he'll come back, though he just said he might for the first time that I've heard. But anyway, he is just an amazing person. Megan bravely decided to go sit over by him to learn from him.

So many of the progressives are scared to even get pictured with him, and to even really work with him, because he's so hated by conservative Nebraska. I watched her, and that spoke volumes to me about her substance and her knowledge of who

YOU HAVE TO THINK ABOUT HOW PRECIOUS LIFE IS. AND THE ONLY THINGS WE HAVE WITH US AT THE END ARE THE RELATIONSHIPS WE'VE CREATED AND THE LOVE WE'VE BUILT AROUND OURSELVES.

she is, and her determination to do what's right. And so I think that was a huge part of why I was attracted to being her friend.

M: Well, he calls Patty his goddaughter, and they're very close. We both have a deep respect for him. I actually have a drawing on my door—it's a rhinoceros—that Senator Chambers drew for my daughter, Alice. It has a poem on it. It says, "Someday sweet Alice may have a fine palace, and life there will be like a song, for she shall find pure peace of mind and live contented and long."

Patty kind of laughed about how we have this important, rare, special women's friendship, and we kind of came together over our mutual respect for this 84-year-old man who has been an important mentor to both of us. Patty and I have, I think, long political careers ahead of us, and his is sunsetting. That in itself is a little bit of intergenerational wisdom being passed down as well.

What are some of the most meaningful lessons you've learned from each other?

M: From Patty, I've learned that it's not as important to follow the rules as they're written as it is to understand patterns of behavior, and have respect for others, and compassion for others. I think there are a lot of leaders who maybe have a big fancy title, or who people think are leaders because of some title they have, but who don't do leadership. They don't do the verb of leadership because they aren't willing to challenge the system that puts them at the top, and that's why it's so hard for people with authority to experience the work of leadership.

P: Megan and I are here to continue to push the envelope, to continue to try to expand knowledge, expand hearts, and make sure people are educated on the issues. She is fearless in doing what needs to be done to speak up for what she thinks is right. I would say the majority are more fearful about how to take a stand in that body, and whether they should, and are unwilling to do what they think is right. And Megan is not afraid to do what she thinks is right.

M: It's also really fun being so close to and working with a woman who loves to argue. I would describe myself as scrappy, for sure. When I came into the legislature, I know Patty was a part of this, too, but I wanted to set an expectation for progressives

that we weren't going to give up on fights. That just because we had only twenty-eight votes, just because we had only thirteen votes, just because we had only four votes, what the fuck ever, it doesn't mean that the other side gets away with it easily. It's about using the tools you have, and making a principled stand with rules, with procedure, because it's fun to fight. We argue recreationally, so we're in really good jobs, but actually, I represent 37,000 people whose livelihoods, quality of life, ability to even stay in this state, ability to provide for their families, depend on my willingness to argue, on my willingness to have that fight and to set the record, which is going to be kept in the Nebraska State Library forever, of what we say about why this argument matters.

P: That's unique. In the body and obviously in politics nationally, you don't see that wisdom and that ability, too. It's so important for our future that we have Megan ready to continue battling and speaking her truth.

What do you each hope your friendship brings or gives to the other person?

P: Well, I hope to remain friends for a long time. I hope to be able to be a support to Megan, to continue to help her on her way. But mainly I hope we will remain friends forever. The depth that Megan adds to my life is significant, and of course you want that in any friendship. I care what Megan thinks about what I'm doing. There are people in that body whose opinion about what I'm doing I don't really care about, but I value Megan's wisdom, and her knowledge, and her kindness. And I think one of the main things I try to do is advocate with compassion and kindness. And so I see that in Megan as well. You can be a strong advocate and still be kind.

M: I see Patty as an extension of my family. One time Patty saw me cry on the legislative floor; I think it was when we were working on the LGBTQIA+ workplace bill, and it was spontaneous. I didn't know tears were coming—it was that kind of cry. She related to me with her own problems and vulnerability, and she supported me no matter what. I needed that so much, and she gave that to me. And she has always felt like family to me.

She's just so generous. I don't know what I can give her. I don't have anything. I can't have her over to my nice backyard; I can't get her dinner. I don't know what to do for her sometimes. I want to give her validation, to tell her she's right, she's doing the right thing, she's always been right, her intuition is right, she's loved, she's appreciated, she's important, and she is going to have an impact for generations of people whose lives will be better because of work she did. That's had such an impact, and I want her to know the impact she's had on me, for one. We always say if you can change just one life, it's worth it. That's good. So she's definitely changed my life, and countless others that we will never even hear about.

What advice do you have for someone who is curious about or interested in making new friends of different ages?

P: Holy moly, go for it! No one should have any hesitation. Intergenerational friendships are so important.

My life is so much richer for Megan Hunt. Megan's precious to me, and she'll always be one of our dearest hearts in our household, too. So I love her.

M: I think we get in our own way when it comes to making friends. When you feel like somebody has such a different experience from you, whether that's generational or based on race or religion, you feel like you're not going to have stuff in common. That's because of how we're raised, because of stereotypes that we learn.

It's not because of anything innately different or incompatible within us. You can't think there's something about you that's so unlovable, or so unrelatable, that you couldn't get along with someone else. And a lot of that is just a learned behavior in our culture, that you think you can't be friends with someone. You think you can't understand someone or that there's something about you that people won't like. But none of that is real. You have to think about how short life is, and how precious life is, and the value that we get in life. And the only things we have with us at the end are the relationships we've created and the love we've built around ourselves.

Ann Simpson

and

Anna Sale

CODY, WY, AND BERKELEY, CA

Ann Simpson, 90, is beloved in her home state of Wyoming for her passionate support of the arts and her mental health advocacy. She started the first American Field Service study abroad program in Cody, Wyoming, and created one of the University of Wyoming's most popular art outreach projects, the Ann Simpson Artmobile. Ann's husband, former United States senator Alan Simpson, was the unlikely conduit for Ann's friendship with Anna Sale, a journalist and the host of WNYC's *Death, Sex & Money* podcast. Anna, 41, found herself turning to Ann and Al for unexpected relationship advice at a difficult time in her life, and wound up celebrating with them at her wedding in Wyoming two years later. Ann and Anna sit down to talk about how a romantic connection brought them together and how their friendship has become a real and lasting one despite a nearly fifty-year age difference.

How did you first meet and become friends?

ANN: My husband, Alan, and I were at a hotel in Denver. He was going through his things and he came across this letter. It was from a young man named Arthur telling of his despondency because his girlfriend had broken up with him and he realized that he was at fault. He said she was a big fan of Al's, and if Al would call her and check in with her, that would mean a lot to him. He was desperate. Al read the letter to me, and it happened to be that we had some time to waste, and I said, "Well, why don't you call her? What do you have to lose?"

So he did. She answered the phone and of course, she was stunned. A little terrified, but she did giggle.

ANNA: What I remember is that it was quite a surprise to have a phone call from Alan Simpson about my love life. I thought I knew about Al's work and his sense of humor and the way he talked, but I didn't know a lot about his marriage, and I remember that when he called, he talked a lot about you, Ann. He was saying, "Well, Ann said I should give you a call. Ann said, 'What have you got to lose?'" and I could hear you in the background talking while he was on the phone. I remember saying, "Well, what does *she* think I should do?" He handed the phone to you, and you didn't know me, you didn't know Arthur, but the thing I remember you saying was "I don't know what's going on, but just don't let your pride get in the way."

ANN: I remember that.

ANNA: I thought that was so wise because I am someone who can often let my pride get in the way. I think that advice in particular, to just not be afraid to be curious based on some principle that I needed to uphold—it changed my life.

ANN: It did, but she was a tough sell. She was a little reluctant, you could tell. I loved the fact that she was so honest about her life. There wasn't any coquettishness. She was direct and honest. We just babbled on about our marriage as though we had never had a problem in the world, which was a big, fat lie. She was just so charming, and that wonderful giggle she has is so disarming.

ANNA: I was coming out to Cody, Wyoming, for an event where Arthur was getting an award for

his research. There was a big gathering and I was supposed to have been his date, and then when we split up, I wasn't going to be his date. Al and Ann were both going to be at this gathering in Cody at the Center of the West museum. When we did all finally meet in person, it was on this weekend that ended in an actual ball, like a fairy tale.

What were your first impressions of each other?

ANNA: I felt a certain directness—a warm directness. Ann says that she acted like she and Al never had a problem in the world, and that actually wasn't what I remember. I remember her openness about what it is to be a part of a long relationship where you both are trying to find room for yourselves. I remember her talking about when Al first went to Washington, and figuring out how to take care of the family that they had in Wyoming, while also having responsibilities in Washington. I remember her telling me about what it was like when their three kids were young and needing to ask for more help and support.

I'm not sure if Ann said this when we first met, but there's a quote of Ann's that I say to myself a lot: "Openness creates openness." I really believe that. I believe that if you are open about what has been challenging, it gives others permission to also be open. That helps all of us.

ANN: Because everyone thinks that everyone else has a problem-free life and they're the only ones who are dealing with issues. I learned long ago that if people do talk about themselves, other people will talk about themselves. And not only about the best things that happened, but about some of the worst things.

Was there a moment when you realized that your friendship was going to be something that continued beyond this fortuitous first connection?

ANN: Well, what I was taken with about Anna is that our age was not a factor. Here I was, a good fifty years older than she, and I didn't feel the difference. She can relate to all ages in a very natural way. When you talk to her, it's as if you're the same age. What's an interesting thing to me at 90 years old is that when I am with someone, I am not particularly concerned about the age difference.

I notice that when I mention that to my book club, people are a little uncomfortable. Often they wouldn't challenge me after I'd say something, as if I was the authority. I've not had someone say, "Well, I don't agree with that." But don't treat me with kid gloves. I don't want that. Anna is not that way. She's just so down-to-earth, and you feel as though there's no age difference.

ANNA: In some ways, it felt like we had this wild, weird encounter, and then on top of that, I made them sit down and tell me about it into a microphone so I could make a podcast episode about it. It was just a weird and strange thing that could have just been a strange and funny story, but then it was just so easy to want to spend more time with Ann.

I think when I started to feel like, Oh my gosh, I can't believe that Ann hasn't been in my life my entire life, was the summer when my daughter, June, was born in Cody and we lived right down the street from Ann and Al. Getting to see Ann multiple times a week just by walking down the street, and getting to talk to her about babies and parenting and to have her drop off groceries and be her neighbor was, I don't know—it was the best thing. It was so wonderful. For me, my memory of that time is that our friendship and relationship were already really full and about really deep, big stuff that we had been through together, and then we got to do everyday things together. That was really, really nice.

ANN: It was fun. I am very close to my daughter, so I also feel a certain feeling like that about Anna, a closeness with her. I can relate to her the way I do to my daughter. We speak very openly about things. Sometimes it's more openly than my daughter likes. When she heard Anna's podcast, our granddaughter, who was then about 12 years old said, "Ann said sex three times!" and her father said, "Well, your grandmother talks about sex all the time." I feel it's something that should be openly discussed.

ANNA: That's what I love, Ann. You talk about sex, you talk about mental health, you talk about aging, and you talk about death and mourning. It's particularly remarkable—you are a public figure in Wyoming and you give people permission to talk about all this stuff. I feel so proud to be your friend.

ANN: Oh, well, I feel proud to be your friend, my dear. I think Anna is an extraordinary young woman. She's just very humble about it. That's how people succeed.

Is there anything you were surprised to learn you have in common?

ANN: I don't know, I guess I just always assumed she was very much like me.

ANNA: The thing that I think about a lot when I think about the way I want to live in my community, and the relationship I want to have with my kids and my family, is this way of being that both Ann and Al have, where they are fully invested members of their community. Even as they are participating in these national debates and are friends with everyone on the political scene, they are very dedicated to the community that they're a part of in Cody. I find that to be such a powerful model.

Since I left my home state of West Virginia, I've struggled with finding a sense of belonging in big cities. That's what I think of. I think of, Oh, they've figured out that really hard balance of how to participate and fully feel like you're really putting all of your potential to use on the biggest stages that you could want and wish for, while also being very committed to a particular local community. Does that make sense, Ann?

ANN: Yes, it does. We've always had the theory "Bloom where you're planted."

What are some of the most meaningful lessons you've learned from each other?

ANNA: Ann is willing to be vulnerable, but also very willing to fill up a room. What I mean by that is, she carries herself with a dignity and sophistication that you notice when she is in a room. I find that combination really striking. You feel comfortable with her, but she also doesn't shrink away from being expansive herself to make others feel comfortable.

ANN: I like that. I wish I knew that person. I think with Anna—she's true to herself. She doesn't let people step on her, and yet she's a very giving and loving person. She thinks things through clearly and then she doesn't second-guess everything.

What do you each hope your friendship brings to the other person?

ANN: Well, I hope that she will have a friendship with my daughter, who has so much of me in her,

because I think they would have a lovely friendship. I hope that they will continue to be friends after I'm gone, but I'm planning to be here for quite some time.

ANNA: My biggest hope is that it brings a lot of fun and a lot of ease and also—Ann is in charge of taking care of a lot of people and has been for a long time. A lot of people are used to her being able to just take care of a lot of things. I hope that one of the things our friendship brings her is a place to talk, when she needs to, about some of the parts of getting older that aren't fun or that make it harder to manage as well.

What does your current age feel like for you?

ANN: Well, I feel as though I'm much younger than I am. It's strange, and I think it has to do with being in good shape, and not being in pain.

ANNA: I would say for me, being 41, I do feel like having children for the first time in my late thirties makes midlife an intense territory. I think professionally, I'm aware that I'm mid-career and all the questions *that* raises about what my priorities are, what new things I want to do, where I can lay off a little bit. That's an intense set of questions to be thinking through while also having little kids.

What advice do you have for someone who is curious about or interested in making new friends of different ages?

ANN: I would say just go into the relationship thinking they're the same age. Talk about the things you want to talk about; don't worry about what other people are going to want to talk about. Just because I'm 90 doesn't mean I don't want to talk about clothes.

ANNA: I think one thing I've learned is that there can be an impulse, especially if you're the younger person in a friendship, to need or want a lot of advice. I have loved all the advice and learning that I've gotten from our friendship, but I also am really glad that there's room for talking about a lot of other things. It's not just asking for wisdom. It's enjoying each other.

ANN: You're easy to be with, Anna.

ANNA: Thank you. You are, too.

I HAVE LOVED ALL THE ADVICE AND LEARNING THAT I'VE GOTTEN FROM OUR FRIENDSHIP, BUT I ALSO AM REALLY GLAD THAT THERE'S ROOM FOR TALKING ABOUT A LOT OF OTHER THINGS. IT'S NOT JUST ASKING FOR WISDOM. IT'S ENJOYING EACH OTHER.

Imara Jones

BROOKLYN, NY

Imara Jones, 50, is an Emmy- and Peabody Award–winning journalist and the creator of TransLash, an online and radio news source dedicated to telling trans stories and saving trans lives. Imara has held positions in the White House, chaired the first-ever UN High-Level Meeting on Gender Diversity, and has degrees from both Columbia University and the London School of Economics. In addition to her work with the trans community, Imara has held economic policy posts in the Clinton White House and was named a 2018 Champion of Pride by *The Advocate* magazine.

Where did you grow up, and where do you live now?

I grew up in Atlanta, Georgia, and I live in Brooklyn, New York, right now. I found my way to New York City because I wanted to leave the South. I didn't want to go to college there. So I came to New York for college. And that's when I fell in love with New York. But then I left New York right after college to go to graduate school in London, and after London I moved to Washington, where I worked in the White House for the last two years of the Clinton administration. Then I came back to New York and moved to Harlem, which I loved and adored. But during the financial crisis of 2008, everything fell apart. So I ended up subletting my apartment and going to Brazil. I came back from Brazil and moved into a friend's apartment in Brooklyn, fell in love with Brooklyn, and just stayed here.

What did you want to be when you were younger, and what do you do now?

Well, I first and foremost wanted to be an astronaut, 100 percent. A part of me still has those dreams, wants to explore and go to strange new worlds. For a long time, I thought I was going to be in politics. I wanted to run for office, and I thought I wanted to be president. I don't know now. But I never say no anymore, to anything, because I've learned that the minute you say no to something, life takes it as a chance to create a parody.

At the core of what I do now is working to change the way people think—about the world and about themselves. And my entry point into that is through trans-ness and gender identity, but I actually have a framework for wanting to readjust how we are able to see ourselves and the world that's firmly rooted in liberation and creativity and innovation. It's about freeing ourselves from the dogmas that are preventing us from making progress and going to the places that we need to as a species in order to be able to survive on this planet.

What does your current age feel like for you?

It feels like all the other ages. I don't feel fundamentally different than I did before, I don't think. Which is a weird place to be, but that's kind of the way I feel.

How has your sense of self-confidence or self-acceptance evolved over time?

I think the biggest change is that I've become more comfortable in myself apart from labels and titles and the way other people see me. I know who I am intrinsically in the world without the world telling me who I am.

People can get lost in whatever stories other people are telling about them. And I think as I have gone through the years and gotten older—through all the ways in which life tests you, bends you, and remakes you—I have a better sense of who I am and my own kind of intrinsic worth. So I think my self-confidence is more real, and it's more grounded. Because it's grounded in *me*. My self-confidence has become more self-confident.

What are you most proud of about yourself?

I think two things. First, transitioning. One hundred percent. And second, so far, being able to keep my humanity.

What misconceptions about aging would you like to dispel?

I think age is relative, just like I think youth is relative. I felt older when I was much younger. So as I continue to age, in some respects I feel younger. I think sometimes the concepts that we have around youth and around aging are empty, in a way. And I think that they're more a function of marketing than anything. The idea that when you are aging, you are losing something—it's incomplete. You might be losing some things, but you're also gaining other things.

I am fascinated by talking to women in their sixties and seventies in particular. If you ask them, "Do you want to be young again, and have kids, and be married?" they almost universally laugh. And they're like, "Why would I ever want to go do that again?"

That's the best-kept secret that people never tell you. Getting older, you have freedom again. I'm liberated from all this bullshit. When you get older, you don't need as much runway, because you're not going to do as much dumb stuff. And so you don't need all this time to recover from these terrible errors. Because you're just not going to make them. You know what I mean?

What role do you feel your ancestors, or the women in your family who came before you, play in your life?

I think overwhelmingly they are my role models. They are my guides. They are how I learn and perceive womanhood, both in terms of the things I want to replicate and the things I don't want to replicate.

Knowing what you know now, what would you go back and tell your younger self?

I've thought about this often, and I think the two things I would tell myself are, "Hang on" and "It's all going to change, and that's going to be okay." Everything you think, everything you thought, everything you wanted, everything you *thought* were limitations—it's all going to change, and that's going to be okay. Have faith in the correctness of what is happening, even as it is uncomfortable.

At this point in your life, what have you made peace with that used to be a struggle for you?

Gender. Like, understanding and creating a possibility of myself, of living the gender that I actually was. That was something I used to struggle with, that I no longer do.

Also, learning to be comfortable in silence. That is huge. It doesn't have to be noisy all the time.

How have your ideas of success and happiness changed over time?

I think that it was often, once upon a time, about external markers. Like how other people see you as being successful. And having these markers of achievement so that other people would see you in a certain way, and then that making you feel good about whatever. I think success for me is accomplishing whatever I want to do. And whatever I set my mind to.

But you know, it's not only the achievement of the thing, it's being on the right *road* to achieving that thing. That's also success. Because whatever you achieve is the result of a process. And so it's also appreciating the process.

Happiness for me is being proud of myself—in ways big and small. I've been able to inhabit my gifts to the maximum, and that makes me happy. That makes me feel good.

What impact do you hope your life and your story will have on those around you?

I hope my story gives people a sense of hope and inspiration and possibility. I wanted to be an astronaut, which is about creating through your example and lived experience, this idea that there are new possibilities, new worlds, new frontiers, new things that open up. And I hope that my life does that for other people. Because our sense of what's not possible is what's keeping the whole world stuck. But to cross new boundaries and to achieve those things that seemed impossible—that's how we get to a new place. That's how we get unstuck. And that's how we are able to actually build a better world. As long as we stay stuck, things are going to stay the same. Because that's just physics, right? You have to keep moving faster than the forces that are trying to slow you down.

So we have to go to new places and do new things. And first we have to do all of that in ourselves. Be brave in ourselves. And get out of our boundaries and our limitations that keep us from fulfilling ourselves and living out whatever gifts we have. We have to get into this explorer mindset.

When do you feel your most powerful?

When I'm speaking before a live audience. It makes me feel like I am in the right place.

Ruth Ann Harnisch

HAMPTON BAYS, NY

Ruth Ann Harnisch, 71, is a coach, philanthropist, writer, and executive producer, and was one of the first women to ever anchor the evening news. She was nominated for an Emmy for her reporting on Nashville's WTVF-TV and has continued to share with those in her community the skills she's learned in her many professional pursuits. Her prominent philanthropic work, as well as her work encouraging other wealthy people to invest their money in philanthropy, has focused on innovation, gender and racial equity, and sustainable journalism. A strong voice for women in positions of leadership across all fields, Ruth Ann has used her resources, knowledge, and experience to create and fund opportunities for women across the country.

Where did you grow up, and where do you live now?

I was born in Buffalo, New York. But this feels like a trick question, because is it possible that I have not yet grown up? Because every time I think I am done growing up, it turns out I haven't finished the job. So I am assuming I have not finished growing up. I certainly have not finished growing old!

What did you want to be when you were younger?

At every stage of my life, every *day* of my life, really, I had a slightly different "want to be." I have always lived very much in the moment.

What does your current age feel like for you?

I always feel like myself. And I'm always surprised to see myself in the mirror. This has been true for me throughout my life: thinking I look one way and the mirror telling me something else.

What misconceptions about aging would you like to dispel?

All of them. Name one, I want to dispel it. I want an end to ageism that punishes people of every age. I felt disrespected as a child, a youth, a teen, a young person. There was always somebody ready to dismiss my ideas or my needs because of my age—whatever the age.

What are you most proud of about yourself?

Everything. I'm proud of everything, including my ability to recognize things I need to change if they are not a source of pride.

How has your sense of self-confidence or self-acceptance evolved over time?

Very incrementally. Sometimes it changes in a heartbeat, and other times over years. The COVID-19 pandemic changed everything *again*. So my self-confidence is constantly evolving. Now I know to strengthen it on purpose, like a muscle, with exercise and many reps.

What role do you feel your ancestors, or the women in your family who came before you, play in your life?

Without them, I would not exist, so they play the only role that really counts: They got me here.

They gave me some good maps and some not-very-accurate maps to get around this world. Their voices speak to me from beyond and ago, as I am now just one woman away from being the eldest of my gender in my family of origin, as well as in my husband's family.

When do you feel your most powerful?

I feel the most powerful *now*. If I need a boost, I remind myself with messages like "I was born for this moment" and "Everything in my entire life has led me to be the leader of this situation." And my mother's favorites: "This, too, shall pass" and "Thank you for this and something better."

Can you describe a turning point in your life, and how it changed things for you?

The turning point is any time I make a big decision. I've had so many. The one that perhaps most people can relate to was when I quit smoking cigarettes. I quit, as Mark Twain did, a thousand times until I made a decision. I decided that I had used enough thought space dithering about whether to have one, or one drag, or to try to abstain, or to smoke just with this person, or under these circumstances, or not at all, a quarter of a century of wasting thought space, money, health. I decided I was a nonsmoker. Period. I knew one drag was the gateway to *all* the drags. And that's how I learned to make a decision.

Who or what has influenced your life the most?

In the early years, blood kin and teachers. In the middle years, it was colleagues, bosses, ideas, miracles, M. Scott Peck's *The Road Less Traveled*, and most lately Jocko Willink's *Leadership Strategy and Tactics*. I'm easily influenced. I'm a great audience, an open mind, a fast fan. I know what resonates, and I'm not afraid to change everything.

What would you never do again?

Where do I begin? So many things. The three-person submersible going down to the bottom of the sea and the operator saying, when it's *way* too late to do anything about it, "In the unlikely event that anything should happen to me while we are . . ."

There are physical things I would never do again and relationship mistakes I would never make again and behavior I would never tolerate again.

The Harnisch Foundation's Funny Girls curriculum includes an improv game called Pet Peeve in which each participant just *goes off* on their pet peeve, and the "director" points to others to start *their* rant, and the chorus is very funny. I could play all the parts in Pet Peeve, just ranting about things I would never do again for *days*.

How have your ideas of success and happiness changed over time?

I could write a book, but I don't want to do the work. Short answer: I realized the only person who gets to say what that is for me is *me*. It's the essence of my coaching work: freeing others to be real about what success and happiness mean to them.

I also try to remember what's really important in life: relationships. All the money in the world won't save you if you have no one you trust and who wants the best for you and who is extending themselves out of love for you. It reminds me of a story I always think of.

My childhood in Buffalo was punctuated by the occasional visit to one of a chain of Mayflower Coffee Shops where you could get a doughnut at breakfast. And they had a sign over the exit. On one side of it was a very skinny, unhappy person looking at the thinnest doughnut in all of history. And on the other side was the fattest, happiest person looking at the fattest doughnut. Between them it said, "As you ramble on through life, my friend, whatever be your goal, keep your eye upon the doughnut and not upon the hole."

How can I not always have my eye on the doughnut and not the hole? I think you have to know when you have enough. And most important, remember that relationships with trust are the real wealth.

How has not being a parent affected your life?

I'll say that being without any minor children in my immediate environment during the pandemic while seeing/hearing what parenting has been like for others, I feel the chasm between our experiences. I have the absence of pressure, expectations, guilt, irritation, frustration, etc., that so many are feeling. It's affected me by giving me much more compassion for them and seeking ways to ease their pain.

At this point in your life, what have you made peace with that used to be a struggle for you?

There's not much I'm not at peace with. Politically, I'm not at peace, and I am not at peace with that! The concept of creative hopelessness has brought me much peace and joy from situations that used to be sources of frustration and pain.

What would you like to learn or experience at this stage in your life?

I'd like to experience the peace of having completed "death cleaning" and estate planning. I feel great about my work, myself, my life—now I need to feel free from the details of death that are the obligation of living sentient beings. Nobody should have to make cleaning up the details of my death their full-time job. I want to do what I can to depart with conscious love and good stewardship. I take advanced classes designed for lawyers and accountants to educate myself so I know what I'm doing with the resources I have. I've got a few details to wrap up before the end of 2021, and I hope I beat the Death Clock! Because at any minute I could go. And nobody's going to say, "Oh, she died so young." I mean, some people, older people, might. But "too soon" is not the same as "so young." I'm long past going too young. So I'm preparing for that, legally.

What is a lesson you're still learning or need to learn?

We always teach best that which we need to learn most, so apparently, I'm still learning everything we've discussed!

Knowing what you know now, what would you go back and tell your younger self?

My very much younger self was not someone you could have told anything, and my coach training has taught me not to coach people who are uncoachable. But I really have nothing to say to whatever arrangement of cells and energy existed as me at some prior time. Like, why didn't Glinda just tell Dorothy everything and spare her the Wicked Witch and the flying monkeys? Her excuse was that Dorothy needed to learn these things for herself. I'll go with that.

What has your experience been with ageism, whether internalized or external?

I was in television news. I retired from on-air regular work at the age of 37. I was described as "the old lady of Nashville broadcasting." The grande dame. The pioneer. Shit like that. The internalized ageism that I think a lot of us feel at every different decade marker is real, too. So how do you fight back and counterprogram that narrative in your head?

First of all, I've read and watched enough to know that not every culture and not every era has had this ignorant opinion. But ageism goes both ways, too. When I was younger, I felt dismissed both for being a girl and being young. I felt like, "You think I can't hear you? You think I can't go look that word up in the dictionary? You think I'm not reading the newspaper? You think I'm just looking at the comics?"

The automatic respect for and submission to older people required for no other reason than that they were older also made no sense and was also ageism. These days, parents don't make kids submit to hugs and kisses from older people just because the older people want them. You shouldn't have to automatically do everything an older person says just because they're older.

I'll tell you where ageism about being "old" became obvious first: when my husband and I stopped being hot and became adorable. We don't know when it happened. I think there might have been a "cute" in between "hot" and "adorable." But it seemed like suddenly instead of awe and oh, we went to eww. And, "Aren't they adorable?"

But you know what I say? Go ahead. Go ahead, underestimate me. I'll prove you wrong.

What message do you have for women reading your story here?

I hope anyone of any gender who knows anything of my life will ask themselves the big questions about their own lives. What are the best things about your character? What is most important to you while you're alive? Why? What crossroad events shaped your thinking? Are you living by someone else's idea of a good life, or are you defining it for yourself? Are there any messes you've made, literal or figurative, that you need to clean up to take some weight off your spirit? How do you know for sure that you can count on yourself to live with integrity and keep your agreements with yourself, so that you never let yourself down no matter what else happens around you? How can you be the best leader of your own self in this life?

MY SELF-CONFIDENCE IS CONSTANTLY EVOLVING. NOW I KNOW TO STRENGTHEN IT ON PURPOSE, LIKE A MUSCLE, WITH EXERCISE AND MANY REPS.

Roxane Gay
and
Keah Brown

LOS ANGELES, CA, AND LOCKPORT, NY

Writers Roxane Gay, 47, and Keah Brown, 30, are known for speaking their minds in their work—and on social media. Roxane is a writer, professor, editor, and commentator on all things pop culture. She is the author of the *New York Times* bestselling essay collection *Bad Feminist* and a contributing opinion writer for the *New York Times*. Keah is a disability rights activist, author, and the originator of the hashtag movement #disabledandcute. Her debut memoir, *The Pretty One: On Life, Pop Culture, Disability, and Other Reasons to Fall in Love with Me* was published in 2020. Roxane and Keah's friendship began online and deepened over dinners and discussions of pop culture.

How did you first meet?

KEAH: We met in person at a writing event in Buffalo.

ROXANE: You came to my event and we finally met in person because we had been familiar with each other online. Then you came to LA and we had dinner, just a sort of hanging-out dinner, and I thought that was really fun. Then you came back to LA and we did an event together.

K: I was so nervous. I wanted you to think I'm cool.

What were your first impressions of each other?

K: My first impression of Roxane was, "Wow, she is a complete badass and I have learned so much from her." To be able to share how much her work has meant to me is so important. I was really worried about being annoying, but I also knew that she was shy, so I was like, I think she might like me. Then I was able to relax a bit.

R: My first impression was that Keah was shy and sweet, and I could certainly relate to the shy part because I am shy. She also has a radiant smile and an infectious energy.

Is there anything you were surprised to learn about each other?

R: I shouldn't be surprised by this, but your love of pop culture, just how down you are for pop culture and the depth of stuff you know about and write about, it's amazing.

Can you describe a moment when you realized that your friendship was a significant one and would have an impact on your lives?

K: I knew when I was heading to LA and asked her to dinner and she fielded all my questions. I felt certain that if we were to become friends, it would be lovely. Not for her ability to answer my questions, but because I wanted to be friends with Roxane the person, not Roxane my hero.

R: I knew when we got together in LA. We had a great conversation over dinner, and it was so good to see such an energized young writer with ambition and confidence. She totally knew her worth, which is so rare, and I really enjoy that kind of energy. I knew we would be good friends.

Can you share something meaningful you've learned from each other?

K: I've learned from Roxane that it's okay not to give the internet everything, and to make sure you are remaining true to yourself as much as you are to this sort of weird visibility that comes with the writing. I also learned it's okay to clap back at people who say ignorant stuff. For so long, people would be like, "You're not supposed to respond to them." But if you catch me on the right day, I'm responding, and I will hurt your feelings and I will feel nothing about it. So, thank you for all those things. I think I learned that it's possible to do everything. You gave me that, because when I first started writing my movie, I was like, I can do this because Roxane did it and Roxane's doing it. It just allowed me to see that I can write outside of just more than two genres. So, thank you.

R: I think one of the things I've learned from you is that you can absolutely make your ambitions happen. You put things into the world and then you manifest them and you work really, really hard. I love seeing someone who is open about ambition and unashamed, because that reminds me of myself, but that's not why I like it. I love when women are ambitious—especially Black women. In how you've grown and how you've started to ask for more for your writing because you certainly deserve it, you are walking proof that it's okay to go for what you want.

What makes you proud to call each other friends?

K: I'm proud to call Roxane my friend and to be her friend because Roxane is funny, kind, wonderfully human—and immensely talented. She makes me feel like every dream is possible. Most important, she's just the kind of person I vibe with.

R: Keah is such a great writer and person. She advocates for herself and others and truly is always working to build community. She's also funny and charming and kind but still has an edge. I am proud that such a fine writer, activist, and woman is my friend. With each new achievement of hers, my esteem only grows.

What advice do you have for someone who is curious about or interested in making new friends of different ages?

K: I have quite a few friends who are older than I am. Just be yourself and remember that we're all just trying to make our way. Age isn't the deciding factor it is sometimes portrayed to be. There is work involved in every friendship. As long as you're genuine, it will happen organically.

R: I don't know that I have any wisdom. Making friends is harder the older you get. But I suppose the friends I have made in my middle age are the ones I let my guard down with, so my advice would be to take a chance and make yourself vulnerable with people you think might be good friends.

Who or what has influenced your life the most?

R: That's a good question. It's hard to pinpoint any one thing, but for better and worse, I would say it's probably my parents. I have really great parents, but, as you know, parents are imperfect. They really shaped my worldview and how I viewed myself. They were very hell-bent on what a lot of Black parents are hell-bent on, which is making sure their children survive Blackness in America. So there was a lot of pressure to be great, and that has made pretty much everything about who I am today and my success possible, but it came at a cost.

When do you feel your most powerful?

R: I think I feel the most powerful when I am saying what I want to say, how I want to say it, in the right moment.

At this point in your life, what have you made peace with that used to be a struggle for you?

R: Oh, I don't know that I've made peace with anything that has challenged me. I think the biggest thing I try to make peace with is my body and how my body is treated.

How have your ideas of success and happiness changed over time?

R: The older I get, the more I realize that work will not keep you warm at night and will not make you feel safe, even though you think it will. So, for me, being able to be personally successful, to have functional friendships and relationships with the people in my life and with my wife, that feels like a true definition of success.

What does your current age feel like for you?

R: It feels like I'm finally figuring out who I am, and I'm as at peace with it as I've ever been. It's still very much a work in progress. But with each progressive year in my forties, I feel like, Okay, this is me. You might like it and you might not. But yeah, I am who I am, which doesn't mean I can't grow or change, but that I have a little bit more confidence about who I am.

I also didn't think I would be alive at 45 when I was 25. Like many people, I just thought I would be dead by 30. I've dealt with depression off and on throughout the years, and my twenties were fairly rough. So I just didn't think I was going to make it out of my twenties, for one reason or another, and then I did.

What is a lesson you're still learning or need to learn?

R: I'm still learning that just because someone critiques me or something I do does not mean they're saying I'm worthless and have no business being part of the world. Criticism is hard. But as a writer and so-called public figure, I know that people are always going to have opinions about me, who I am, and what I do, and some of the critiques I receive are going to be reasonable. I'm trying to learn to hear them without feeling completely devastated by them.

People love to doubt your reality when it contradicts their understanding. That's incredibly frustrating for marginalized writers because so many people would like to believe that the world is a fair and equitable place, and it isn't. That doesn't mean you are completely marginalized. Everyone has some amount of privilege, and some of us have a lot of it, but that doesn't mean we're not also disadvantaged in other ways. It's very frustrating that there's no space in public discourse to talk about that, and in ways that are open and honest. People don't really ever want to be contradicted. They don't want their worldviews contradicted. So it makes for a very impoverished public discourse.

What you know about me is what I allow you to know about me, and it's important to not lose sight of that.

What do you each hope your friendship brings or gives to the other person?

K: I hope it brings Roxane joy and gives her the ability to lovingly laugh at the pop culture–obsessed, cheesecake aficionado, very bisexual ball of energy that I am and that you never knew you needed. I also hope I can genuinely bring and give her comfort and laughter. I think those are great functions of friendship.

R: I hope I offer Keah a person with whom she can kiki about pop culture and turn to for advice about negotiating the writing life and publishing world, and a friend who will always have her back when she needs someone.

PEOPLE LOVE TO DOUBT YOUR REALITY WHEN IT CONTRADICTS THEIR UNDERSTANDING.

Aleyna Rodriguez

and

Karen Washington

THE BRONX, NY

Her devotion to social justice first brought Aleyna Rodriguez, 28, to Karen Washington's Rise & Root Farm outside New York City as an intern. Karen, 67, a farmer, political activist, and community organizer who left a lucrative job at the age of 60 to open the farm, coined the term "food apartheid" to bring attention to social inequalities and injustices in the American food system. She was named to *Ebony*'s Power 100 list of influential Black Americans, and in 2014 received the James Beard Foundation Leadership Award. Her work in food justice and supporting farmers of color in the Bronx is what connected her to Aleyna, who is now the director of the Mary Mitchell Family and Youth Center. Karen and Aleyna bonded deeply as mothers, and as women who had experienced great loss and wanted to find the good in the world and share it with those in their community.

How did you first meet?

ALEYNA: This is our eighth year knowing each other. I met Karen when I was a sophomore at the University of Vermont. I was born and raised in the Bronx, but I left to get my higher education. When I went to college, I had a little bit of culture shock, where I was like, Oh my God, I have to go back home. So I focused all my studies in the Bronx. I got an internship at a program run by Heidi Hynes called La Canasta at the Mary Mitchell Center. And when that ended in the summer, Heidi introduced me to Karen. She was so nice. I loved everyone at the market. And then I went back every summer.

KAREN: This young woman walked in the door and asked if she could volunteer. And as soon as I met her, I knew she was the nicest person. Certain people come into your life for a reason. And there was something about her that clicked. She came right on in and didn't even miss a beat. I knew she was a gem, so we figured out a way to hire her. And now, after our friend Heidi's passing, Aleyna is becoming the heir to the Mary Mitchell Center. So the progression was there, the stars were aligned, and she's a treasure.

What are some of the most meaningful lessons you've learned from each other?

K: Let's face it, there are times when the world gets you down, but there's something about Aleyna, this reservoir of inner strength, that holds everyone together. She may not see it now, but she has this inner strength that's burning to get out, and I can see it. She has a light that I'm trying to nurture, because I know she's going to do great, great things.

A: I've learned so much from Karen. Karen is my mentor, professionally, but also in my personal life. I've been through a lot in the last two years. I was married, and my husband left while I was pregnant. And then Heidi passed, and then my dad passed from COVID. Karen has been there through it all. And she's talking about this inner strength and this inner light that she sees; that's how I keep on going. She was a single mother, and she's come so far and puts everything back into the community without batting an eyelash. She doesn't think twice about it. It's just, "Okay, this is what the community needs. I'm going to get it done." Meanwhile, she also took care of and is still taking care of her family and those that she adopted into her family. And her dedication to taking care of those around her has definitely been passed on to me. Karen helped me realize that it's okay to wake up every morning and keep going. Times will be hard, but she's always going to be here for me.

And she doesn't do any of this because she feels she *has* to but because she *wants* to give all this love that she has. It has definitely helped me become who I am today and be in the role I'm in now.

Can you describe a moment when you realized that you were going to be in each other's lives for a long time?

K: I remember taking Aleyna to her grandmother's house. I just drove the car there, made a U-turn, and dropped her off. And then I sat back and thought, This is a person I know is going to be family. Something just clicked in that moment, and I knew she was going to be a part of my life.

A: There is this particular moment that I remember, after Karen had gotten Rise & Root Farm. We were out in the field, picking tomatoes and talking about life. And she was discussing the public speaking she does. It wasn't something she had envisioned doing, but she had started to enjoy it, and now she's trying to make a platform for my generation to come and do these talks. She put me on the spot and asked if I would give a talk. I thought I couldn't do it. I didn't know what to say.

But I said yes. And I did it. I challenged myself because of Karen. And because if she worked so hard to create this platform for the next generation and she believes in us, I should challenge myself to be the next voice, and try to be the person that Karen is. So when she retires and starts to lie back and enjoy her life with her family and her grandchildren, which she so rightfully deserves to do, she can trust that there's a community behind her supporting her every step of the way and her work won't go unfinished.

What do you each hope your friendship brings or gives to the other person?

K: I hope I pass on the gift of love, the gift of understanding. Life is very, very short. When you wake up in the morning, give God thanks and praise, be thankful for your life, but then try to make a difference in someone's life with a kind word, thought, or deed. And I hope that's something I can pass down to her and that she will continue to do throughout her lifetime.

A: I hope I can give Karen the warmth of knowing that she can come to me and I'll be here for her, and I'll always be there for her family. Like Karen, I try to wake up every morning and smile. I just try to smile at folks, even if I don't know them; even with a mask on, people can tell I'm smiling. I want to follow her example and bring light to people's days.

Why do you think you came into each other's lives when you did?

K: I think because we've gone through the same thing: husbands leaving, two kids to raise, and not seeing the light at the end of the tunnel but understanding that as a mother, your first and foremost duty is to take care of your kids. So I think I'm trying to look at her, see what she's going through, and give her some hope that there *is* light at the end of the tunnel. Because things happen for a reason.

A: We have been on such similar paths, and we also share a love of social justice, environmental justice, and food advocacy. When I met Karen, I realized that there's so much more work to be done, and I want to be a part of that. So when she decides to retire from this work, I hope she knows she's left me and then someone else that hopefully will follow me that I can mentor and bring it down the line, to show that after all this work that she's done, her name will never be forgotten. I think that's why I came into her life.

What role do you feel your ancestors, or the women in your families who came before you, play in your lives?

K: I always go to the ancestors. I always go to the ancestors before I speak. I talk to the ancestors all the time. Being an African American, I long for my past. People come through Ellis Island and they can trace back, but my ancestors came here enslaved. I crave the knowledge of who my great-great-grandparents were. And so what I hold on to is the nameless and the faceless, but they are always in my heart. There's always this spirit of belonging, of being there, of nurturing. I don't know their names, but I feel their presence, and I feel that they carry me to do the work I'm doing. And so being a farmer and starting the farmers' conference and all these different things that I've done in my speaking engagements—everything I've done has been possible because I stand on the shoulders of kings and queens, and I never, never want to forget them. I am what I am because of them.

I had this conversation with my son the other day. I said, "One day when I die, the first people I want to see is that line. I want to see the ancestors." Sometimes I can feel them, like when I'm in a room and I've done really well, I can feel them clapping. And I can just feel the energy, the positive energy that makes me feel comfortable saying things that are hard for people to hear when it comes to racism. But they know I say it in an effort to be truthful, and I come from a place of love. I have to go to the ancestors to give me strength, and I have to go to the ancestors to know, again, that they're with me.

A: I'm half Puerto Rican and half Dominican— there's two different sides to that. So I'm learning about each side. That's something I'm learning from Karen, and hoping to build better connections with my ancestors and my culture and my family.

Do you have a message for younger women reading your story here?

A: Follow your heart always. Follow what you think is best, even if that road seems unfamiliar, because taking risks and taking chances doesn't mean there is going to be a bad end. Change is okay. And growth will happen, no matter what age you are.

K: I want to stress the power of women. Women of color, women of different ages and different ethnicities. We've found the common thread, talking about our relationships, our experiences, and really being able to feed off one another and have that divine friendship. Even though there's a difference in our ages, we both learned from each other; we will both give a little bit of our heart, a little bit of who we are to each other, and that's sacred. I think that's what keeps us going. And we should all aim for that.

And always remember to say you love each other. Aleyna and I always, at the end of the conversation or on a call, make sure we say that. Always say I love you, all the time.

What are you most proud of about yourself?

K: I don't take life for granted; it's a gift. And I want to stay humble with that, to cherish just being simply me and being thankful for life. I also always do my best to support my community. You can't say you've made it in this world if the people you left behind are still struggling.

A: I think for me, it's my positive energy. I think that's also what helps me get through my days. I think positivity is the way I'm healing through everything. I hope I spread it to other folks who are going through similar situations.

Patti Paige

NEW YORK, NY

Artist, author, and baker Patti Paige, 69, is known for her beautifully precise cookies. Patti has run a custom bakery in New York City for over twenty years, informed by her love of painting and using baking as a means of artistic expression. She has created custom work for *Martha Stewart Living*, the *New York Times*, and *New York* magazine; Tiffany & Co.; the Metropolitan Museum of Art; Ina Garten of Barefoot Contessa; and the White House's famous Easter Egg Roll, which featured her intricately designed cookies. Patti's book *You Can't Judge a Cookie by Its Cutter* celebrates her love of not only baking but also finding the joy in using your hands to make beautiful things.

What does your current age feel like for you?

When I think of my grandmother and mother, I realize that I always thought of them as *older*, and I didn't understand that despite your age, you are always just the same person. I feel the same now as I did when I was a kid; I don't really feel my age. So I wish I could go back and relate to those women differently. I realize that they were just the same as I am; they just looked different on the outside.

And people can treat you differently when you look different on the outside. It starts out slowly. For example, I was at a sale event thing with my daughter, and I was struck by how everyone who came up to our booth only looked at her, talked to her, asked her questions—even though there were two of us there. Nobody asked me anything. That's when I started to notice how people treat you when you look older. They can ignore you.

I feel like I can do anything, but I'm aware that things have changed, in terms of how other people see me. And I think the only people who can relate to it are people my age; they all know what I'm talking about when I say that. People might look at your hands, or your skin, and they get an idea of what you are capable of. And it's limiting. But now I treat older people differently because I wish I could go back and see my mother and grandmother and know more about how they probably felt on the *inside*.

Where did you grow up, and where do you live now?

I grew up on Long Island. My mother and father each grew up separately in Brooklyn. And then they moved to Levittown, Pennsylvania. Then to Rockville Centre, New York, where I grew up. And now I live in New York City.

What misconceptions about aging would you like to dispel?

The concept of invisibility. I have started to feel it more lately. The people I work with have always been younger, and as I've gotten older, I've found myself stepping away from their conversations. I imagined I was somehow squelching their fun by stepping in to talk. But that's just one of the insidious ways ageism affects everybody. It doesn't just affect younger people—it affects older people as well.

When I worked on the photo shoot for my first cookbook, it was clear people didn't want my hands to be in the book. They ended up using a younger woman's hands for the shoot, and it was torture for me. People thought nobody would want to look at a million pictures of somebody's raggedy hands.

But now I'm learning that I don't care anymore. As I've gotten older—and I wish I'd felt this way all along—you really care so much less what anybody thinks. You have to learn it for yourself, you know what I mean?

How has your sense of self-confidence or self-acceptance evolved over time?

For me, self-confidence ties into not caring what other people think, but also into trusting your own instincts more. But to be honest, I think I've always been the same person in terms of self-confidence. I've always been an overthinker, but I've also always had the confidence to persevere and just do something.

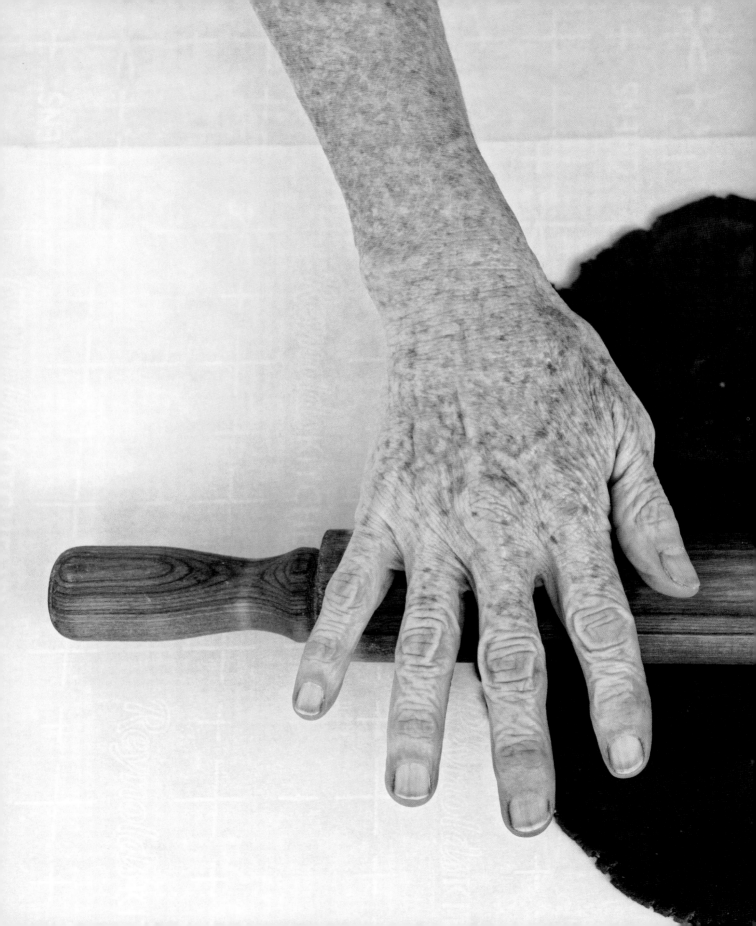

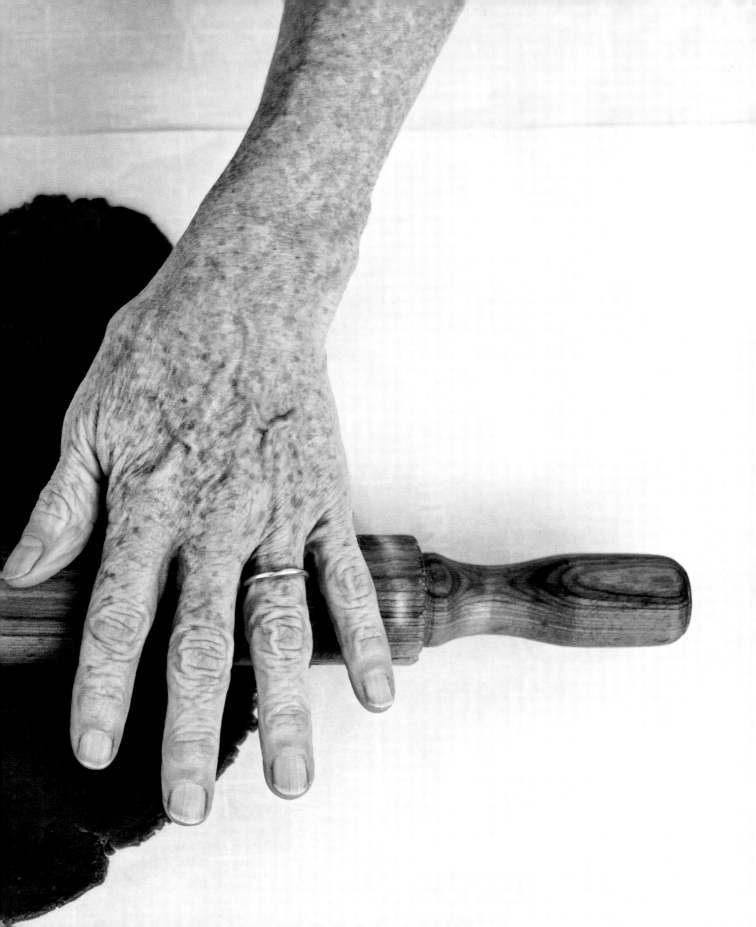

TIME IS SHORT. I JUST WANT TO DO WHAT I WANT TO DO AND NOT BE DRAGGED DOWN BY PEOPLE'S EXPECTATIONS.

I started my business with just an idea, moved into an empty building, built a wall, and gave myself a big space to get started. I would travel by myself, because I felt like I didn't want to be dragged down by anybody. I wanted to be able to move and do as I liked. So I guess I've always had a certain amount of confidence, but I would say it's a weird mixture of confidence and worrying.

But now that I'm older, I see things differently. The things that are the most popular from my business (very perfect and precise cookies) are not of as much interest to me anymore. I'm starting to do things with pressed flowers now. I just want to take squares of cookies with natural colors, plant-based colors, and do my thing. I don't care if it's what people want anymore. Time is short. I just want to do what I want to do and not be dragged down by people's expectations—and I guess that's a form of self-confidence.

Who or what has influenced your life the most?

One thing that has been life-changing for me was buying a house in the country. I had no idea what I was doing. But this is the first thing I've ever owned, and I'm just so comfortable and happy here. We used to bring our dog up here, and the second you would open the door, she would run out and be in heaven. That's how I kind of feel when I go up there.

My clients have been a huge influence on me, too. I've had clients who have been with me from day one who I am still friends with, who I still talk to, who are like extended family. They call me up and they don't have to say their last names, even if I hear from them only every couple of years. I've had long conversations about divorces and separations and kids. Some of them I've never met in person. Some have died. It's an intimate relationship that is interesting and has definitely impacted my life.

What's the biggest risk you've taken in your life, and how has it shaped you?

Quitting. I used to teach part-time with this program Learning to Read Through the Arts at the Guggenheim museum. It was exhausting. I was working three days a week and then doing my art the rest of the time. But at a certain point, I just had to say, "Okay, I'm going to do this thing for real." I

transitioned, with no real baking experience, from making regular cookies at home to selling to big stores, without any real business plan. I was kind of putting all my eggs in one basket, but I was only 26, and at the time, I didn't really think of it as being a big risk. I just went ahead and did it.

For a long time, I felt bad about leaving my art world work hanging. It was very hard for me to accept that I wasn't doing that anymore. But pretty soon I'm sure I'll end up leaving my cooking thing hanging and go on to something new. But instead of stopping, I'm going to do it my way. Just do what I want. Say no to things, not feel like I say yes to everything. I know that's a problem for a lot of people, but it's really fun when you get to the point where you feel comfortable saying no. It's a great feeling of freedom.

How have your ideas of success and happiness changed over time?

I thought of success as just doing well and being happy with what you're doing and having other people respond well. I guess now I think of it as having more time to do what I want and not feel so compelled to be working all the time. At this point, success feels like something a little bit slower.

What are you most proud of about yourself?

I'm pretty independent, and I think of that as a positive. I'm independent and self-sufficient, and I guess I'm pretty determined to get the job done.

What impact do you hope your life and your story will have on those around you?

I hope they feel like, Maybe if this person just followed her instincts, I can, too. You can actually follow your instincts and even back into something, and it can work out or lead to something wonderful. It's kind of a cool way to live your life if you can do it.

Ann Wood

Artist Ann Wood, 60, has always dreamed big. As a young girl growing up on a farm in Iowa, she taught herself to sew and create all sorts of artistic projects with the support of her parents. She followed her big dreams to Minnesota, where she attended art school and would eventually settle to run Woodlucker along with her husband, Dean Lucker. Through good times and bad, Ann learned to find beauty in small moments of nature. Her intricately detailed paper botanicals are now beloved across the world and were recently exhibited at the Kunstmuseum Den Haag in the Netherlands.

Where did you grow up, and where do you live now?

I grew up in a really small town in central Iowa. In fact, my graduating class was eighteen people—and that was three towns together.

My parents had a farm, and I was your quintessential farm kid. I had animals and whole herds of cats that my brother and I would go out and play with every day. A lot of my time outside was spent growing things and gardening. I was super involved in 4-H, which was my *life* as a kid. Making things and sewing and gardening. I came up to Minneapolis to go to college at the Minneapolis College of Art and Design, and now I live in St. Paul.

What did you want to be when you were younger?

I had one of those points in life where I drew a picture and I *knew* that I wanted to be an artist. Now, I had no reference to anybody or anything that could have told me how to be this, but I was lucky to have parents who believed I could do anything. They were difficult, but they really believed I could

do anything. So they provided any type of art materials I wanted. My dad bought me this really expensive sewing machine when I was 11. He said, "My girl's going to learn how to sew." So he went up to the little town, and he said, "Which one's the best? She needs that one."

I had a couple of lessons from a neighbor farm lady, but it grew into something that I just kind of figured out. Sewing was like that for me as a kid—it was intuitive. I've always really followed my intuition about everything.

What does your current age feel like for you?

I feel in between a young person and an old person. I'm trying to figure out how to grow into my older years. My mom was 40 when I was born. She always said, "I can keep up with those young ones." She shifted careers later in life and went from teaching to working in a nursing home and helping older people. She worked there until she was 82 years old. So I didn't really look at age as a negative thing. I grew up with a good example of someone who lived for who they were, rather than what age they were.

I had a long period of time where my parents were ill and helped them for about ten years in that whole realm, which was very difficult and trying on all kinds of levels and, ultimately, very beautiful and healing.

During that time, I got a start in fashion blogging with women over 40. I needed something really positive at the time, because my husband and I lost all of our parents within a very short period of time. That connected me to women older than me. And I realized that they were *all* so worthy, and what they did was worth noticing and appreciating. After the death of my parents, I didn't know what to do, but being around all these amazing women, I realized I could change my work and my life if I wanted to. So that's when I started making paper flowers.

How did you choose paper flowers as the focus of your artwork?

My dad, in his last days of his life, he'd want to go outside and look at plants and talk about them. He'd say, "Look at that sumac over there. Isn't that the most beautiful thing you've ever seen?" He found so much joy and beauty and happiness in those small moments of nature. And what I took from that is that the world around us is infinitely beautiful and inspiring, and I wanted to continue to reach outward with that message through plants and flowers.

What misconceptions about aging would you like to dispel?

Well, it happens to all of us. I thought somehow I could skirt the issue in my life, but you can't. So you have to make these sorts of deals with yourself. Like, where are you going to put your energy and what has to change? I used to be able to work until 11:00 p.m. or midnight every night, no matter what. But I can't do that anymore.

I want to make sure that I'm using my time in a way that matches my values. Who you want to spend your time with and what you want to be doing at age 60 reminds you that you better make sure you're making the most of every day.

How has your sense of self-confidence or self-acceptance evolved over time?

I've always been someone who just dives right in, and I'm trying to keep that in the forefront of my decision-making now. I don't want to be fearful just because I'm an older person now. I don't want to start worrying about what other people think.

Being part of an online community, I feel like I swim in a sea of young people. It can be disconcerting sometimes, because I get constantly barraged with people telling me what I should do or produce or put out into the world. But they don't seem to realize that I've already done all that. I've had a production business. I've done every craft show in America. So for me, at this age, I just want to do things I *haven't* done. Because I lived a full creative life before the online world happened—it's just not documented. No one's seen the sea of stuff I created before the internet existed.

Has getting older helped you feel more secure in saying no to things?

Yes, definitely. I probably say no to 95 percent of things. Because for me, most of the things that make me excited are generated through my own creativity. If our time is limited, I want to be doing what I like and what makes me feel inspired.

I've never been someone who was very good at doing commissions. Some of the worst work I've ever done has been because of accepting commission work for money. I'm much better at just saying, "I make *this*. Do you like it? If you don't like it, then go on to the next person." It's more about me doing what makes me excited and hoping other people will like it.

When do you feel most empowered?

When I'm talking about my art. I could talk to *anybody* about my art. I feel the most fearless in that situation, because I know what I make and who I am, and it's a take-it-or-leave-it situation. I've met thousands of people through my art, and I've heard everything from "Oh, that's the greatest thing in the world" to "This is the ugliest thing I've ever seen." I mean, I've heard that. People have said that to me. You just go, "Well, I guess I'm not for you." So that's all right. My most empowered position is being creative. I'm normally pretty introverted, but when I'm standing there talking about my work, I'm amazed at how extroverted I can be.

How has your idea of happiness changed over time?

The pandemic has changed my idea of happiness greatly. My favorite part of the day now is after work, when my husband, Dean, and I go out to a cemetery about a mile from our home, and we walk there for about an hour. We walked all through the winter and all through the summer. We see these deer every day. There are two males and about six or eight females and a couple of youngsters, and we've see them do all kinds of things. We've seen their society and watched different groups of deer meet.

So I think that this COVID time has required me—and, I believe, a lot of people—to enjoy the simpler things in life. Cooking food, gardening, walking, being with our families. Less high-speed life. Less shopping. Less going out and looking at things. Less buying of objects, too. I'm just finding I require much less, and I honestly have everything I need. I don't think I had realized that before. My life already contains everything I need. There is something really comforting about landing on that thought.

How has not being a parent affected your life?

I never really felt like Dean and I had room for a family, necessarily. We were so devoted to our art careers. I mean, the idea of making your living as an artist and being one your whole life is just absolutely daunting for me, and we made it work through sheer grit.

Now as I can see and witness aging, I realize how important it could have been for us to have children. That's the one thing in my life that I think I do wonder what would have happened if I had said yes to. But we have our extended families on both sides, and we have good friends. So you know, you've got what you've got and you do the best you can.

When I was 40, I started mentoring a young woman. A friend of mine brought her niece to me and said, "She needs a job, and she wants to learn what it's like to be an artist." We've been friends for seventeen years now. She is as close to a daughter as I'm going to have.

When my dad died, I talked to her that day and I said, "You know, the thing that I'm really going to miss is talking to my parents every day," because I did that. She said, "Well, we'll talk every day." That's what we've been doing. She's amazing. For someone like me who doesn't have a child, it's been a really, really important relationship for me.

What role do you feel your ancestors, or the women in your family who came before you, play in your life?

Both of my grandmothers, their husbands died very young and they were alone their whole life. Actually, on both my husband's and my side, all our parents came from one-parent families. I think in the generations after that, especially in the children of the children whose parents died, that spawned a lot of entrepreneurial spirit. My brother and I have both grown up with our own businesses. All five of Dean's siblings had their own businesses, too. So I think the legacy of the people who were from the greatest generation was this feeling that you were just going to make it on your own and figure out how to do things. There was a toughness built in. There was a "not giving up on yourself" built in, I think, through those experiences. It's a kind of generational courage. So I think resilience is something I inherited from them. I feel that through what I know about my own history.

At this point in your life, what have you made peace with that used to be a struggle for you?

I'm dyslexic, so writing is an extreme challenge for me. I used to be really terrified of writing things, because I knew I was a lot smarter than what my words could portray. Now I've gotten so the phone has really helped me, because I can dictate everything. It's another way that technology has helped people like me.

What are you most proud of about yourself?

That I had the courage to go out and try for a really obscure, hard dream. That I've always set the bar really high for my bigger dreams, and many times they've come true. I feel I have a certain sort of magic dust that if I choose to allow myself to believe I can do anything, it could happen.

When I started hanging my paper flowers on the wall, I thought, I want to see this in a museum. That felt like an impossible dream. But that was one experience I really wanted to have. I wanted to hear my shoes as I walked on a terrazzo floor and look up and see my work. It was almost like I could see myself doing this. And it happened—sort of. This year I got to show my work at the Kunstmuseum Den Haag, but then because of COVID-19, I couldn't fly to see it in person. So I didn't get to hear my shoes on the floor, but it *did* happen.

I think during this time, it's been a challenge to keep your dreams alive, when you're not really leaving your house. So I think that's probably my strongest skill: thinking big, dreaming big, and then shooting for the moon.

Knowing what you know now, what would you go back and tell your younger self?

I would go back and tell myself that life can be bigger than what it is in its current state. I mean, I was a kid on a farm waving at a plane. Seriously. My brother and I would walk out to the creek, and we'd be waving at planes, wondering if we were someday going to be able to get on one of those. So I think it goes back to telling myself to just follow where my gut leads me. Follow what's in your gut and believe that you can do it.

Miss Major Griffin-Gracy

and

Raquel Willis

LITTLE ROCK, AR, AND NEW YORK, NY

Miss Major Griffin-Gracy, 81, is an activist and community leader who has been fighting for transgender rights, with a focus on women of color, for over forty years. She served as the original executive director for the Transgender, Gender Variant, and Intersex Justice Project and participated in the 1969 Stonewall riots in New York City. She was the subject of the 2015 documentary *MAJOR!*, and has cared for and supported several generations of young trans women. Writer, speaker, and transgender rights activist Raquel Willis, 30, is the director of communications for the Ms. Foundation for Women. She is a former national organizer for the Transgender Law Center, the former executive editor of *Out* magazine, and the winner of the GLAAD Media Award for Outstanding Magazine Article. Miss Major and Raquel are friends and compatriots in the fight for trans rights. Their friendship is also a chosen family that inspires both women to live authentically as themselves.

How did you first meet?

RAQUEL: I remember it was at a conference. It wasn't that long ago; I think it was 2014, but everything feels like ten years ago now.

MISS MAJOR: I don't remember conferences. They come and go. But I remember meeting you.

R: I was such a baby, and I remember it was such a powerful moment because it was like looking at royalty. You know? Here was this queen of power and resistance.

What were your first impressions of each other?

MM: It's hard to say because that's way before I can remember. But I remember that I got really close to Raquel when she interviewed me for *Out* magazine, because she asked me really good questions. And she was very gentle with me. She was very gracious with me. And so I was curious about her, and I got to know her. And now I don't know what life was like before I knew her.

R: You have contributed so much to the possibility of me even doing what I can do as a young Black trans woman. Moving through the world and talking to you—it's like documenting history. To be able to sit at your feet and learn from you, it's powerful.

What are some of your most fun memories together?

MM: We got to work together on a shoot for *Out* magazine, and seeing her work out in the field is simply marvelous for me. I enjoy it a lot. Because I get to see her use her skills, and it is empowering to me, too. It made me feel very proud to know her and to be a part of what it was that she was working on. That was really special for me.

R: That was an unforgettable day. That was my first major assignment, and I knew in the moment that there was never going to be a moment that topped that experience. There might have been ones that came close, but when you were in front of the lens and you were in all the glam—that was just such a powerful moment, because we knew your experience was the most important experience. Period. It was so powerful to be in that space with you.

Can you describe a moment when you realized that your relationship was going to be a significant and long-lasting one?

MM: Well, you know, I approach everything like that. Because all of my girls are important to me. They give me a reason for living. And as they get closer to me, I get more involved in their lives.

R: I don't know the tea about Mama Major's experiences with other folks (we don't all get along). But either way, it's like meeting family. Because we *are* each other's family, even before we meet each other. At the end of the day, we know we are connected in this fight. So when I meet other Black trans folks, and of course when I met you, I knew we were always going to be in the same ecosystem. And it's even more beautiful that we did share camaraderie and there is that relationship that evolved where she checks in on me and I try to check in. I always need to be better with checking in on everybody in my origin family. There is a sweetness that has come out of us knowing each other.

What are some of the most meaningful lessons you've learned from each other?

R: I'm thinking, What is Major going to learn from me? [*laughs*] You are so unapologetic about your Blackness, about your trans-ness, about every part of your identity and what you've been through. Like having experienced what it's like to be in prison— and then to be a testament to resistance and power. All of that. Being around during the Stonewall era. I mean, when those things were happening, you literally were from the future.

We are just catching up. The culture is catching up to where you've always been. You told us that these white cishet men out here, from their heads to their toes, don't know *nothing*, and have been entrusted with all the power and all the resources. But it's really been Black trans women like you who have solutions. And fought for those solutions to be heard when that fight was unheard of.

You've taught me so much about being *unapologetic*. Naming things as you see them, not couching it in niceties and trying to make it all cute. Like, no! These are what the truths are. And for me as a journalist and obviously as a Black trans woman, that is the perfect legacy to lean on.

MM: Well, you know, for me, one of the most important things is balance. Because life is going to throw stuff at you that's really going to challenge you. But *this* helps keep me stable. My friendship with you has kept me calm because I've got to be who I am and be cool to you. I appreciate you so much, honey.

R: The balance she has in her life is amazing. You know you are the boss bitch, honey! And everyone knows it! I mean, you've created organizations, you've contributed so deeply to social justice. You have raised a lot of kids and have a little one on the way! For me, as a young Black trans woman, it's nice to see that you've been able to have so many major things that so many of us are still striving for.

MM: *You* can get them if you want to. It's not an easy business, but you can go about it right and get it.

What do you each hope your friendship brings or gives to the other person?

MM: I hope that knowing me and the closeness we have helps her keep her calm and not get excited unnecessarily about stuff. And that she focuses on what she wants, because it's important to me that she gets everything she deserves. I wish that for all of my girls. To have that wherewithal to accomplish it and get ahold of it, and not just in passing but really latch on and hold on to it. That's my hope.

R: I hope that our friendship provides a window for Mama Major to see that the cavalry is coming, or that the cavalry is here. And I hope that you feel celebrated. And that we are modeling what it looks like to celebrate people in real time. So I hope our relationship provides a window of what that can look like.

What makes you proud to call each other friends and family?

MM: Are you kidding? Everything about her! Everything about her says that if she's committed to somebody, she's a true friend. And I would trust her anytime.

R: She is a pillar in our community, in our world! That's all I can say—yes! Of course! I want to be around the magic and be in the same space with the magic that is Mama Major. And the love! And the gentleness you were talking about earlier is just something that you elicit or that you pull out of the people around you. And I like that feeling, too!

WE ARE NOT
IN THE BUSINESS
OF PRETENDING,
OF FAKERY, OF
ANY OF THAT.
AND I THINK
OUR EXPERIENCES
ARE A TESTAMENT
TO THAT.

How would you describe how you each feel in the other's presence?

MM: Well, for me, it's my everyday feeling. I don't go out of my way to meet people in a sense. When they meet me, I remain who I am. Always. I think one of the things that is innate about her is that she understands that, and she adapts to it. And that's a wonderful, wonderful thing.

R: To approach Mama Major is to show up as yourself. I'm not the girl who's forever cheery. And I like to have space in our conversations to just be. I'm not coming expecting a perfect response or for this five-step advice. A lot of times when I'm talking to Mama Major, it's about understanding what she thinks about where we are in the world, currently. And so that is where I draw the most, I think, advice, if it happens. Like, how would you compare this to when you were my age or earlier in your life and the world then? Those are like the nuggets I really live for.

But again, there's no expectation there. Most people don't want to be throwing brilliance out at you even if it comes effortlessly all the time. And I feel that way about Mama Major. She's not always trying to be in the space of holding people's hands, and trying to assure them that the world isn't crumbling. It's like, actually, yeah. Some shit *is* crumbling. And she's not afraid to say that and keep it moving. And I think that's refreshing. There isn't like this pretense around what's going on in the world, or how hard life can be. It just is what it is.

We are not in the business of pretending, of fakery, of any of that. And I think our experiences are a testament to that. Whether we were owning our Blackness and transness in the '60s, like Mama Major was, or a decade ago, like I was, there's always work that happens before the world is watching.

And in this work, there is a through line of authenticity, and I'm so honored to be able to share in that legacy with you.

MM: You, too, honey.

Paula Greif

HUDSON, NY

Artist Paula Greif, 69, discovered a passion for ceramics later in life. After going through a divorce, she took a pottery class that led her down the path to starting her own business (her pieces are collector's items that sell out the same day they are posted online) and opening a shop in Hudson, New York. Prior to her career in ceramics, Paula worked as an artist and art director at *Rolling Stone*, *Mademoiselle*, Barneys New York, and MTV and helped create iconic rock videos for bands like the Smiths. Never content to rest on her laurels, Paula is always learning and trying something new. She sat down to talk with her former studio assistant Sula Bermúdez-Silverman about what she has learned in her life so far.

Where did you grow up, and where do you live now?

I was born in Brighton Beach, Brooklyn. The beach and the water are a big part of who I am. Our family culture was the beach. Our block was an eastern European first-generation Jewish neighborhood. My mother grew up in a Yiddish-speaking home. We moved around Brooklyn and Queens and Long Island and Westchester, but now I live in Hudson, New York.

I ended up here on a fluke, although I've kind of modeled my life on Lucie Rie, who was an Austrian Jewish potter working in London. She left Vienna during the war and moved to London, where she lived in this little town house. She had a store and workshop downstairs and she lived upstairs, and I wanted that life. And now I have it, except I'm not running from the Nazis—so far.

What did you want to be when you were younger?

I always wanted to do something creative because I was always a good artist. At summer camp, I was always the person who drew the sets for the plays, and in junior high, I was on the yearbook staff. I always moved in that direction—but I never really wanted to be an artist alone. And even now, I struggle with that, kind of being alone, making art, making things for myself. I really always liked the team part of stuff.

How have your ideas of success and happiness changed over time?

Well, I have a pretty high failure rate, which I accept. I think that acceptance part has made me a lot happier. I just feel like if two out of every ten things I make are really good or work really well, I consider that a good year. I keep my expectations kind of low, and I'm happier.

How has raising a child affected your life?

I have a pretty complicated kid, so it's made my life complicated. It's one of the things that sometimes works and sometimes doesn't work. I'm doing the best I can at parenting. I have an amazingly talented daughter, but she has her ups and downs, and so do we.

What's the biggest risk you've taken in your life, and how has it shaped you?

I think the biggest risk I took was in my early thirties. I'd always had a full-time job, and I left that job to start freelancing and doing rock music videos. It was a huge risk because, well, I'm kind of a square cake, and I like security. But it worked out really well. And I've never had a full-time job again.

I guess I also took a big financial risk when I was younger, too. I took out almost all the money I had in my bank account to buy one of Basquiat's drawings. He came to my house, and he had three paintings rolled up over his shoulder that he said he wanted to sell for $200 each. We went to an ATM, and I had $600. I thought, I can't spend all the money I have. So I bought one for $200.

I guess I've had a pretty colorful life for someone who is a square cake. I don't know how I pulled it off, but I've always kind of been where a lot of the action is.

If you could go back in your life, what would you like to do over—and what would you never do again?

My marriage. I wish I could do it over and do it differently. And then I would *never* get married again.

What is a lesson you're still learning or need to learn?

I'm still learning how to relax and not be so rigid. Even my work is like lines, lines, lines, circles, squares. I can never just relax and be messy and loose—I always get back to the line, line, line.

Then again, I've learned a lot from things that have been failures. Something comes out of the kiln in a different way than I planned, and later I realize that there's always some new idea in that that I can use. So I guess I'm not as much of an uptight person as I thought, because if I didn't really allow myself any of those failures, I wouldn't be able to let them push me in a different direction. So that's the good thing about failure and flops.

When do you feel your most powerful?

I don't know if that's a word I would even use for myself. I feel powerless, which is a good place to be, for me, because it's a form of letting go. It's not being controlling. To me, being powerful is when you're in control and you're the boss. I like to want to be part of something bigger. I don't need to be bigger than anyone else.

What role do you feel your ancestors, or the women in your family who came before you, play in your life?

Huge, huge. My parents are first-generation Jewish Americans and that immigrant culture contains a lot of strength, but also a lot of loss and pain. My mother lost her mother when she was 9. And I just think about my parents coming here from Europe, how brave they were to move to a whole new place and learn a new language. You figure out how to use the skills you have to survive. It's inspiring.

I was the first generation to really get educated. My father went to City College, but none of the women before me were educated. But I know that if they had been, they would have run the world.

What would those women think of what you do now?

I think they would be excited, but being from the kind of culture I'm from, I think they also would have been critical. It's complicated. It's always a "You should . . ." or "Why didn't you . . ." mindset. I don't even know how to describe that, but anyway, that's that.

How has your sense of self-confidence or self-acceptance evolved over time?

I think it's been pretty consistent. I'm kind of just okay. I think that's the reason I've been able to go from one thing to the next, to go from graphic design to music videos to commercials to doing what I'm doing now, art directing. I think I feel confident in my talent, and that's been really consistent. I don't think I'm a big genius, but I think if I apply my talent to something, it seems to work out pretty well.

What are you most proud of about yourself?

I think I'm a really loyal friend. That's the thing I'm most proud of, my loyalty—I still have friends from junior high school. I still stay connected. I have friends forever. And every old boyfriend, I'm still friends with, and still loyal to them also.

Do you have a message for younger women reading your story here?

One thing I feel like I've done well is to learn new things and learn new skills. I think that's what I would encourage everybody to do: Learn something new and run with it. I mean, I never even studied ceramics. I took a goofy class in my neighborhood and learned about it. I think learning new skills keeps life moving forward in a cool way.

What does your current age feel like for you?

Well, I'm 69 and didn't feel any particular way about my age until recently. I have a boyfriend who is ten years younger than me, so that's kind of nice. That feels good. I'm just starting to have things happen physically that make me think, How could this be happening to me? But I feel good. I feel like I'm fit and I can do almost as much as I want to do. I don't know. Sixty-nine doesn't feel that old these days. Your brain and your body are on two different tracks. I think your brain feels like you're you, you're the same person, and then your body says you're someone else. I think it's best to just stick with who your brain tells you you are.

Knowing what you know now, what would you go back and tell your younger self?

I would say to my younger self, "You're not going to believe how interesting life can be if you just keep kind of jumping in, being brave and trying new things."

I just thought what you were supposed to do was get a job and start work at 9:00 a.m. and leave at 5:00 p.m. I didn't even realize that there was another way of functioning in the world. But I'm glad I learned how to work and have a real job first. I think it's important to have real jobs and know how the world works. Then bursting out of that world was great. I didn't know I was going to do that.

What inspired you to burst out of that world and find your own path?

I don't know how it happened, but I went to a Clash concert at the Palladium. There was something about the music—it made me feel empowered to do something else. I just thought, Man, there's so much more to do in this world. Listen to the *sound* of this. There was so much more out there, and I had to get out of here. And I did it. And it worked out.

Helen Williams

and

Camille Banks-Lee

NEW YORK

Helen Williams, 81, has devoted her life to supporting and advocating for music and the arts in education. As a beloved music teacher in Ossining, New York, Helen taught choir and musical theater and mentored future music teachers in her community. It was in Ossining that she met her friend Camille Banks-Lee, 50, a licensed psychotherapist based in New Rochelle, New York. Camille was drawn to Helen's direct, no-nonsense communication style, which has remained a hallmark of their friendship. Their shared passion for family has helped them through difficult times and created a strong bond they both cherish.

How did you first meet?

CAMILLE: We met when I was interviewing for my first job at the age of 23. I had just gotten my master's from Fordham University, and I was interviewing to be a teacher. Helen was on the selection committee of six staff members. I was late, as usual, and wasn't sure if I should even show up because I was so late.

HELEN: Well, it all worked out, and the rest is history.

What were your first impressions of each other?

H: I thought Camille was smart and capable and *spunky*.

C: I knew that Helen was no-nonsense and blunt and straight to the point. On many occasions, she would pin my blouse when she thought I was showing too much cleavage!

Can you describe a moment when you realized your friendship was going to be a significant one in your lives?

H: I was at Camille's wedding and gave the blessing for her husband as the right suitor. She had been dating another guy, and I told her I felt that her husband would make a better partner.

C: And she was right.

What are some of your most fun memories together?

C: Helen loves to dance, and her parties are simply the best in the world. We have gone to New Orleans and danced the night away in New York City. Music is such a significant part of her life.

What are some of the hardest times or moments you've gotten through together?

C: Attending the funeral of Helen's husband was one of the most difficult things I've ever had to endure. He was such a strong complement to her and such a tremendous person. He built an in-ground swimming pool for her by himself!

Can you share something meaningful you've learned from each other?

C: Helen is always mentoring other women, and it's taught me a lot about sharing and giving to others. She has so many goddaughters, and some of them are jealous because all of us want our special time with her.

What makes you proud to call each other friends?

H: We're both proud of each other for coming from humble beginnings and hardworking women who support other women. That means a lot.

Was there anything you were surprised to learn you have in common?

H: We both like bargain shopping and getting dressed up for fun!

What advice do you have for someone who is curious about or interested in making new friends of different ages?

C: You would be surprised at how many things you can have in common with someone of a different age. But it's about letting your guard down and letting each other into your life. Sometimes people don't want to be vulnerable because they don't think they have anything to learn.

What do you each hope your friendship brings or gives to the other person?

C: I hope that I never embarrass Helen and that she wants to continue to do for others what she did for me by becoming my friend and mentor.

H: I hope she learns not to be late anymore!

Why do you think you came into each other's lives at this time?

C: When I first started teaching, I didn't have a real compass for knowing what my life was going to look like. But spending time with Helen and her family and seeing all the ways that she continues to be alive and love life has been significant for me.

H: My only regret in life is that I wish I had had more children. But spending time with Camille is like having more children—but better, because I don't have to financially support her!

What does your current age feel like for you?

H: I'm 81, and I feel *mature*. I stay active and independent, and I continue to look forward to making memories and having a good time. So it feels like I'm still continuing to grow.

C: I'm 50, and I feel more nervous that I don't have enough time left. But spending time with Helen, celebrating life, gives me more optimism about what time is left.

What message do you have for women reading your story here?

H: Remember that it's important to remain active and to have younger friends!

C: It's never too late to learn something new, and always have something to look forward to so you can continue to be inspired and have gratitude.

WE'RE BOTH PROUD
OF EACH OTHER
FOR COMING FROM
HUMBLE BEGINNINGS
AND HARDWORKING
WOMEN WHO
SUPPORT OTHER
WOMEN. THAT
MEANS A LOT.

Acknowledgments

The book you're holding in your hands is the work of hundreds of women, photographers, writers, friends, and family who opened their hearts and homes during an uncertain, and often terrifying, time. Their hard work, honesty, and generosity allowed this book to come to life, and it is with that gracious energy that I hope it enters *your* life as well. To honor the spirit of that group effort, 50 percent of this book's profits will be divided among the women featured in this book, in perpetuity.

Photographer Sasha Israel and I began working on *Collective Wisdom* in January 2020, right before COVID-19 became a global pandemic. Between January and February, we traveled to San Francisco; Washington, DC; and Jackson, Mississippi, to complete what would be our only in-person interviews for the book. Our final plane rides were filled with Clorox wipes, masks, and the assumption that after a few weeks, we would be back on the road to resume our shooting and interview schedule. But we soon realized that nothing would, or could, go back to the way it had been before.

I am endlessly grateful to Sasha for her hard work on this project. Working with her is a joy and privilege. Thank you to all of the photographers who worked together to help complete this book. I also had the pleasure of working with several writers—Tyra Blackwater, Sula Bermúdez-Silverman, Siena Chiang, Anna Paige, Miss Rosen, Elle Simone, Harron Walker, Matika Wilbur, and Kaitlyn Yang—who traveled locally to conduct interviews with people for whom Zoom interviews were not an option. Thank you to them all.

At times I was worried that this book would not come to fruition. Opening up to talk about vulnerable life moments can feel like too much when you're just trying to survive a pandemic— often separated from your support systems of friends and family. The women in this book not only shared their stories, they opened their hearts at a time when that felt *especially* challenging. For their honesty, courage, and support I am endlessly grateful.

Thank you to the team at Artisan for their support. I am so grateful to be a part of this publishing family. Lia Ronnen, Allison McGeehon, Suet Chong, Jane Treuhaft, Shubhani Sarkar, Sibylle Kazeroid, Shoshana Gutmajer, Nancy Murray, Hanh Le, and Bella Lemos, *thank you*.

To my Design*Sponge family, who has supported me in this new post-blog chapter, I love you all so much. Caitlin Kelch, Kristina Gill, Kelli Kehler, Garrett Fleming, Sofia Tuovinen, Lauren Day, and Erin Austen Abbott—I am so happy that our blog family continues to cheer each other on. I believe in all of you, always. And thank you, Kelli, for project managing this book and reminding me that it's okay to ask for help. You always know I need it before *I* do. Thank you.

To my friends and family, thank you for always making me believe that the projects I imagine are possible. Mom, Dad, Rochelle, Doug (and Steve!), thank you for supporting this book and helping me visualize it. Julia, Hope, and Winky, thank you for being the greatest family I could ever ask for. To my friends Albie, Gail, Sicily, Elle, Tanya, Rachel, Stacey, and Lacey—thank you for your support.

I hope this book will bring anyone reading it the same sense of hope, perspective, and community that it brought to me while working on it. Each person's story comes with a lifetime of experience and understanding, and I hope everyone reading will be able to find something to connect with, learn from, and pass on. Here's to women everywhere sharing their stories, building bridges, and passing on wisdom for generations to come. May we always honor those who share with us and pay that love and generosity forward.

—GRACE BONNEY

Grace Bonney is the author of the bestselling books *In the Company of Women* and *Design*Sponge at Home*. Her website, Design*Sponge, is now archived in the Library of Congress. She also founded *Good Company*, a print magazine and podcast about creative entrepreneurs, and *After the Jump*, a podcast about creatives. Bonney lives with her wife and their pets in New York's Hudson Valley, where she is working on her master's in marriage and family therapy from Syracuse University. Find her on Instagram and Twitter @designsponge.